MORESHET MOSHE

"תורה צוה לנו משה מורשה קהלת יעקב"

מורשת משה

לקוטים מדרשותיו של הרב הגאון ר' משה סוויפט זצ"ל
ראב"ד דק"ק לונדון והמדינה

MORESHET MOSHE

Selections from the Sermons of the late

Rabbi M. Swift

Senior Dayan, London Beth Din.

Formerly Rabbi, Brixton and Brondesbury Synagogues, London;
Berea Synagogue, Johannesburg;
Young Israel Movement, Los Angeles.

First Published 1992
ISBN 0-87306-583-2

Feldheim Publishers
POB 35002
Jerusalem, Israel

Feldheim Publishers
200 Airport Executive Park
Spring Valley, NY 10977

Printed in Israel

FOREWORD

"Jewish life, Jewish observance, and Jewish thinking are not taught; they are transmitted." This was the philosophy of our beloved and revered father, Dayan Moshe Swift. It was his dream to transmit Judaism to all Jews everywhere, and he did so in a language they could understand and with a zeal that was never extinguished during his lifetime.

The publication of this second volume of *Moreshet Moshe* is the fulfilment of that dream. For here are compiled his sermons to congregants all over the world, his speeches to Bar Mitzvah boys, his charges to young couples under the *chuppah*. Here are hundreds of Torah ideas and ideals, so masterfully delivered that they left everyone moved and inspired by the Dayan's oratory, his scholarship, and his love for Torah and his fellow man.

Amongst a wide variety of accomplishments, Dayan Swift זצ״ל was particularly renowned as an inspiring and forthright public speaker and *darshan*. Those of us who were privileged to hear him speak during his half-century of service to world Jewry remember the enthusiasm and rich content of his speeches as if they had been given just yesterday. With his passing, a fire was extinguished among the Rabbinate of Anglo-Jewry. Yet a way has been found to keep the flame burning brightly: from a myriad of rough notes written for countless occasions during more than fifty years, these two volumes of *Moreshet Moshe* were compiled. And

V

so has Dayan Swift's greatest desire been fulfilled: to leave behind a legacy of original thoughts and *Divrei Torah* that would inspire young men entering the Rabbinate and would also reach the layman who thirsts for knowledge. These volumes are written, these speeches were phrased, in a language that everyone can understand and appreciate.

How fortunate we were to find, in Dayan Isaac Lerner, the perfect person for the mammoth and painstaking task of editing, compiling, and polishing this work: the two volumes of *Moreshet Moshe*. As a close friend of the author, as well as his colleague on the London *Beth Din,* Dayan Lerner knew how to capture the very essence and spirit of Dayan Swift's sermons. He has given unstintingly of his time and energy to bring his work to fruition, for which he deserves our eternal gratitude.

We know that oratory without substance is meaningless, oratory without sincerity is hollow, and oratory which is not captured in the written word is lost forever. The substance of *Moreshet Moshe* is eternal Torah; its sincerity is unquestionable; and now it is captured in the written word, to be an inspiration to all who read it.

Rachelle Gruber (nee Swift)

ACKNOWLEDGMENTS

בשבח והודאה לבורא עולם

We wish to express our happiness and our profound gratitude to God for having been זוכה to achieve our goal: perpetuating the memory of a great champion of Torah-true Judaism.

Thanks are again due to Rabbi J. Shaw לאי״ט for his painstaking correcting, and to my daughter Freda for typing the manuscript. It is a pleasant duty to thank all the colleagues and friends who offered their encouragement and who assisted in tracing the source of the more obscure quotations.

I.L.

Teves 5751

CONTENTS

ויקרא

צו

שמיני

שלח לך

קרח

חקת

בלק

פינחס

מטות

מסעי

דברים

ואתחנן

עקב

ראה

נצבים

וילך

האזינו

וזאת הברכה

VAYIKRA

ויקרא

i

The Small Aleph

The Book of *Vayikra* presents a remarkable contrast to that which preceded it. *Shemos* is the book of Revelation. In it the power and the presence of the Almighty are made manifest to all[1] by the historic events it describes. Man, woman, and child, even the lowliest handmaid, saw the miracles of the Exodus from Egypt, from דם וצפרדע to חשך and מכת בכורות. All experienced the crossing of the ים סוף and witnessed the revelation at Sinai. Everyone shared in the erection of the משכן, the visible symbol of the Divine Presence in the camp of Israel. All this openness reaches its climax when the cloud of Divine glory descends upon the newly-erected Sanctuary. No longer was God's presence revealed to Israel by awesome acts of retribution upon their persecutors, or by supernatural sounds on a lonely mountaintop. The *Shechinah* came into the camp to dwell amidst the hearts and homes of Israel: ויכס הענן את אהל מועד וכבוד ה' מלא את המשכן, "and the cloud covered the Tent of Meeting and the glory

---

כאמור בהגדה של פסח: ובמורא גדול זו גילוי שכינה כמו שנאמר "או הנסה וכו' במצרים 1
לעיניך" (דברים ד', ל"ד).

of the Lord filled the Tabernacle."

In this moment of rejoicing comes the anticlimax: ולא יכל משה לבא אל אהל מועד, "and Moses was not able to enter into the Tent of Meeting." The lines of communication were blocked. There was the glory of God, a thick cloud that no eye could penetrate. The door was sealed against intruders, even Moses — ולא יכל משה לבא.

There are areas, and not necessarily in the remoter regions of the universe, but here in the very midst of life, that are beyond the reach of man, even the scientist, the philosopher, and the greatest thinkers. God's world is too vast, too big and unimaginable. It is infinite, it is timeless, it is limitless; man is too small, too limited, too finite. That is how the Book of *Shemos* ends. The book that tells the great story of God's revelation and His redemption of His people from Egypt ends with God's presence dwelling in the midst of Israel, but behind the scenes, hidden by an impenetrable screen. Yet He is not sealed off: ויקרא, a new book, begins with God's call to משה רבינו.

Here we are confronted with a strange phenomenon. Speaking mouth to mouth, a person-to-person conversation, is usually denoted by the term ויאמר, whereas ויקרא denotes calling in a loud voice audible to all within its reach. "No," say the Rabbis, משה שמע וכל ישראל לא שמעו; it was not audible to Aaron, nor to all the people of Israel. No one else heard the call but משה רבנו. Yet this call concerned the services and sacrifices in the Sanctuary; to whom was it addressed if not to the people of Israel? But only משה רבנו had broken out of himself, so to speak, detached himself as it were from his personal ties and surroundings; only he was prepared to sacrifice himself, to give himself up rather than give up the House of Israel.[2] He alone heard the call from the silence of the glory of God. To him

2 See Ex. 32:32, where Moses freely offers his life in return for God sparing the Jewish people.

time broke out of the Divine eternity; to him God became visible through the clouds of doubt by day and the fires of hate by night. בכל מסעיהם, "in all their journeys" that had been and were yet to come it was ויקרא אל משה. There God stood in the presence of the whole House of Israel, and yet no one heard His voice but Moses.

How proud would any man feel to be 'on call' for that voice any time of the day or night! Not only in times of sorrow or celebration, not only at a *Bris* or a Bar Mitzvah, not only under the *chuppah*, but at any time to feel inspired and uplifted, בכל מסעיהם, in all circumstances. Yet when it came to writing the Torah, Moses wrote the *Aleph*, the last letter of ויקרא, in miniature — a tiny *Aleph*, a clear indication of his realisation how small the finite is when it is placed side by side with the Infinite God. How great is the contrast between the *Aleph* of ויקרא and the *Aleph* of אנכי ה' אלקיך! Man shrinks into nothingness when he pauses to think what he is, how long he will last, what he possesses. Incidentally, it has been observed that in our holy language there is no single word for 'have.' In Hebrew we resort to a compound circumlocution, יש לי, meaning "*I* have nothing; there is something which is 'to me.'" Modesty or humility was to משה רבנו not a part of his character, a kind of distinctive feature; it was a fundamental principle of his faith, the very essence of his being. I have reached such dizzy heights, I have spoken to God, I heard His voice, He called me at any time — yet ואנחנו מה, what am I? My *Aleph*, my אנכי is so small, Your אנכי so big.

That ויקרא with its small *Aleph* is a clarion call to every one of us. The voice can be heard, however small one is, so long as the attachment between us and the Caller has not been broken. That first call from the Sanctuary began with the message "Speak unto the Children of Israel and say unto them, אדם כי יקריב מכם קרבן." When man feels moved to bring an offering to God, מכם: it must be an offering from man's very self. Not everyone can give as much as

Moses gave, but at least we can give מן הבהמה ומן הצאן, something from our material possessions, as an outward expression of innermost dedication.

The Holy One, blessed be He, does not ask of man that which is beyond his reach. As the Sages say, אמר הקב"ה לישראל עשר בהמות טהורות מסרתי לכם, "the Holy One, blessed be He, says to Israel, 'I have given you ten pure animals which you may enjoy.'[3] Three of these are within your reach: the ox, the sheep, and the goat. כלום הטרחתי עליכם שתהא מחזיר בהרים ובקעות כדי שתביא קרבן, Did I ask you to go out into the mountains and valleys to find Me a sacrifice from all ten species? It is enough if you bring your sacrifice from among the three that are easy to get, those that you care for and feed." Says God, I don't want you to go out of your way for My sake. Don't trouble too much for Me, but don't leave Me out! Give Me three out of ten animals as your occasional sacrifice, give Me one day out of seven, one hour out of twenty-four, that little extra price for kosher meat and matzah instead of *treifah* and *chametz*. Eating on Yom Kippur, eating *chametz* on Pesach — these cut off one's soul from eternity, they snap the link, sever the attachment.

Eternal life is planted in our midst; it is right here by means of right living, right giving. Become one with God, one with the People of Israel, the Torah of Israel, and the land of Israel, in peace and tranquillity to celebrate, all of us together, in the not-too-distant future, the great פסח לעתיד in a world of peace and calm.

---

3 תורה שלמה בשם מדרש הגדול: אמר ר' יהודה ב"ר סימן, אמר הקב"ה עשר בהמות טהורות מסרתי לכם וכו'. ובדעת זקנים (על פסוק ב'): בתורת כהנים מסיק למדנו ענוותנותו של הקב"ה שלא הטריח בניו להביא חיות מן היערות אלא בהמות המצויות להם.

ii

At the Foot of the Bed

(Ha-chodesh)

The four prerequisites to Pesach are expressed in the four Sabbaths that precede the festival. *Shekalim* expresses communal consciousness: no Jew can be free, alone, detached from the community. *Zachor* celebrates national consciousness: the Jewish people must know who are its friends. *Parah* speaks of consciousness of God: distinguish between sacred and secular, pure and impure. *Ha-chodesh* expresses family consciousness: Jewish living and Jewish dignity begin with the family. Four ideas, then: duty to the community, duty to the world, duty to God, and duty to the family.

The lamb that constituted the Pesach offering was not the responsibility of the community, nor of the individual. It was the obligation of the father of the house: שה לבית אבות שה לבית. It was led through the streets of the Egyptian cities on the tenth of Nisan and guarded for four days, until the eve of Pesach, the 14th of Nisan, when the sacrifice was brought. That night it would be eaten in family groups. And where was it kept for four days? Not in the stable out of sight, not in the backyard out of mind, but קשורה בכרעי המטה,[1] brought into the home and tied to the foot of the bed.

What a strange thing to do, to bring a lamb into the house and tie it to the bed! But what a profound thought lies in that strange

1 בתורה שלמה מביא זה בשם מדרש הגדול ומכיל' דרשב"י: ועי' פי' הרמב"ם על משנה כלים י"ט ב' "החבל היוצא מן המטה" וגם פי' רש"י (חולין נ"ד ע"ב) על משנה זו המובאת שם: בפי' הר' קהתי על משנה זו מביא המאמר בשם פסיקתא דרב כהנא.

performance. There in the closed confines of the home, there where no strangers are about, in the intimacy of home life — there was the lamb to be kept, as a symbol of Jewish self-sacrifice and purity. From that place where the pure and holy Jewish lamb is born and reared — thence was the Pesach lamb taken on the 14th of Nisan to the altar of God. And when was it taken, at what time of day? בין הערבים, between the two darknesses, which Rashi explains as meaning between the darkness of the day and the darkness of the night. At noontime the Pesach lamb was offered, as a sign that no darkness can prevail over that other lamb, the Jewish servant of God, whose sacrifice and purity began בכרעי המטה, before it was even born. There is an abundance of truth in the old English saying, "Life is how you make it," but it should be taken more literally.

An American scientist declared some years ago that he and his colleagues had finally discarded the last vestige of the mechanical theory of the human body, and that now they were coming closer to the discovery of how life begins. The question was put to him, "What about the soul?" He answered, "We have not got around to investigating that scientifically." It might have been a much better world to live in if, to use the man's own expression, they had first got round to investigating the spiritual aspect of life and only then the physical. But the scientists have been much more concerned with establishing their kinship to the ape than their kinship to God.

It is only a question of priority, which comes first; for life is indeed how you make it. Our Bible begins with בראשית ברא אלקים את השמים ואת הארץ: first God created the heavens, and then the earth. In our *Rosh Chodesh* prayer we proclaim אתה יצרת עולמך מקדם — "You were there first." Then too, the angels on Jacob's ladder were going up and down; but they went up first. It is truly sad if the only answer to the question "What about the soul?" is "We've not got round to that yet." This attitude has made religion anaemic instead of dynamic; seemingly, heaven cannot keep pace with earth.

Leviticus 1 was written by the same Author as Leviticus 19. Readiness to sacrifice for God's sake is in the same blueprint as readiness to sacrifice for man's sake: the entire Book of Leviticus is called ויקרא. For everything is a question of how near you are when called upon. It is a question of proximity, of intimacy between man and his God. On three occasions in the Torah the expression ויקרא is used in the Divine summons to Moses: at the burning bush, on the peak of Sinai, and here, at the door of the אהל מועד, Israel's portable Sanctuary in the wilderness. These were the moments when Moses was as close as a human being can be to God: at the burning bush, the call to leadership; on Sinai, the call to Torah study and observance; before the משכן, the call to sacrifice. And Moses answered: Here I am, with spiritual and physical self, with body and soul, ready to answer the call.

There is a wonderful Midrashic note on that word ויקרא with which the third Book of the Torah begins. The *Aleph* of ויקרא is written in miniature, a small *Aleph*. The Midrash explains why: because Moses, the humblest of all men, was embarrassed when writing the Torah. He did not wish to disclose to the world that he was so near to God that a mere call brought him into living communion with Him. He wrote the *Aleph* small as an indication that he wanted to write ויקר instead, which would mean that he had an appointed time to speak with his Maker. The Midrash goes on to ask what happened to the ink that was left over in the quill: נשאר לו מעט דיו בקולמוסו והעבירו על ראשו ועי״ז זכה לקרני הוד,[2] "He wiped the quill on his forehead, and that spot of ink caused a radiance to shine from his head." One drop of Torah ink can shine from a human being like a beacon: the constant readiness, anywhere at any time, to serve, to practise, to learn, to

2. בחומש תורה שלמה מביא טעמים שונים מהזוהר ועוד מקומות ובתוכם מה שכתוב כאן.

teach, and to observe. The will to be 'on call' to God, always ויקרא,
can come from the tiniest jot of the Torah, if it but penetrates to
one's physical life. It is a kind of spiritual living that radiates like a
torch, that shines forth like beams of light dissipating the darkness
of Egypt, turning the home into an אהל מועד, making it a meeting-place
between man and God.

This, then, is the שה תמים, the Pesach offering that is the symbol
of Jewish life. This is the Pesach offering that פרשת החדש speaks of,
the offering brought בין הערבים, between the dusks of our history. It
begins in the home, for there the beams of Divine light have their
origin, and from there they spread through the world.

Ezekiel's message in the *Haftorah* of *Ha-chodesh* is, מאחזתו ינחיל
את בניו, "from his own possessions shall he give his sons inheritance,"
למען אשר לא יפוצו עמי מאחזתו, "that My people may not be scattered every
man from his possessions." May the possessions of the father be the
possessions of the child: the light of God and freedom projecting
from every home, to pave the way for the fulfilment of Pesach in
joy and happiness for all.

ii(b)

The Mighty Voice

ויקרא אל משה וידבר ה' אליו מאהל מועד, "The Lord called to Moses and
spoke to him from the Tent of Meeting." The Rabbis tell us, מלמד
שהיה הקול נפסק ולא היה יוצא חוץ לאהל, "We learn from here that the voice
broke off before it left the confines of the Tent." It was no קול נמוך,
no low voice, our Sages add;[1] it was קול ה' בכח, a loud and mighty
voice. Yet it never penetrated beyond the walls of the Holy
Sanctuary. There is a voice that the Jew alone can hear, within the

ספרא י"א. 1

confines of his own home and his House of Prayer and Study. It is the voice of אדם כי יקריב מכם קרבן, that springs from Jewish self-sacrifice, from Jewish idealism. It is a call to our youth alone: the voice of faith, of practice, of tradition in the Jewish home. And that voice will eventually let sound the voice of freedom and song in the streets of our own homeland.

iii

Torah — A Book We Live From[1]

In traditional Jewish life a Rabbinical Diploma is more than a testimony to a man's degree of scholarship. *Semichah*, as it is called, literally means the laying-on of the ordaining Rabbi's hands upon the ordinand. Moses laid his hands upon Joshua in a communication of Divine Spirit, a transmission of Divine teachings, a handing-over of Divine truths. "Here they are as I received them. You take over; you transmit them, you teach them, you communicate them." A Rabbinical Diploma is a religious distinction, a spiritual quali-fication. It is a degree in יראת שמים, the fear of Heaven. It is a testi-ony to the Rabbi's belief in the Written and Oral Word of God. It certifies the Rabbi's acceptance of Divine authority. No wonder, then, that Jewish law demands that respect and high regard be shown to the Rabbi. For by reason of the authority vested in him to convey the word of God as it was handed down, and to apply the word of God as he received it, he is described as שותף של הקב"ה, a partner with God.

1 On the occasion of a former pupil's Rabbinic ordination.

In Jewish life the Rabbi is not an interpreter but a transmitter.
He does not make the law, he applies it, he administers it. Of course
a man must think and reason and search and attempt to explain;
the ability to do so is one of our greatest gifts. Only a fool would
deny himself or others that right, but he is a bigger fool who will go
no further than where his limited reasoning will take him. Once you
do that, you reduce everything to being relative. Then there is
nothing you are sure about, nothing absolute. Apply human reason,
and chastity will have a thousand definitions and morality a
thousand meanings.

Society today is paying a heavy penalty for having destroyed the
absolute in its aims and the certainties among its aspirations. Take
God out of them and put man in, and what have you got? By whom
is good determined now, and justice defined? If you do not believe
that God said it all, then you might as well throw the whole thing
overboard: for who is to choose what to accept and what to reject?
But if God did not say it, Moses did not write it, Isaiah did not preach
it, Ezra did not dictate it, and Hillel and Rabbi Akiva did not interpret
it, who then did? Decent, believing, honest people have been drawn
astray by waves of misleading propaganda because they find so little
time for serious studies. They are told that there is nothing
fundamental and nothing we are really sure of, just because reason
and logic fail to explain everything. Our goals are blurred by
confusion, a smog that blinds the eyes of youth. They are driven off
the tracks by double-talk about מצות, pretending that some come
from God and some don't, and that there is nothing absolute about
anything.

What can we expect of a society that has removed from its midst
the fundamental concepts of goodness and virtue? Is there anything
we can say "No" to with certainty, unless we know that God said it?
Heaven itself is being blasted from its lofty columns, and we rush

about in a mad world in search of security and serenity, family integrity and communal cohesion.

Torah is not merely a book we learn from, it is a Book we live from. That is why the Rabbis say that when you begin teaching a child *Chumash*, you should not begin from Genesis or Exodus, though these may most appeal to the child's emotions, but from *Vayikra*, the Book of Leviticus: יבאו טהורים ויתעסקו בטהורים, "let pure souls come and occupy themselves with pure things."[2] How ridiculous that must sound to the so-called modern mind! What can a child understand of an altar and sacrifices, of sin and repentance, of purity and impurity, of כהן, לוי, וישראל? But the Torah is the fountain of life; it is milk for the child's soul. The Torah is זורע צדקות, a seed planted in the soul. It has more to do with the נשמה than with the brain. Our Rabbis sing the praises of the Jewish mother who brought her infant son in its cot to the *Beis Ha-midrash*, the House of Study: שהיתה מוליכה את בנה לבית המדרש כדי שיתדבקו אזניו בדברי תורה.[3] Not so that he could hear and understand — what can one teach a baby in its crib? — but כדי שיתדבקו אזניו, so that the words of the Torah might cleave and stick to his ears. Let the Torah penetrate! It will enter his נשמה, it will mould his character, it will shape his thinking. It will bring the שכינה into his life and create a bond with God.

Let the holy, pure words penetrate the innocent, pure ears: ויקרא אל משה, "God called to Moses"; וידבר אל משה, "He spoke to Moses"; ויאמר אל משה, "He said to Moses." Divine communion, a relationship with his Maker: man and God, body and soul, spirit and flesh. You can be sure that that child will grow up with a different attitude towards chastity, a different outlook on morality, a positive acceptance of purity.

2 א"ר אסי מפני מה מתחילין לתינוקות בתורת כהנים ואין מתחילין בבראשית אלא שהתינוקות טהורין והקרבנות טהורין יבואו וכו' (ויקרא רבה ז', ג').

3 ירושלמי יבמות פרק א' הל' ו'.

Not Moses' scholarship, nor his leadership, nor even his communion with God filled his being with that *Shechinah* whose light shone forth from him. Only that drop of ink did it, for Torah and more Torah make the Jew what he is. It was once remarked, "Well done is better than well said." It is not what you say about Torah but what you do about it that makes the difference, what you take from it and put into yourself, with your head and your hands, in living and in practice. This may well be the message of שבת פרשת החודש. Count your days from שבת — God created the world. Count your months from Nisan, the month of Pesach — God brought you out of the land of Egypt. Make the Torah a concrete part of your daily life, a living influence.

Any attempt to explain the Torah fails because אנכי ה' אלקיך, "I am the Lord your God." Any attempt to explain the phenomena of history must fail because ויוציאנו ה' אלקינו משם, "God our Lord took us out of Egypt" — it was God Who did it. Pesach is God in history, Shavuos is God in the Torah, Sukkos is God in nature; their observance is God in the Jew. Let us renew our faith, reaffirm belief, and readjust our living in conformity. Rabbi and layman, parents and children, let us go hand in hand, showing the world the way to live, leading men everywhere to sane thinking and righteous living in a world of peace and calm.

iv

What Is a Jew?

(Ha-chodesh — Bar Mitzvah)

The *Haftorah* עם זו יצרתי לי (Is. 43) is read on those occasions when the *Sidrah* of *Vayikra* falls on the הפסקה, the Sabbath intervening between the Four Special Sabbaths and *Shabbos Ha-gadol*. This

Shabbos ought not, however, to be regarded merely as an interval in the weeks of preparation for our Pesach festival of freedom; for its *Haftorah* gives us the prophet's vision of what יציאת מצרים, the Exodus, means to the Jew, and moreover, what it really means to be a Jew.

The Deliverance from Egypt is undoubtedly the greatest, most momentous, event of all time for our people. Its importance is portrayed not only by the Special Sabbaths, and by the domestic preparations preceding its annual commemoration; it occupies a most prominent place in our Prayer Book and in our religious conduct at all times. The Ten Commandments begin with the words אנכי ה' אלקיך אשר הוצאתיך מארץ מצרים, "I am the Lord thy God Who brought thee out of the land of Egypt." Every morning and every evening, when we read our *Shema*, we conclude with the verse reminding us that the Almighty brought us out from the land of Egypt. In our *Kiddush* on Friday night, in our ברכת המזון after meals, when we put on our תפלין in the morning: again and again יציאת מצרים is recalled.

Why is so much attention focused upon this one incident in our great and varied history? As if in answer the prophet proclaims, עם זו יצרתי לי תהלתי יספרו, "This people I formed for Myself that they might tell My praise." There are two Hebrew words which are frequently found together: ברא, "to create," and יצר, "to form." ברא means to create something יש מאין, out of no antecedent material. יצר means to take a material which is in existence, but shapeless like clay, and to cast it into a definite shape.

In this lies the secret of Jewish existence. Since the dawn of our history, there is hardly a country in the world where the Jews have not lived. Someone once said, "There is definitely no life on the moon, or the Jews would have been there." We have been nearly everywhere; we have learned everybody's language, absorbed everybody's culture. We would have disappeared from the map a long time ago; we would have been swallowed up by Romans, Persians, Spaniards, Germans, French, Italians — we would have had no shape. But the prophet proclaims, עָם זוּ יָצַרְתִּי, "This people I formed, I have patterned them, I have shaped them לִי, for Me, that they might tell My praises." Pesach came and I brought them out of the land of Egypt לִהְיוֹת לִי, "to be for Me." I shaped them to be Mine.

Do we ever pause and think what the world would be like without the Jews? It was the Jew Abraham who brought the whole idea of God into the world. Abraham rose above Sodom and Amorah. Isaac set the example of sacrifice for God's sake; he rose above the Philistines of his day. Jacob rose above the allurements of Laban, and Moses destroyed Egyptian idol-worship. Our first ancestors set the example of Jewish steadfastness displayed by our parents and grandparents, by Jews throughout the ages.

We may be proud of the Jewish contribution to science, art, and medicine, and of all the Jewish Nobel Prize winners. But we ought to be still more proud when we think back to the time when the people of the world followed primitive heathen cults, and we taught them "Thou shalt not murder, thou shalt not covet." This is the meaning of Isaiah's prophetic message. יְצַרְתִּי לִי, "I formed you for Me." I brought you out of the land of Egypt and took you to Sinai. The prophet goes on, שְׁמַע יַעֲקֹב עַבְדִּי, "hear, Jacob my servant" — there we became God's servants, and וְיִשְׂרָאֵל בָּחַרְתִּי בּוֹ, "Israel whom I have chosen." We became God's chosen people, with a special task to fulfil as Jews: to show by our actions, by our living, by our conduct, by our behaviour, that we are different. We were formed by God, we were chosen by Him, we were selected by Him to be His servants. In all our comings and goings we have to demonstrate that we are Jews. Outside the home, the *mezuzah* on the door; in the street, our decency, modesty, and respect; at work, in school, and in business, our integrity and honesty; in the home, our respect for our parents and teachers, for Shabbos and Yom Tov. In all our doings we must show that we are God's chosen ones. We ought never be upset if someone points a finger and says, "Look, there's a Jew." We should be happy and proud that it can be seen.

Becoming Bar Mitzvah means being proud of being a chosen one, being resolved to be a Jew in the fullest sense of the word, resolved to practice Judaism and live it, thus bringing joy and credit to our community.

v

The Sanctuary and Sacrifice

The Book of *Shemos*, Exodus, ends with the construction of the משכן, the Sanctuary, the model on which the sanctuary of the ideal Jewish home is built. The Torah is careful to define the Sanctuary that Israel built in the wilderness: אלה פקודי המשכן משכן העדות. It is only called a משכן when it is משכן העדות — when it bears testimony to the God Who dwells within it. A Jewish home is not only a father, a mother, and their children — it is that too, it must be that, but it must also be a testimony to the presence of God in the home. Such a home is not easily made; but that is why the next Book of the Torah is ויקרא, whose opening words speak of Divine offerings and sacrifices. A Jewish home that is also a משכן can only be maintained if there is a קרבן. Sometimes it is כי יקריב מכם, a sacrifice from one's own self, your own person, your self-restraint, your time, your energy. Sometimes it is מן הבהמה, מן הצאן, a sacrifice from your earnings, your belongings, your possessions. Neither a Jewish home nor a Jewish community can be maintained on air and talk. Those who can serve must serve, those who can give must give, those who can do both must do both.

The Mishnah in *Avos* (Chap. 4) says: שלשה כתרים הם, כתר תורה כתר כהונה וכתר מלכות, "There are three crowns: the crown of Torah, the crown of priesthood, and the crown of sovereignty"; וכתר שם טוב עולה על גביהם, "the crown of a good name excels them all." The question needs to be asked: surely the crown of a good name makes a total of four crowns; why, then, does the Sage speak only of three? His reason was to indicate that the three crowns are placed on our heads by others: the crown of Torah by a teacher, the crown of priesthood by one's father, the crown of sovereignty by the people. Not so the crown of שם טוב. A good name is neither conferred nor inherited; it is acquired by one's own efforts. It is achieved, it is won by sacrifice and effort. By making this sacrifice, a Jewish family does not merely acquire a "good name"; it converts a mere home into a Sanctuary, משכן העדות, a living testimony to the Divine Presence.

TZAV

צו

i

Faithful and Faithless

(Shabbos Ha-gadol — Bar Mitzvah)

An encounter with a group of rebellious students has prompted a sequence of thoughts that lends added significance to the designation of this Shabbos: the special *Shabbos Ha-gadol.* The question arose as to why a man who was chosen to lead Israel from bondage to freedom suffered from an impediment in his speech. Moses was כבד פה וכבד לשן, "slow of speech and slow of tongue." Why, of all men, did he lack the language and the eloquence to stand before kings and statesmen? Surely this shows that the battle of faith cannot be won by debate, by argument and dialogue. The faithful cannot argue with the faithless and hope to win: a Jew cannot enter into dialogue with the Freudian and the Marxist and expect to gain the upper hand. Faith is a fact, not susceptible of reason nor logic.

There were two revelations in Jewish history: one was Pesach, the other Shavuos. Pesach was the revelation of God Himself: אנכי ה' אלקיך אשר הוצאתיך מארץ מצרים, "I am the Lord thy God Who brought thee out of the land of Egypt" — אני ולא אחר, "I and none other." There were moments when they were able to point at Him with a finger. Shavuos was the revelation of God's will: וידבר אלקים את כל הדברים האלה לאמר, "God spoke all these words, saying —." There were moments when they stood back because they heard the Voice with their own ears.

Faith is either accepted or rejected. If you want to see it, you can see it and believe; if you want to hear it, you can hear it and believe. Or you can take the way of innocent, child-like faith, implicit and undemanding of proof. But Moses did not enter into dialogue, for Pesach was faith without חכמת. It was an affirmation that God created the world. At His bidding the Red Sea parted and then returned לאיתנו as nature went back to normality. The sun set when it was told to, and turned to darkness at a word; the water dried up and turned to dry land; life stopped beating and turned to death. The יד חזקה, the hand of God, was revealed in nature; the זרוע נטויה, the outstretched arm from on high, led Israel out to freedom.

Has anyone attempted to explain Jewish history rationally, and succeeded? This מה שהוא, this tiny crumb among the nations, is like a grain of *chametz* that can never be neutralised; no matter how it may be crushed, pounded, and scattered, it still ferments. So this little nation, though a whole world may seek to crush it, still it rises again. What is it, faith or reason? What are these *mitzvos*, faith or reason?

The popular passage of the Haggadah, כנגד ארבעה בנים דברה תורה, lends itself to an interpretation quite different from that of the regular English version. Usually we read, "With reference to four sons does the Torah speak." But the word כנגד, rather than "with reference to," literally signifies "opposite to," as if to say, "in spite of the questions of the חכם, the rebellion of the רשע, and the neglect of the תם." Despite them all, the Torah speaks out. You can always find these question-masters going around confusing people. You find them in every generation. For indeed the Haggadah does not say, חכם מה הוא אמר, "what *did* the wise one say?" but מה הוא אומר, "what *is he saying?*" Do you think there is a new type of חכם — a new type of אפיקורוס? It is the same in every generation. He speaks of God, of theology, of ה' אלקינו; but he leaves you with all the questions and he has no answers. No wonder the author of the Haggadah enumerates them all: אחד חכם, אחד רשע, אחד תם, ואחד שאינו יודע לשאול. Can we not count to four by ourselves? Of course; but the Haggadah wants you to know that every חכם is always the same *one* חכם, every רשע is always that same *one* רשע, always the same one that we have met before. It has been the same right down through the ages; but כנגד ארבעה בנים, against them all the תורה stands firm: דברה תורה, the Torah speaks.

כי אני ה' לא שניתי, "for I the Lord change not." In the *Haftorah* of *Shabbos Ha-gadol,* the prophet Malachi, last of the prophets, proclaims in these words the last of all prophecies. Remember, he says, there will be no more prophecy after this. As it was, so it shall be: "I, the Lord, change not." ואתם בני יעקב — "And you, the children of Jacob, because My arm is outstretched in you, because My will is revealed through you, לא כליתם, you too are not consumed. You, the Jews, shall never die; as I am, so are you."

The Ibn Ezra, that immortal critic, explains this invincibility. How can these people never be consumed? כי אם מת האב נשאר הבן, "because if the father dies the son remains." Continuity, perpetuity, eternity, father to son to the end of time; because God is in your history. זכרו תורת משה עבדי אשר צויתי אותו בחורב על כל ישראל, "remember the Torah of Moses, My servant, which I commanded him at Sinai" — not for that generation alone, but על כל ישראל, "for all Israel," for all time. Malachi's last word is the unchangeable God, the unchangeable Torah, the unchangeable people.

Here is the great triangle: God, Torah, and the Jew. We proclaim
it Shabbos after Shabbos, and now it is highlighted by this *Shabbos
Ha-gadol.* In the *Amidah* prayer of Shabbos night we recite ויכולו,
proclaiming God as the Creator of the world. In the שחרית service of
Shabbos morning we recite ישמח משה, recalling God's giving of the
Torah. In the *Minchah* service of Shabbos afternoon it is מי כעמך ישראל,
"who is like Thy people Israel," the chosen people, the people of
God. This is the way to the final redemption. For the message of
Malachi is neither a prayer nor a hope, but the last word in prophecy
and history. When we see fulfilled והשיב לב אבות על בנים ולב בנים על אבותם,
when fathers and children join hands and hearts, when we know
that our continuity is assured and God is revealed as unchanged,
when the faith of the fathers is the faith of the children and the
Torah is lived equally in the parents' life and the children's; then
will the Jew lead the world — through his family, his home, and his
community — back to sanity, peace, and tranquillity.

The *Sidrah* begins with the words צו את אהרן ואת בניו, "Command
Aaron and his children"; and so we find throughout the Book of
Vayikra the expression אהרן ובניו or ובני אהרן, constantly recurring.
Rarely do we find אהרן on his own. There is a salutary lesson here
for every Bar Mitzvah. For throughout our history we were thrown
about from place to place, until we have been in practically every
country in the world; and yet the כהנים can still trace their origin
right back to Aaron. For it was never just אהרן; it was always אהרן ובניו,
preserving the family link between father and son. This stands out
more prominently than ever in the Book of *Vayikra*, because it is
the תורת כהנים, the Book that spells out the law of priestly sacrifices.
For sacrifice is at the root of the Jewish family: wherever and
whenever we have made sacrifices, we have succeeded in handing
on our sacred traditions. Beginning with our first father Abraham
and his son, willingness to sacrifice has been the strength of our

people. This is the call that goes out to every Bar Mitzvah, demanding of him to ensure the continuity of our people and to bring joy to every Torah-true Jewish family.

i(b)

The Infallible Torah[1]

We started off on our march through history with a pair of Bar-Mitzvah boys, as the Torah tells us: ויגדלו הנערים, "the lads grew up."[2] The ebb and flow of Jewish life throughout the ages has depended largely on how those two boys, Jacob and Esau, grew up. For a child is either a link connecting one generation with another, or, God forbid, a breach between them.

Jewish history is a winding procession, parents moving out and children moving in. The significance of this progression may perhaps be reflected in the *Haftorah* read when this Shabbos coincides with *Parashas Parah*. Its opening words run: בן אדם בית ישראל ישבים על אדמתם, which may be rendered thus: בן אדם בית ישראל, it is man's son that makes the House of Israel; and when the House of Israel is made up of people who know that they are sons of men, then ישבים על אדמתם, they dwell on their ancestral land: there is continuity of inheritance.

This interpretation brings added meaning to the *Sidrah*'s opening verse: צו את אהרן ואת בניו, "Command Aaron and his sons." There is no object in building a temple and consecrating it if צו, the

---

1 An extract from an address at the New Synagogue, Egerton Road, in honour of the Bar Mitzvah of a colleague's son.

2 בראשית כ"ה, כ"ז.

Divine command, does not apply to son as it does to father. The Divine directives are given to two generations, to the present and the future, to parents and children. Of even greater significance in this respect is the *Sidrah*'s final verse: ויעש אהרן ובניו את כל הדברים אשר צוה ה' ביד משה, "and Aaron and his sons did all the things that the Lord commanded by the hand of Moses." Not ויעשו, "they did" in the plural, as we would expect grammatically, but ויעש in the singular form, as if to emphasise that each one on his own did as he was commanded. When Aaron was no longer able to do it, his sons did it.

Each individual must stop when the time comes, but continuity can be maintained through the take-over of the new generation when the inevitable time comes to hand over the reins. However, there is a whole *Sidrah* to go through before the sons of men can reach ויעש. There is so much to be done: there is קח את אהרן ואת בניו, "take Aaron and his sons"; there is דבר אל אהרן ואל בניו, "speak to Aaron and his sons"; there is ויקדש את אהרן. . . ואת בניו, "and he consecrated Aaron. . . and his sons." Children do not grow up, they are brought up. The bringing up of Jewish children is the historic עולה, the burnt offering whose fire has burned on through the night of Jewish history.

זאת תורת העלה, היא העלה על מוקדה על המזבח כל הלילה. This — the Torah — היא העלה. This is the offering that burns through the night. The Torah can never be reduced to ashes, and the ashes of the Torah's sacrifices never go to waste. והוציא את הדשן, והרים את הדשן; we have got those ashes heaped up all over the world. But it is not the will to die for God's sake that has kept us alive; it is the will to live for God's sake that has kept the light burning through the night. זאת, וידבר ה', תורת העלה; it is the Divine character of a mitzvah that gives it its worth and makes it indestructible. No mitzvah, however much we may sacrifice for it, is lasting unless it finds its origin in וידבר ה' אל משה לאמר, "and God spoke unto Moses, saying...." When all of the Torah is performed like the עלה, in submission to Divine authority, with surrender to Divine discipline and unfaltering faith in its infallible expression — then היא העלה. This alone keeps the fire alight where all about is darkness. Shabbos observed because it is God's bidding, *tefillin* donned because it is His behest, family life respected because it is Heaven's command; when all established standards of society are uprooted, these remain firm. When the Jew learns that human reasoning is an enterprise of pathetic futility, because the Torah can never be explained, then לא תכבה, the light of Jewish life will burn inextinguishable until the sun of Redemption rises upon the whole world.

ii

The Law of the Burnt Offering

(Shabbos Ha-gadol)

צו את אהרן ואת בניו לאמר זאת תורת העלה, "Command Aaron and his sons, saying, 'This is the law of the burnt offering.'" The *Sidrah* begins with a passage concerning the burnt offering, which the *Kohen* had to attend to all night long, and from which he was allowed no portion and enjoyed no benefit. Here alone does the Torah use the strong expression צו, "command Aaron and his sons," upon which the Rabbis comment, ביותר צריך הכתוב לזרז במקום שיש חסרון כיס.[1] This sacrifice involved a loss for the *Kohen*: he had nothing out of it, yet gave up his time for it. He might easily become lax and neglect it; therefore the Torah says צו את אהרן ואת בניו, a command, a compelling injunction.

1. רש"י שם, מתו"כ.

It is the command, the mitzvah, which seems inexplicable, which is difficult to observe and expensive to honour, that has made our religion what it is. A thing which has no trouble attached to it and no cost involved in its doing is never appreciated and rarely respected; and herein lies the beauty of Pesach. It involves trouble, expense, and toil, and yet is honoured more than almost any other time.

We must endeavour to go on this way, never weakening the festival's influence, ever strengthening its observance. When all the pre-Pesach preparations are zealously carried out, then when they reach their climax at the Seder table, the children will see a difference. There will be something unusual and distinctly Jewish about the Seder, prompting the age-old question, ‏מה נשתנה הלילה הזה‎? They will ask it with deeper meaning, and our answer will be ‏בחזק‎ ‏יד הוציאנו ה׳ ממצרים‎.[2] It is the hand of God in the life of the Jew, in his history, his faith, and his observance, that makes him what he is. And this is what will, ‏במהרה בימינו‎, very soon, in our own days, lead the world to the knowledge of God, to peace and to freedom for all men.

iii

Another Kind of Chametz

(Shabbos Ha-gadol)

It is interesting to note that neither the wonderful prophetic message of Malachi, which forms the *Haftorah* of *Shabbos Ha-gadol,* nor the *Sidrah* of *Tzav* which frequently coincides therewith, refers

‏סוף פר׳ בא‎. 2

in any way to Pesach, *chametz,* or matzah. There is, however, another kind of *chametz.* It is of equal importance to the ordinary kind, and yet its laws are frequently ignored, even trampled on, and in the best of circles, too. The Rabbis called it שאור שבעיסה, the leaven in the dough. It is the *chametz* within our own beings. This, the greatest and most dangerous *chametz* in human life, is referred to quite clearly in our *Haftorah.* The prophet Malachi proclaims the Divine warning:

וקרבתי אליכם למשפט . . . "And I will approach you for judgment, and I will be a swift witness against the sorcerers, against the adulterers, against false swearers, and against the oppressors of the hired man's wages, the widow and the orphan. . ." Yeast is a most potent substance; a small quantity stimulates the entire dough to rise and ferment. And spiritual *chametz* is equally powerful. Like the viper's venom that injures from a distance, so, our Sages say,[1] slander that is hissed in one place may slay countless thousands at the other end of the world. Physical *chametz* causes fermentation in the dough, rendering it unfit for consumption on Pesach, Israel's festival of redemption. Worse than that is spiritual *chametz,* for it paralyses the soul of man; the fermentation it causes in human society renders man unfit to celebrate Israel's future redemption.

And has the *Sidrah* anything to say about *chametz?* ופשט את בגדיו ולבש בגדים אחרים, says the *Sidrah*; after cleaning the altar of ashes, "[the *Kohen*] shall put off his garments and put on other garments, and carry out the ashes. . . to a clean place." On this verse Rashi comments אין זו חובה אלא דרך ארץ. It was not compulsory for the *Kohen* to remove his garments and put on others for the dirty work of taking

---

ירושלמי פאה פ״א ה״א: אומרים לנחש מפני מה. . . את נושך אבר אחד וכל האברים 1
מרגישים, א״ל אמרו לבעל הלשון שהוא אומר כאן והורג ברומי, אומר ברומי והורג בסוריא
וכו׳ (וכעין זה בבבלי ערכין ט״ו ע״ב).

out the ashes; it was דרך ארץ, good manners, not to dirty the clothes he had worn while serving at the altar. Rashi draws his example from daily life: בגדים שבישל בהם קדרה לרבו אל ימזוג בהם כוס לרבו, "the clothes one has worn while cooking a stew for his master he should not wear while pouring out a glass of wine for his master." To use the same methods in the synagogue as we use in business; to speak in the same brusque and earthy way inside God's house as outside — to wear the same garment for carrying out the ashes as we do for service at the altar — is not only an infraction of the Holy Law but a breach of דרך ארץ. In the service of God's temple, in discussions and deliberations of our community's affairs and its well-being, ולבש בגדים אחרים; we should go about these matters in a sincere, honest way, with only the *Kehillah* at heart, without introducing personal feeling or personal remarks into the confines of our discussions.

This is the combined message of *Shabbos Ha-gadol* and the *Sidrah* of *Tzav*. Pesach is the mountain of freedom: it is an uphill struggle whose pinnacle is Sinai. "Who may ascend the mountain of God, and who may stand in His holy place? He that has clean hands and a pure heart." While we are welcoming our great Pesach festival with zealous preparation, rigorously removing the *chametz*, so too all spiritual *chametz*, everything that ferments, that sours the soul, all רכילות and לשון הרע should be eliminated from our homes and from our lives. Then will Pesach fulfil its purpose, and והריקותי לכם ברכה עד בלי די, "I will pour out blessing for you beyond all sufficiency." Then we will share with Israel the world over the true festival of redemption.

iv

What Is Freedom?

(Shabbos Ha-gadol — Bar Mitzvah)

It is strange, not to say surprising, that Pesach, the festival of freedom and emancipation, is surrounded by so many laws and customs. Discipline seems to be woven into its fabric. Not a crumb of bread, not a drop of *chametz* spirits, not a bean or lentil in the house. A special list of supervised foods which alone are permitted during the week of Pesach. From a precisely given moment of *erev* Pesach until the whole week has passed, good Jewish housewives will not tolerate a single crumb of leaven. Eight days under the strain of such a strict discipline, and this is called זמן חרותנו? So many restrictions! What kind of freedom is that?

Moreover, from the *Haftorah* of *Shabbos Ha-gadol* it seems that the restrictions are not limited to food and drink. The message of the prophet Malachi would seem to be more appropriate to *Shabbos Shuvah,* the Shabbos between Rosh Hashanah and Yom Kippur, than to *Shabbos Ha-gadol :*

וקרבתי אליכם למשפט. . ., "And I will approach you for judgment, and I will be a swift witness against the sorcerers, against the adulterers, against false swearers, and against the oppressors of the hired man's wages, the widow and the orphan, those that divert the stranger from his due, and fear Me not, saith the God of Hosts." Is freedom concerned with moral discipline? Is there a *chametz* of the soul? Are immorality, unchastity, and dishonesty also a kind of leaven? If there is need of a "spring cleaning" in man's soul, what has it to do with Pesach? Unless, of course, we say that freedom is not a licence but a blessing, not a free-pass but a privilege.

Freedom does not mean that you are free to assign your own meanings, make your own definitions, declare your own principles — like politicians, who have taken the word "justice" and turned it to suit their own whims. Or like some professors and educationists who have taken the word "chastity" and defined it to embrace everyone's susceptibilities. Or like some business people who have taken the word "integrity" and put it in line with their own schemes. Do you wonder that the world is in such a mess, or that our own community is getting itself into an equal mess? When the most sacred things are given such a variety of meanings, what else could one expect?

The first prerequisite to זמן חרותנו, the festival of freedom, is the recognition that there are duties and obligations, "thou-shalts" and "thou-shalt-nots": definitely defined fundamentals that are absolute and immovable. There must be clear definitions that can never change. Truth can only have one meaning; if it has a number of meanings it is no longer truth. So it is with morality and chastity and integrity. It is not surprising that the Rabbis make a play on the word חרות, the Hebrew word for freedom. חרות is freedom; חרות, it is engraved: חרות על הלוחות, engraved on the Tablets, חרות על הלב, engraved on one's heart. Man is free to do good or evil as he chooses, but he is not free to say what is good and what is evil. His deeds, whether good or evil, are his to decide; the definition of good and evil is not his to decide.

כי אני ה' לא שניתי has been the prophet's call on *Shabbos Ha-gadol* down the ages, "I the Lord change not." You can choose whether to accept Me or to reject Me, but you cannot choose to define Me. זכרו תורת משה עבדי אשר צויתי אותו בחורב: this too is Malachi's call to the ages. "Remember the Torah of Moses My servant, which I commanded him at Chorev." To accept the Torah or to reject it is part of your freedom, but to say what is Torah and what is not — that is not your prerogative. This, then, is the message of *Shabbos Ha-gadol*: without discipline, freedom leads only to anarchy.

The Shabbos before Pesach is called *Shabbos Ha-gadol* because on this Shabbos the Israelites in Egypt became really great. They had suffered oppression and servitude for over two hundred years under the selfish tyranny of the Pharaohs; then came the tenth of Nisan. The lamb they were commanded to take that day was the symbol of the Egyptians' god, because the lamb represented everything they needed and required and believed in. Wool represented riches, flesh represented their mundane requirements. The lamb became their god the way we say of some people today that "money is their god."[1] They think that they can buy the world with it, and the next world, too. No Shabbos, no Yom Tov, no *tallis,* no *tefillin,* no *kashrus,* no education; just money.

It needed a lot of courage to take a lamb on that tenth of Nisan, that fateful Shabbos, and walk through the streets of Egypt while the Egyptians looked on. Then to take it into their houses and keep it for three days for everyone to see, and then to slaughter it in public, and roast it whole with the windows open as the smoke rose and the scent penetrated even the Egyptians' houses. It needed a lot of courage, even greatness, to defy the society in which they lived, to ignore the people who had ruled over them, to take their god and abolish it, to take their worship and destroy it. That is what they were preparing to do on that Shabbos before Pesach, and in the face of such greatness the Egyptians were completely helpless. And so it came to be known as *Shabbos Ha-gadol,* the Great Shabbos.

Every Bar Mitzvah boy can show greatness by his courage, for sometimes he must be the only one against everyone else. To *daven*

---

1 חולק פ״ד ע״ב: מאי דכתיב ועשתרות צאנך, שמעשרות את בעליהן. ויש לציין שעשתורת ל׳ ע״ז היא.

each morning, to leave school early on Friday afternoons, not to be ashamed to wear *tzitzis,* to refuse to play sports on Shabbos, to tell the truth when everybody is lying, to show respect to parents and teachers when so few do. To be one in a million needs courage; but that is true greatness.

The *Sidrah* concludes with the words, ויעש אהרן ובניו את כל הדברים אשר צוה ה' ביד משה, "and Aaron and his sons did all the things that the Lord commanded by the hand of Moses." It was not easy for Aaron, the older brother, to listen to Moses and do as he was told, with his sons watching. Rashi tells us, להגיד שבחן שלא הטו ימין ושמאל, the Torah sings praises of Aaron, who did not deviate from all he was told. It needed courage, but Aaron did it. He did as he was told, because it was God Who commanded Moses.

To be Bar Mitzvah means to do as you are told because it is the mitzvah of the Torah; to be afraid or ashamed shows a lack of courage. The Shabbos of his Bar Mitzvah is every Jewish boy's personal *Shabbos Ha-gadol,* when he attains his religious majority and becomes a גדול, a grown-up in the eyes of Jewish law. It presents him with a challenge to show courage and tenacity in keeping to the path of Torah and *mitzvos,* to be a learned Jew, an observant Jew, a respectful son, a credit to the community and a glory to God.

v

The Marvel of Jewish History

(Shabbos Ha-gadol)

Every period of history, in fact almost every generation, sets certain standards of life, thereby taking part in the progress of human advancement. It is obvious that in the onward march some things must be discarded; but a snobbish contempt for everything produced by our forbears is a most undesirable thing. The great secret of progress is to preserve the best of the old, and carry that into the new. This has been the marvel of Jewish history, in striking contrast to the history of the nations of the world.

It is a sad business when old treasures no longer inspire, for a new interpretation is often better than an entirely new conception. From this angle the cycle of Jewish history has been amazing, and nothing else can compare to it. Right from the very beginning, from the earliest prophets through the age of the Talmudic Sages and down to our own day, our history has been like a revolving door with one central hinge. Generations have come and gone, but always there was a central anchorage; they were able to carry the old into the new. Old altars were not replaced by new ones; they were woven into the texture of the new generation's life. You can take a thread and stretch it out right across Jewish history, and you will get a straight line from the days of the prophets down to this day. With all the upheavals and changes of the world, that thread never snapped.

When a great personality of the "old school" (so to speak) dies, it is often said that "with him the old order dies." The Patriarch Jacob stood on the edge of a new order for his people: the beginning of the Egyptian slavery to which we turn our thoughts on Pesach. His greatest fear was that with his death the old order would die, too, and specious new concepts would take its place. מי אלה, he cries to Joseph, who has brought his sons to be blessed by their aged grandfather. מי אלה, he asks in trepidation, מהיכן יצאו אלה שאינן ראוין לברכה,[1] where do these come from who are not fit to assume my heritage

1. בראשית מ״ח, ח׳ ורש״י שם.

and have my blessing conferred upon them? "They were born in Egypt," Joseph replied. The influence of Egyptian culture, Egyptian training. That was the beginning of the Egyptian oppression.

The same fear seems to echo in the words with which Malachi, the last of the prophets, concludes his message in the *Haftorah* of *Shabbos Ha-gadol*. הנה אנכי שלח לכם את אליה הנביא לפני בוא יום ה' הגדול והנורא, "Behold, I am sending you Elijah the Prophet, before the coming of the great and terrible day of the Lord." And what will be his first move? והשיב לב אבות על בנים ולב בנים על אבותם, "and he shall turn the fathers' hearts towards the children, and the children's hearts towards their fathers." He will have to forge some kind of a hinge, a joint between the old and the new. Something will have to be done to enable the new to be built on top of the old. The old Jacob must recognise the new Joseph. It is the first prerequisite to Jewish emancipation that old values be not cast off, old treasures be not abandoned, but woven into the texture of the new generation, so holding a happy balance between the two.

Malachi preached to a generation of Israel like our own. It was a period of transition in Jewish history. The old state had been destroyed, and now the Jews were coming back and a new state was emerging, and Malachi speaks to the social upheaval that attended the transition. He refers not only to the godless, but also to those who believed in God but behaved indecently, those who made no distinction בין צדיק לרשע, between the righteous and the wicked in gaining their ends. Youth was breaking away from the old order, because the two had nothing in common. This was the kind of internal *chametz* which had to be eradicated before the פסח לעתיד could be enjoyed. And so the prophet declares, not a new order for the age, but a restoration: ושבתם וראיתם בין צדיק לרשע בין עבד אלקים לאשר לא עבדו, "you shall *again* discern between righteous and wicked, between the servant of God and him that serveth Him not."

The thing that drives the young away from the anchorage of their fathers is simply the confusion that results from a lack of self-discipline. An overly-flexible Jewish community breaks to pieces the landmarks upon which the younger generation would have built its future; whereas the old Jewish discipline, firm and unbending, is like an escalator carrying forward into the new day the ancient ideals which will motivate it.

Pesach is a particularly appropriate time to think of these things. The whole observance of Pesach depends upon our standard of discipline. With new methods and modern machinery, so many things can be enjoyed on Pesach which our fathers never knew of. But this does not mean, as some have said, that "if all these things are permitted, we might as well have bread on Pesach." New things and new pleasures are harmless as long as they keep within the limits of the Law; but let us not uproot the old landmarks. The signs are widespread, alas, of contempt for things of the past; but the message of *Shabbos Ha-gadol* is: honour the past and build the future upon it. Then והשיב לב אבות על בנים — a meeting-place will be formed between parents and children. Those who have abandoned their heritage will return to it, values lost will be retrieved, and Israel will dwell securely in their land, free from all encumbrances in a world of peace and calm.

vi

Solidarity

(Shabbos Ha-gadol)

"Religion," a preacher once said, "stands committed to the principle that salvation has a dual aspect: both individual and collective." If religious apathy and neglect of religious observance creep into Jewish life here and there, the danger to the individual is very real, but Jewish survival as a whole is not yet threatened. And what if it goes farther? What if the home is broken into fragments, if the community disintegrates, if the link of Jewish brotherhood snaps, if there is no solidarity between Jew and Jew? Then it is more than a threat to the individual: our very survival is in jeopardy, for our existence as a people is at stake now.

In a time like this, those who are concerned with their own *tefillin* and guard their own *kashrus*, building a private paradise for themselves while all around them can rot and go by the board — such people are possessed of an inverted sense of values. What good is personal salvation, if collectively all hope is lost? "The community can die of hunger as long as I am secured with my matzah." Well, and what good will it do him?

No wonder the first approach to the Seder, the celebration of our redemption from Egypt, is כל דכפין ייתי וייכול, "let anyone who is hungry come and eat." Redemption depends on how wide you open your door to the stranger, how much you are prepared to give to the hungry, how you express your solidarity with your brother Jew. היקבע אדם אלקים, the prophet cries: "Shall a man rob God?כי אתם קבעים אתי, for you rob Me, ואמרתם במה קבענוך, and you say, 'How have we robbed You?' המעשר והתרומה, You give no tithes." For in everything but charity we alone are the winners or the losers. Your *tefillin* and your Shabbos and your Yom Tov and all your religious observances belong to you: if you fail to practise them you deprive yourself, not others, of their eternal value and gracious influences. The Torah is your own: if you keep it you share its benefits, if you fail you are the one to suffer the consequences. But your material possessions belong to God: if you refuse to share them with others less fortunate, if you refuse to give the dues and the tithes for the preservation of the Holy Land, then אתי אתם קובעים, you rob the Almighty.

No other season in the Jewish year is so surrounded with activity for the poor as is Pesach, for our future redemption depends on just this. We must always show solidarity with Jews the world over, and in the Holy Land particularly. Give to God that which already belongs to Him, and by doing so ואתם בני יעקב לא כליתם, our eternal survival is guaranteed, for as members of one great family we will find courage and fortitude to continue. We shall not be consumed; we shall live to see the true redemption of Israel, in the Holy Land of Israel and in the *galus*, and of men the world over.

SHEMINI

שמיני

i

In the Work of Your Hands

(Bar Mitzvah)

Our *Sidrah* describes events that occurred on the eighth day of the initiation of the *Mishkan,* the Tabernacle erected by Israel during their journey to the Promised Land. Aaron and his sons were being installed into the priestly service. With zeal and devotion, the new High Priest and his sons brought the sacrifices and offerings on the altar. Yet in spite of the honour bestowed upon him on this most auspicious occasion, Aaron was grieved: קרבו כל הקרבנות ונעשו כל המעשים, ולא ירדה שכינה לישראל.[1] "The whole House of Israel have assembled to witness the sanctification of this beautiful edifice, to which they have generously donated, and the offering up of the sacrifices they have brought; and yet the שכינה has not descended upon them."

The Divine Presence of God was still not felt after all that had been done. "Come, Aaron," said Moses, "you blessed them, saying יברכך . . . וישמרך, 'may the Lord bless you and keep you,' but that is not

רש"י על ויקרא ט', כ"ג. 1

the blessing that makes them live better lives." So they both went into the *Mishkan* to ask for Divine assistance, and came out to bless the people once again. But this time it was a different kind of blessing: not a blessing that comes from Heaven without any human effort, but a blessing that we bring upon ourselves. יהי רצון שתשרה שכינה במעשה ידיכם, "may the *Shechinah* rest upon the work of your hands," may you bring the *Shechinah* down, may you receive the blessing of God, through the work of your hands.

You cannot just open a Prayer Book and say, 'Dear God, this is what I want to say, it's all written here'; you have to say it. We cannot sit back and pray that Israel should be saved from the enemies that surround her; we have to help save her. You cannot spend every day playing games, and expect Jewish learning just to fly into your head; you have to learn. שכינה במעשה ידיכם — religion means to be active.

The *Haftorah* delivers the same message with even greater emphasis. King David went out to bring the Ark of the Torah to Jerusalem, the capital of Israel. But instead of carrying the Ark on their shoulders, they placed it in a wagon. True, it was a new wagon and beautifully decorated for the occasion, but the Torah's place is not packed away in the Ark and borne on wheels; it is in human life, to be borne on our shoulders, in practice and service. No wonder a great calamity befell those responsible for this lapse.

The story is told of two air-force men who were shot down and stranded on the high seas, floating on a raft. With nothing in sight and no provisions, they thought that the end had come. One of them stood up on the raft, looked up to Heaven, and prayed: "Please, God, if You will save us, I promise we will never . . ." "Hold on," his comrade interrupted him, "don't make any promises! I think I see land ahead." As our Bar Mitzvah boys set sail on the high seas of life, we pray that they may always see dry land, but we hope that nevertheless they will remember the promise of this great day in their lives: to practise and observe, to learn and respect, thus ensuring that the *Shechinah* will rest upon the work of their hands.

ii

Pleasing God

(Bar Mitzvah)

Our *Sidrah* tells how the consecration of the *Mishkan* was marred by the sudden death of Nadav and Avihu, two of the sons of Aaron. There was an unfortunate sequel to this tragic event: a misunderstanding arose regarding portions of the day's sacrifices. They were intended to have been eaten by the כהנים in joyous celebration of that great day, but Moses found later that they had been left untouched. When he protested, Aaron replied, "Such things have befallen me! If I had eaten the sacrifice today, הייטב בעיני ה'? would it have been pleasing in the sight of the Lord?" וישמע משה וייטב בעיניו, "and when Moses heard that, it was pleasing in his sight." These final words might well be translated as a direct reply to Aaron's question, הייטב בעיני ה'? The Torah tells us, וישמע משה, "Moses understood," וייטב בעיניו, "and it was pleasing in His, God's, sight."

We always hope and pray for God to please us; now for the first time the Torah speaks of us pleasing God. So many people try to find favour in the eyes of their fellow men, but so few know what it means to find favour in the eyes of God! In order to please God we must follow the wise advice of the Proverbs: בני תורתי אל תשכח, "My son, forget not my Torah; let thy heart keep my commandments." ומצא חן ושכל טוב בעיני אלקים ואדם, "and so find grace and good understanding in the sight of God and man."[1] By being a good and honourable Jew one not only pleases family and community, one makes God happy, too.

That is what becoming Bar Mitzvah means: to become a child of the *mitzvos,* loyal and faithful to the observance of God's commandments. The same loyalty that a son owes to his parents, a Bar Mitzvah, a son of the *mitzvos,* owes to the practice and observance of our sacred Jewish traditions. By study of the Torah and loyalty to its *mitzvos,* a Bar Mitzvah will surely be doing that which is pleasing in God's sight, and we may hope that God will in turn please him with every Heavenly blessing.

iii

Jewish Distinctiveness

In our annual cycle of Torah reading, the *Sidrah* of *Shemini* is always read on a Shabbos close to the festival of Pesach. It is the season of the year when we are either in the throes of the exacting preparations for the festival, or else just returning to our normal routine, a time when we are more conscious than ever of the differences that make Jewish life what it is.

The four questions of the מה נשתנה focus our attention on just a few of those differences, a few paradigms of the numerous observances that pervade and characterise our lives throughout the year. A famous sage[1] once said that the difference between the words חמץ and מצה is one single dot. Both words have the same letters,

---

1. משלי ג'.

1. בפי' הגר"א ז'ל על הגדה של פסח.

מ and צ, only *matzah* has a ה and *chametz* has a ח. These two letters are almost the same, the only difference between them being the little dot that closes the gap at the top of the left leg of the ה, joining it to its ceiling and making it a ח. Such a tiny difference! Yet it makes all the difference in the world.

This example serves to demonstrate the many differences, seemingly small, that are nevertheless of vital importance in Judaism. For matzah is composed of the same basic ingredients as *chametz*; it is the zeal and care of its preparation that make all the difference, so that it will be fitting for the celebration of our festival of freedom. It may seem a small matter how a dough is prepared and baked, but the consequences are of major importance to the Jewish soul, for eating *chametz* on Pesach is one of the major Torah prohibitions. Thus the מה נשתנה serves to emphasise that we *are* different from all others: we eat differently, we drink differently, we sit differently, we live differently.

The concluding portion of the *Sidrah* of *Shemini* deals with the basic dietary laws, which are a prominent feature of these differences throughout the year. That passage ends with the revelation of these laws' significance to the Jew: והתקדשתם והייתם קדושים, "you shall hallow yourselves and be holy, כי אני ה' המעלה אתכם מארץ מצרים להית לכם לאלקים, for I am the Lord Who brought you up from the land of Egypt to be your God, והייתם קדשים כי קדוש אני, so you shall be holy, for I am holy." Now, elsewhere in the Torah and in our prayers the expression is always אשר הוצאתי אתכם מארץ מצרים, "Who brought you *out* of the land of Egypt." Only here does the Torah use the expression המעלה אתכם, "Who brought you *up* from the land of Egypt." I not only brought you out, I brought you up, on to a different level, the level of להית לכם לאלקים, "to be your God," that God can be seen in you; והייתם קדשים, "you shall be holy, for I am holy."

Kadosh, in Hebrew, means literally "set apart." The Oxford Dictionary defines "holy" as meaning "inviolate from ordinary use." I brought you up, I lifted you out of the masses, to be out of the ordinary. להבדיל, the *Sidrah* concludes, to make divisions in your lives, to remember the differences.

In Yiddish-speaking circles the Hebrew word להבדיל is used as a colloquialism. We say להבדיל when speaking of an animal and a human; להבדיל when we mention the living and the dead; and also להבדיל when we talk of a Jew and a non-Jew. Make no mistake; this is no derogatory remark. It is an unforgivable sin to belittle or offend any human being. Our Sages say, חביב אדם שנברא בצלם, "every man is beloved in God's eyes, for he was created in His image."[2] If so, then to belittle, to abuse, or to offend a Jew or non-Jew, black or white, is an offence against God. Yet the Rambam, Maimonides the great humanitarian, the healer, thinker, and philosopher, rules that wine touched by a non-Jew, even an infant, must be removed from a Jewish table. His ruling, furthermore, is based on the Mishnah, of which the supremely tolerant Hillel was a master.

Were these Sages merely intent upon setting up ghettoes? Or was it because המעלה אתכם...והייתם קדושים, "I have lifted you up; you must be holy"? You are to be different, you live in a different world. If you refuse to accept some of these differences, or if you remove them, then you abdicate; you move out of your Jewish world.

The prime purpose of the difference of Jewish home life is vividly demonstrated by the mitzvah performed by Israel on that first Pesach in Egypt. They proved themselves worthy of redemption by boldly distinguishing their homes from the Egyptians' homes, with the blood of the Pesach sacrifice on their doorposts. Our Sages ask in amazement, Did God have to go out Himself to see which homes

אבות פ״ג. 2

had the blood on the doorpost? הכל גלוי לפניו, "is He not the Knower of all things, is not everything revealed to Him?" אלא אמר הקדוש ברוך הוא, נותן אני את עיני לראות שאתם עסוקים במצוותי, "Rather, the Holy One Blessed be He said, 'I only want to put My eye on you, to see you performing My *mitzvos*.'"[3]

"I want to put My eye on you," I want to lend you My eyes. I want you, through your performance of the *mitzvos*, to come to see things through My eyes. I don't just want to see you, I want to see if you can see Me.

Does keeping to ourselves, with our Shabbos and Yom Tov, our *kashrus* and day schools, our synagogues and Land of Israel, only serve to put us in ghettoes? Or does it rather mean living openly in accordance with our distinctiveness? The *Sidrah* of *Shemini* calls out, המעלה אתכם, lift yourselves up! Be out of the ordinary! Preserve Jewish distinctiveness, on Pesach and throughout the year. With our Jewish observances — those little differences that make all the difference — we will bring about the true redemption, for Israel and for all the peoples of the world.

3. רש"י: מכילתא.

TAZRIA—METZORA

תזריע-מצורע

i

The Sublime Task of Women

The Rabbis tell the story[1] of a Roman Emperor who said to Rabban Gamliel, "Your God is a thief, for he caused a deep sleep to fall upon Adam, and then stole one of his ribs whilst he was unconscious." The Rabbi's daughter told him, "Leave him to me; I will answer him." She then asked the Emperor to send an officer to investigate a complaint.

"What is the complaint?" asked the Emperor.

"Thieves broke into our home during the night and stole a silver vessel; but they left a gold one behind."

"Would that such thieves would visit me every day!" exclaimed the Emperor.

"Well then," she replied, "a single rib was taken from Adam, and a woman was given him in its place."

---

1 בסנהדרין ל״ט ע״א הלשון בגמרא הוא: ״אמר לו כופר״ אבל בר״ח הגירסא ״אמר לו קיסר״ וביילקוט שמעוני על הפסוק ״ויפל ה׳ תרדמה״ (בר׳ ב׳ כ״א) ״מטרונא שאלה את ר׳ יוסי ור׳ יוסי בעצמו השיב לה במשל כזה: ״אם הפקיד אדם אצלך אונקיא של כסף בחשאי והחזרת לו של זהב בפרהסיא זו גניבה?״

Here is a remarkable compliment paid to women. Though it was written some two thousand years ago, you will find nothing comparable to it in all the vast store of literature written since then. For from time immemorial the Jewish woman has enjoyed individuality and distinction. Her dignity and her honour have been guarded and respected as in no other nation. She is the gold, the jewel of man's heart, not to be contaminated, not to be slighted or abused, but held pure and sacred. While man wages a war for life, woman holds the fortress.

There is a place and a purpose for everything in life. The flower that buds here cannot bud there; the fruit that ripens there cannot ripen here. The wild beast has his habitat in the forest and the domesticated one in the field. The sun shines by day and the moon by night. The coloured man lives in his part of the world, the Caucasian in another. Man has his purpose and woman has hers.

Each of the two, man and woman, occupies a distinct place and controls an allotted sphere. Jewish law recognizes this distinction, and exhorts us to keep it. In Jewish law, the mixing of linen thread with wool makes the garment unusable, and the mixing of different seeds makes the fruits uneatable. To harness a horse with an ox to the plough is a violation of the Holy Law. For we must know that the world is an orderly machine; there is a scheme and a plan to it. It is not a conglomeration of elements thrown out haphazardly to function at their own convenience, however they may fall out.

Was it not within the Creator's power to give a single command that the world come into being? But He did not do so. Instead He made His world over six days, according to a Divine plan of progress: Sunday one thing, Monday another, the fish in the sea and the birds in the skies. One creature was not to interfere with another: עשה

שלום במרומיו, "He makes peace in His heights."[2] Heaven, say the Sages, is made of fire and water. Confuse these two, and destruction is the result; let each be king over his domain and construction comes about. The first page of the Bible is a grave warning to man: beware lest you interfere with the elements. If politics violate human property, if sexual appetites violate human sanctity, if science mixes fire and water, then the world will go back to תהו ובהו, to waste and void.

When Noah sought to save himself from the flood of incest and corruption, he took with him into the Ark זכר ונקבה, male and female, preserving for each its legitimate place. When Abraham fought to save himself from the avalanche of selfishness in his days, he stood at the door of the tent, while Sarah remained within. The battle against idolatry was won by the man who destroyed them without and by the woman who guarded sanctity within. Isaac went out to the field to pray, and Rebecca was escorted into the home. The battle with Laban was won by Jacob, out among the flocks, and by Rachel, in the home. The battle with Egypt was won by Moses among the men and by Miriam among the women. Ruth gave up all the temptations of a glamorous world so that David could issue from her; Hannah staggered the Greeks with her seven sons, whom she trained to קדוש השם, the sanctification of God's name. Haman was hanged by Esther, who fought the battle in the palace while Mordechai stood at the gates. The woman in the home has brought glory to our name. Yes, man fights the battle of life, and woman fights the battle of the domestic sanctuary.

Three sublime duties rest particularly upon the Jewish mother. Man's duty is to find the bread, and woman's is to give the חלה portion and share the bread with those in need. Man's duty is to practise

2. איוב כ"ה, ב'.

the mitzvah of *tefillin,* showing the world the light of God;[3] woman's
duty is to kindle it in the home. Man's duty is to procreate and bring
children into the world, and woman's is נדה, to purify the seed and
sanctify the birth.

In the combined *Sidrahs* of *Tazria* and *Metzora* we learn of a
gradual sequence of impurity, beginning with childbirth,
progressing to disease in the flesh, then in garments, culminating
in disease in the walls of the home and the inevitable desolation of
man's life and the destruction of his property. When an Israelite saw
something suspicious in the walls of his house, the Torah
commanded him to come and tell the priest, saying, כנגע נראה לי בבית,
"something like a plague hath appeared to me in the house." The
spot that begins the disease, the Rabbis say, appears in the house
מתוכו ולא מאחוריו, "within it and not without."[4] The walls of a home can
be made so thick that no influence from without can penetrate them;
but if ever a mark of that influence is seen within, on the inside,
then it will spread so rapidly that the entire home must be
demolished. There are some homes that are plagued from within,
stricken with a leprosy of indecency and immodesty that spreads
like an infectious disease. A home where no light of faith has been
kindled by the mother, a home where no mother's concern for נדה
has ever exerted its purifying influence, a home without Torah,
wherein no meal is ever prepared for a stranger.

A modern wit has described our homes today as "a filling station
by day and a parking place by night." If mother is not there to make
the home, what else is left but this? But mother has gone into
business, and mother has gone into industry, and now some want
mother to step into synagogue affairs besides, and never mind that

עי' מנחות ל"ה ע"ב, והוא ענין גילוי שכינה. 3

תורת כהנים.4

the home is being desecrated by a godless generation. Yet the synagogue is man's affair, and the election of its officers is his concern. Is there any lack of her own affairs to which woman should devote herself? There are the societies and organizations where valiant work needs to be done, in caring for the distressed and providing charity for the poor. And there are children waiting at home to be taught the meaning of Shabbos and sent to Hebrew classes. Then we will have a generation that will fill the synagogues and revitalise Jewish life. We call upon mothers to reinstate themselves in the high position they have always held in the Jewish community. Let the flexible rib take on the eternal strength of Torah in the execution of woman's sublime task, so that the home may become the true sanctuary, spreading its gracious influence throughout human society.

ii

Torah Involvement

In Hebrew there is no word for religion. There are words for 'traditional,' and for 'observant,' but not for 'religious.' Ours is not a religion, nor even a civilisation; Judaism is a science. The Torah, in a spiritual sense, is a scientific fact; וחי בהם, we live by the *mitzvos*, כי הם חיינו, because they are life itself. Take them away, these מצוות, and there is no Jew. The synagogue may be full, but remove the מצוות, the precepts of the Torah, and the Jew is no longer. The Torah is life.

The Rabbis talk,[1] for instance, of 365 negative precepts in the
Torah, which are equivalent to the 365 days in the year, and of 248
positive precepts, equivalent to the limbs and organs of the human
body. There are, the Rabbis say, 613 pips in a pomegranate,
equivalent to the 613 *mitzvos* in the Torah. The *tzitzis* that we wear
on the four corners of our garments remind us of the 613 duties
incumbent upon us, because ציצית in its numerical value amounts to
600, and together with the five knots and eight threads in each
fringe it comes to 613.

What did the Rabbis mean by all this? Were they playing games,
as one does with schoolchildren? Not at all. They were conveying
the whole philosophy of Judaism. And what is that? It is Torah in
every day of the year, it is Torah in every fibre of our being. It is
Torah in every pip, every element of nature. *Tzitzis* symbolises
Torah in every thread of our garments; *mezuzah* is the symbol of
Torah on every doorpost. ודברת בם בשבתך בביתך ובלכתך בדרך ובשכבך ובקומך,
"thou shalt speak of them when thou sittest in thine house, when
thou goest on thy way, when thou liest down, and when thou risest
up." Torah requires total involvement. It forges a link whereby we
are chained inseparably to God. That is why we *daven Shacharis*
when the sun rises; that is why we *daven Minchah* when the sun
declines; that is why we *daven Maariv* at twilight when the sun has
set. These are not just prayers; these are involvement,
acknowledgment that we are one with God in every nook and cranny
of life, everywhere, every day, in every place.

The Rabbis say that we should begin teaching a child *Chumash,*
not from the Book of בראשית, Genesis, but from the Book of ויקרא,
Leviticus. *Bereishis* is very important, needless to say: it tells us that
God created man. But *Vayikra* is even more important, for it teaches

מכות כ"ג ע"ב. 1

us how man creates Godliness. How man comes to be down here
we know from the Book of *Bereishis;* but how he can reach
heavenwards we learn from *Vayikra* זאת תורת הבהמה, זאת תורת האדם, זאת
תורת המצורע, "this is the law of the animal — this is the law of man —
this is the תורה of the leper." Religion means to bring even the animal
into the service of God, to bring Torah — so to speak, God — into
the animal. Bring the Torah into man, make him Godlike! Bring the
Torah even into the leper! The garment, the house, and the leper
himself can all become pure.

The Rabbis say, כשם שיצירתו של אדם אחר כל בהמה חיה ועוף, just as man's
creation came after that of the animals, כך תורתו נתפרשה אחר תורת בהמה
חיה ועוף, so man's Torah was placed in order after that of the animals.[2]
Hence we find in the previous *Sidrah* the laws of כשר and טרפה,
permitted and forbidden animals, and in this *Sidrah* we find טמא and
טהור, the laws of pure and impure in man, in his person, his garment,
and his home. For we believe that there is a Divine purpose in the
Creation, and we see it expressed in this order. That Divine purpose
can only be achieved when the Divine Creation takes its course,
when Divine order is observed and the Torah of each creature is
rigidly honoured.

The opening passage of these twin *Sidros* deals with the laws
relating to childbirth. We notice that initially the Torah does not
refer to children either as sons or as daughters. They are described
as זכר ונקבה, "male and female." When, for the first time, does a זכר
become a בן, a son, and נקבה, a female, become a בת, a daughter? במלאת
ימי טהרה לבן ולבת, "when the days of purity are fulfilled, then they are
son and daughter." In homes where there is קדושה וטהרה, where there
is prayer and charity, learning and communal involvement, those
who follow after are the heirs to the house. Where there is nothing,

2. רש"י: ויקרא רבה.

they are merely "males and females." Relationships are severed, if not now then surely later. Links are broken, chains are snapped. But where there is טהרה, purity, there is בן ובת, son and daughter. Even if, like the sons in the Haggadah, they ask questions, they will have the strength and resistance to hold on until God Himself comes to rebuild the House of Israel in the future redemption.

iii

A Festival of Demolition

(Shabbos Ha-gadol)

וידבר ה' אל משה ואל אהרן לאמר, כי תבאו אל ארץ כנען אשר אני נתן לכם לאחזה, ונתתי נגע צרעת בבית ארץ אחזתכם "And the Lord spoke unto Moses and unto Aaron, saying, 'When you come into the land of Canaan, which I am giving you as a possession, and I put the affliction of leprosy in a house of the land of your possession. . . .'"

The *Sidrah* proceeds to advise us what steps are to be taken to stop the disease from spreading and contaminating the whole area, or even the whole country. Anyone coming into the house is contaminated, as is anyone who sleeps in the house, or anyone who eats in the house. Every item, every person, is to be purified. The dust of the house is to be taken outside the city along with the bricks and mortar: the house is to be completely demolished.

The Rabbis[1] comment that the Torah says, "When you come into the land, ונתתי, I will put the disease there." It will not be there of its

---

ספרא: "בשורה היא להם שבאים עליהם נגעים." ועי' מלבי"ם ותורה תמימה שם, וכן ויק"ר 1 י"ז ו.

own accord; I will cause it to be there. Why? Because during the forty years that the Israelites were in the wilderness, the Amorites concealed their treasures of gold and silver in the walls of their houses, so that even if they were conquered the Israelites would not possess their treasure. Therefore, God brought a plague onto these same houses, forcing their new tenants to demolish them and so uncover the hidden treasure.

It seems difficult to believe that the Rabbis really meant to say that such a phenomenon would occur merely to make the Jews rich, by disclosing fortunes in their walls. It is noteworthy, indeed, that the Sages do not speak of this as a בשורה טובה, not good tidings but a בשורה, an announcement to them as they set foot in their new land of hope and promise. If you want to fulfil your mission, if the purpose of the Exodus, יציאת מצרים, is to be realised, if the festival of freedom is to mean what it says, then, as we say in the Haggadah, חייב אדם לראות את עצמו כאלו הוא יצא ממצרים, every man must strive to extricate himself from his own מצרים, his personal shackles that enslave him: those material possessions without which he imagines he cannot live. The first thing that had to be done as they set foot in the blessed land of hope and promise, אשר אני נתן לכם, "which I give you," was to demolish those walls that hemmed them in: those theories, those policies, those ideas upon which the Canaanites based all their hopes and fortunes.

That is why this passage of the Torah begins וידבר ה' אל משה ואל אהרן לאמר, כי תבאו אל ארץ כנען — "the Lord spoke unto Moses and unto Aaron, saying, 'When you come into the land of Canaan....'" Did not the All-Knowing know that neither Moses nor Aaron would enter the land of Canaan? But the Divine Voice spoke not to that generation alone; it was for all time, it was a clarion call down the ages: "Jew, yours is a different way of life, a different way of thinking, a different way of living. Your riches are not their riches, your blessings are not their blessings."

ונתץ את הבית את אבניו ואת עציו ואת כל עפר הבית והוציא אל מחוץ לעיר... והבא אל הבית... והשכב בבית... והאכל בבית יכבס את בגדיו. The house shall be pulled down, the bricks, the wood, the mortar shall be thrown out beyond the city's confines; he who goes into the house, he who sleeps in the house, he who eats in the house — these shall wash their garments.

Their homes are not your homes, their beds are not your beds, their food not your food. זאת התורה, this it is that the Torah expects of you if Pesach is to fulfil its purpose. No wonder that their final act as they left Egypt was to sacrifice the lamb, the sacred Egyptian lamb, the materialism of the Egyptian way of life. Throw the dough on your backs, not in front but behind, so that the bread will, as it were, run after you rather than you running after your bread. It was faith that brought them out of the land of Egypt, faith that gave them courage to plunge into the sea, faith that provided them with food in the desert and water in the wilderness.

See what the world looks like: justice can be exchanged for oil and truth twisted to serve power and riches. But now is יציאת מצרים, the festival of demolition. Get out of Egypt, in every age and in every generation, Jews in Israel, Jews in the Diaspora — Jews each and every one! Then will we see real redemption, in a world of peace and calm.

iv

A Plague in the House

(Shabbos Ha-gadol)

Much of this *Sidrah* is devoted to the various forms of a disease which can afflict the Jewish home. The Torah calls this disease צרעת, leprosy, in the walls of the home. Instructions are given to the owner of the house and the כהן, how to proceed when the rot appears and if it spreads. ובא אשר לו הבית והגיד לכהן לאמר, "and the one to whom the house belongs shall come, and he shall tell the priest, saying," כנגע נראה לי בבית, "something like a plague hath appeared to me in the house."

The Rabbis stress the significance of the Torah's expression בבית, "in the house." Not outside the house: מתוכו מטמא ואין מטמא מאחוריו, the infection can only affect the home if it is found בבית, in the house, not if it appears outside. Things between you and God must be in order; there must be none of the hypocrisy which children are so ready to detect. There must be honesty between you and God, between husband and wife, between sons and daughters. What the father does the son will do, and what he does not do the boy will not do; and likewise with mother and daughter. Things catch on: if the inside is clear and strong, no outside disease will contaminate it. Nothing will penetrate those walls. The disease is only מטמא מתוכו, only from the inside, not מאחוריו. You see to it that the first five of the Ten Commandments are observed — those between man and God — and then you can be sure that the second five, between man and fellow man, will be observed too.

Malachi cries out in the *Haftorah*, זכרו תורת משה עבדי אשר צויתי אותו בחורב על כל ישראל, "remember the Torah of Moses My servant, which I commanded him at Sinai for all Israel." Not just for a Chassid, not for the Rabbi alone, but על כל ישראל חקים ומשפטים. First חקים, statutes: those things between you and Him, between man and God. Then משפטים, judgments: those things between man and man. The *chametz* in the house and the *chametz* outside of it — honesty in religious service and honesty in secular dealings. This is the true *Shabbos Ha-gadol*, the Shabbos grown so great as to exercise its influence על כל ישראל, defining and demonstrating to the whole world the true meaning of religion. Then the prophetic promise will be fulfilled:

והשיב לב אבות על בנים ולב בנים על אבותם, "and he shall turn the fathers' heart towards the children, and the children's heart towards their fathers."

iv(b)

Israel: A National Possession

כי תבאו אל ארץ כנען אשר אני נתן לכם לאחזה, "When you come to the land of Canaan, which I am giving you for a possession." The *Sidrah* announces to us a Divine gift: *Eretz Yisrael* is to be an אחזה of the Jewish people. The word אחזה denotes something more tangible than a ירשה, an inheritance. It means property in which each has a share, to which each can hold on.

This is the opening verse of the passage detailing the laws of leprosy affecting houses. We notice that, in the main, the law's instructions appertaining to the other forms of leprosy and uncleanness are written in the singular. There is the man or woman who is unclean, and the laws of his purification; the garment that has been eaten into, and the laws governing its cleansing. But when the Land of Israel is affected, "the house of your possession," ובא אשר לו הבית והגיד לכהן, then the owner, the occupant of the house must come and tell the priest of the misfortune. What happens next? וצוה הכהן, the priest shall command ופנו את הבית, that *they* empty the house. If the priest should see that והנה פשה הנגע, the plague has spread, then וחלצו את האבנים, *they* shall break out the stones והשליכו אתהן, and *they* shall cast the stones out. The safekeeping of the Land of Israel, the sanctity of its soil, the building of its houses — these are no individual responsibilities. ופנו, וחלצו, והשליכו — the whole portion is written in the plural. The security and the spiritual problems of Israel are not to be the concern of the individual alone. If his life becomes intolerable and his home uninhabitable, it is to be the concern of all the 'shareholders' in Israel.

The Sages speak of the hidden treasures to be uncovered when houses are demolished during treatment of the plague. What a strange thing! As though there were no other method of uncovering gold concealed in the walls, a wind or a storm or a tiny hole somewhere, that could expose the treasures. But you cannot sit back and expect oil to spring from the Negev, or gold to flow in Tel Aviv and the word of God from Jerusalem. These are treasures which are everybody's business. It starts with ובא הכהן, ושב הכהן, וראהו הכהן, ויצא הכהן, וצוה הכהן. There is seeing and coming and going and commanding; and then, ופנו והשליכו ושפכו ולקחו: public responsibility, communal sharing, combined operations involving the priest, the occupant, and the people.

That *Eretz Yisrael* will remain אחזתכם is a Divine assurance. But Torah and Israel demand energy and sacrifice. With bowed heads let us remember those who have died that Israel may live. With unbending determination we must resolve that we shall play our part in these historic times. Then will God grant peace in Israel, in a world that enjoys calm and tranquillity.

ACHAREI MOS—KEDOSHIM

אחרי מות-קדושים

i

The Blessing of Old Age

(Bar Mitzvah)

The Torah, in this *Sidrah*, prescribes the special rituals required for the Day of Atonement, when the High Priest was to enter the Holy of Holies. By way of warning against any deviation, there is an opening reference to the tragic death of Aaron's two sons when they deviated from the prescribed procedures during the initiation of the *Mishkan,* as told in the *Sidrah* of *Shemini*. The Zohar says, "He who is affected to tears while reading this portion of the Torah, taking its teaching to heart, will win forgiveness for his sins and the blessing of old age for his children." What is there in this portion that should stir the reader's emotions, bringing tears to his eyes; and how will all this ensure that his children will not die in his lifetime?

On reflection, we notice that in these opening words of the *Sidrah* the Divine Author repeats Himself: "The Lord spoke to Moses אחרי מות שני בני אהרן, after the death of the two sons of Aaron." The Torah could have stopped there, but it continues, בקרבתם לפני ה' וימתו,

"when they drew near to God and died." To die in the eyes of man and to live on in the eyes of God, to die and yet to live on in the continued service of one's successors, is to proceed to life eternal: בקרבתם לפני ה' is the dying hope of all men. When life and work are transmitted to succeeding generations, when children and grandchildren carry on the home and the synagogue, when the spirit of the past lives on, rekindled in the new places of study and prayer — that sort of death is a mere passing phase in the cycle of life, that goes on and on. It means that one does not come to the end of the road in his own lifetime.

But אחרי מות, when death strikes and there is none to carry forward the mission and purpose of life, then בקרבתם לפני ה' וימתו, when they draw near to God they die a second time, for then the end comes abruptly and it is all over.

To read this portion and to take its message to heart: to try, to hope, and to pray, to strive that our generation may carry and transplant the past into the future, means that death can never strike the final blow. The tragedy of our age would be the second death of our martyrs at our own hands. The Shabbos they observed, the *kashrus* they regarded, the purity they practised, the ideals they honoured, the Jewish life they lived and suffered to build anew — to forget these is לפני ה' וימתו, a spiritual death for all time. That is why we pray for Israel, and that is why we must strive to build vibrant communities and see to it that our schools and Yeshivos do not have to go cap in hand to seek support.

The Zohar's saying is of obvious significance for every Bar Mitzvah. It is reinforced by the rousing call with which this *Sidrah* concludes: ושמרתם את משמרתי, "keep My charge." The word משמרתי means 'My guard'; God is telling us, guard My fences. Jewish life is like a garden of roses: so many beautiful colours, so many lovely fragrances. The *tefillin* every day, the Grace after every meal, the

Shabbos every week, the honesty and respect, the study and the practice. It is good to build a fence around a garden of roses; otherwise, people tread upon them and trample them. That is why we see so many things today disregarded: the fences have been pulled down. Your parents and grandparents laboured to build fences that would retain the beauty of Jewish life; ושמרתם את משמרתי, guard those fences and keep God's charge.

ii

Compartmentalism in Jewish Life

A famous thinker once said, "Nine-tenths of all the bad things in the world are done because not to do them would be held ridiculous." Compromise and understanding in individual or communal conflicts are usually reached by adjustments on both sides, particularly when new and unexpected conditions make adjustment necessary. That is the lesson to be learned from the well-known Rabbinic saying, קשה זיווגן כקריעת ים סוף,[1] "the pairing together of two people in marriage is as difficult as the parting of the Red Sea." It is strange that the Rabbis use as their metaphor an example of something divided rather than something united. The parting of the Red Sea was the division of the waters, and זיווג is the combination and the uniting of two entities. But to couple together two individuals, sometimes with opposing elements, means to fit them in with each other — to make a קריעת ים סוף, cutting away such parts, such superfluities, as prevent a harmonious unity.

---

1. סוטה ב' ע"א; סנהדרין כ"ב ע"א.

Only that mutual cutting away can make unity possible in any human endeavour; unless each one is prepared to give something up, cut something away, nine-tenths of the world go one way and the other determined tenth is held ridiculous. History is moving forward rapidly towards a great goal, and science is pushing it on with all the impetus at its command. And we stand by, passive onlookers refusing to adjust ourselves and unable to keep pace, with the result that we are being dragged unwillingly to an abyss from which God alone knows whether we shall be able to extricate ourselves. We have become completely unconscious of the severe defeats we have sustained in the things for which we live and die. For the huge mass of our people, those things have ceased to exist.

We have created compartments within ourselves, a spiritual compartment and a physical compartment, and we refuse to attempt to fit them together. The world of religion lies in one compartment, and the everyday world of work and play lies in the other. If nine-tenths is in one and one-tenth in the other, there is no need to say which is held ridiculous. Religion has stopped thinking in terms of Monday or Wednesday, and now thinks in terms of Saturday or Sunday. Instead of it being something that helps us to live with an aim or a mission in this world, it has become something to do with death. It looks up to Heaven with its back turned on the earth, its only aim or mission 'up there' somewhere. No adjustments, no cutting-away of superfluities has been attempted in order to bring the two worlds into contact, to make men realise that if religion is to have any meaning, if there is to be anything 'over there' when we move on from here, it must be part of a vast circling venture that will be realised only when men begin thinking in terms of the Kingdom of God on earth as well as in Heaven. Unfortunately, this is only בקרבתם לפני ה' וימתו, something that is contemplated only when we are about to face God in death. No wonder the *Sidrahs* אחרי

מות-קדושים are usually read together: אחרי מות, of which our mothers used to speak as the great after-death for which they lived, can only come when קדושים תהיו, when life and work are hallowed in the world into which we are born.

ושמרתם את חקתי ואת משפטי אשר יעשה אתם האדם וחי בהם, "and you shall keep My statutes and My judgments, which if a man do, he shall live by them." The Rabbis said of this, וחי בהם ולא שימות בהם.[2] This is the essence of true religion: "do them for the sake of life, and not for what you get after life." אחרי מות can only be when קדושים תהיו, and there are to be no separate compartments. את חקתי ואת משפטי: the statutes, the spiritual things which none can understand, and the ordinances, which all can understand, must go together in the forefront of civilisation. אשר יעשה אתם האדם: not only Rabbi and priest, but every man must do them, וחי בהם, and he must live by them. Then and only then can the blessings of both worlds be man's reward.

"Pity the wicked," a great Chassid once said; "for the righteous to attain גן עדן is much easier than for the wicked to attain גיהנום. For Gehinnom is attained by strife, hatred, passion, and crime, but גן עדן is attained by means of patience, charity, rectitude, and love." Such paradise is the eternal repose of men and women who are prepared to make adjustments, to hold the balance, to close the gap between themselves and the outside world, to pursue science, to catch up with it and to control it; to pursue communal enterprise and to limit it; to pursue insane politics and purblind nationalism and to bring them together into one compartment with spiritual values; to follow the pattern of the great Law-giver.

The question that faces world Jewry in the new and glorious phase of its history in the reborn Jewish state, and the question that faces us as Jews in the *galus,* is this: are we to follow nine-tenths of

2. יומא פ"ה ע"ב.

the world, with corruption and confusion that are leading mankind
to a disaster such as it has never experienced; or are we to remain
that final tenth, held ridiculous it may be, but retaining our Jewish
dignity and national prestige, and maintaining the mission that is
our life's struggle. Will we allow the great storms that are sweeping
the world to penetrate our hearts and homes and desecrate our
sanctity, or will we make adjustments from without and from within,
and so maintain the balance? The fight is on between inner values
and outer influences, between וחי בהם and ימות בהם. Bankruptcy is
bound to be the result of this terrible conflict unless adjustments
are made and the gap is closed.

In the whole detailed account of the annual ceremony of
purification in Israel's ancient Sanctuary, which forms part of this
Sidrah, the most interesting aspect of the service is the garments in
which the High Priest was attired as he entered the Holy of Holies
to perform this yearly ritual. כתנת בד קדש ילבש ומכנסי בד יהיו על בשרו ובאבנט
בד יחגר ובמצנפת בד יצנף בגדי קדש הם, "He shall wear a holy linen tunic, and
linen breeches shall be upon his flesh, and he shall gird himself with
a linen girdle, and wear a linen turban; they are holy garments; he
shall bathe his flesh in water and put them on." Again and again the
Torah insists on the simplicity of his garments. The material of which
they are made is repeated four times: his tunic linen, his breeches
linen, his sash linen, his head-covering linen. חמש פעמים היה מחליף מעבודת
פנים לעבודת חוץ,[3] five times he proceeded from the service inside the
Sanctuary to that performed outside, and from the outside service
to the inside, changing each time from the golden vestments of all
year round to the simple linen garments. With each change from
gold to linen and from linen to gold, ורחץ במים את בשרו, he immersed
himself in the מקוה.

רש״י: יומא ל״ב ע״א. 3

In the life of each of us there is עבודת פנים and עבודת חוץ. Service to each other in the confines of our homes and community — עבודת פנים; service in the life of society, to fellow men and the world at large — עבודת חוץ. The great thing in life is to draw the line between the interior service, in the Holy of Holies, and the service outside, in our daily occupations and businesses — to hold the balance, to avoid confusion, to retain glory within and dignity without. If outside the High Priest was attired in garments of gold, inside he was to be robed in linen; and each time he came in, he washed and changed. We dare not prostitute the sanctity of our homes, the high sense of moral values and clean living, by giving way to every temptation that offers itself outside. If outside there is suspicion, inside there must be trust; if outside there is splendour, inside is simplicity. You would not walk into your lounge with the mud on your shoes that you brought in from outside. You cannot talk to your wife in the language you speak to your business associates. Your home, your synagogue, your school, your state: guard them against the mud that is flung about outside.

This must be the pattern of Jewish enterprise: עבודת חוץ with בגדי זהב, and עבודת פנים with בגדי בד. To the outside world present dignity, prestige, and splendour; in this mad rush for political supremacy, ours must be a pattern of pure gold. Jewish distinctiveness, shaping and building the national character; the Torah of Israel and the faith of Israel exerting its influence on the People of Israel in the State of Israel, a gracious influence that will lead the world to a sane and righteous order. And within ourselves — in our own world, in home life and communal institutions, we must robe ourselves in the glory of Jewish practice and observance, of service to God and service to people. Alas, in all too many communities the עבודת פנים has collapsed. The purity of family life, with its profound influence on the home, has lost its place; ורחץ במים את בשרו, even for many of our brides, no longer exists. Shabbos in many homes has lost its character, except for a lingering Friday evening. *Kashrus,* that through the ages has influenced the course of history, has for too many become a mere rubber stamp sealed in the abattoir, the Pesach label of the provision merchant. Careers for the children have completely supplanted religious idealism in the character of the young in such families. The בגדי זהב have replaced the בגדי בד, and עבודת פנים, the interior service, is falling to pieces.

Snobbish contempt for everything produced by our forbears has devalued Jewish life and cheapened Jewish values. Yet the only education that will avail men in their present dilemma is a religious education. A non-Jew of some importance has said, "For too long have we been educating children in a fashion in which the primacy of the spiritual has been banished." Give us the child until his adolescence, and we will hold the balance between Torah and worldliness, between nationalism and Jewish values. How many parents are prepared to make just a little קריעת ים סוף, to sacrifice just a little of the career, for the sake of a Jewish future?

What we require is adjustment between the religion and faith that we gave the world and the new freedom the world has given back to us. The gap between the two is wide open, but we can close it by coming back to עבודת פנים. We have captured the imagination of the world with the things we have done — such great things, and done by so few; we shall never allow those things to be undone. From without we are clothed in בגדי זהב: the world has begun to respect us again. From within, too, let us recapture the ideals that we have lost, and the young people who are going astray. We need only come back to the בגדי בד, clothing ourselves in the garments of simple faith and Jewish values. Then shall we see in our days a generation growing up, in the גלות and in the land of Israel, that will bring blessing to our people and glory to our name.

iii

Into the Wilderness

The *Sidrah* tells of the two special offerings brought on Yom Kippur. One was the שעיר לה', the lamb which the High Priest sacrificed on the altar of God; and the other, the שעיר לעזאזל which was taken out into the wilderness and cast down from the top of the mountain.

They may be compared to two types of homes and two types of children. One child with an anchorage, with a home, with a מזבח of Shabbos and Yom Tov, *tallis* and *tefillin, kashrus* and purity. The father with the child at the altar, unflinching: that child is שעיר לה'. The other child, with no מזבח in the home, no anchorage, nothing to hold on to, no קדושה, no טהרה, no *kashrus,* no Shabbos, no צדקה. Nothing: a child המדברה, out in the wilderness, with no Torah education, no Jewish training, exposed to all manner of dangers. Like the שעיר לעזאזל, which died before it reached halfway down, עד חצי ההר,[1] so this child: before he reaches half his age his soul is crushed, his Jewish body torn limb from limb.

The Torah tells us that the שעיר לעזאזל was sent out into the wilderness ביד איש עתי. The English translation is "by a man appointed" for this purpose; המוכן לכך מאתמול, Rashi says, a person who was prepared and appointed the day before to do this task. A child acts today on what he was taught yesterday, a child will act tomorrow according to the influence exercised upon him today; a child is מוכן מאתמול.

There is something in the word עתי even more significant. איש עתי can mean a man of the times, a man who says, "It is today that

1. משנה יומא ו', ו'.

counts, forget yesterday, yesterday belongs to the past, yesterday is dead." איש עתי is a modern man: live with contemporary society! Traditional synagogues are antiquated, Torah living is full of restrictive practices; Jewish observances were good for the ghetto. An איש עתי leads the children out into the מדבר. He drives to the mountaintop of materialism — good living and open spaces! — only to topple down a hopeless abyss, to be lost and swallowed up for all time.

iv

Holiness: A Collective Responsibility

The *Sidrah* of *Kedoshim* begins וידבר ה' אל משה לאמר, "And God spoke unto Moses, saying," דבר אל כל עדת בני ישראל ואמרת אלהם קדשים תהיו כי קדוש אני ה' אלקיכם, "Speak unto all the congregation of Israel, and say unto them, 'Ye shall be holy, for I the Lord your God am holy.'" Instead of the usual דבר אל בני ישראל, "speak unto the Children of Israel," here the Torah uses the unusual expression דבר אל כל עדת בני ישראל, "speak unto the whole congregation of the Children of Israel."

This chapter, Leviticus 19, is one of the outstanding chapters of the Torah. No one would believe that it was written so long ago. It contains the golden rules of Judaism, the most sublime concepts of morality, of integrity, and of decency, uttered by the Almighty four thousand years ago, when human standards were at their lowest ebb. And it was addressed to the whole congregation; no one was left out.

The Ten Commandments were proclaimed in the singular: אנכי ה' אלקיך, "I am the Lord your God"; but in Leviticus 19, אני ה' אלקיכם is in the plural. In the Ten Commandments it is לא תשא, "thou shalt not bear the Name in vain," but here it is לא תשבעו in the plural. There זכור את יום השבת, here את שבתותי תשמרו. There, כבד את אביך ואת אמך, "honour thy father and thy mother"; and here, איש אמו ואביו תיראו, "ye shall revere" collectively. Why was it necessary for the Torah to repeat the same golden rules in the plural, imposing an especial injunction upon the community as a whole?

The standards of decency, of morality, of faith adopted by each individual are matters between himself and his Maker. The Torah is the greatest democracy; man's most sacred privilege is his freedom of will, his ability to obey or to disobey. The moral and religious discipline of each man is in his own hands: he builds or he destroys at his own cost. The Ten Commandments, addressed to the individual, do not begin with the words קדוש תהיה, "you shall be holy." That will depend upon your actions, and you will take the consequences. Vastly different, however, is the Jewish people as a collective body or national entity. פרשה זו נאמרה בהקהל, "this passage was proclaimed in full assembly," the Rabbis point out.[1]

There is a very necessary preamble to Leviticus 19: קדשים תהיו כי קדוש אני ה' אלקיכם, "ye shall be holy, for I the Lord your God am holy." A Jewish state, a Jewish community, a Jewish assembly must bear a Jewish character, because they bear the seal of God. "My country, right or wrong!" a non-Jewish politician once said. Not so with the Jew. If my country is wrong, she has got to be put right; if the congregation as a whole is misguided, it must be redirected. There is a beautiful Rabbinic message on this verse of the Torah. "Ye shall be holy, for I am holy," says the Torah; יכול כמוני, ask the Rabbis, should men be like God Himself, secluded from society, hidden in a faraway corner somewhere, not to be seen or known? No; the Torah demands no renunciation of human relationships. תלמוד לומר

1. רש"י; ספרא.

כי קדוש אני; that kind of קדושה, of holiness, you must leave to God. Your duty is ונקדשתי בתוך בני ישראל, in the midst of Israel as a whole, in the assembly. בהקהל, in the congregation, the spirit of holiness must prevail. For the individual there are the duties and the devotions; for the community there must be a collective sense, a consciousness of holiness.

It is interesting to note that wherever the ideal of holiness is spoken of in the Torah, the plural is used. Whether on the Israeli scene or the local scene; whether it be a struggle for Judaism or for Zion; whether it be an organisation for culture or for play — if it is a collective Jewish body, that seal of holiness must be its character, that ideal of Jewishness must be its overall cast.

v

The Kernel of the Law

פרשה זו בהקהל נאמרה מפני שרוב גופי תורה תלויין בה,[1] "This portion of the Torah — Leviticus 19 — was proclaimed אל כל עדת בני ישראל, to all the congregation of the Children of Israel, because most of the fundamentals of the Torah are dependent upon it." The Rabbis regard this chapter as the kernel of the Law, for most of its essentials are summarised therein.

There is an interesting build-up in the course of these two *Sidros*. אחרי מות opens up with the ceremony of purification, the atonement of sin, the introduction of Yom Kippur, the purity of meat food, the extraction of the blood, the prohibition of unlawful marriages, the sin of incest, the guilt of unchastity, the crime of immoral practices.

1. רש"י; ספרא.

This is אחרי מות: the evil things that make men impure and unrighteous, and from which God Himself recoils.

The second *Sidrah* begins with קדשים תהיו כי קדוש אני ה׳ אלקיכם. Here is the most remarkable lesson of all that the Jew brought down to mankind. It is the keynote of civilisation; it is more real than any hypothesis of science; it is demonstrable, not in cold fact, but in living souls. Here is the best sermon ever spoken. Compared to it, all our pulpit exhortations appear childish. There is no language comparable to it: five simple words that defy definition, but contain everything worthwhile: קדשים תהיו כי קדוש אני, "ye shall be holy, for I am holy." A new light irradiates the horizon of human thought and outlook; God is not only to be worshipped, He is to be imitated.

"In all the world," a preacher once said, "nothing is so daring as the self-identification of finite man with the cause of the infinite God." Man dares to aim so high, because in all the world there is no nook or corner where holiness may take up its abode except in the recesses of the human soul. Man must strive at a purity that is Divine, for by his deeds he reveals the Divine that is implanted within him. There is no theory of man's evolution; there is a practice of Divine Revelation. Be like God! How? By those deeds set out in the portion of *Kedoshim*. Read them, and live by them: reverence for parents, consideration for the needy, prompt payment to employees, honourable dealings with fellow men. No tale-bearing, no malice; love your neighbour, be friendly to the alien, be just to rich and poor alike. Honest measures and just balances, and abhorrence of everything that is unclean and heathen. Deeds that affect us in everyday life, every phase of human and national life, civil and religious, physical and spiritual.

To attempt to preserve the Torah's ethical and moral standards whilst abolishing its halachic and ritual laws is as ridiculous as to attempt to preserve the ritual laws and observances whilst ignoring the ethical and moral ideals. No wonder *Acharei Mos* and *Kedoshim* are usually read together. ושמרתם את חקתי ואת משפטי אשר יעשה אתם האדם וחי בהם, "ye shall keep My statutes and My commandments, which if a man do, he shall live by them." The Rabbis point out the lesson: ליתן שמירה ועשייה לחוקים ושמירה ועשייה למשפטים,[2] both the חקים and the משפטים, the ethical and the ritual, the physical and the spiritual, must be treated alike, with the same שמירה and עשייה, the same observing and performing. We have seen the tragedy of regard for one without the other: abstract loyalty to the lessons of the prophets so tragically incompatible with the most barbaric decrees, idolising God and despising man. We have seen this tragedy in our own individual and communal life: men who stress the necessity of synagogue decorum, men who are ready to participate in a long service, joining in the songs and praise of synagogue worship — and who are equally ready afterwards to abuse and offend a fellow man. Friendly with God but unfriendly with man, rife with tale-bearing, malicious hatred, and ill-will.

We have seen, too, the tragedy of men who shout from the rooftops about the greatness of Jewish ethics and Torah ideals, and yet are equally ready to violate Torah law and Torah precepts. ושמרתם את חקתי ואת משפטי, both the ethical and the ritual, the physical and the spiritual, must be guarded and practised, וחי בהם, so that man may live by them. This is the message of *Acharei Mos— Kedoshim*.

To summarise a man's life,[3] to estimate a man's service, this question must be answered: "How much of God did he imitate? How much קדושה did he leave behind?" I think of my father on this solemn, yet not unhappy, day. How much קדושה did he leave behind? I

---

2. רש"י; ספרא.

3 This sermon was delivered at the Brondesbury Synagogue on the Shabbos coinciding with the first *Yahrzeit* of Dayan Swift's father, ז"ל.

remember so well how every spare moment was used. The spare moments were few after a hard day's work, scraping out a living for a large and growing family; in those days shops were open to midnight, because every shilling counted. But there was never a day without a *blatt Gemara.*

How I remember the early hours of the morning, cold, dark, and miserable. So cruel, and yet so kind, to lift us out of the blankets, so as to learn a little before school and to *daven* like a *Yid.* School hours were sandwiched in between learning, morning, noon, and night; and yet we survived, and when we occupied positions our medical reports were, "T.G.," beyond question. When he bade me farewell as I left him to study abroad for five years, he showed no רחמנות, because it was in my interest to go. His feelings were only revealed in his encouraging letters. Jewish knowledge was life-blood for him; he knew that without it there is no future.

He imitated God: firm when it was necessary to be firm, and kind when it was proper to be kind. All he left was a good name and a good *Kaddish,* because his life was full of קדושה. He lived by the Torah, וחי בהם—לעולם הבא;[4] such a life defies dust and death. That is why I am happy today.

Let each one, then, ask himself: "How much קדושה am I leaving behind, how much love, how much harmony am I accomplishing by 'doing justly, loving mercy, and walking humbly with God and man'?"[5]

4. רש"י.

5. מיכה ו', ח'.

vi

Simple Faith

A *Yizkor* sermon on faith in God and faith in ourselves prompted a young congregant to say, "I wish I could grip myself as you suggested, and have that simple faith and belief in God, without my mind being troubled with politics and economics and the great international problems that beset us." His words may well remind us of the story of the cynic who once took hold of an old Jew, who was faithful but ignorant, and said to him, "Tell me, what is it you believe in?" The old man answered, "I believe in what the Rabbi believes in." "And what does the Rabbi believe in?" "The Rabbi believes in what I believe in." "Well, tell me," the cynic went on, "what do you both believe in?" The faithful old Jew would not be shaken; who can shake an old stalwart? He answered, "The Rabbi and I, we both believe in the same thing."

Though some may well disagree with the implication of this story, it serves to illustrate a commendable attitude. It stresses the view that the healthiest state of mind is that of implicit and simple faith, that come what may cannot be shaken. A faith without חכמה is the only kind of faith that can stand the test of modern times. Whichever way you may choose to follow, the road of the scientist or the road of the theologian, any attempt to prove anything, any attempt to explain the goings-on of this world of ours, has always failed and always will fail. There is a borderline beyond which no mind can penetrate. If anything, science is proving beyond doubt the accepted belief of the ancient Israelites in a supernatural power beyond all things. Every new thought in the field of scientific development is another step, slow but sure, in unfolding the Divine plan.

Faith is not a philosophy; faith is a fact, and it cannot be called upon only for special occasions, for startling events, or for sudden catastrophes. It is a state of mind that calls out continually, without break, השמים מספרים כבוד א–ל ומעשה ידיו מגיד הרקיע, "The heavens recount the glory of God, and the firmament declares His handiwork," אין אמר ואין דברים בלי נשמע קולם, "there is neither speech nor language, their voice cannot be heard," בכל הארץ יצא קום ובקצה תבל מליהם, "their sound is gone throughout all the earth and their words to the end of the world."[1] That is faith in the pure and simple sense. No platform speeches, no pulpit addresses can prove it, but nature itself speaks, in its quiet yet voluminous voice: 'God is through all the earth.'

The Chofetz Chaim, of blessed memory, used to say, מען דארף נישט זיין פרום, מען דארף זיין קלוג. One doesn't need to be religious, only intelligent. The biggest חכמה is simple faith, if you are looking for serenity of mind and peace of soul in this restless world. The greatest tragedy of modern times is that a line has been drawn between אמונה and חכמה, between what we call *frumkeit* and *klugkeit*. We have been trained to believe that you cannot gain entry into the other world with חכמה, you can only get there with *frumkeit*. This came about because for nineteen hundred years we were hounded about the world, and for us there was no די וועלט. What kind of life did those before us enjoy, who kept on telling us about יענע וועלט? Restricted within ghetto walls, hemmed in from all sides, in so many lands quite cut off from the outside world. Their only recreation was the תהלים and the Book; these took their minds off their troubles. Generation after generation grew up believing that this world is nothing but a grim vestibule we have to go through to get into the World to Come.

---

1. תהלים י״ט, ב׳,ד׳–ה׳.

From time to time in our historic march, great men arose with new, refreshing outlooks. We had the golden age of Spain with its philosophic giants, we had halachic genius in the sixteenth and seventeenth centuries, we had Rabbinic scholars in the eighteenth and nineteenth centuries, as well as the Chassidic emotionalists. All these were efforts to lift the Jew up from being sunk in the drabness of his existence. Now we are living in an age of nationalism, which tends to lift us up with a sense of freedom and independence; but between all these factions and ideologies we have been torn to pieces. A wide gap has been left between אמונה and חכמה, between faith and practice. We are moving about in different worlds at one time; there is no harmony and no spiritual adjustment. God is no longer perceived in nature, and there is a wide open space between the natural and the supernatural. Take away simple faith and there is nothing to hold on to.

קדשו את עצמכם למטה ואני אקדש אתכם למעלה ובעולם הבא,[2] "You make yourselves holy on earth, and I will make you holy above and in the World to Come." This is the Rabbinic exposition of the Divine exhortation repeatedly expressed in *Sefer Vayikra*. There is a clear link between מטה and מעלה, between this world and the next. If God's purpose had been simply to get us into the next world, we should never have been born into this struggling world where men grab from men and nations from nations. He could have put us right into the world of eternity, and that would have been the end of all our troubles! But His purpose is קדשו את עצמכם למטה ואני אקדש אתכם למעלה. They go hand in hand. There has got to be a spiritual adjustment, in the ordinary things of life, in the simple everyday things למטה, the things that are down here. They can be uplifted, raised to the level of eternal value. Enjoy life to your heart's content, but recognise

יומא ל״ט ע״א; רש״י ויקרא י״א, מ״ד. 2

God in it! Eat that which is permissible; make a blessing and offer Him thanksgiving. Toil and labour, by all means, but give up some of your time to spiritual things, to prayer, to study, to communal activity. Earn and become prosperous: no one begrudges it, God wants it; but give of your means and your earnings to your people, to your Torah institutions. קדשו את עצמכם למטה, create a link between Heavenly and mundane things, bring God into everyday affairs, ואני אקדש אתכם למעלה; that is the only way to עולם הבא.

It should not surprise us to find in the Torah that the first Sanctuary set up in the wilderness, when the Jew was in transit, on his way to the land of promise, was dedicated by the sacrifice of oxen and sheep. Similarly, throughout the glorious days of Israel's nationhood sacrifices played a prominent part in the service of the Temple. The purpose of sacrifice is to raise up this animal life of ours to a spiritual level. Bring them to the altar, acknowledge God in the lowest things in life, and life becomes a dedication of our all to His service, paving the way for אקדש אתכם למעלה. The purpose of a Temple, the ideal of a synagogue, and the beauty of a home, is קדשו את עצמכם למטה: make things holy, give them value and meaning. Have simple faith, believe that God is in all these things.

ויאמר משה זה הדבר אשר צוה ה' תעשו וירא אליכם כבוד ה',[3] "and Moses said, 'This thing which the Lord commanded shall ye do, and the glory of God will appear unto you.'" The glory of God does not fly in through the window; it is manifested in אשר תעשו, in man's actions. It makes no difference who you are, Rabbi or layman, or what your profession is, student or businessman; if what you do is אשר צוה ה', according to the will of God, then וירא אליכם כבוד ה', your home becomes a Temple and you become a priest, and the glory of God rests upon you.

3. ויקרא ט', ו'

יהי רצון שתשרה שכינה במעשי ידיכם; this was the blessing conferred upon Israel as the Sanctuary was dedicated. "May it be God's will that the שכינה rest upon the work of your hands." So few realise that it is upon מעשי ידיכם that the שכינה must rest. You can stand all day in your *tallis* and *tefillin,* but if מעשי ידיכם are not clean there is no שכינה in your life.

You can be builders of the Holy Land, but if you do it for personal aggrandisement —

you can become members of a synagogue council, but if you do it for the sake of personal glory and not in the interests of the congregation —

if you work with your hands but do not give of the fruits to God and to His institutions —

then you drive away the שכינה from מעשי ידיכם. Our constant striving must be that וירא אליכם כבד ה', the glory of God should appear unto us.

vii

Be Holy

קדשים תהיו, "Ye shall be holy." What does the word 'holy' mean? Holy means set apart, קדוש means to be detached, separated, an individualist. In Hebrew the word קדוש is used for something which cannot mix. Sometimes such a thing must be destroyed: a harlot is a קדשה — she is to be removed from society. A saint is a קדוש — he lives apart from society. He is not swept by the current of events, he refuses to ride on the bandwagon, even though he may be held ridiculous.[1]

1 See *Acharei Mos—Kedoshim,* ii.

Nachmanides, the Ramban, in his famous commentary,[2] says that to honour the commandments and refrain from the things we are forbidden to do still does not imply holiness. You are not a קדוש by rejecting forbidden foods: that is no more than how it should be. You are a קדוש by bringing קדושה into the things that you may do. To be holy does not mean to be an isolationist — פרשה זו בהקהל נאמרה.[3] Live with society, and mix with society, and be community-minded; but do not submerge your identity, do not crush down your individuality. Do not be afraid of being regarded as ridiculous by those lacking understanding. "Be like God," is the call of the *Sidrah*, "imitate Him." God is the greatest mixer; He is with everybody, but He is apart. He cannot be crushed, He cannot be submerged.

קדש עצמך במותר לך.[4] Holiness does not lie in prohibitions, in the things we must not do. On the contrary, holiness lies in the things we may do and can do. Enjoy the things you have, enjoy the sensations of your senses, but do not wallow in them like an animal: that is unbecoming and profane, that is not clean and holy. How wonderful it is to be a Jew, and to live that way in this uneasy world into which our children are being born. Homes with *Kiddush,* marriages with *Kiddushin;* domesticity with purity and *kedushah.* Children identified with God as soon as they rise in the morning: מודה אני לפניך. Our eating identified with God: הזן את הכל.

והייתם קדושים: be separatist in your outlook, be individualist in your loyalties. Remain staunch to your values, וחי בהם, live by them, and transmit that קדושה to generations to come.

---

2. רמב"ן על ויקרא י"ט, א'.

3. רש"י; ויקרא רבה; ספרא.

4. יבמות כ' ע"א.

viii

Do Not Unto Others. . .

(A Lag Ba-Omer Address to Children)[1]

In the different periods of our history, many things happened to the Jewish people during the weeks between Pesach and Shavuos: events that are written in blood and tears. It is, in fact, a period of mourning, and that is why we have no weddings or joyous functions during these days. Of special significance to children is the well-known story of Rabbi Akiva and his pupils.

Rabbi Akiva had an amazing life. He started to study Torah when he was quite a middle-aged man; not like some, who at the age of thirteen or fourteen think they are too old for study. When he was forty he realised how important it was for him to know what the word Jew means, the name that he bore, and what this Torah was, which it was his duty to practise. After twelve years of hard, intense study, he became one of the leading teachers of his age.

Twelve years of learning: not once a week or twice a week, but all day until the night, and even then he never ceased. It was Rabbi Akiva who said, "As a fish cannot live without water, the Jew cannot live without Torah."[2] Not like some today, who learn so little and think they know so much. Not even willing to question or to try to understand, they cannot be bothered with those things for which Rabbi Akiva eventually gave his life. במסרקות של ברזל,[3] with iron combs his flesh was torn from his body; but despite his terrible pain, he

1 From an address to the children of the Brixton Synagogue during the war years.
2 ברכות ס״א ע״ב.
3 שם.

brought a smile to his lips and said, "Now I understand the true meaning of בכל לבבך ובכל נפשך ובכל מאדך, 'with all thy heart and with all thy soul and with all thy might.'"

To love God with all your heart does not mean to love God for the sake of the things you can get out of religion; it means to offer God, out of love, all the things you can sacrifice for your faith, even so far as surrendering your heart and soul. There is a story of a man who said he loved fish. He went to the market, bought it, cut it up, cleaned it, cooked it, and ate it. When he was asked why he did all this, he said, "I love fish." But that is not loving fish, that is loving oneself. Rabbi Akiva said that to love God is not to make Him a convenience for yourself: to keep Shabbos because it is restful, to eat Jewish food because it is pleasant to taste, and to pray because God will answer you. We must do these things because God expects us to do them. That is loving God בכל לבבך, giving everything and expecting nothing; that is true love.

There are children who love their parents, and they love their sisters, their brothers, and their friends. But how often do they irritate their parents, and even ignore them? How often do they annoy their sisters and their brothers, and how often do they offend their friends? That is not love, that is selfishness. To love deeply and truly is never to demand your own way, but always to give the other person the benefit of the doubt. That is the first letter in the alphabet of our religion, and it is embodied in three important words in the *Sidrah* of *Kedoshim:* ואהבת לרעך כמוך, "love thy neighbour as thyself."

'Thy neighbour' means every man. It was Rabbi Akiva, not the one who gave the sermon on the mount, it was the Old Testament, not the new, that gave these three words to the world. Here is the "golden rule of Judaism," plain for all to see in the Book of *Vayikra,* Chapter 19, verse 18. Rabbi Akiva described these three words of the *Chumash* as כלל גדול בתורה,[4] a great principle of the Torah, and in this he echoed the previous teaching of Hillel, דעלך סני לחברך לא תעביד,[5] "Do not do to others what you would not have done to yourself."

The opposite is equally true: "Do to others what you would like done to yourself." Be truthful because you like others to be truthful to you, have respect for others because you want others to respect you. This was the new light that our Rabbis shed on this verse. The very principle of all religious and ethical teachings the world over: we Jews established it. Others have adopted it, and now they say it belongs to them; but it is ours. We are the fathers of that religion.

How tragic it was that in Rabbi Akiva's own college this principle of love and respect was not maintained. לא נהגו כבוד זה בזה,[6] say the Rabbis: the pupils did not hold each other in proper regard and respect, and punishment was meted out to them. A plague broke out soon after Pesach and lasted until the thirty-third day of the Omer — Lag Ba-Omer. Children can never grow up to respect elders and parents if they fail to respect one another when they are young. Regardless of what other boys and girls do, our Jewish boys and girls should be better. We have got to be different. The pupils of Rabbi Akiva were expected to be different, because we gave the world that principle: love thy neighbour as thyself. Lag Ba-Omer became a great day in Jewish schools because on Lag Ba-Omer the plague ceased and the Rabbi's pupils turned over a new leaf.

With respect for one another and true love and respect for parents, we will have healthy Jews and Jewesses, and in future years Lag Ba-Omer will bring us all happiness and peace.

4. ירושלמי נדרים ט', ד'.

5. שבת ל"א ע"א.

6. יבמות ס"ב ע"ב.

EMOR

אמר

i

Into Eternity

וַיֹּאמֶר ה' אֶל מֹשֶׁה אֱמֹר אֶל הַכֹּהֲנִים בְּנֵי אַהֲרֹן וְאָמַרְתָּ אֲלֵהֶם לְנֶפֶשׁ לֹא יִטַּמָּא בְּעַמָּיו: And
the Lord said unto Moses, "Speak unto the priests, the sons of Aaron,
and say unto them, 'None of them shall defile himself for the dead
among his people.'"

Besides some of the ideas underlying the whole Book of ויקרא,
one of the most important aspects of Jewish thought and practice
is enunciated in these opening words of the *Sidrah* and in the
following chapters.

The Book of Leviticus begins with some of the detailed laws of
the קרבנות, animal sacrifices, and it proceeds with the laws of *kashrus,*
purity and holiness. Much human sacrifice would have been avoided
in the world had men taken to heart the message of animal sacrifice
and learned the lessons of purity and holiness. Fundamental in all
our teachings is the belief that God abides in man. Finite and infinite
are blended into one; time and eternity are fitted together in the
process of the Divine purpose. Man is touched and affected by the
Divine in him. The nobility of his deeds, the holiness of his thoughts,
the purity of his living, all reflect the Divine Spirit in him. He imitates

God, he develops a Godlike-ness. Holiness and purity involve all his faculties and regulate his every thought and deed. They endow him with the capacity to follow the Divine pattern. So body and soul, finite and infinite, become one. Time moves on into timelessness, and death into life eternal.

"None shall defile himself for the dead." We have just heard the portion of קדושים, in which the Torah repeats again and again "Be holy, because I am holy." Immediately following, this instruction goes out to the priests and the high priests, those men who serve in the Sanctuary, whose bodies are consecrated and whose lives are dedicated to the service of God, whose day-to-day activities are concerned with holiness and purity. The food they eat is to be pure, the marriages they contract are to be restricted and sanctified. Their priestly vocation brings them into closer communion with God; therefore in their daily services no attention is to be given to the dead. The very touch of a dead body contaminates them. The area in which the dead are confined and rest is out of bounds to the *Kohen*. Such defilement debars him from his sacred office, because the service of God is the service of the נשמה, the service of the soul. In its pathway there is no death. The *Mishkan* and the *Kohanim* who minister in it, by their purity and holiness, bear testimony to the eternal character of the soul.

The *Kohen* is to direct mankind into the stream of the life that is eternal. He is to neutralise the finite and give force to the infinite. Service to the dead is not to occupy his attention. No wonder that here, rather than in any other place in the Torah, the Rabbis recommend להזהיר גדולים על הקטנים,[1] that the adults should teach the young. The young, who would turn their minds from attending the living to attending the dead: they must be taught the fundamental

1. יבמות קי'ד ע'א.

principles of purity and holiness, that way of life which, if it is followed, goes on and on. *Kedushah* in deed and in thought, in attitude and in practice, must rule their senses and regulate their actions, turning them into instruments of service to God Eternal, and so to the life that is eternal. They must strive to rise above the mundane, physical things that are finite and end in decay. Therefore, "none shall defile himself."

It is not the *Kohen* alone to whom holiness applies: it is equally incumbent upon איש איש מבני ישראל ומן הגר הגר בישראל,[2] "every man of the House of Israel, and of the stranger who abides among Israel." The House of Israel is set upon holiness and purity. From the House of Israel there emerges ממלכת כהנים, the Kingdom of Priests, and גוי קדוש, the holy nation. Whilst the Torah distinguishes between the *Kohen* and the ישראל, and removes for the Israelite many restrictions which apply to the *Kohen*, nevertheless the Israelite must live a life in which ונקדשתי בתוך בני ישראל, God's name is sanctified. With this קדוש ה', the sanctification of life, the Israelite, too, moves from the finite to the infinite and into life eternal.

Even there אמר does not stop. If life can be hallowed, so can the days, the seasons, and the blessings of nature. Festivals are described as מועדי ה', "the seasons of the Lord." The assemblies of Jews that come from all over to the Holy City to offer thanksgiving for God's beneficence are known as מקראי קדש, "holy convocations." These are the instruments of the Divine purpose: sacred events and historic epochs that direct the people to celebrate holy and festive days in Jerusalem. And the goal is purity and holiness, the moralisation of life and the perfection of living, the movement from the finite into the infinite, from time into eternity.

2. קדושים כ', ב'.

The *Sidrah* continues with the נר תמיד, the perpetual light in Israel's Sanctuary, nowadays kindled in every Jewish place of worship, the symbol of the נר ה' נשמת אדם, the inextinguishable spirit of the soul, the spark of eternal life that knows no death. The *Sidrah* goes on to speak of the Land of Israel, describing it as "the land which I give you," the land that is God's gift. The Land of Israel is the instrument of the same Divine purpose. It possesses the elements of the same קדושה; it is the Holy Land, and its people are the people of God. Time and nature are the instruments of God: our light will never be extinguished, our land will never be destroyed, our people will never die, because the people, the land, and the Holy One are one.

ii

The Old Must Instruct the Young

(Lag Ba-Omer)

The Talmud tells briefly of the plague that raged amongst the disciples of Rabbi Akiva: שנים עשר אלף זוגות תלמידים היו לו לר' עקיבא כלם . . . מתו מפסח ועד עצרת, "Twenty-four thousand pupils of Rabbi Akiva perished between Pesach and Shavuos."[1] Though the Talmud does not refer to it, tradition has it that on Lag Ba-Omer the plague ceased; and so the day became known as the Scholars' Festival. Other sources say that when the Israelites were in the desert of Sinai, the manna began falling on the 18th of Iyyar, and that is the reason that the day is especially marked in our Jewish calendar.

1. יבמות ס"ב ע"ב.

In Israel, Jews from all over the country make a pilgrimage to the grave of Rabbi Shimon ben Yochai, the author of the Zohar, who died on Lag Ba-Omer. It is said that before his death he revealed many secrets that were hidden in the words of the Zohar. So from time immemorial history and traditions have surrounded this day, and it is a good thing that we should be made acquainted with some of them. These are events that go to make up the amazing story of our people, and give added meaning to the pages of our glorious calendar.

It is a tragic coincidence that the anniversaries of a whole series of attacks upon the Jewish people, times when massacre succeeded massacre and persecution succeeded persecution, fall during these very weeks between the joyous festivals of Pesach and Shavuos, between the festival of freedom and the festival of the giving of the Torah. It seems to be a message to us, calling out that the terrible price we have paid and are paying for our freedom can only be worthwhile if it leads to the culmination of מתן תורתנו, the new civilisation that Shavuos has to offer.

והיה העולם שמם[2]; the Rabbis say that when Rabbi Akiva was faced with this terrible disaster, the destruction of his life's labours, the collapse of his academies of learning and the death of twenty-four thousand of his disciples, "the world was desolate," שנשתכחה תורה, Rashi explains. The Torah was on the verge of being forgotten: who would teach, and who would learn? From without the Romans were cutting them to pieces; from within the plague was killing them one by one. Torah concepts and Torah outlook would soon be a thing of the past, because, as Rabbi Akiva himself had said, "A fish cannot live without water, so the Jew cannot live without the Torah."[3]

2. שם

3. ברכות ס"א ע"ב.

What did he do? Did he stop at that comment, and let frustration grip him? Did he weep over the graves and hug their tombstones? עד שבא ר' עקיבא אצל רבותינו שבדרום ושנאה להם, ר"מ ור' יהודה ור' יוסי ור' שמעון ור' אלעזר בן שמע, והם העמידו תורה אותה שעה.[4] "No, the great Sage moved to the south, set up new schools, and reared new disciples, and whilst he suffered a martyr's death they re-established the study of the Torah, and brought new light into the darkness of Jewish life." These great men knew well that Pesach, with all the blessings and freedom it brings in its wake, means nothing to the Jew unless it leads, through study and knowledge, through practice and observance, to the greater blessings of Shavuos. שתשתכח תורה מישראל, that the Torah might be forgotten, has always been the greatest fear of the Jewish people, and ignorance, עם הארצות, the greatest danger. If these were to prevail, we would have a beautiful world with no character and no discipline, a beautiful home with no moral values or ethical standards; a people that do not pray, a people that do not learn, a people who have no sense of control. Pesach without Shavuos means העולם שמם, a void that can never be filled.

No other people possesses such a proud record of קדוש השם, of martyrs among Rabbis, teachers, and scholars. They concealed themselves in cellars, they hid themselves on the rooftops to carry forward the torch of knowledge and the light of learning. A far greater threat than the darkness of oppression has been the darkness of ignorance in Jewish life. We have no need to look back into history; turn back only one generation! Our fathers would have preferred to tackle twelve Cossacks rather than have one son an *am ha'aretz*. They would much have preferred to leave after them a *Shas* that children would use rather than fortunes that children would misuse. When pleasures were rare and comforts were scarce,

4. יבמות ס"ב ע"ב.

cheder gelt was always available, and the misery of all the poverty they endured never squeezed out the light of learning.

The *Sidrah* begins ויאמר ה' אל משה אמר אל הכהנים בני אהרן ואמרת אלהם, "And the Lord said unto Moses, 'Speak unto the priests, the children of Aaron, and say unto them, לנפש לא יטמא בעמיו, none shall make himself unclean through contact with the dead.'" The *Kohen* who came in contact with the dead was rendered unfit to perform the duties of the Temple. Only in the case of near relatives: a wife, parents, children, brothers, and unmarried sisters, was the rule set aside.

The Rabbis ask, Why is the word אמר, "speak," repeated twice in the verse? The answer is, כדי להזהיר גדולים על הקטנים,[5] it was a special admonition to the *Kohanim* that the adults must instruct the young. It seems strange that the Rabbis found no other place in the Torah but here, in the discussion of contact with the dead, that the Torah admonishes the *Kohanim* to teach the young. It is not only strange, it is significant, and bears a message for us all.

One is apt, during a period of mourning, in time of personal grief, to become absorbed in the loss one has sustained. The Torah recognises human weakness and personal feelings, and makes allowance for the *Kohen* who has lost a near relative. One is apt, however, in such times of distress, to become unconscious of what is going on about him, and allow the children, at least figuratively, to "roam the streets." We are sometimes so concerned with burying the dead that we neglect to keep an eye on the living. We may say קדיש for the deceased without making a קידוש for the one who is alive; or spend money on tombstones without spending any on the education of the young. להזהיר גדולים על הקטנים, the warning goes out in the *Sidrah*: in your deepest grief, remember your duties to the young. Rabbi Akiva turns his back on the graves of twenty-four

5. יבמות קי"ד ע"א; ספרא.

thousand pupils, and sets out to build new schools of learning, to educate new pupils.

This is the message of Lag Ba-Omer: in the midst of your mourning between Pesach and Atzeres, make a scholars' feast! Set up new schools, rear new pupils. Lag Ba-Omer is a challenge to the עם הארצות that prevails in some communities. Throughout the ages, Jewish communities all over the world were made up of two elements, those that learned and those that provided the means for others to learn. עץ חיים היא למחזיקים בה[6] has a double meaning: the Torah is a "tree of life" for those who "hold on to it," those who learn it and observe it; and it is a tree of life for those who "support it and provide for it." The community was divided into Rabbis, scholars, and students on the one hand, and *ba'alei batim* on the other who gave the means. One who did not belong to one or the other of these groups was virtually an outsider. Parents even saved up their *groschen* to be able to provide for a Yeshivah-*bochur* for their daughter. Learning, and support for learning, was the basis of all social rank.

We, too, must do all that is in our power to be the מחזיקים in both of its senses. Like Rabbi Akiva's new disciples, the Sages of the south, הם הם העמידו תורה; we, both of our elements together, must endeavour to replenish the stock which has been so sadly depleted by the tragedies of our own times. We must ensure that the Torah will live anew in a strong and vigorous Jewish community.

משלי ג׳, י״ח. 6

iii

Significant Anniversaries

The *Sidrah* of *Emor* is read during the month of Iyyar, in which there are two significant dates. The first of these is the fourteenth, indicated on the calendar as *Pesach Sheni*. This festival was instituted for the benefit of those who were unable to bring the Pesach offering on the fourteenth of Nisan. Although it is unusual for a celebration to be postponed for a whole month, nevertheless, since Pesach was instituted to keep the liberation of the entire people alive in Jewish memory, no one was to be precluded.

There is also a lesser-known anniversary on this same day. Just as Lag Ba-Omer, a few days later, is known as הלולא דרבי שמעון בן יוחאי, marking the departure to eternal life of Rabbi Shimon ben Yochai, the fourteenth of Iyyar is known as הלולא דרבי מאיר בעל הנס.[1]

Rabbi Shimon ben Yochai was one of the last surviving pupils of the martyred Rabbi Akiva after the Bar Kochva revolt. Tens of thousands lost their lives in the revolt against the Romans in the second century, in a vain effort to save the Holy Land from their oppression. That is why the period between Pesach and Shavuos is one of semi-mourning. It was Rabbi Shimon ben Yochai who rekindled hope in the hearts of the people when all seemed lost. It was he who coined the phrase, כל מקום שגלו שכינה עמהם,[2] "Wherever Israel is exiled, the *Shechinah* is in exile with them." This consoling conviction gave new hope to a grief-stricken people. Rabbi Shimon's travels to and from the Holy Land forged a link between Israel and

---

1 ראה ירושלמי סנהדרין פ״א הל׳ ב׳ בענין סמיכת זקנים: בראשונה היה כל אחד ואחד ממנה את תלמידיו כגון ר׳ יוחנן בן זכאי מינה וכו׳ ור׳ עקיבא את ר׳ מאיר ואת ר׳ שמעון. ונראה מזה שאלו השניים היו תלמידי ר׳ עקיבא המובהקים (ויש מביאים ראיה מזה שרק אלו סמך!).

2 מגילה כ״ט ע״א.

the Exile, and Jewish survival was due in many respects to that great figure in Jewish life of the second century. On Lag Ba-Omer, the anniversary of his death, thousands of Jews flock to Meron, near the ancient city of צפת, to pay homage at his tomb.

Not many are so well aware of הלולא דרבי מאיר בעל הנס, the anniversary of the passing of Rabbi Meir, "Ba'al Ha-nes." Though the name of Rabbi Meir is the most widely known of all the famous men of that age, this day seems to have been overlooked.

In tens of thousands of Jewish homes, in cities, in villages, and in hamlets, there hangs on the wall a collecting box, known as קופת רבי מאיר בעל הנס. When and how they were instituted seems to be unknown; but perhaps we can find a clue in the facts of his life.

Rabbi Meir, too, was a pupil of Rabbi Akiva. He was the most remarkable scholar and saint of his generation. If it was Rabbi Shimon ben Yochai who forged a physical link between Israel and the Exile — and indeed it may well be that to him we owe our return to our national home — it was Rabbi Meir *Ba'al Ha-nes* who forged a spiritual link. He was responsible, more than any other man, for the development of the *halachah* and Jewish way of life throughout the Diaspora, without which the physical link would have snapped. He was responsible for the re-establishment of the Sanhedrin and the setting up of numerous academies, without which the spiritual and moral structure of the people would have collapsed.

His feats of memory were supernatural. When books were burned and destroyed, he wrote entire volumes from memory. Of him it was said that he was able to produce a hundred and fifty reasons to prove a thing legally right, and as many more reasons to prove it wrong.[3] It was he who infused new life into the development of the *halachah*. As a scribe he earned three shekels a week; אכל ושתי

3. עירובין י"ג ע"ב.

בחדא מתכסי בחדא ומפרנס אורחתא לרבנן בחדא,[4] two shekels were spent on his
household needs, and one was given to maintain a fellow student.
When he was asked why he did not provide for his children in later
years, he replied, "If they are good, God will provide for them; if
they are not good, they must find for themselves." His love for
learning outweighed everything else in life.

The Rabbi Meir *Ba'al Ha-nes* boxes were instituted centuries ago
to raise a common pool to which all Jews contributed. They helped
in this way to maintain those who throughout the years of exile
remained in *Eretz Yisrael*, holding on to the land for future
generations. There they practised and studied the Torah of God and
the intricacies of the *halachah*. When Rabbi Meir died, he begged
of his pupils, "Bury me by the shore of the sea, that the sea which
washes the land of my fathers may also wash my bones."[5] What a
manifestation of a profound and indestructible love for Jewish soil!
His remains lie in Tiberias, and thousands of Jews flock to his tomb
on the eve of the fourteenth of Iyyar, to pay homage to his blessed
memory.

It is interesting that these two pupils of Rabbi Akiva, Rabbi
Shimon ben Yochai and Rabbi Meir *Ba'al Ha-nes,* were both
immortalised by these two outstanding days in the Jewish calendar.
Here is an expression of a wonderful combination of the love for
Israel's land and the love for Israel's learning. Both of these two
Sages lived at the most critical time in Jewish history, both suffered
heavily in the Bar Kochva revolt, both saw with their own eyes the
annihilation of Jewish communities, and both knew all too well that
unless the link with the land were maintained and world Jewry were
linked together with one *halachah* and one Torah, one Talmud and

קהלת רבתי ב', כ"ב. 4

ירושלמי סוף כלאים. 5

one culture, the people would never survive the vulture that aimed at their destruction. It is right and proper that we should pause on these two days to think of the influence these immortal men still have on our lives.

The *Sidrah* of *Emor*, with its dual injunction, אמר ואמרת, calls upon the *Kohanim* להזהיר גדולים על הקטנים, that the older ones amongst them shall warn and instruct the young. Here is a salutary lesson for the whole "priestly nation," that only by due regard for Torah education can the future of our people be assured. A story is told of a child whose father was recovering from a severe illness, and was being trained to walk again on his frail feet. As he tried to walk, he fell, while those standing by watched with anxiety and distress. "Daddy," the child asked, "when our little baby was learning to walk and fell down, even if he hurt himself everyone laughed and was happy; but now that you are learning to walk and fall down, people cry and look sad?"

"I will tell you, my child," the father replied. "When Daddy teaches a child to walk, then there is reason for happiness; but when a child teaches Daddy to walk, there is reason for sorrow." The message of the *Sidrah* is להזהיר גדולים על הקטנים, that it is for the old to teach the young. Today we frequently see a new situation: young people, interested and alive, drawing the old people back into the community. Sad it may be to see so many of the older generation who have fallen by the wayside, but one day all will be well if we keep alive the memory of those two famous men, Rabbi Meir *Ba'al Ha-nes* and Rabbi Shimon ben Yochai. Their memory is symbolic of that love of Torah learning and of the Holy Land through which we hope one day the world will be filled with the knowledge and the way of God.

iv

Guardians of the Torah

(Bar Mitzvah)[1]

Like the *Sidrah* of *Emor*, the opening words of the *Haftorah* this Shabbos are directed to the *Kohanim*. The prophet Ezekiel, in Babylon, looks forward to the restoration of Israel to its ancient homeland and the rebuilding of the Holy Temple.

There were many thousands of priests in the Temple days, but only one family of *Kohanim*, the prophet tells us, would be chosen as fit to serve in Israel's second Sanctuary. Only the descendants of that one family would serve as priests in the future, because בתעות בני ישראל מעלי, "when the Children of Israel went astray," these chosen *Kohanim* were the few who stood on guard against the desecration of our sacred values. אשר שמרו את משמרת מקדשי, "they kept My charge"; when everything was being violated, they stood at their posts. המה יקרבו — when everybody was moving further away, they drew near; ועמדו לפני — when everyone was being swept by a current of ignorance and assimilation, they stood firm.

Those words were spoken by the prophet who foresaw that the time would come when, like today, the Jews would return to their own country. During the years of exile among communities of different faiths and practices, whose languages and beliefs are not like the Jews' own, thousands would surely be led astray. Torah study would be forgotten, Shabbos would lose its character, and Hebrew would be like a foreign language. Only a few would hold on to the true traditions of the Torah, keeping a synagogue that

1 An extract from an address at Young Israel of Los Angeles.

looked like a synagogue, seeing to it that Yeshivah pupils learned Torah and did not merely attend "Sunday school classes."

Further on in the *Sidrah* we find the oft-repeated Divine exhortation to all Israel: ושמרתם מצותי ועשיתם אתם, "and you shall keep My commandments and do them." The word ושמרתם literally means to guard. Now, there are two ways to guard a thing. The story is told of a king who had two magnificent trees in his orchard. He appointed two men, each of whom was to guard one tree. One of these men had a fence built around his tree, with iron railings, and he commanded soldiers day and night to see that no one got near it. The other one left his tree exposed, but he spent all his time on nurturing it, pruning it, watering it, and ensuring that it had plenty of sunlight.

What happened when the royal owner returned? He broke through the fence the first man had erected, removed the iron railings, and discharged the guards. At last he reached the tree; but it was dead. Its leaves had fallen, its blossoms had decayed, its trunk was dry and rotting. As for the other tree, that had been tended without fences and railings, the sun had shone on it and nature had nurtured it. There it was, a beautiful, blossoming, fruitful tree, that provided its owner with all its blessings.

Likewise, there are two ways of ושמרתם, of guarding the Torah. You can guard this *Sefer Torah* of ours, close it in the Ark with beautiful lights surrounding it, adorn it with gold and silver ornaments, and insure it against loss and damage. No one touches it the whole week round; but see what happens when a few generations have gone by. The Torah's language is foreign, its *mitzvos* are thought antiquated, its study is neglected. It itself is regarded as decadent and old-fashioned. But there is the other way of guarding: ושמרתם — זו משנה,[2] to learn it and study it, to practise it and live by it. In this way it is always fresh and fruitful.

Why is Lag Ba-Omer a minor Jewish holiday? It was in Rabbi Akiva's time, when the Temple had been destroyed and the Yeshivos had been closed down. The People of Israel were driven from their country, and then thousands of Yeshivah students perished between Pesach and Shavuos. Not the destruction of the Temple, nor the exile of our people, was the biggest worry to Rabbi Akiva; his main concern was that, God forbid, עתידה תורה שתשתכח מישראל,[3] the Torah seemed likely to be forgotten. It is the removal of that threat that we celebrate on Lag Ba-Omer.

The prime message to give a Bar Mitzvah is ושמרתם — זו משנה; the way to preserve Jewish identity is by learning Torah. If you learn, you will put on your *tefillin;* if you learn, you will keep Shabbos; if you learn, you will respect your parents. If you learn, you will be a *mentsch,* bringing real *nachas* to your parents and credit to the whole community.

iv(b)

Synagogue Leadership

The task of synagogue leadership is made very clear in this week's *Haftorah.* Reading it, one could almost imagine that Ezekiel were living today, in our own age. Repeatedly he says המה יקרבו אלי, "they will draw near unto Me," these are the type, המה יקרבו אל שלחני, "these are the type that can draw near to My table." And what type

2. רש"י; ספרא.

3. שבת קל"ח ע"ב.

is that? אשר שמרו את משמרת מקדשי בתעות בני ישראל מעלי, which is translated as "they that kept the charge of My Sanctuary when the Children of Israel went astray from Me." But משמרת מקדשי does not literally mean "the charge of My sanctuary." A משמרת is a guard or fence; then אשר שמרו את משמרת מקדשי means "they guarded the fence that guarded My Sanctuary." That type, המה יקרבו ושמרו את משמרתי, "they shall draw near and watch over that which watches over Me."

It is the easiest thing in the world to trample upon the bed of roses once the fence is broken. Leadership means to be a שומר, alert and on guard to see that nothing is tampered with, nothing is desecrated: אשר שמרו את משמרת מקדשי בתעות בני ישראל מעלי, "they that guarded that which guarded, which preserved and protected, My Sanctuary, when the Children of Israel went astray from Me." Anyone can be a warden when there is nothing amiss, when no one goes astray. Greatness is shown by standing firm בתעות בני ישראל מעלי, when the people go astray. A thousand members with a thousand opinions, calling for all kinds of attractions from outside the synagogue to be brought inside. Foreign languages and foreign music, innovations that will never strengthen קדושה, our holiness, but rather weaken it.

והיה בבואם אל שערי החצר הפנימית, "when the Kohanim enter in at the gates of the Inner Court, בגדי פשתים ילבשו, they shall be clothed in linen garments" — they shall not wear the same garments that they wear outside. The task of the leader is not to bring the street into the synagogue, but to take the synagogue outside into the street.

Amongst the various instructions the prophet gives regarding the priestly clothing when entering the Holy Place, there is one that is seemingly strange, and yet most meaningful. לא יחגרו ביזע, "they shall not gird themselves with anything that causes sweat." When we speak at a meeting, when we address the Council, we should remember that we are not in business; we are not even at home;

we are not in the street. We are dealing with holy things, with the
guarding of that which guards God. Clothes, language, and manners
must be suited to the occasion — no heat, no sweat, no politics, no
lies, no selling your soul for honours. Let us not confuse the common
with the sacred. Let some things remain holy, untampered with. Let
something belong to God, which we shall not tear to pieces. He does
not need our unclean things; we need His clean ones.

To lead a congregation this way is, as Ezekiel says, להניח ברכה אל
ביתך, "to bring blessing into your house." To look back on years of
truly dedicated service and to be able to say, "this I have lived to
do," or to look forward and say, "this I shall try to do," is to bring
blessing to the community and blessing upon our lives and our
homes.

BEHAR—BECHUKOSAI

בהר-בחקתי

i

Strangers or Settlers?

Reading this *Sidrah*, it is astonishing to find this homeless People of Israel, who only a few days ago shook off the shackles of bondage, endowed with the greatest laws ever set before man. The laws of property and estate, the laws of employer and employee, the laws of debtor and creditor — that such things were thought of in those primitive days is the greatest proof of תורה מן השמים, that these laws were Divinely inspired.

It would be a different kind of world to live in if the approach to the great social problems that beset us were not political but Biblical. Such an approach has never been adopted, because it deprives man of his so-called freehold claim on his possessions. The world does not belong to us; we belong to the world. The seventh day of the week is more than a day of rest, to recover from six days' labour and to go back fresh when the week begins. It is יום השביעי שבת לה׳ אלקיך, it is a Sabbath unto the Lord. Time belongs to Him: מען לעבט נישט אייביק, no one lives forever. The seventh year, ordained in this *Sidrah* as the "Sabbatical year," is more than a year of rest for the soil, so that a good crop can be enjoyed when the earth is rested and refreshed. וּבַשָּׁנָה הַשְּׁבִיעִית שַׁבַּת שַׁבָּתוֹן יִהְיֶה לָאָרֶץ שַׁבָּת לַה׳, "in the seventh year shall be a Sabbath of rest for the land, a Sabbath unto the Lord." כְּשֵׁם שֶׁנֶּאֱמַר בְּשַׁבַּת בְּרֵאשִׁית,[1] it is the same conception as the weekly Sabbath, the Rabbis tell us. Time belongs to God, and property belongs to Him, too: מען חאפט נישט אַריין די וועלט, no one can snatch the whole world. And when you have counted seven times seven, you will honour not only the Sabbatical year, but the Jubilee year, too. כִּי יוֹבֵל הִיא קֹדֶשׁ תִּהְיֶה לָכֶם, "for it is the Jubilee year, it shall be holy to you"; תּוֹפֶסֶת דָּמֶיהָ כַּהֶקְדֵשׁ,[2] all its produce and all its profits remain הֶקְדֵשׁ, they bear the same character as the Holy of Holies in the Temple. Slaves are to be freed, debts are to be annulled, land is to return to its original owner. There is no freehold.

Here is an amazing introduction of God into human personality and into man's possessions. Man is not here for ever; you cannot enslave him all his life. Property does not belong to you for ever; you cannot cling to it all your life. וְכִי תֹאמְרוּ מַה נֹּאכַל, "and if you should ask," the Torah continues, "what shall we eat if Shabbos deprives us of a day's profit? וְצִוִּיתִי אֶת בִּרְכָתִי לָכֶם, I will command My blessing upon you." This is a strange and rare Biblical expression, that God will "command His blessing." But here is the secret of our faith: no man is a master of nature. God holds the key, God gives life and God will command that it be sustained. כִּי גֵרִים וְתוֹשָׁבִים אַתֶּם עִמָּדִי, "remember that you are only strangers and settlers with Me on earth." No man comes to stay.

The Dubner *Maggid* gave this phrase of the *Sidrah* a remarkable interpretation. He said that man is either a גֵר or a תּוֹשָׁב, a stranger or a resident. If he remembers that he is but a גֵר, here for a span of sixty, seventy, or maybe eighty years, but nevertheless a גֵר, then

---

1. רש"י; ספרא

2. רש"י מהספרא, וכן איתא בסוכה מ׳ ע"ב.

God is a תושב for him, resident in his heart. But if he considers himself a תושב, a settler, a resident who has come to stay, then God is a גר, a stranger in his heart.

This *Sidrah* enshrines a glorious message: think of the number seven. The seventh day, Shabbos; the seventh year, שמיטה, the Sabbatical year; seven times seven years, the Jubilee. The seventh decade of life, man is ready to move on. Think of these things, and then when the seventh week after Pesach arrives, זמן מתן תורתנו, the anniversary of the Revelation of the Torah will be a true celebration. It will be a joyful acknowledgment that the law of God controls our lives, making us an example of true faith and righteous living to men the world over.

ii

The Jewish Social Order[1]

If I had the power and the influence, I would tell the world to turn to ויקרא כ״ה, Leviticus Chapter 25, this *Sidrah* of *Behar*. I would post it up on the walls of government buildings, on civic centres, in every home and every commercial office. Here, tucked away in this little book of ours, are the most realistic of all laws, applicable to all people. The most amazing thing about this Leviticus 25 is that it originated בהר סיני, in the wilderness at Sinai. We had no land, we possessed no industry, we had coined no currency. Yet this great social order, applicable to the land, the soil, distribution and equality, rich and poor, master and slave, employer and employee, wage and class, landowner and stranger — נאמרו כללותיה ופרטותיה

1 An address at Young Israel of Los Angeles, 1954.

ודקדוקיה מסיני,[2] all the laws, down to their minutest detail, were promulgated at Sinai. And they were promulgated even in greater detail than were the laws of *tefillin* and *sukkah*. For when you take off your *tefillin* and go out into the street, when you leave your *sukkah* and go out into the open, it is there that you face a world of reality, and it is there that the heart of Judaism beats most.

Some find it difficult to understand why the Rabbis recommended that we begin teaching a child *Chumash* from the Book of *Vayikra* rather than from *Bereishis*. It may well be that therein lies the source of ignorance today. We attract the child with the story of the Creation, with the romances of the Patriarchs, with Isaac's love for Rebecca and with Joseph's achievements in Egypt. By the time we reach *Behar* the Torah is dressed in legendary garb, like a fairy tale that does not seem to fit in with reality. Religion has become one thing and the science of right conduct another thing, as though the Torah is not concerned with the stiff problems that Mammon holds in store for the child when he comes face to face with the world.

The Rabbis hold a different view: והלא כל המצוות נאמרו מסיני, "Were not all the *mitzvos* promulgated at Sinai?" they ask. Why are the laws of the land in this *Sidrah* singled out in so pronounced a fashion? These were not the only laws that were given in detail at Sinai; אף כולן, all the others were, too; but these were singled out as the prime example. The Torah speaks to the farmer and tells him how to nurture the soil; it speaks to the industrialist and tells him how to treat his employee. This is a social system that would remove poverty and slums. It is an economic system that provides for fair distribution. This is the *Chumash* from which the child should first be taught. It is the only answer to the conflict between God and Mammon.

_____

2. רש"י; ספרא.

There is nothing like it in any other book in the world. You need not call it religion: it is a social order. Men are fools who think that they can secure the economic future of their children and their future generations, when all around them is frustration and suspicion. The Russian millionaire sold *charoses* in the streets of Palestine in 1921; the German industrialist went cap in hand collecting coins to set himself up anew. How their castle of illusions was shaken! They had forgotten one thing, and other communities forget it, too: והארץ לא תמכר לצמתת כי לי הארץ, כי גרים ותושבים אתם עמדי No land belongs to man in perpetuity. No man lives forever. We are strangers and settlers on earth — מען רייסט נישט אײן די וועלט — it goes back to its owner in its own good time.

Give the soil a rest; it does not belong to you. Let the land return to its original owner; it is not your eternal possession. Make a Statute of Limitations, and discount your debts at given times; do not hold the less fortunate in your stranglehold for all time. Set the slave free in the Sabbatical year. Let man and earth breathe the air of jubilation in the Jubilee year. When circumstances require a man to sell his home, give him an opportunity to redeem it. If a man becomes poor, ומכר מאחזתו: do not force him to sell all his possessions, but מאחזתו, only part of them. וכי ימוך אחיך ומטה ידו עמך, "if thy brother wax poor, ומטה ידו עמך, let him still be one with you." Do not look down upon him. If he has to work for you, treat him like a man. This is Torah; this is the Bible; this is the Jewish social order. You need no "isms" to face the challenge of society; you need to go back to the Bible.

This is the vital message of this *Sidrah*. Let Jews return to this order, let the world see that this is our aim and mission. Then nothing would expose us to shame. We would stand out as an example of true and righteous living, helping to bring the world back to a social order of peace, tranquillity, and calm.

ii(b)

Torah in the Atomic Age

וצויתי את ברכתי לכם, "I will command My blessing to you." In those four words lies one of the great secrets of God's dealings with man. The blessings of nature are no mere compensation for man's deeds; וצויתי is a command. Put God into life: in domestic relations with purity, in commercial relations with honesty, in national relations with integrity, in religious relations with observance. Put Shabbos into labour, put *kashrus* into food, put religious training into children. Bring Torah into communal relations, with synagogue and schools, Yeshivos and Israel. Bring God down into the arena of life, and צויתי, nature will be compelled to serve you. Recognise, by observing the Sabbatical year and the Jubilee, that the world and worldly possessions belong to Him; then the things created by His command at the beginning, the sun and the moon, the birds and the earth, the fruit and the harvest, will be at your service by His command.

A thousand interpretations have been given to that strange Rabbinic saying, אלמלי נתנה רשות לעין לראות אין כל בריה יכולה לעמוד מפני המזיקין,[1] "if the human eye could see the מזיקין, the millions of demons that surround us, no one would have the strength to face them." We may well wonder whether the Rabbis had any knowledge of those demons which science is producing out of nature these days: nuclear forces, atomic energy, radioactivity, מזיקין that the eye cannot behold, yet here they are, in the very air we breathe. Build with God, live with God, and they shall serve you with blessing. Take God out of life, remove Him from the atom, ואין כל בריה יכולה לעמוד, mankind lies

1. ברכות ו' ע"א

prostrate in the face of annihilation. As Jews, then, let us return to the Biblical order of living, so that the world may see in us and through us a true example of righteous living.

ii(c)

The Great Guest

There is an outstanding Midrash on this *Sidrah*, that calls for careful consideration. The Rabbis tell us, הלל הזקן בשעה שהיה נפטר מתלמידיו היה מהלך והולך עמם, "When Hillel the Elder concluded his studies with his disciples, he would walk along with them. 'Master,' they said, 'whither are you bound, where are you going?' לעשות מצוה, 'To do a mitzvah,' he replied. 'What mitzvah is that?' they asked. 'I am going to the bath-house to clean my body. If the king's statue is washed by a man appointed for the purpose, אני שנבראתי בצלם ובדמות על אחת כמה וכמה, I who was created in the image of God, all the more must my body be cleaned.'"[1]

On another occasion, as Hillel concluded his studies and walked along with his disciples, they asked once again, "Where are you going?" לעשות מצוה, he replied. "What mitzvah are you going to do this time?" they asked. לגמול חסד עם הדין אכסניא בגו ביתא, "To do kindness for the guest I have in the house." "Have you a guest every day?" "Yes," he replied. "Is not the soul a guest in the body? Today it is here, and tomorrow it is here no longer."

This is not a fatalistic attitude, as if to say, "Why worry if we are only guests here?" It is the attitude of a sound thinker, who knows והארץ לא תמכר לצמתת, that there is nothing here of a permanent nature.

1. ויקרא רבה ל״ד, ג׳.

No war has ever improved man's condition, and no political system
has ever secured stability for human society. What one generation
builds, another destroys. But what a different world it would be to
live in if men were to realise that this is an אכסניא, a "guest house,"
where they are not masters of the situation but the situation is
master over them. You get what you are given, not what you wish
to take. That is a striking introduction of morals into economics. It
is a great pity that the Bible has become the book only of the
synagogue (and, להבדיל, of the church), a textbook for preachers but
not for the laity.

iii

An Old Fallacy

There is an old fallacy in Jewish life that has done more harm
than good. People say, וואס צו גאט איז צו גאט, אונד וואס צו לייט איז צו לייט, "What
is for God is for God, and what is for people is for people." You
cannot make such a simple separation of the issues in Jewish life.
The real thing in our lives is וואס צו גאט איז צו לייט, אונד וואס צו לייט איז צו גאט,
"What is for God is for people, and what is for people is for God."

The third book of the *Chumash,* generally known as Leviticus,
deals primarily with the sanctities of life — things to do with the
soul: the dedication of the *Mishkan* and its sacrifices; the laws of
purity and impurity; the clean and the unclean animals; marital
relations and prohibited marriages; Sabbath and festivals. There
are six *Sidros* in this book wholly concerned with the relationship
between man and God; but what a mistake the Jew makes who
believes that this alone is the ladder that leads to Heaven. This same
Book of *Vayikra* also teaches respect for parents, respect for the

human personality, respect for property; it teaches us to respect the poor, it forbids usury, it commands honest weights and measures and freedom for the slave.

The final chapters of *Vayikra* contain the *Tochachah,* which concludes with the words, אלה החקים והמשפטים והתורת אשר נתן ה' בינו ובין בני ישראל, "these are the statutes, the ordinances, and the laws which God made between Him and the Children of Israel." The Torah does not use its usual expression, אשר נתן ה' לבני ישראל, "which God gave to the Children of Israel"; instead it says בינו ובין בני ישראל, "between God and Israel." The ladder from Heaven to earth, the contact between God and the Jew — the lines of communications are the חקים and the משפטים, those laws of life with which *Vayikra* begins and those laws of life with which *Vayikra* ends, the Written Law and the Oral Law. These alone create a relationship between man and God.

חקים are wonderful things: to *daven,* and best of all with a *minyan;* to learn and to keep Shabbos; to eat kosher food and to honour domestic purity. We cannot survive without them. These glories have a transforming effect on human nature. They are חקים, statutes of Jewish life; but they are only one rung on the ladder. Finance, too, is part of Jewish civilisation. Righteous, honest communion with man, and man's communion with God. As you use your arm for *tefillin,* your body for *tallis,* your stomach for kosher food, so use your means in the right direction. If you keep one dime which you can give away and do not give, if you believe that what is left over belongs to you, and you are not prepared to finance the civilisation in which you believe, then you are severing the link between Heaven and earth.

אם בחקתי תלכו, "If you will walk in My statutes" — חקים שבהם חקקתי את השמים וארץ. . . חקים שבהם חקקתי את השמש ואת הירח. . . חקים שבהם חקקתי את

הים,[1] "those statutes with which I marked out the heaven and the earth, the sun, the moon, and the sea." ונתתי גשמיכם בעתם, "I will give your rains in their seasons." Everything in life has its place and its season. There is no suggestion here that the rains will cease; nature will go on, but out of place and out of time. אם בחקתי תלכו, if everything in life plays its part, your body and your soul combined, שתהיו עמלים בתורה,[2] if your life's labour is a fruitful Torah life, then nature will respond in its time and place. For heaven and earth were moulded by the same statutes. Let us all play our part, each one of us with the things with which he has been blessed; then the blessing of Heaven will be ours.

iv

Walking with Mitzvos

(Bar Mitzvah)

It has been suggested that the reason why so many Bar Mitzvah boys come and go, and that is all you see or know about them for years, is because they think that Bar Mitzvah means to do six hundred and thirteen *mitzvos* every single day! They don't intend to be Rabbis, so why should they carry such a burden? And so, having started on the wrong foot, they don't do a thing. But that is all wrong. Bar Mitzvah does not mean to become a man overnight, nor to do all the *mitzvos* in a day. Bar Mitzvah means to enter into the covenant; it betokens a pledge of allegiance, of becoming a member

ויקרא רבה ל"ה, ד'. 1

רש"י; ספרא. 2

of the House of Israel. Consequently, you have to begin trying to be fit and worthy of it. It requires of you nothing more than to try to do your best.

I am sure that if everyone tried his best to put on *tefillin* in the morning, they could do it; but they do not even give it a try. If they tried to say המוציא לחם before they eat, they could do so; but they do not even make an effort. Some do not even say "Thank you" to their parents, or to their wives, for making breakfast in the morning. If so, how can we expect them to say הזן את העולם כלו? Imagine what the community, and our Bar Mitzvah boys, would look like if all tried their best to do what they can as Jews!

Think of those boys and girls in Israel who have to do far more than their best. The flower of our youth who are parachutists, submarine crews, and pilots, so many of them with *tzitzis* under their uniforms and *tefillin* in their sacks, doing far more than their best: giving their very lives. Guarding their people and their soil, their land and their freedom. Bar Mitzvah boys are asked to do no more than their best, to keep the commandments and to stand on guard against ignorance and indifference. They are asked to try their best to learn every day; to respect their parents, their elders, and their teachers; to observe the Shabbos and the Yamim Tovim.

The *Sidrah Bechukosai* is the last in the Book of *Vayikra*. In it, Moses addresses the people just before they leave the Sinai desert to start their march to the Promised Land. Then follows the *Chumash Bemidbar,* the start of their journey. As they are about to set out, Moses assures them of God's blessing and protection: אם בחקתי תלכו, "If you walk in My statutes, ואת מצותי תשמרו, and keep My commandments, ועשיתם אתם, and do them." Three words are used in this verse: 'walk,' 'keep,' and 'do.' What does it all mean, to *walk* in My statutes, *keep* My commandments, and *do* them? The Torah means simply that becoming a really good Jew is a gradual process.

You do not start off by doing everything in one go. You start with תלכו, walking slowly in the statutes, so to speak. As you get up in the morning you rise as a Jew with שמע ישראל and שמונה עשרה. You walk about as a Jew, and as you go, תשמרו: you watch your step, you see how it is done, you try your best not to allow anything — neither your work, nor your school, nor your career — to interfere. תשמרו, with careful watching it then becomes ועשיתם אתם: you are bound to do them. They become second nature, they become part of your life; and as the years roll by, you will never leave them. They give you faith and hope and confidence; you will find comfort in sorrow, satisfaction in living, and courage in the face of the enemy.

Whatever the future holds in store, be it a profession, work, or commerce, leave a little room for the Almighty to help you by trying your best. Be a brother to your fellow Jews by observing the *mitzvos*, and so share in our destiny, for it is a glorious one.

v

The Tochachah

The most prominent feature of the *Sidrah* of *Bechukosai* is the prophetic warning and admonition, which is read in the synagogue quietly and quickly, because of the long list of penalties and horrors that is foretold for sinful man. There is a series of five groups of penalties of increasing severity: sickness and defeat, famine, wild beasts, siege, and exile. All these shall strike those who "walk contrary to Me and will not hearken to Me."

In some synagogues no worshipper is called up to the reading of this portion of the Torah. In others the beadle or the *ba'al korei*, the regular reader, is given this *aliyah*. Why is it? Why are we so afraid to face the truth in its nakedness? Why are we so afraid to face the realities of life, the facts seen plainly? How abundantly these warnings have been borne out by Jewish history, over and over again. How true the prophetic messages, in our *Sidrah* and in its *Haftorah*, from Jeremiah, have proved to be. And yet we are still so uncivilised, still so foolish, as to run through the warnings as if we were fleeing from the very devil — as if they were intended for some other person, not for us. It is not generally realised that most of the negative precepts in the Torah are written in the singular form, as if addressed to each separate individual. But in *Bechukosai* the blessings for obedience and the curses for disobedience are both written in the plural form. They do not apply to one who reads alone; they apply to one and all.

Why, the commentators ask, does not Scripture temper its expressions and speak in a milder tone of God's displeasure? Why does the Torah enter into such dreadful details when describing the consequences of disobedience?

". . . And I will set My face against you, and you shall be smitten before your enemies; they that hate you shall rule over you. . . and I will bring a sword upon you, executing the vengeance of the Covenant. . . and you shall be delivered into the hand of the enemy."

What destruction, what devastation is foretold for the disobedient! Even the wartime bombing hardly compared with what is to come if God's word is to be fulfilled. Yet what an insensate question it is to ask why punishment was so detailed. When Rabbis speak about *kashrus,* dietary laws, many people laugh. The doctor says, "In those days conditions of living were different: food was not so hygienic. Today life is different; we can live without *kashrus.*" When Rabbis stress what the Torah says of Sabbath, many ridicule them. The engineer tells us, "In those days conditions were different: there was no machinery, there was no electricity. Today we have no manual labour; it is all done with the switch." When the Rabbi talks about *mikveh,* about the purity of family life, many mock. They say, "In those days there were no baths; the water was not clean, so they went to bathe in rainwater." When the Rabbi talks about synagogue prayer, he is told, "In those days men were ignorant and could not read." When the Rabbi talks about the Revelation on Sinai, he is told, "In those days there was no science; men looked to Heaven for salvation." When the Rabbi talks about honesty in business relations, of morality between the sexes, of equitable sharing with the poor, many dismiss his words and give their own self-serving interpretations. Yet the Divinely written word is as clear as the shining sun to the man of God.

Yes, it is true that the language of the Torah is Biblical, and the meaning is sometimes hidden. Therefore, this one time the Torah says, "I will speak in a language which all can understand. Ignorant and wise, no doctor, no scientist, no engineer, no philosopher can change it. 'If you walk in My statutes and keep My commandments, I will give you peace; you shall lie down and none shall make you afraid. . . But if you will not hearken unto My voice, I will lay your cities waste, and make your sanctuaries a desolation, and I will scatter you among the nations.'" What simpler, plainer language can there be? No interpretations can change these simple words. The bitter experiences of man, and of the Jew in particular, have confirmed every word; no one in the world can change it.

This would be my reply to the age-old question, "Why does the Torah enter into such dreadful details?" How our cities have been laid waste and our sanctuaries made desolate in the wartime devastation! What answer can the scientist, the philosopher, and the medical man give? What can they tell you, these men of wisdom? But the simple man of faith turns to the *Tochachah* and says, Here is the solution to the world's tragic problem.

When will man awaken, when will he be stirred from his selfish complacency? Why not face the facts, instead of trying so hypocritically to evade them? There is only one solution to the world's problems: back to the uncivilised age when the word of God was respected. Back to בראשית ברא אלקים. God before self, synagogue before home, truth before falsehood.[1]

vi

Two Mouths

(Lag Ba-Omer)

The passage of the Talmud which tells of the death of Rabbi Akiva's disciples, during the weeks between Pesach and Shavuos, contains the answer to a pertinent question: why did they die? The answer is stated right there: מפני שלא נהגו כבוד זה בזה,[1] "because they did not treat each other with respect and honour." Torah forces were split, the Orthodox fighting each other on every front. Who was this Bar Kochva? Some said he was a new star, a *Mashiach*; others said בר כוזיבא, he was a crook. We would have expected Orthodox forces at such a critical moment to join hands, to foster a spirit of unity, to respect each other's loyalties, to study together

1 A sermon prompted by the ravages of the bombing of London, when numerous synagogues, including the Great Synagogue, Duke's Place, were destroyed. The sermon was followed by an impassioned plea for the revitalisation of Dayan Swift's own synagogue (Brixton), and a tribute to various devoted congregants (deceased) who maintained the synagogue's activities when the area was depopulated by evacuation.

1. יבמות ס"ב ע"ב.

ways and means of combating the evil of Roman domination. Instead, לא נהגו כבוד זה בזה.

And that was not all: what was the cause of their death? כלם מתו מיתה רעה, "it was a horrible death called אסכרא." The English translation of אסכרא is croup, a disease of the air passages. מתחלת בבני מעים וגומרת בפה,[2] the Rabbis say, "it is a disease that begins in the stomach and becomes fatal when it reaches the mouth." How are we to interpret this cryptic reference to a strange disease that begins in the stomach, מתחלת בבני מעיים? Perhaps it refers to differences that began with *kashrus:* what one said is kosher the other said is *treifah.*

Or perhaps we can go further than that. מתחלת בבני מעיים — small beginnings, internal grievances, an argument over a little כבוד, over an *aliyah* or a criticism of the Rabbi or the lay leaders. וגומרת בפה — it is an awful disease in communal circles; it ends up in the mouth, with לשון הרע, condemnation of each other, strife, scandal, and blackmail. Without the slightest compunction, one shouts בר כוזיבא about the other: "This one is a crook, that one is an imposter, this one is a money-grabber."

Make no mistake; that awful disease אסכרא, that begins בבני מעיים, with internal grievances, applies to our smaller circles, and it applies to the wider issues in which we are involved. It is often a small grievance, that might begin with something absolutely unintentional. Perhaps we might have overlooked a "Good Shabbos"; perhaps something was said in a moment of emotion or upset. Yet it is sufficient to set the whole house on fire. We get resignations and splits, then the movement loses its dignity, and the whole ideal collapses.[3]

שבת ל"ג ע"ב. 2

3 This sermon was delivered at Young Israel of Los Angeles.

Yes, it is an awful thing, this disease of אסכרא. The twenty-four thousand pupils of Rabbi Akiva died of it. They should have known better. Jerusalem was burning, and sectarian splinter groups were springing up. There were Sadducees and Pharisees, and later there were Karaites. But there was one pupil of Rabbi Akiva, one disciple, whose *Yahrzeit* is on Lag Ba-Omer — Rabbi Shimon ben Yochai, who survived and stood like a giant, high above the friction and dissension. His deep distress at the dissension in his day is reflected in a remarkable saying of his in the Talmud Yerushalmi:

אילו הוינא קאים על טורא דסיני . . . הוינא מתבעי . . . דיתברי לבר נשא תרין פומין, חד דהוי לעי באורייתא וחד דעבד ליה כל צורכיה,[4] "Had I stood on Mt. Sinai when the Torah was given, I would have asked the Lawgiver to create two mouths for man, one with which to learn Torah, and the other for his everyday needs." No wonder Lag Ba-Omer, the anniversary of Rabbi Shimon's death, stands out so prominently as a break in the period of mourning. It is a sad reminder to the Jew to make use of two tongues: one for use in our everyday needs, and the other for Torah matters. In synagogue, in *kashrus* affairs, another tongue, a tongue of respect and decency.

With this in mind, we can understand the significance behind a seeming difficulty in the *Sidrah* of *Bechukosai*. The *Sidrah* begins with the blessings of God upon those who abide by His teachings and walk in His ways, and goes on, alas, to the curses that come in the wake of disobedience. But with what does the *Sidrah* conclude? With a subject that has no connection with curses or blessings: איש כי יפליא נדר, the laws of vows and the redemption of sacred undertakings. What is this word יפליא? The Rabbis say פלא הוא, "it is wondrous, it is astonishing that הפה יקדיש מה שהוא חול, a man can sanctify

---

4: ירושלמי ברכות פ"א הלכה ב' ושבת א' הלכה ב. אבל ראה שם בירוש' שחזר בו רשב"י:
ומה אין חד הוא עלמא קאים ביה מן דילטוריא דיליה, אילו הוו תרין כמה וכמה.

with his mouth that which is profane."[5] How can man bear to profane that which is sacred with the same פה, the same mouth? איש כי יפליא נדר בערכך נפשות —remember that what you say with your mouth must be evaluated according to its effects upon human souls.

This is the final message of Lag Ba-Omer: כבוד זה בזה, respect for each other, unity of purpose. Let the mouth with which we learn Torah be the same mouth that controls our communal service. Let us show that dignity of character, that unity of purpose, that cleanliness of expression, which will bring about a revival of Jewish values and a return to a Jewish way of living.

vii

Faith and Practice

(Bar Mitzvah)

Judaism is frequently referred to as a religion, which is a somewhat inaccurate definition. If religion means believing in God, thinking about God, something to do with intellect or emotions — a kind of theory — then there is nothing Jewish about it. A thousand people can have a thousand different emotions, and that is all wrong. Religion to the Jew is living, not thinking; it is a civilisation, not a theory; it is a plan, not a persuasion.

Every year when we introduce the month of Sivan, the month we came to Sinai, that occasion always comes on the Shabbos when we read the *Sidrah* of *Bechukosai*. This is our introduction to Shavuos; it is the approach to Sinai — ביום הזה באו מדבר סיני. It is the

ראה אבן עזרא במדבר ו', ב'. 5

road that leads to Torah. If all that the Jews needed was a faith, a new way of thinking instead of a new way of living, Sinai with all its problems would have been quite unnecessary. Israel saw enough at the Exodus to persuade them to believe; but faith is not enough. Faith is the means, not the end; faith is the approach, not the goal. Thank God for faith; it would be an awful world to live in without it. But it is not the be-all and end-all. The end is the Torah, the goal is Sinai.

The *Sidrah* of *Bechukosai* deals primarily with the consequences of sin and disobedience. Some people call it "the קללות and the ברכות," the curses and the blessings. Of course that is not true: God does not curse. The real name given to that part of the *Sidrah* during which the reader lowers his voice is "the תוכחה," the warning. It is not a series of curses; it is not reward for good and punishment for bad. Reward and punishment have to do with the Hereafter, יענער ועלט; the Torah is concerned with this world. The Torah is אם בחקתי תלכו, "If you will walk in My statutes."

There are warnings about things which come in consequence: you reap what you sow, you take out what you put in. אם בחקתי תלכו, "if you will walk in My statutes, ואת מצותי תשמרו, and keep My commandments, ועשיתם אתם, and do them, ונתתי גשמיכם בעתם ונתנה הארץ יבולה ועץ השדה יתן פרי, then I will give you your rains in their time, and the land shall yield its produce, and the trees of the field shall yield their fruit." God and man and nature at one: He put of Himself into us, and He planted His creative powers into nature. If we do, God does; if we do, nature does. There is reaction, there is reverberation, there is reflection. If you walk in God's statutes, He walks too.

The Hebrew word for the Code of Jewish Law is הלכה, which means to walk, from the verb הולך — the walk of life, the way of living. Law in Jewish life is not an imposition; it is not even an obligation. Law is conduct. The name given to our Code books, the

Books of Law, is not ספר דינים; it is שלחן ערוך, which means a prepared table: a table with all the dishes, all the food spread on it. How to walk, how to dress, how to eat, how to do commerce, how to live — it is all in the book: turn to the relevant clause, and there it is. Even the word "Torah" is a simple word meaning to guide along a path or route. אם בחקתי תלכו, "if you walk in My statutes," then God must react; that is in the nature of things. ואת מצותי תשמרו, "and if you keep My commandments," then God must keep His word too. That is religion to the Jew. It is not believing alone, and it is not praying alone. It is very important to believe and pray, but religion to the Jew is practice, doing. God says, If you will walk, I will walk; if you keep, I keep; if you do, I do. This is the approach to the third month, Sivan, to the month of Sinai. Get into line, take the route which Sinai directs, stray neither to the right nor to the left, and you will go on and on to the end of time.

In the *Sidrah* we are told that if a man consecrates part of his field, of which the value will be given to the service of the Temple or for some holy charity, the field has to be evaluated. לא כפי שוויה, it is not assessed by what it is worth,[1] but ערכך לפי זרעו, according to the quantity of seed that can be grown in it. Torah values are measured not by what a person possesses, what he has got, but what he can produce, what he can do. What kind of Jew is he? What does he give to God? What does he give to the community? It is לפי זרעו, how much Jewishness he sows. Not what you have, but what you give; not what you are, but what you do. This is the Torah's guidance to every Bar Mitzvah setting out on the path of Jewish life.

---

1. רש"י; ספרא.

BEMIDBAR

במדבר

i

Princely Names and Princely Conduct

The *Chumash Bemidbar* begins by naming the heads of the tribes, who were charged with the task of taking the census of Israel as they began their journey from Sinai to the Holy Land. But surely, it is sometimes said, the Bible is of a sublimer character than a mere reference book for documentary purposes. Why, then, are all these names recorded? A simple answer would be that this seeming redundancy in the Bible gives historic proof of its authenticity, because pedigrees and names can be investigated. The Rabbis, however, find an interesting link running through all these names that conveys a moral to us even in our own day.

ויקח משה ואהרן את האנשים האלה אשר נקבו בשמות, "And Moses and Aaron selected those men who were pointed out by name." It means that there was something in their names that distinguished them. Their name was a reflection of their personality. Even when reading the daily press, one can frequently judge at a glance whether certain people named are of Jewish, or Indian, or English, or African origin. Moses selected men אשר נקבו בשמות, men each one of whom had the name of God embodied in his name. The head of the tribe of Reuben was אליצור — "God is my rock"; that of Shimon was שלמיאל — "at peace with God"; that of Judah בן עמינדב — "the Divine Kinsman is generous." The head of Yissachar was נתנאל — "God has given"; of Zebulun אליאב — "God is father"; of Ephraim אלישמע — "God has heard"; of Menasseh גמליאל — "He is also my God" or "God is my reward." Princes were selected whose names personified all that they stood for.

A person's name invariably throws light on the character of his home, his family and even his generation — all of which play a vital role in the development of an individual's personality and character. These names in the Torah, a famous Rabbi said, are an invaluable documentation of early life in Israel, throwing light on the religious feelings of the ancient Israelites. And it is even more than that: it is a reflection of what was foremost in the minds of the people of that age. One sometimes enters a home and finds portraits hanging on the wall of father and grandfather. The host will say, "This is my father, Reb Yosef, and this is my grandfather, Reb Yaacov." Do you know what will happen in the next generation or two? "That is my father, Paul, and that is my grandfather, Peter" — a gallery of apostles! As though the Old Testament contains an inadequate list of names, so that we must go to the new "testament!" ויקח משה ואהרן את האנשים האלה אשר נקבו בשמות; that may well be a sound reason for the listing of these names in the *Sidrah*. גמליאל and פגעיאל in their names reflected their thoughts and characterised their pride of race, of origin, of Jewishness.

In the latter part of the *Sidrah*, the Torah records in minute detail the functions that were allotted to the Levites. Some were given the task of carrying the Ark, others the candelabrum, others the altars and the walls and covering of the Sanctuary itself. Again the question is asked, "What difference does that make to us today?" Particularly remarkable is the detailed description of the duties allocated to Elazar, the son of Aaron the High Priest:

ופקדת אלעזר בן אהרן הכהן שמן המאור וקטרת הסמים ומנחת התמיד ושמן המשחה פקדת

המשכן וכל אשר בו בקדש ובכליו, "And the charge of Elazar the son of Aaron the priest shall be the oil for the light and the sweet incense, the meal offering and the anointing oil, the oversight of the Tabernacle and of all that is in it, as to the Sanctuary and as to its vessels."

Elazar was not an ordinary priest: he was נשיא נשיאי הלוי, the prince of the princes of the Levites. The Rabbis wonder האיך היה טוען כל אלו, "How could he carry all these things and at the same time supervise the entire transport?" They tell us that he carried the oil in his right hand, the incense in his left, the meal offering slung over his arm and the flask of oil suspended from his girdle! את סבור מפני שהיה אדם גדול היה נותן לאחרים; a dignified man such as he, surrounded by priests and servants, did he not ask others to assist him? אין גאוה לפני האלקים,[1] "There is no pride before God": the prince must carry these things and march at the head of the people. However would the Temple have been borne across the sandy desert if these Levites had said, "We have our hands full, it is beneath our dignity"? Jewish service demands the carrying of burdens alone sometimes. The Land of Israel would never have been built and schools would never have been erected if pride had been the ruling motive of our leaders. אין גאוה לפני המקום, in God's eyes there is no pride. With hands full, with loins girded, sitting on all committees, supervising everything that goes on — this way and this way alone were achievements accomplished.

The task was a difficult and strenuous one. The family of Kehas, whose duty it was to carry the Ark, started out in large numbers, more numerous in fact than all the other Levitical families. They began the journey with about 2,900; and when the last census was

במדבר רבה ד' בסוף. 1

taken they were diminished by some 117 in number. Should they not have thrown over the task and taken an easier one? חס ושלום, the Rabbis say:

לא היו בני קהת מניחין את הארון ורצין לשלחן ומנורה, אלא אף על פי שמתמעטין היו נותנין נפשם על הארון.[2] God forbid, they did not abandon the Ark, in spite of their depleted numbers, and run to some easier task. That is the reason for the detailed record of the allotted duties given in this *Sidrah*. חס ושלום, no task undertaken can be abandoned, אף על פי שמתמעטין, although our numbers are depleted and resources meagre.

It is very easy to leave the Torah in the Ark and take to other interests and philanthropic endeavours. You gain numbers that way and you win adherents. It is not so easy to take the Ark on your shoulders and walk through a wilderness, depleted in numbers and with little support. The secret of Jewish survival has been vested in those Jews who realise that not the energies we have exerted for others have been of help to us — nay, they are frequently condemned. It is what we have done for ourselves: bearing Jewish names with pride, bearing Jewish burdens without pride. Burdens borne by us alone in the march from Sinai: these alone have taken us through the wilderness of life to a Jewish land of honour and freedom.

ii

A Divine Census

The fourth book of the Torah takes its English name, Numbers, from the original Hebrew name חומש הפקודים, the *Chumash* of numberings. It is so named because its opening portion deals with the census that Moses was commanded to take of the Israelites as

במדבר רבה ה', א'. 2

they were about to leave Mount Sinai for the Promised Land. It was a task that even the father of the prophets found daunting. Whilst it was comparatively easy to count those who were to be numbered from the age of 20 and over, the tribe of Levi, whose duty it was to serve in the Sanctuary and to bear the לוחת, were to be counted מבן חדש ומעלה, from the age of one month upwards. האיך אני נכנס לתוך אהליהם לדעת מנין יונקיהם, "How can I enter their tents to ascertain the number of their babes?" Moses asked. א״ל הקב״ה עשה אתה שלך ואני אעשה שלי, "the Holy One, blessed be He, said to Moses, 'You do your share and I will do Mine.'" הלך משה ועמד על פתח האהל והשכינה מקדמת לפניו ובת קול יוצאת מן האהל ואומרת כך וכך תינוקות יש באהל, "Moses went and stationed himself at the entrance of each tent. The Shechinah went before him, and a Divine Voice issued from the tent saying, 'So-and-so many babes are in the tent.'" That is the meaning of the verse ויפקד אתם משה על פי ה׳,[1] "and Moses numbered them according to God's word."

What a wonderful message is revealed in that beautiful Rabbinic note! If Moses is to count the Children of Israel outside the home, then the Shechinah must penetrate inside the home. If Jewish children are to be numbered, if boys and girls are to grow up bearing the ארון, the Ark of God's Covenant, on their shoulders, then השכינה מקדמת לפניו ובת קול יוצאת מן האהל, the Shechinah must precede each child's birth and the voice of God must be heard in the tent. כך וכך תינוקות באהל, there are Jewish babies born in this tent, in קדושה, in טהרה, in holiness and purity. ויפקד אתם משה על פי ה׳, "and Moses numbered them according to the word of God."

If a child is to survive the street, if assimilation is not to swallow him up, if you are to count him as a Jew כאשר צוה, "as he was commanded," then Jewishness must pervade the home, the Shechinah must permeate the atmosphere. It begins with the quiet,

<hr>

1. רש״י; במדבר רבה ג׳, ט׳.

intimate, holy and pure relationship between father and mother. It continues with prayer in the home, with Friday night and Shabbos in the home, with *kashrus* and purity in the home — בת קול יוצאת מן האהל. Those who turn Friday night into a "temple night," where the womenfolk light the Shabbos candles in the temple[2] — the light of Shabbos, the soul of the Jewish people, is taken from their homes: no בת קול, no *Shechinah,* nothing. Who knows if their children will be counted within the House of Israel in a few decades to come? Only if, like the Levites of old, our youth will bear the לוחות on their shoulders, can they be sure of surviving the tides of assimilation that are sweeping away the pillars of *Yiddishkeit* one after the other.

---

2 This address was given at Young Israel of Los Angeles, condemning a current Conservative innovation.

NASO

נשא

i

Study in Jewish Life[1]

Study in Jewish life is part of Jewish devotion. Where there is no learning in addition to prayer, where there is no study in addition to devotion, there is a decline in Jewish life. It is overlooked by so many that the first thing we do, or ought to do, in the morning as we rise from our sleep is to wash the hands and offer thanksgiving to God for the preservation of our physical health: שאם יפתח אחד מהם או יסתם אחד מהם אי אפשר להתקים. The closing up or opening up of the minutest element in this fleshly frame of ours would make it impossible to exist. Then we pause in our daily devotions, and before we turn to praise or to prayers we make a *berachah* on the Torah. Just as vital as is God's care for our physical preservation, so is the Torah for our spiritual preservation. Immediately after the *berachah* on the Torah — before we come to רפאנו, "heal us," and before we come to סלח לנו, "forgive us" — we offer up a prayer which seemingly has no connection with our daily work and toil, which are uppermost

---

1 From an address given at Berea Synagogue, South Africa, on the Annual Shabbos in honor of the Chevras Mishnah and Talmud.

in our minds as we start the day: ונהיה אנחנו וצאצאינו וצאצאי עמך בית ישראל כלנו יודעי שמך ולומדי תורתך, "may we, and our offspring, and the offspring of Thy people Israel, all know Thy name and study Thy Torah." We must remember, in the midst of a day's toil and labour, the duty of study.

The study of the Torah is not the exclusive prerogative of any caste or class, as medicine is the prerogative of the doctor and law of the lawyer. The average layman would never dream of taking a book on anatomy out of the library or of making a study of botany; but come into a *shiur* on Shabbos afternoon and you see laymen, ordinary everyday Jews, sitting over an intricate problem on a question of the transfer or acquisition of property, or marriage and divorce laws, or diseases of the skin. They are all students doing research in a Talmudic laboratory: the laws of oaths and vows, of general litigation and of ritual ceremonies — they all find a prominent place in it. It is the greatest democracy that man has ever known. A modern commentator on the Siddur quotes a non-Jewish author who said of the Jewish religion, "because it was a literature-sustained religion it led to the first effort to provide elementary instruction for all the children of the community." It is the first thing we pray for in the morning that כלנו יודעי שמך ולומדי תורתך, "we may all know Thy name and learn Thy Law." No other people has attached so much importance to study.

During the summer months we study the פרקי אבות, the Ethics of the Fathers, beginning with that familiar Mishnah: משה קבל תורה מסיני ומסרה ליהושע, "Moses received the Torah at Sinai and handed it over to Joshua, and Joshua to the Elders, and the Elders to the Prophets; and the Prophets handed it to the Men of the Great Assembly." It might have remained only with them, had they not warned the people העמידו תלמידים הרבה, "raise up many disciples." This is not a study for the Rabbi and teacher alone; it belongs to the masses.

Learning is a mass institution. It belongs to the people. The word Rabbi does not mean 'minister' — he is not the only one in charge of religious affairs. The word Rabbi means 'teacher,' and everyone has as much to say as he in religious affairs, so long as the structure of the Torah remains intact. That is why the Rabbis, when giving their advice והעמידו תלמידים הרבה, "raise up many disciples," use the term והעמידו, derived from the word עמידה, "to stand." They meant "raise up disciples who will stand firm, unbending."

And that is why the Rabbis add, ועשו סיג לתורה, that the fence around the Law must never be breached. The high esteem in which the Rabbi was held in the community was not due to any Papal conception that he stood nearer to God than the masses. There are no boundaries in Jewish life: everyone can break through and get as near as he is able. The only boundary is that of the Torah. The Rabbi is the interpreter and the guide, a teacher by qualification and by sound belief. If the community stands up as he passes by, it is not for the person but for the personality. He does not represent God, that is a blunder, every man is God's representative; the Rabbi represents the Torah. For that alone he has to command the respect of the people.

The first verse of the *Sidrah* conveys this great Jewish principle. Levi, the third son of Jacob, had three sons, גרשון קהת ומררי. Although קהת was the second of the three sons, he was given priority, because his duty was to bear on his shoulders the Ark of the Covenant of God. His was the Torah as they journeyed from place to place; but that does not mean Gershon was to be ignored. If the children of קהת were numbered first, it does not mean that they became the יחסנים, the privileged class: נשא את ראש בני גרשון גם הם, "take the number of the children of גרשון also." The *Sidrah* demands, אף על פי שבני קהת

קהת although the family of" [2],נמנו תחלה לא להניח לבני גרשון שלא יימנו לגמרי
was counted first, it must never be suggested that the children of
גרשון were not to be counted." נשא את ראש בני גרשון גם הם: they are also
somebody.

The Jewish view is adamantly opposed to any particular caste
or class. Each one has a duty to perform: one bore the Torah, others
learnt the Torah, one created atmosphere, the other maintained the
structure. The synagogue *shiur* represents the view that the Torah
belongs to all!

ii

The Priestly Blessing

(Bar Mitzvah)

The priestly blessing contained in the *Sidrah* is called ברכה
המשלשת, the threefold blessing. It is divided into three parts: יברכך ה'
וישמרך, "the Lord bless you and keep you," יאר ה' פניו אליך ויחנך, "the Lord
cause His countenance to shine upon you," ישא ה' פניו אליך וישם לך שלום,
"the Lord lift His countenance to you and give you peace." The first
part of this blessing is paraphrased by the Rabbis, שיתברכו נכסיך, that
your possessions may increase — that you should be rich and
prosperous and affluent. But riches and prosperity do not always
bring blessing. Sometimes one must be guarded against one's own
possessions; a man must be guarded against the society he builds
up around himself. It is particularly so with young people today,

2 הלשון במדרש רבה ו', ב' הוא: "גם הם" שאף בני גרשון כיוצא בהם של בני קהת אלא
שהקדימו הכתוב כאן בשביל כבוד התורה.

whose earning capacity sweeps them off their feet. Parents are disregarded, the community is disregarded, and they become their own enemies. So the *Kohen* blesses the people and says וישמרך, "may God keep you safe and guard you against yourself and your possessions."

In the *Maftir* we are told of the consecration of the Sanctuary, when the נשיאים, the leaders of the tribes, brought their offerings. The house of God was ready for service, and Moses went in. ובבא משה אל אהל מועד לדבר אתו, "and when Moses had come into the appointed tent to speak with Him" — he went to be inspired and hear the voice of God — וישמע את הקול מדבר אליו, "and he heard the voice speaking unto him." Where did that voice come from? From the heavens, or the walls, or the Ark? No, not at all. It came מעל הכפרת אשר על ארן העדת, from above the covering that was upon the Ark of the Covenant. Not from the Ark itself but from above the covering, מבין שני הכרבים, "from between the two cherubim." They were two figures of children, a boy and a girl, above the Ark, suspended over the covering. From between those two figures וידבר אליו, the voice came. From there God spoke to him.

You can fill the Ark with gold, adorn the Torah with all the riches you possess, you can build the most beautiful Temple, and all the נשיאים, the princes and the leaders, can bring their offering — and the voice of God may still not be heard. It is מבין שני הכרבים, from the children who learn and study and observe and honour and obey, that the voice will be heard. It is from boys and girls who are observant and respectful that real happiness and joy come, for God's voice is audible where Torah is learned and practised. It must be וישמע את הקול מדבר אליו: the voice of Torah must be heard every day.

The second part of that threefold blessing is יאר ה' פניו אליך, "may God's countenance shine upon you." What is the light of God? It is the Torah. In conferring blessing upon Israel, it is the priestly prayer that the light of Torah may never go out. It expresses the hope that as our youth grow up that light may grow within them, radiating joy and blessing to the whole community.

iii

A Tale of Woe!

ויהי ביום כלות משה להקים את המשכן, "And it came to pass on the day that Moses had finished setting up the Tabernacle." The latter part of the *Sidrah* is concerned with the erection of the *Mishkan*. It was Moses' practice to erect and dismantle the Tabernacle each day during the seven days of initiation:[1] in the morning he set it up and in the evening he took it down. But on this day, when it was to be consecrated by service and sacrifice, an end came to these daily dismantlings. Henceforth it stood constantly, day and night, at the heart of Israel's encampment. It is a sure lesson to Israel that the Temple, the Sanctuary of sacrifice and service, of prayer and devotion, set up in the course of their wandering to the Promised Land, must stand prepared at the end of the day. When the sun sets and darkness engulfs the wandering Jew, the Temple must stand ever ready to illumine his path through the night until the sun rises and he can again see the light of day.

But what will be when the sun shines and the day is drawn out, and Israel's stay in the *galus* is prolonged by a false sense of security? The history of Jewish freedom has proved beyond any doubt that

---

1 The expression ביום כלות משה להקים implies that the setting up of the *Mishkan* took place over a number of days, hence the inference that the *Mishkan* was erected and dismantled each day of the seven days of initiation (see Rashi).

in every country where the Jew has enjoyed a measure of security, in the long run it has been false. The turn of events in countries where he has enjoyed the light of day and basked in the sunshine of political equality has brought about a hatred that cannot be quelled. It has swept every land, infected every continent, and found its adherents in every social order and all forms of government. It has been tragically but rightly described as the "eternal hatred for the eternal people." But for the time being it is security, nevertheless: His Sanctuary stands erect without having to be dismantled at the setting of the sun.

But there is another curse that prolonged daylight produces, a tragedy far greater than the setting of the sun and the dismantling of God's sacred Temple. It is implied in the first word of our text. The Rabbis draw attention to that word: ויהי. They say that wherever this word occurs in the Bible אינו אלא צרה, it always refers to a period of sorrow and grief.[2] Surely then, our Sages wonder, the creation of the Sanctuary as a permanent and lasting foundation was cause for שמחה, happiness and rejoicing. How does צרה come in at a moment of such exaltation?

The Rabbis say:[3] "It is like a king who has a quarrelsome wife; he said to her, 'Go and make queenly garments for yourself.' She does his bidding, and goes and occupies herself with the planning and fashioning and making of the garments — כל זמן שהיא עסוקה אינה מריבה, whilst her time is fully occupied she leaves the king alone; but when the queen completes her task and the garments are ready for attire she presents herself to the king. כיון שראה אותה המלך התחיל צווח וי וי, in spite of his delight at the beauty of the clothes he began to cry 'Woe, woe! Now that her occupation has come to an end she will

2. מגילה י׳ ע״ב.

3. במדבר רבה י״ב, ו׳.

again resume her quarrelsome ways.' כך אמר הקב"ה, כל זמן שהיו בני עסוקים במשכן לא היו מרננים, whilst Israel were engaged day in and day out with the erection of the Temple they had little time to murmur and complain; but ביום כלות משה להקים את המשכן, on the day when the setting up of the Tabernacle had come to an end, Moses was afraid: now they will resume their quarrelsome ways." ויהי היה ביום כלות משה; it was a day of sorrow when the *Mishkan* came to stay.

None but the Rabbis, with their prophetic vision, could find in that small word ויהי a true picture of Jewish life through the ages. It has been said — and it is true, alas! — that the intensity of Jewish persecution is itself a factor making for Jewish survival, and if it were to cease the Jew would disappear. Some have surmised that the process of so-called emancipation might, if unopposed, have ended in the complete extinction of the Jewish people.

When the sun rose in the morning and set at night, and the day was too short for settling down to enjoy the light, we were far too preoccupied to abandon our glories and surrender our hopes. Everywhere, as we were on the go, we followed the same pattern of life: כל זמן שהיו בני עסוקים לא היו מרננים, we were conscious of a distinction that was ours alone. We *davened Minchah* in the trains, and we put on our *tefillin* in the camps, and we kept Shabbos in the ghetto. But when there was no further anxiety of transit and transport, when political equality presented the Jew with all the opportunities of a modern life, when public schools and universities opened their doors wide, there was no longer a need for Moses to dismantle the *Mishkan.* Religious indifference became widespread. Everywhere there was a diminution of Jewish content. Each generation knew less of Jewish culture and observed less Jewish teaching—ויהי היה ביום כלות משה, woe to the day when the preoccupation with Sanctuary-building ended and the Temple came to stay.

This trend has marked the life of the Jew wherever he has come in contact with the blandishments and opportunities of Western civilisation. Where are the remnants of those families, the descendants of those Jews who arrived here two centuries ago to enjoy the freedom of this country? But why go back so far? Where are the grandchildren of those who came here eighty or one hundred years ago? They set up beautiful sanctuaries that they had dismantled in the countries where they were oppressed. There the sun set, here the sun rose; but כלתה, it was the end of all their sanctity and glory.

Statistical records would probably prove that proportionately to the Jewish population we have lost far more Jews in this emancipated country than we lost elsewhere in our oppression. וי, woe to those generations! They have left after them some, a handful perhaps, still identifying themselves as Jews, but in the main they were never able to sustain and nourish Jewish consciousness. So you will find, in our synagogues today, children of foreign parents who wrapped themselves in *tallis* and *tefillin,* who remained poor rather than violate the Shabbos, who starved rather than break the laws of *kashrus.* Yes, they were still עסוקים במשכן, occupied in maintaining Jewish sanctities; for them emancipation was no sunrise.

Israel is virtually the only reservoir of Jewish spiritual strength left in the world. Anglo-Jewry must ensure that the synagogue, as of old, shall continue its benign influence of charitable endeavour. It must promote Jewish day schools, never ceasing to support Yeshivos and other educational institutions, and ensure that our children do not partake of *treifah* school meals. Otherwise the synagogues will become an empty shell of what once was the centre of Jewish life and culture, with hardly a שומר שבת to be found or a weekday *minyan* for a *Kaddish.*

The Rabbis tell us that Reuben, the eldest of the brothers, the head of the tribes of Israel, was jealous of Judah, who had been chosen to bring the first offering to the Tabernacle on the occasion of its dedication. Reuben protested this breach of etiquette, expecting at least to be second on the list, but to his dismay, it was Yissachar who was called to bring the second day's offering: ביום השני הקריב נתנאל בן צוער נשיא יששכר. In the next verse the words הקרב את קרבנו appear, only on this one occasion in the order of the service of dedication. Twelve times, one for each of the tribal princes, the Torah repeats the same formula, the repetition of the same ceremony day by day in unaltered language; only this time it is different. In answer to Reuben's protest, the Divine Author chose the word הקרב, without the *yod*, so that it implied הקרב, the imperative form. In spite of all claims of priority, the order of proceedings came from on high; it was not Moses' choosing, but a Heavenly command.

This is a salutary lesson to Jewish leaders, that in the service of the Temple יחוס and כבוד are to be eliminated. Everyone is an equal in God's house; *kavod*-hunting and the distribution of the so-called "better *mitzvos*" are our own inventions, מפני דרכי שלום, only for the sake of peace. So Reuben, the elder, was given רביעי, and Zebulun, the younger, was given שלישי. This was the order of service at the dedication of Israel's *Mishkan*: first Judah, because he was ready to throw himself into the water at the crossing of the Red Sea; then Yissachar, because יודעי בינה לעתים,[4] among them were scholars and men of learning. Then came Zebulun, because he supported the scholars, the Rabbis and the teachers. So was Israel's Temple dedicated. It is to these elements in our midst that we owe our survival. So let us go forward with the sanctuary we possess, bearing always in mind the Rabbinic teaching that these sanctuaries too will

4. דברי הימים א', י"ב, ל"ג.

one day be returned to the Land of Israel with the People of Israel, there to live with the Torah of Israel in a world of peace and tranquillity.

iii(b)

Bar Mitzvah: Accomplishment or Commencement?

The Bar Mitzvah ceremony, frequently the climax of much practice and preparation, is usually regarded as the occasion for the showering of profuse praises upon the young man for his performance. All too often his accomplishment is regarded literally as a task fulfilled and completed. The Midrashic comment ויהי ביום כלות משה[1] expresses a necessary note of caution. When the Jew says, "Look at my accomplishment; כלות, the *Mishkan* is at an end, there is nothing more to do," then ווי, ווי, צווח הקדוש ברוך הוא, "Woe is Me! Woe is Me!" cries the Almighty.

The whole of Jewish history is reflected in that remarkable little verse. Wherever there is כלות there is ויהי. Complete emancipation in the *galus* meant extinction, because it put an end to the continuous driving force of Jewish life. The old schools were closed, the old traditions ceased, the old synagogue was abandoned. There was a כלות, an ending of ancient Jewish glories. Any kind of כלות causes a sigh of depression. Hence when Moses set up the *Mishkan* he immediately appointed נשיאי ישראל, leaders, העמדים על הפקדים, men to stand at the helm and see that the work of the *Mishkan* would go on every day. Twelve times the Torah repeats ויהי המקריב ביום הראשון...ביום השני...ביום השלישי. We may well wonder why the Torah,

1 See the previous section.

usually so concise with not one letter redundant, should repeat the same thing twelve times? It is to emphasise that every day the same work must go on; otherwise the whole Torah will become redundant. We are never finished. It is learning every day, it is giving every day, it is collecting every day. There was no rivalry between the עמדים על הפקדים, whether it was נחשן, who was prepared to sacrifice his life, or נתנאל his time, or זבולן his money. All wereעסוקים במלאכת המשכן, doing a job for Torah.

When the Bar Mitzvah is called to the Torah, he should regard it as a call to be one of the עמדים על הפקדים, never to become tired of learning and doing his Jewish duty. The *Haftorah*, speaking about the birth of the mighty Samson, says ויגדל הנער ויברכהו ה', "the child grew up and the Lord blessed him." Blessings come with ויגדל, with growth and progress, with ongoing development. With effort and endeavour, this can be achieved and God's blessing assured.

iv

Victory Shabbos[1]

Two precious columns in our sacred Torah scroll — which contains not one single redundant letter — are devoted to the repetition twelve times over of the identical gifts and offerings of the twelve princes of Israel at the dedication of the Sanctuary. What a mighty lesson to leaders and to statesmen, to Rabbis and to laymen! In the service of God and the community none must try to outrival the other. Such harmony reigned among the princes of

---

1 A sermon at Brondesbury Synagogue on the Shabbos coinciding with a military parade in London in honour of the Allied victory in World War II.

Israel, such unity of spirit, our Sages comment, that God valued the service of each as if he brought not only his own gifts but those also of his companions.[2]

What better message than this on Victory Shabbos, when, at this hour, a procession of military prowess and human strength is pouring through the wide and open thoroughfares of this great metropolis. Twelve months have passed since the cessation of hostilities. Hunger and famine threaten the world; human beings who, by the common rights of man, are entitled to freedom of thought and action are still imprisoned behind barbed-wire fences. The nations of the world have not yet undertaken not to outrival one another. The disunity of the United Nations threatens the very foundations of those things for which millions gave up all. A more fitting procession on this victory day would be the columns of orphans and homeless, the bereaved and the mourners, the blind, the infirm, the maimed, the disfigured; an exhibition of the suffering element of a maddened, selfish society, whom the tanks, the bombs and rockets have torn limb from limb. Why, the streets of London could not contain them! And no military salutations could comfort them. For the world has not yet rid itself of the men who revel in bloodshed and oppression, of the men who enjoy wading through rivers of tears and blood. It is too soon to hope that swords have turned into ploughshares.

It was to defeat these wicked men that Britain stood alone, and it is to Britain — in whom our faith has not yet been shaken — that the call for justice goes out today above the din of greed-caused wars. God is on the side of those arms which are lifted in His cause and thrown into battle for His purpose. Of these arms Britain has reason to be proud this day. But it is for the Jew that this Victory

2. במדבר רבה י״ד, כ״ז-כ״ח.

Shabbos has special significance. We gave of our best in this battle for human rights. The mass grave, the first, and, we hope, the last, is the earth that covers some of the six million of our people — one third of the world's total Jewish population; and it was the best we possessed.

In the *Sidrah* we read ויהי ביום כלות משה להקים את המשכן, "And it came to pass on the day that Moses had completed the setting up of the Tabernacle." "Did Moses, then, build the *Mishkan*?" the Rabbis ask; בצלאל ואהליאב וכל חכם לב עשו את המשכן, "surely Betzalel and Oholiab and the wise-hearted men made the Tabernacle?" ותלאו הכתוב במשה לפי שמסר נפשו עליו,[3] they reply, "because Moses devoted his life to it, to show the workmen how to shape it and how to build it, the Torah attributes its completion to Moses."

Many there were who gave of their strength and genius to the building of Israel's spiritual centre, but none like Moses שמסר נפשו עליו, who was ready to give up all to accomplish it. Its entire setting up was, therefore, attributed to him. Many there were in six years of universal carnage who contributed to victory; Britain, of all nations, held on when others succumbed. But none were so crushed under the weight of that terrible war as the Jew שמסר נפשו עליה. None gave so much that victory might be achieved. In the victory of the Allied nations we claim a rightful portion. By our unequalled devotion and unparalleled sacrifice we were the ones to show them תבנית כל דבר ודבר,[4] the shape of things. We brought them together and urged them to do justly, to walk humbly and to respect the sanctities of human life. Would that the world realised how much it owed to this people, who throughout its blood-soaked history struggled on in defiance of the so-called established order of society, moving the

רש"י: במדבר רבה י"ב, י"א. 3

רש"י: ומדרש הנ"ל. 4

world forward to the right-ordering and integration of life. It is an order of life that must be seen in the Jew. This is our mission.

The test has been a severe one. "Such another victory and we are undone," a great general once said. Such another victory and who knows how many would survive to hold up the torch of freedom, the torch of law and order. By the grace of God we are here.

Well might the words of today's *Haftorah* apply to the fathers and mothers of our generation, as they applied to the parents of Samson: לו חפץ ה' להמיתנו לא לקח מידנו עלה ומנחה ולא הראנו את כל אלה, "If the Lord wished to kill us, He would not have received a burnt offering and a meal offering from our hands; neither would He have shown us all these things." We have seen such things in our own lives as would rouse the most indifferent from his slumber. Our burnt offerings have been so grievous as would stir the faithless from his apathy. Not for nothing have we been spared. If the Lord desired to kill us, He would not have received all we have offered. He has spared us that we may live — with that infinite patience demanded of us — a Torah life, practising it ourselves, transmitting it to our children and offering it to mankind. Then will this victory day fulfil its purpose: the victory of justice over injustice and righteousness over evil, for the salvation of men the world over.

v

Wondrous Things[1]

So many things have happened to the world and to the Jew; wondrous things! Like Manoach and his wife in the *Haftorah*, ומפלא לעשות ומנוח ואשתו ראים, we saw them with our own eyes. The similarity

1 Delivered at the New Synagogue, Stamford Hill, 1958.

with the *Haftorah* goes even further: ויעל מלאך ה' בלהב המזבח, the angel of God who appeared to these anxious and expectant parents disappeared, ascending in the flame of the altar; and Manoach and his wife saw it. She said unto him, לו חפץ ה' להמיתנו לא לקח מידנו עלה ומנחה ולא הראנו את כל אלה, "If the Lord desired to kill us, He would never have received offerings at our hand, neither would He have shown us all these things." We, too, saw not one מלאך but hundreds of thousands, ascending in the flames of the altars of a foul and decadent civilisation. לו חפץ ה' להמיתנו — we were not far away, and the same could have happened to us. But instead we brought them as offerings, and we were spared to see wondrous things. The Jewish State — with all its evident weaknesses — reborn again. Our synagogues back to normal, our day schools and Yeshivos rising out of the debris. In this very locality, a *Yesodei Hatorah* school transplanted with the old spirit that we thought was crushed for all time. Yeshivos like Gateshead, the old schools of learning like Volozhin and Mir, that we thought were gone for all time, thriving on these very shores.

But we must also note the conclusion of that verse of the *Haftorah*: וכעת לא השמיענו כזאת, even now so many of us have not heard of these things. The sorrow of destruction never moved them, and the joy of reconstruction never stirred them. They are the type of people who never apply the events of history to themselves. If a state emerges, let others build it. If day schools arise, let others maintain them. If Yeshivos are replenishing the losses, let others support them — וכעת לא השמיענו כזאת, even now they are unconscious of מפלא לעשות, these wondrous things.

ותלד האשה בן ותקרא את שמו שמשון. The secret of Jewish survival is to apply history to one's self. From the flames of the burning altar, the couple that had been spared had but one thought: that salvation must come from themselves. They produced a son who bore on his shoulders the weight of Jewish suffering and the glory of Jewish triumph. Not everyone can be in the forefront of Jewish battles; but that does not absolve the masses from playing their part and sharing their responsibility. איש איש על עבדתו ואל משאו,[2] every man to his task. To carry one single socket, so long as it belongs to the Sanctuary, is עבודת הקדש, a holy service.

In the opening passage of the *Sidrah* the command went out to Moses: נשא את ראש בני גרשון גם הם, "Count the children of Gershon, too." Because the children of Kehas were given priority, that does not mean that Gershon should not be numbered; they too have a task to fulfil, of a lesser standing. In the great work of Sanctuary-building, in the wilderness of history, those who bear the Torah, those who maintain it, those who observe it, and those who honour it are numbered alike among the heroes and saviours of our people.

Repeatedly in these opening chapters of the חמש הפקודים, the Book of Numbers, we are told that Moses numbered them and appointed them to their sacred tasks על פי ה', "according to the word of God." If Jewish children are to be numbered, if Jewish children are to be distinct, singled out from among the mass of youth that runs amok, that shoulders no responsibility, that bears no loyalty, that loses all dignity, that understands no decency, then על פי ה', the word of God must mould their character. Then there is Jewish distinctiveness, Jewish individuality that no power in the world can crush. In this crazy world in which we live, if we are to save our children from being dazed by the new satans — these bluffing sputniks that encircle the earth — and from the strife and turmoil that has thrown men and nations into confusion, we must follow the Divine behest. The command to the *Kohanim* concerning the priestly blessing contained in this *Sidrah* was, ושמו את שמי על בני ישראל, "let them put My

במדבר ד', י"ט. 2

name upon the Children of Israel, ואני אברכם, and I will bless them."
Impress the name of God upon the children, imbue them with Torah
study and Torah ideals.

Born into Jewish homes in which the שכינה abides, imbued with
Torah teaching and Torah ideals, children go forth like the כרובים,
the cherubim, those youthful figures that stood above the Ark. In
the final verse of the *Sidrah* we are told that from between them
the voice of God was heard. Like the cherubim above the Ark, our
children will be beyond the reach of a devil-ridden society that is
bringing the world to destruction. Born in purity, with the covenant
of Abraham in their flesh and Torah and prayer on their lips, it will
be said of them, as was said of the mighty Samson, ויגדל הנער ויברכהו
ה', "and the lad grew and the Lord blessed him." They will be blessed
with strength and with courage to save themselves and, like Samson,
to save their people for the fulfilment of its Divine mission.

vi

Memory and Maturity[1]

"Thoughts drift back to bygone days,
Life moves on but memory stays."

Memories of an infant synagogue now become merged into the
reality of a mature and developed congregation. The young boys
and girls in whom we planted seeds have now grown and blossomed.
זורע צדקות מצמיח ישועות — these seeds are like any other seeds: you plant

1 In 1969, at Young Israel, Beverly Hills, revisited after an interval of thirteen
years.

righteousness and salvation must blossom.

ומפלא לעשות ומנוח ואשתו ראים, "and wondrous things happened, and Manoach and his wife saw it." In the *Haftorah* we read of a seemingly small event in the life of a husband and wife, that changed the course of history. Manoach and his wife were both participants and onlookers. Samson was to be born to them, and Manoach brought an offering on the rock, and he stood with his wife watching, ומפלא לעשות, and it was inexplicable: a flame appeared on the rock and the angel disappeared בלהב המזבח, in the flame of the altar. In those days when we mixed the cement and water with our own hands, when some of you were boys and girls and you carried the wood on your own shoulders, who would have thought that these were humble offerings from which a flame of faith, of enthusiasm and vitality would emerge and blossom, building more on the old foundations?

ומפלא לעשות ומנוח ואשתו ראים; there is a tremendous lesson in those few words. What is expected from us is to bring the קרבן, the offering, whatever we can; and the flame will arise of its own accord. In the birth of a new community, in the establishment of a new *Mishkan*, it is important to have those who learn and those who carry the burden of Torah on their shoulders. It may well be that one group must sometimes be given priority over the other. What good is a *Mishkan* without a *minyan*, a synagogue without *shiurim*? So נשא את ראש בני גרשן גם הם, "take the number of the sons of Gershon also." Everyone who assists — it makes no difference what he carries, the curtain or the sockets — no one is to be left out. The secret of success, of Jewish הצלחה, is to do something about the situation and then leave the rest to God. Bring an offering on the altar, and the flame will emerge on its own. Be a participant first, and then you can stand by and see. The Rabbis say that the little box in which the infant Moses was placed to save him from Pharaoh's decree was floating ששים אמה, 60 cubits from the edge of the bank of the river; ותשלח את

אמתה, and yet Pharaoh's daughter stretched out her arm ותקחה, and she reached it. How was it possible? You do what you can and leave the rest to the Almighty. But do what you can!

ויהי ביום כלות משה להקים את המשכן, "And it came to pass on the day that Moses had set up the Sanctuary," אמר משה לפני הקדוש ברוך הוא איך אפשר הקמתו על ידי אדם, "How is it possible," Moses asked, "for man to set it up on his own?" Of course, Moses meant the physical weight, too — the walls, the beams, the ceiling curtains — but the words seem to suggest a deeper meaning. Is it possible in this world of ours, this age of demolition: demolition of old values, sacred standards, historic pillars; is it possible to set up such walls of *Shechinah* that can resist the storms of change that erupt in our society? Moses looked about him: who is there that can accomplish this? On the one hand היו מבקשין להעמידו ולא יכולין להעמידו, "there were some who wanted to raise it up but were unable to do so. On the other hand היו חושבין להעמידו והוא נופל,[2] there were some who thought of raising it up, but it fell." If they only thought of it, how could it fall? The Rabbis probably meant היו חושבין להעמידו, they thought they *had* put it up, but it fell.

Neither of these two schools of thought can succeed. היו מבקשין, those who want to but do little about it, who like the idea but leave it to others, onlookers and not participants, they never succeed. ולא יכולין להעמידו; it just does not go up that way. There are also those who really believe they can put it up on their own. They have got the material, they have got the answers, they have got the quack remedies. But how long can these self-made, man-made, changing attitudes last? והוא נופל: such walls must collapse. They are detached from eternity.

אמר לו הקב"ה עסוק אתה בידך והוא נזקף וקם מאליו, "The Holy One, blessed be He, said to him, 'You get busy with your hands, והוא נזקף, it will straighten out and of its own it will stand firm.'" So long as the Jew

תנחומא פקודי י"א. 2

continues to build schools and Yeshivos, centres for prayer and study, וקם, no power in the world can destroy the walls of the *Mishkan*. That is when there are מצות מעשיות, when we obey the Divine command עסוק בידיך, when the Jew is engaged in doing *mitzvos*. Not merely in theory, not only חושב, not only מבקשין, but בידיך; then ונזקף, the *Mishkan* rises and the walls are immovable. No wonder we find no other expression anywhere but ביד משה. Not בפי משה, not בלב משה, but "in the hand of Moses." Living, to a Jew, is מעשי ידיכם, performing *mitzvos* with the hands, the limbs, the body; and indeed this was Moses' prayer when the *Mishkan* was complete: שתשרה שכינה במעשי ידיכם, that the *Shechinah* should continue to abide in your actions.

Everybody believes in the Kingdom of God; stop any man in the street who is not an atheist, and he will tell you he believes in the Kingdom of God. They preach about it and talk about it in all their services, but we add one little monosyllable to that phrase מלכות שמים. It is עול מלכות שמים, "the *yoke* of the Kingdom of God," and it means what it says: a yoke. שמע is not enough, and ואהבת is not enough. There must be ולמדתם וקשרתם, וכתבתם, ועבדתם, ועשו להם ציצית וראיתם, "teach them, bind them, write them, you shall serve, make for them *tzitzis,* see them." Not a limb is left out. This business of being a Jew is a continuous performance. It means doing all the time, otherwise it does not work. When the Jew closed his *Gemara*, put away his *tefillin,* sealed up the *mikveh,* stopped building centres for prayer and learning — כלות, decadence set in. The walls crash, standards break, foundations are uprooted and nothing is left.

Congregational activity is never finished. It must be a continuous performance, a never-ending process of *Yiddishkeit* going on and on. עסוק אתה בידך והוא קם מאליו; with constant endeavour the *Mishkan* will rise and stand, never to collapse, bringing credit to the community and Jewry at large.

BEHA'ALOSECHA

בהעלתך

i

Playing Second Fiddle

The *Sidrah* takes its name from the opening paragraph concerning the kindling of the menorah, the daily duty entrusted to Aaron and his sons to light the golden candelabrum in the Sanctuary. דבר אל אהרן ואמרת אליו בהעלתך את הנרת אל מול פני המנורה יאירו שבעת הנרות, "Speak unto Aaron and say unto him, 'When thou lightest the lamps, the seven lamps shall give light in front of the candlestick.'" The word *Beha'alosecha* is in the causative form, and consequently בהעלתך את הנרות literally means "when thou causest the light of the lamp to go up." To keep the light of faith and knowledge aflame, the priest, the teacher and guide of the people, must cause others to go up. He must endeavour to elevate them by kindling the light and love of Torah in their hearts and minds.

An eminent teacher once said to his school inspector, "My job is to try and make myself useless. I am trying to carry forward my pupils to a point where they can do without my help and be teachers unto themselves." The happiest day in the life of Moses came in this *Sidrah*, when Joshua nervously complained of the men who were prophesying in the camp without Moses' knowledge. Joshua was afraid that the dignity and authority of Israel's teacher would be abused by men prophesying who were unknown as leaders. But such was the remarkable greatness of Moses, the profound lover of Israel who never gave a thought to his own honour and position, that he longed that all should be as he was, and better. 'ומי יתן כל עם ה נביאים כי יתן ה' את רוחו עליהם, "Would that all the Lord's people were prophets, that the Lord would put His spirit upon them."

It was Moses' greatest yearning that all in Israel, irrespective of rank or class, might be endowed with the Divine Spirit. In short, he was working to make himself useless and unneeded. A good violinist, someone once said, is a man who has the ability to play first fiddle, but is willing to play second. Happy is the Rabbi who can say, "My congregation do not need me; they can do it all themselves."

ii

On Surrendering Self-Interest

The test of a person comes when he is confronted with the problem of what comes first, me or the cause. Is the cause bigger than me, or do I say, never mind the cause, I must get my way? It is a challenge that faces us all from time to time. The happiness of a home, sometimes its very survival, depends on it. Shall I give way and surrender my will, or must I get my own way? Young couples about to set out on married life's journey may well think of this, so often does the home depend on this בטל רצונך, giving way. Homes and families, businesses and governments, have collapsed because of the obstinacy of one who would not surrender his own will. The criterion of greatness can be seen in a person who is prepared to lose himself in the cause, to suffer indignity in the interest of the cause.

Two incidents in this *Sidrah* are an ample illustration. One is in its opening verses and the other in the closing verses. Aaron, the High Priest, suffers an indignity. He is the highest in the priestly hierarchy in the camp of Israel, yet he was not invited to participate in the consecration of the *Mishkan*. He was downcast, for all he was asked to do was בהעלתך את הנרות, the menial task of lighting the menorah. ויעש כן — שלא שינה,[1] "and Aaron did so," the Torah tells us; and the Rabbis add, "without changing a thing."

Again, when Miriam spoke evil about her brother Moses, she was stricken with leprosy, and the entire nation was held back from journeying on to the Promised Land. Moses might well have felt bitter and resentful. He had done so much for the people, and now to suffer such indignity! Yet no, ויצעק משה אל ה' לאמר קל נא רפא נא לה, "And Moses cried unto the Lord, 'Heal her now, O God, I beseech thee.'" It was a complete surrender of the respect due to his high office and of his own dignity in the interest of his people. The cause means more than the man.

Our own sovereign, the Queen,[2] in her selfless devotion to the duties of her high office and her total dedication to the service of society at large, is an inspiring example to us all to work for the well-being of others. By our so doing, may peace reign among nations and tranquillity among men.

---

1. רש"י; ספרי.

2 This extract is from a sermon given in 1977 at Golders Green Synagogue on the occasion of the Silver Jubilee of the Queen's reign.

iii

Jewish Unity and Jewish Shame

One of the difficulties confronting Moses in the construction of the *Mishkan* was how to make the menorah, the golden candelabrum. The Divine instruction was עד ירכה עד פרחה מקשה הוא: it was to be designed with seven branches and lights, all pointing to the centre, and all its parts were to be beaten out of one piece. Separate branches, yet beaten out of one piece; and he could not do it until כמראה אשר הראה ה' את משה, God Himself showed him and explained its construction.

People are frequently dismayed and depressed by the disunity and factionalism in Jewish life, particularly in Israel. There have never been gathered, in so short a time and in such limited space, so many people from so many lands, who speak so many languages and are possessed of so many views. In all these years we could not get Chassidim and *Misnagdim* to see eye to eye, or in Germany Orthodox and Reform, or in England Zionist and anti-Zionist. Can we expect a few years' residence in Israel to suffice to alter out of all recognition the life and thought of any man or any people? To get together all these elements and to weld them into one can only be כמראה אשר הראה ה'. Given peace and given the means, the way will be shown and unity will be achieved. Time will heal, and the people will regain confidence in God alone, Who has wrought all these miracles.

In the *Haftorah* the prophet Zechariah talks of the two Satans: יגער ה' בך השטן ויגער ה' בך הבחר בירושלם הלוא זה אוד מצל מאש. There is the enemy of the people and the enemy of the land. For centuries the Jew has been confronted by two problems. One is where to live and the other is how to live. With the emergence of Israel and its ever-open door, the problem of where to live has been solved. Thought must now be given to the problem of how to live.

The preservation of Jewish dignity and Jewish decency deeply affects our national prestige, demanding that our indifference to religious values should at least not be exposed. The private life of the individual is God's affair; it is our duty to teach, to preach and to persuade — we can do no more. But the public life of the Jew is the concern of the whole Jewish community. At any non-Jewish function, the priest or the bishop is there to offer a thanksgiving for food; and the Jew, who brought the word of God into the world, has lost all sense of responsibility in this connection. No wonder that in some circles Jews and atheists are addressed in the same language. Jewish decency and national prestige are badly shaken.

It was for this that Aaron prayed when Miriam was stricken down with leprosy for having spoken evil against her brother Moses. There she was, the great Jewish prophetess, the ideal of Jewish womanhood, exposed before the whole community, her sin revealed: ויאמר אהרן אל משה בי אדני אל נא תשת עלינו חטאת אשר נואלנו ואשר חטאנו, "and Aaron said to Moses, 'I pray thee, my master, do not lay upon us the sin that we have done in our folly.'" Here is a peculiar expression and rare to find in the Bible: אל נא תשת עלינו חטאת, "do not place upon us the sin." It was not for forgiveness that he prayed; it was that the sin might not be exposed. The tragedy is not the sin itself and the consequences she was called upon to bear. The tragedy is the knowledge and the publicity to which the sin gives rise: אל נא תשת עלינו חטאת, "lay no sin upon *us*." Oh, that the sin may not be put upon us and revealed to the world!

We make many mistakes in life, and parents are often called upon to suffer for children; but the greatest suffering is when the world talks of our shame. The sin can be forgiven, but the shame is a blot that can never be erased. והענן סר מעל האהל והנה מרים מצרעת כשלג:

whilst the cloud covered the tent, she bore her suffering; but when the cloud was removed, the world saw her shame. אל נא תשת עלינו חטאת, Aaron prayed, "Oh, that the shame and disgrace be removed." The indifference shown by a gathering of people involves the serious crime of *chillul Hashem*. Public opinion must be aroused to bring the name of God back into the open. אל נא תשת עלינו חטאת, let not our sin be exposed! *Chillul Hashem* must be avoided; then will *Kiddush Hashem* take its place, and Israel will stand revealed as a God-fearing nation, leading the whole world back to the paths of faith and righteousness.

iv

Marital Problems

Winston Churchill, in the course of one of his public statements about conditions in England, once said, "It is not enough to float; we must swim against the stream." This phrase is strikingly similar to one used by a famous *Maggid*. The *halachah* is that when a fowl falls from a rooftop to the ground, if it can rise to its feet and walk it is kosher, but if it cannot rise it is *treifah*. And if a fowl falls from a ship into the sea, if it floats it is *treifah*, but if it swims against the stream it is kosher. "So is the Jew," the *Maggid* said; "if he floats and the winds carry him at will, then he is *treifah*, but if he swims against the stream he is kosher."

The secret of Jewish survival is Jewish עקשנות: the Jew's stubbornness, his dogged resistance, his unbending character. When the world set up images, he defied them; when child murder was prevalent, to him a child became his most cherished possession. When filial respect meant nothing, he shouted from the mountaintop "Honour thy father and thy mother." When the lights of the world were extinguished, the Jew kindled the light of Shabbos. When polygamy was common and woman was cheapened, he instituted monogamy, and a wife became a sacred being, not a tool. "Be careful," the Rabbis say, "not to make a woman weep, because God counts her tears."[1]

We swam against the stream when the current was strong in the opposite direction. The absolute and unchanging character of Jewish law in marital matters, which we have practised for thousands of years, has helped in no small measure to uphold and to strengthen the Jewish home, which basically is a spiritual conception rather than a physical one.

The *Sidrah* refers to the murmurings of the Israelites in the wilderness. The stream of events then, too, went against them. They would have to go hungry in the wilderness if they wanted to reach the Promised Land. לו יאכלנו בשר, they cried, "Would that we were given meat to eat." There was no kosher meat available; זכרנו את הדגה אשר נאכל במצרים חנם, "We remember the fish we ate in Egypt for nought." Food was plentiful, though we were slaves.

חנם does not mean, the Rabbis tell us, that they received food חנם, for no money, but חנם מן המצות, without any Heavenly demands. We had it easy: no *kashrus* to restrict us, no Shabbos to limit us. We floated, we could do what we liked. What has this Torah done for us? The kitchen must be controlled because of *kashrus,* earnings must be limited because of Shabbos. That distinctiveness in Jewish life meant that something must be given up.

To build a state, either you give and become free, or you don't give and remain slaves; you cannot build schools unless you give and become educated; otherwise, חנם, you don't give and remain

___
1. בבא מציעא נ"ט ע"א.

ignorant. Decency and dignity, morality and discipline make demands. אשר נאכל במצרים חנם means a good-for-nothing life. What do you get out of it? And what do you leave behind?

וישמע משה את העם בכה למשפחתיו איש לפתח אהלו, "And Moses heard the people weeping over their families, every man at the door of his tent." Ostensibly it was no more than a food problem: בלתי אל המן עינינו, it was the same manna every day, the same dish of food at every meal; they got tired of it. But there was a much more serious problem: the same wife every day, or the same husband — restriction in marriage, special requirements for divorces, major domestic issues. When these laws were made known וישמע משה את העם בכה למשפחתיו, "And Moses heard them cry *because of* their families," על עריות הנאסרות להם.[2] The law demanded of them איש לפתח אהלו, "every man to stand at the door of his own tent." A house must be guarded no less than a state that guards its frontiers against invasion, or else tears and weeping will be heard within its walls. There is nothing worse than a home that is exposed: שאין פתחי אהליהם מכוונים זה לזה,[3] the beauty of the Jewish homes was that their doors did not face each other. Each one respected the privacy of his neighbour and minded his own business. That was the distress in the wilderness: בכה למשפחתיו איש לפתח אהלו, they realised that in order to build a home in a world where morals were low and woman cheap, each one would have to turn to his own home and take charge of his own affairs.

Today more than ever the Jewish call must be איש לפתח אהלו, go back to the door of your own tent, do not leave it exposed. There are genuine cases of incompatibility; Jewish law never demands such personal suffering, there is provision made for it. But where reconciliation is impossible, then איש לפתח אהלו — build another tent.

---

2. רש"י; ספרי; שבת קל"א ע"א.

3. רש"י במדבר כ"ד, ה'; בבא בתרא ס' ע"א.

Do not retain the strings by blackmail, trying to get what you can out of a victimised wife or a victimised husband. Every human being has a right to live, but discipline and morality must be the watchword. Society will have to recognise this if it is not to sink into the sea of immoral corruption.

The home in Jewish life is the sanctuary: the husband the priest and the wife the priestess, the table the altar and the food the sacrifice. So let it be, איש לפתח אהלו, every man guarding his sanctuary, remaining always a proud example of clean living and righteous thinking, and an example to men the world over.

v

Reacting to Slander

The pathetic episode in the life of Miriam, told in the *Sidrah*, cast a dark shadow over the majestic appearance of one of Israel's greatest women. The righteous woman whose son was killed על קדוש השם; the great heroine who was responsible for the safety of Moses at the time of his birth in Egypt; Miriam, who led the women of Israel in song and prayer at the crossing of the Red Sea and in whose merit a well of drinking water accompanied the Israelites during their wanderings in the wilderness. What sin did she commit that should have deserved this tragic affliction? ותדבר מרים ואהרן במשה, Miriam instigated Aaron to join her in speaking evil of Moses and in scandalising his domestic life. What could she say of this super-man whose selfless devotion to his people is unequalled to this day? Could she accuse him of dishonesty, of self-aggrandisement, of כבוד seeking? If jealousy sets in it is like a cancer, it is malignant and spreads: so she attacked his private life, which, in fact, had received Divine approval.

What was Moses' reaction? He stood silent with his characteristic modesty. To squeal, to go about justifying his actions and vindicating himself, is not the way of a great man; he gets on with his task and ignores the false accusations. You do not surrender a cause and turn your back on an ideal because of a few slanderers in your institution. What could be expected from a people who had just been taken out of bondage — not into a free, happy country but into a desert. Sometimes there was no water, sometimes no food, here was an Amalek and there were false prophets. To keep a balance without being swept off one's feet was the greatest achievement.

We would have no Israel today had it not been for fanatics who were exposed to the vilest accusations. There would have been no Yeshivos in America had it not been for the old Rabbis, who ignored an American philosophy of assimilation and went from door to door gathering funds and pupils. That was the strength of Moses: hold on at all costs, try to do even more, to pray and to pray hard for those who rose in opposition.

All who believe in the preservation of true Torah ideals must refrain from any temptation to slander one another and expose one another. There must be a sincere endeavour to create a disciplined, orderly, dignified unity. We must not sell our ideal short, we must not barter our dignity for selfish prejudice and sectional interest. Like Moses, we must not abandon the ship because we are sometimes accused of something we did or did not do. בהעלתך את הנרות, we must strive to kindle a light that will spread to illumine the spiritual darkness of ignorance and prejudice, to the glory of God and of Israel.

vi

A Call to Prayer[1]

This has been an anxious but exciting time. Our own interests, and even world news, have been overshadowed by the mighty operations that have been proceeding satisfactorily with the invasion of Europe. Our thoughts have been, and still are, directed to the gallant men fighting on the beaches of France — now on its very soil — in the liberation of Hitler's enslaved continent. Our intercessions go up to the Almighty for a speedy ending of all the misery that the European peoples, and the Jews especially, have known for well-nigh ten years — that men the world over may be freed from all human aggression.

It is to England's glory that as it steers through the stormy seas it does not rely entirely on physical power and military genius, but combines with these operations the spiritual strength of its faith in God, the God of justice and righteousness. The King's words on what is probably the greatest day in English history must remain always in the minds of the people: "We shall not ask that God may do our will, but that we may be enabled to do the will of God." Indeed, this echoes an utterance of the Rabbis some two thousand years ago, in the second chapter of the Ethics of the Fathers, read in all our synagogues on summer Sabbath afternoons: בטל רצונך מפני רצונו כדי שיבטל רצון אחרים מפני רצונך, "Nullify thy will before His will, that He may nullify the will of others before thy will." The will of the enemy can be made as nought if the will of God permeates our own lives. It is to this Jewish idea of hinging ourselves on to God by good conduct,

---

1 Given at Brixton Synagogue shortly after the D-Day Landing which led to the liberation of Europe from the Nazi tyranny.

by continuous and widespread care, that we are asked during the coming days and months to dedicate our lives. Is it too much to demand of the Jew, to return to that instrument of faith — prayer — which our fathers brought into the world? Here it is, in the very words of the *Sidrah*: ויצעק משה אל ה', "And Moses cried unto the Lord, אל נא רפא נא לה, 'Heal her now, oh God, I beseech Thee.'" Heal now this world that is sick unto death. Our fathers used to call it to *'daven'*; upon it depends the whole structure of Jewry, and upon it depends the freedom of men. It is the link that binds us with God.

A call has been made, not from religious leaders alone, but from military leaders too, for continuous and widespread prayer flowing from the lips of men and women, from every place of worship, from home and factory, to strengthen the hands of those brave sons of civilised people as they battle their way through to victory. There is no need for us to announce that the synagogue is open daily. We have so far never failed; when the Blitz was at its height this place of worship stood undaunted with its continuous daily prayer. It is the solemn duty of every Jew, שחרית מנחה מעריב, morning, noon and night, to recognise as the sun rises and sets, as night falls, that with Him alone is the fountain of light. With Him no battle is in vain, with Him no battle is lost. If the fighting men want our prayers, then for God's sake let us pray. For our children's sake let us *daven*. Let us start all over again; for those who are giving up all let us give up a few moments of the day. Thus will "the Lord give strength unto His people," and thus will "the Lord give His people the blessing of peace."

vii

Contentment

(Bar Mitzvah)

A class of young artists was asked to paint a picture of contentment; the picture judged as best in expressing and portraying contentment was to be awarded a prize. One student painted a countryside, with cows in a pasture. Another student sketched the afternoon sun, trees and grass. Another portrayed a mother feeding her child, and another, a man with a pipe and book in his hand. But the prize was won by one who pictured a bird sitting on a twig that overhung a raging, tempestuous waterfall dashing over huge rocks. The twig seemed to sway under the impact of rushing air and spray, but the bird lifted its head and sang with a heart full of song.

The Jewish people may well be likened to that bird, sitting on the twig of the Torah, overhanging a world rushing and restless, fighting and struggling, never able to keep the balance between changing ideologies. In the picture it seemed as if at any moment the swaying of the twig would unbalance the bird; but no — there it sat, calm and restful, singing to its heart's content. It has looked many times as if the Jew would lose his balance and be swallowed up by the tempests that have raged in the countries in which he lived; but that never happened. We may well wonder why. The answer is contained in the *Haftorah* that accompanies this *Sidrah*: לא בחיל ולא בכח כי אם ברוחי, "not by might, nor by strength, but by *My* spirit."

The prophet Zechariah speaks not just about "a spirit," but רוחי, "*My* spirit," the spirit of God. How can the spirit of God be put into ordinary men and women? By the *mitzvos*, the commands and the duties of the Torah to which every Bar Mitzvah boy should be loyal. Our uniform is our *tzitzis,* our arms and equipment the *tefillin,* our academies the Hebrew schools, our strength our kosher food, our exercises our Shabbos, our duties our respect for parents and teachers, our decency our cleanliness of character. These things give us the spirit of God.

That little יוד, that איד, added to the word רוח makes all the difference in the world. When amongst friends, the difference is the איד; when out in the street amongst people, it is the יוד. That is the meaning of Bar Mitzvah: to become a איד, adding the יוד to whatever you do. You will never be able to do it correctly unless you learn. Through Torah learning and Torah living, true contentment is attained and the dual acclaim heralded by the prophet — חן חן — is attained: חן in the eyes of God and חן in the eyes of man, bringing credit and joy to the whole community.

SHELACH LECHA

שְׁלַח לְךָ

i

Careless Talk Costs Lives!

The Midrash connects the opening passages of this *Sidrah* with the closing passages of the previous *Sidrah* by means of a comment that reveals a peculiar human weakness which, if allowed to spread, can do untold injury to man and society. The *Sidrah* begins with the account of the מרגלים, the spies, who were sent out to explore the land of Canaan, to investigate its potential, השמנה היא אם רזה, whether it is a fat land or lean, and to enquire into the strength of its inhabitants, החזק הוא אם רפה, whether they are strong or weak. These twelve representatives, one for each of the tribes, were sent to examine the character of the land and the attitude of the inhabitants. Their mission proved the turning point in their history.

All but two forfeited their right of possession of the land. Not only the spies, but the multitude of the people, influenced by their evil report, proved themselves unfit for the tasks of a free nation. A community whose faith can be shaken by a few scandal-mongers cannot undertake a venture that demands courage and determination. It was a national calamity: לשון הרע, the evil tongue, brought disaster in its wake.

The story of the spies follows the account, at the end of the previous *Sidrah*, of the occasion when Miriam spoke to Aaron impugning the good name of Moses. The story of her downfall is pathetic. She succumbed to a temptation of slander, and brought death near her door instead. What a tremendous lesson this must have been to the people! Their journey to the Promised Land was delayed for seven days until Miriam recovered from her illness. The Rabbis say that the delay was a reward for Miriam's having waited in the bulrushes, praying for Moses' life. In return Israel now waited at Miriam's tent, praying for her life. A good deed is never forgotten, but the thought of a good deed can be obliterated in the rubbish heap that the slanderer's tongue throws out.

One would think that this would have been a lesson to the Israelites. צפוי היה לפני הקדוש ברוך הוא שיאמרו לשון הרע על הארץ,[1] the Almighty foresaw, the Midrash says, that they would return from Canaan with an evil report. What did they expect to find? Milk and honey flowing down the gutters? Hospitable inhabitants to welcome them with open arms? A land without a fight, industry without an effort, housing without means? Of course they would come back slandering the land! לפיכך סמך הקב״ה הענין זה לזה,[2] the Holy One, blessed be He, deliberately set the sequence with Miriam's tragedy as a prelude — a fair warning to slanderers who would delay the entry to the Promised Land to beware. Let them not say, 'We never knew of the punishment meted out to slanderers.' But if Miriam's לשון הרע made a break in their journey for seven days, the evil report of the spies broke their journey for all time. One spoke evil of an individual, but the others spoke evil of a land and misled an entire people.

---

1. במדבר רבה ט״ז, ה'.

2. שם.

The Chofetz Chaim illustrates the disastrous consequences that can ensue from the seemingly trivial לשון הרע with the story of a family that perished because someone spoke evil of a horse! It was put about that the horse from which the family drew its livelihood was scrawny and feeble. Because of this the driver was no longer hired. When he thus became unemployed the family of eight was subjected to starvation!

The iniquity of Joseph's לשון הרע brought him down to the prisons of Egypt. The iniquity of Bar Kochva's לשון הרע brought about the downfall of Bettar. Great martyrs went to their death because of the evil tongue. Likewise the entire generation that left Egypt was annihilated because of the לשון הרע, the report of the spies. What an awful weakness in man the Torah reveals! The industrialist cries out like the מרגלים, 'We shall never cope with it, ארץ אכלת יושביה הוא, it is a land that eats up its inhabitants; it will not produce enough to support them; economic conditions will not satisfy the hungry people.' Traditionalists cry out, 'We shall never change their mode of life, כי חזק הוא ממנו, they are stronger ממנו,[3] even than God Himself; there is no Shabbos and there is no *kashrus*.' This is not the first time that our people have gone up to conquer a land. Just as it was then, so it is today. Some come back with evil reports, slandering the land and its inhabitants. והתחזקתם, "be of good courage, ולקחתם מפרי הארץ, see the right side of things, take of the fruit of the land."

In every struggle — be it for the nation, for the land, for the community, or for the family — there must be faith in God and unity of purpose. והתחזקתם ולקחתם מפרי הארץ, with courage you will take of the fruit of the land, and the future will bring success to your endeavours and blessing to your work.

רש״י; סוטה ל״ה ע״א. 3

ii

The Supreme Slander

There are three cases of לשון הרע, slander, referred to in the Torah, prior to the one in this *Sidrah*, which outdoes them all. Each of them made a tremendous impact on Jewish history; indeed, some may be said to have changed the course of history. No wonder the Torah unashamedly exposes them to Jews and to the world at large to the end of time.

First was Joseph: his father's favourite, the apple of his eye, the first son of his beloved Rachel. Telling his father about his brothers' deeds, causing jealousy and hatred, was a לשון הרע that brought about the collapse of Jacob's household in Canaan and the beginning of Egyptian bondage. Then there was Moses, to whom the call came to go as God's messenger to liberate His people. Moses turned to Heaven and pleaded, והן לא יאמינו לי ולא ישמעו בקלי, "They will not believe me and they will not listen to me." The third לשון הרע was that of Miriam and Aaron, who slandered Moses. It held back the whole People of Israel on their journey to the Promised Land.

Now we come to a לשון הרע not against man, not against brothers, not against a people, but against God Himself. Of the twelve spies, only Caleb and Joshua returned with hope and faith and confidence that if God wills it we shall succeed. The others spoke well of the land: "It flows with milk and honey — but we shall never conquer it. The occupants are giants, its cities are like fortresses. לא נוכל לעלות אל העם, we will never be able to go up against the people, כי חזק הוא ממנו, they are stronger ממנו," mightier than Him. כלפי מעלה אמרו כביכול; אפילו בעל הבית אינו יכול להוציא כליו משם[1], it was as if they spoke against God,

רש"י; סוטה ל"ה ע"א. 1

saying, "Even the Owner of the land could not obtain entry to take out His belongings from there."

What a slander! Once they took God out of the picture they never stopped there. ויציאו דבת הארץ אשר תרו אתה אל בני ישראל, "they spread an evil report about the land which they had spied out to the Children of Israel." They spread the לשון הרע far and wide, to the whole community. "Do you know who occupies the land?" they cried. "Do you know whom we saw there, whom we met there? ושם ראינו את הנפילים בני ענק מן הנפלים, We saw the *Nephilim*, the sons of Anak, who come of the *Nephilim*." Who were these *Nephilim* who exercised such a powerful influence over them? Rashi quotes the Sages as saying שנפלו מן השמים בימי דור אנוש, "they were creatures that fell from heaven in the time of Enosh, at the beginning of the Creation." Our Sages may well have meant שנפלו מן השמים, the *Nephilim* dropped from heaven — they were men without a soul, without Heaven in them. They fell from heaven, like animals without נשמות. *Nephilim:* low, depraved, animal-like. How will we fight these people with mere faith? ותשא כל העדה ויתנו את קולם ויבכו העם בלילה ההוא, "and all the congregation lifted up their voices, and the people wept that night."

כל העדה, the whole congregation wept. A whole congregation lost its faith! Our Sages say: אמר להם הקדוש ברוך הוא, "the Holy One, blessed be He, said to them, אתם בכיתם בכיה של חנם ואני קובע לכם בכיה לדורות — אותו הלילה תשעה באב היה,[2] 'You wept this night for no reason; I will make this a night upon which you will have reason to weep for many generations' — that night became the night of Tisha B'Av." What an awful punishment was meted out to those spies, and to that generation which lost its soul and was willing to surrender and submit itself to a people that had no soul, who long before had fallen from Heaven, as it were. Our ancient Sages say that none of that

2. תענית כ"ט ע"א.

generation enjoyed a share in the eternal life: אין להם חלק לעולם הבא.[3] People without a נשמה have no portion in *"Yenner Velt."* This was the meaning of the Divine decree, במדבר הזה יתמו ושם ימתו, "in this wilderness they shall be consumed, and there they shall die." Not only will you be consumed in the desert, but after death you will die again: ושם ימתו. Cut out the נשמה, and you have cut yourself off from eternity.

Is it not wonderful that the Torah does not continue with this theme of the tragic journey through the wilderness? It turns in another direction; it holds out hope to the young children: דבר אל בני ישראל ואמרת אלהם כי תבאו אל ארץ מושבתיכם. They will reach the land of promise because אני נתן לכם — *I give it to them.* The first duty must be to recognise, to acknowledge God in history, אני נתן לכם; God in their possessions, ועשיתם אשה לה' עלה או זבח; God in their produce and their food, באכלכם מלחם הארץ, "when you eat of the bread of the land, set apart a portion for a gift unto God." God in labour: preserve the Shabbos and protect it from desecration. Finally, ועשו להם ציצית, "bid them make fringes on the corners of their garments": surround yourselves with God.

The tears of that night are still with us. They are caused by the country that crushed the נשמה, the soul of the Jew. They thought that the Jewish soul would never recover. But no, that will never happen. He will bring back all the scattered ones of Israel to the land of promise, with souls restored and trust returned, to the astonishment of the world and the glory of God.

---

3. סנהדרין ק"י ע"ב.

ii(b)

The Bar Mitzvah Aliyah

The spies, in their report, related that they had seen the נפילים, the sons of ענק. There is some mystery about this word נפילים; some English versions do not even translate it. The Rabbis say that the נפילים were those שנפלו מן השמים,[1] who fell from heaven during the early days of man. They fell short, they fell foul, they could not hold up the Heavenly things, the things that heaven wants. They gave in to all their earthly wants and gave up all their Heavenly things. That is why in the days of Noah there was a flood — they were corrupt and immoral and violent. They were like animals, looking down to earth, never looking up to heaven.

To the spies, this handful of Israelites who had just been standing at Sinai, who were taught to look up like men, with *tallis* and *tefillin*, Shabbos and Yom Tov, it came as a great shock to see these "fallen ones." How could they come to terms with men who had stooped so low and who never looked up to Heaven? It was the great Caleb who took up the challenge and silenced the people, ויהס כלב את העם. He said, עלה נעלה, "We will go up." Just the opposite: even if the whole world around us is going down, and sinks as low as נפילים, we will go higher and higher. עלה נעלה — אפילו בשמים,[2] even up to the heavens. We will lift up and elevate this earthly existence, we will put Heaven into it, we will put a נשמה into it. With the spirit of God in us we will conquer and we will win.

This is the meaning of Bar Mitzvah: instead of נפילה there should be עליה. The first עליה of the Bar Mitzvah is to bring God into

1. יומא ס״ז ע״ב.

2. רש״י; סוטה ל״ה ע״א.

everything: to be like the first Caleb, to adopt his slogan: עלה נעלה!
Even though he may become a man of the world, yet he must possess
that רוח אחרת, that "other spirit," full of Godly feeling, following
loyally in our great Jewish heritage and tradition.

iii

The "Other Spirit"[1]

a) Torah commentators are concerned with the distinction
Moses made between Joshua and Caleb as they embarked on their
mission to spy out the Promised Land. ויקרא משה להושע בן נן יהושע, "And
Moses called Hoshea the son of Nun, Joshua." According to the
Midrash, Moses here pronounced over Joshua the prayer י"ה יושיעך
מעצת מרגלים,[2] "May God deliver thee from the counsel of the spies."

Why did Moses omit the loyal companion Caleb from his
prayers? It may well be that Moses thought his devoted disciple
Joshua was in greater danger. Because of his known association
with Moses, the risk that the spies would suspect him of dissent was
greater than for Caleb, who was one of the rank and file and whose
true sympathies could be concealed until an opportune moment.
Indeed, in the sequel it was this that gave Caleb the opportunity of
speaking up against the majority with the bold assertion עלה נעלה
וירשנו אתה, "We shall go up at once, and possess the land." And it was
this that earned him the Divine commendation ועבדי כלב עקב היתה רוח
אחרת עמו וימלא אחרי והביאתיו אל הארץ אשר בא שמה וזרעו יורשנה, "But my servant

---

1 This section gives several short extracts with variations on the previous
theme.

2.רש"י; סוטה ל"ד ע"ב

Caleb, because he had another spirit with him and has followed me fully, him will I bring into the land whereinto he went and his seed shall possess it."

The Rabbis suggest that the expression רוח אחרת implies that Caleb played a double game: שתי רוחות אחת בפה ואחת בלב, למרגלים אמר אני עמכם בעצה, ובלבו היה לומר האמת,[3] "to the spies he said, 'I am with you in your plan,' but in his heart he had no other intention than to tell the truth." People sometimes think that in order to achieve an end, to reach the ideal goal, it is necessary to silence the opposition by telling them they are right. But one can only permit himself to do that if he is convinced that in the end he will win. Caleb did it; but Joshua, the leader, the future successor to Moses' exalted office — his associations, his deeds, his word must never be doubted. For him Moses prayed י"ה יושיעך מעצת מרגלים, "May God save you from being mixed up with them and concealing the truth."

When Caleb and Joshua opposed the rest of the spies, the whole community wanted to throw stones at them: ויאמרו כל העדה לרגום אתם באבנים. The Rabbis in their wisdom say, נטלו אבנים וזרקום כלפי מעלה,[4] "They never aimed the stones at the two men; they threw them in the direction of Heaven." These days there are all kinds of stones thrown at the Heavens: at religious authority, at the Shulchan Aruch, at Divine law. But worse than anything are the stones that come from the mouth and are thrown כלפי מעלה, over the air, making a *chillul Hashem,* penetrating thousands of Jewish homes and ears. We must not be misled! We must echo Moses' prayer for Joshua and lead an uncompromising Jewish way of life that will redound to the glory of God, the glory of Torah and the glory of Israel.

רש"י: במדבר רבה ט"ז, י"א. 3

סוטה ל"ד ע"א. 4

b) Any fool can follow in the wake of the masses, and any weakling can swim with the tide. The spies were no mere individuals, but selected men, singled out; they were all worthy men when they left for their mission of investigation. If ten of them recoiled at the thought of coming to grips with the gigantic problems they discovered, should the remaining two be caught in the same net of cowardice and faithlessness? If ten of them were afraid of difficulties, should Caleb and Joshua too decline to set their face against such misguided conceptions? — ועבדי כלב עקב היתה רוח אחרת עמו Caleb had two spirits. With one he lived at peace with his colleagues, but with the רוח אחרת, with the other spirit, וימלא אחרי, he followed faithfully in the footsteps of faith and loyalty. He took counsel with the other leaders, but he fearlessly voted against them.

Where there is a conflict between heart and conscience there is only one way for the conscientious Jew: וימלא אחרי. Conscience must prevail. This was his reward: וזרעו יורשנה, his children, therefore, will possess the land. Can we expect children to grow up courageous and loyal if parents waver, and are possessed of a kind of non-committal Judaism that turns the synagogue into a kind of church with empty, meaningless ceremonial — if they have no faith in their future and no attitude in their present? Can good Jews and God-fearing Jews be so far misled as not to protest against this form of idol-worship, that turns our religion into a body without a soul, an empty shell without תורה שבעל פה, without hope in our return to ארץ ישראל, with a Jewish burial the only goal of one's labours?

We pray first and foremost that the spirit that animated Caleb and Joshua may animate our children. That Torah learning may find a place in their hearts and minds. That the light of faith and loyalty may radiate from the Land of Israel across the seas to penetrate our hearts and homes. That וזרעו יורשנה, our children may possess it, in our own day for the benefit of mankind the world over.

c) The great tribute that was paid to Caleb was not even paid to Joshua. Joshua never mixed with the masses; he was being trained as Moses' successor. Caleb lived among men and mixed with them, but stood out courageously. רוח אחרת עמו, "he had another spirit, וימלא אחרי, he followed Me."

וימלא means more than follow; it means 'he was filled with Me.' To be filled with God means to have רוח אחרת, to be different and to live differently. With such a person religion is more than outward ceremonial: it is part of his very life, in the home, on the door, on the flesh and on the limbs. וימלא אחרי is to have God all over you. אם חפץ בנו ה', "if God delights בנו, in us, if He is in us, והביא אתנו אל הארץ, then He will bring us to the land."

There is a choice: to have God in us and to live like men, or to put Him outside of us and live an animal-like existence. To die and leave behind mortal remains, or to die and leave behind a פגר, a carcass. The Torah permits itself to use this strong expression. It describes that generation as פגריכם אתם, "you are carcasses," and אין להם חלק לעולם הבא,[5] that generation, the Rabbis say, had no portion in the World to Come. None can enjoy the fruits of a life's toil and labour unless an impress is made on the generations that follow. If life's energy and life's possessions leave a mark on the soil of Israel where the Jewish body is being rebuilt, if life's work and life's earning leave a mark on the schools of learning where the Jewish soul is being recaptured — then when men die the soul lives on, and it makes no difference how long we live. Life is measured not by years but by achievement — achievement that is carried forward in the years that follow. That achievement, כי יכול נוכל לה, the spirit of 'it can be done' — that achievement alone can bring national prestige and uplift Jewish dignity that will command the respect of the peoples of the world.

5. סנהדרין ק"י ע"ב.

iv

New Interpretations

Much has been said in recent years of the need to interpret Jewish law and values in modern terms, and to explain them in a way that would be attractive to the modern world. There is some truth in that. Throughout our long history, some of the finest literary, philosophical and halachic contributions have been written in the language of the countries in which we lived, and interpretations given to make the Torah intelligible to the people of the day. Through interpretation and translation the Bible has become the most powerful, penetrating force that man has ever known. Its impact on civilisation from the early days on has no parallel. It is the most amazing thing that could have happened to man, that a people so small should produce a book so small, with such tremendous influence on countless millions. Untold myriads have drawn inspiration from it. If the seven oceans were turned into ink there would not be enough to write a thesis on the influence of the Bible on civilisation.

The most amazing thing about the Bible, as an American once wrote, is its vocabulary. Shakespeare employed about twenty thousand different words, Milton employed about ten thousand words, and the Bible, the vast panorama of Biblical thought, is conveyed in little more than six thousand words. Whilst it is true that Hebrew is so rich in nuance and meaning that no translation can do it justice, nevertheless, the fact that the Bible has been translated into so many different languages and interpreted in so many different ways has been instrumental in furthering its far-reaching influence on the world.

All this may have been to the good, but nevertheless, the solution to our aching problem is not one of interpretation and translation. Modern emphasis on science, on politics, on sport will not be counteracted by modern interpretations of the Bible, because it is studied and read today less than ever before. Today it is a question of conviction or no conviction, of belief or no belief. We cannot fight distractions with interpretations if we want to retain the masses to Judaism. We can only fight distraction with self-sacrifice, with practice and observance. We are living in an age of action, not of thought. Any experienced public man: orator, actor, singer or musician, will tell you that the masses are attracted more by the policies and the acts than by the speech or the voice.

Make no mistake: the modern trend away from religion is not motivated by reason or logic or lack of interpretation. One does not need to be such a חכם to be an אפיקורוס, an agnostic, or an atheist. It is much easier to disprove a thing than to prove it. Today it is not חכמה; it is just a take-it-easy philosophy.

A Talmudic comment on the concluding portion of this *Sidrah* puts it very well. It relates to the mitzvah of *tzitzis* and is recited every day in our prayers. The Torah says, ולא תתורו אחרי לבבכם, "that ye go not about after your own heart," and the Talmud explains, זו מינות, וכן הוא אומר אמר נבל בלבו אין אלהים.[1] To turn after your heart means to be an אפיקורוס, a non-believer. A negative needs no conviction. The Rabbis went deep down into the psychology of the human being: אפיקורוס has nothing to do with conscience or with the brain; it is to do with the heart — אמר נבל בלבו, "the *fool* said in his heart, 'There is no God.'" One need not be a חכם; a fool can say it too, because it has to do with the heart and not with the head and the brain. To counteract the feelings of the heart, the whims and the desires, the

ברכות י״ב ע״ב על תהלים י״ד .1

passions and the emotions: a million new interpretations will not achieve it. The hands must fight it, the eyes must turn away from it, the feet must walk in the opposite direction. To talk of new interpretations in modern terms is just a pious sentiment that leads nowhere. וזכרתם את כל מצות ה׳, "Remember all My commandments": fringes on your garments, curb your appetite, contain the take-it-easy conception. Commandments and duties are the only bulwarks against the tide of the heart.

The validity of this contention is nowhere more vividly portrayed than in the Rabbinic comment on the *Sidrah,* that the enraged Israelites who attempted to stone Caleb and Joshua נטלו אבנים וזרקום כלפי מעלה.[2] They may have appeared to be throwing at Caleb and Joshua, but, say the Rabbis, their aim was really directed Heavenwards. What a foolish thing to do, to throw stones in the air! Of course it is not logical; but it does not need logic or reason to reject faith, to denounce tradition, to upset loyalties. זרקום כלפי מעלה — to ridicule authority, to defy moral discipline, is to follow the inclinations of the heart, leading a shallow, unconvincing, meaningless life while throwing stones at higher values.

It is going on all around us; more than an interpretation is needed today, a return is needed to basic practices and observances. נשמע will follow נעשה. The giants of opposition can be defeated and indifference can be overcome by a readiness to fight back with faith and confidence in oneself. We must take spiritual stones and throw them earthwards, rather than Heavenwards, so that Heaven can penetrate our homes and our lives. Let conscience dictate to the heart rather than the heart dictate to the conscience. Then will the Jew be the architect of a new society: a society in which deeds and not words will be the ruling motive, thus creating a better Jewish

2. סוטה ל״ה ע״א.

community and making the world a better place to live in.

v

Tzitzis

(Bar Mitzvah)

וראיתם אתו וזכרתם את כל מצות ה', "See them and remember all the commandments of the Lord." The Sages are prompted by this Torah verse to declare, שקולה מצוה זו כנגד כל המצות כולן,[1] "this mitzvah is equivalent to all the *mitzvos*." Rashi, on this text of the Talmud, says that this is tangibly represented by the composition of the *tzitzis*, which thus visibly serves as a reminder of all our religious duties. For the Hebrew alphabet, besides its usage for the formation of words, also serves to indicate numbers. The letter 'yod' represents number ten; the letter 'tzaddi' equals ninety; 'tav' equals four hundred. Hence the Hebrew word ציצת, "fringes," with twice 'yod,' twice 'tzaddi,' and one 'tav,' equals six hundred. Together with the eight fringes and the five knots in them, this gives the total six hundred and thirteen — equivalent to the תרי"ג מצות, the combined total of the two hundred and forty-eight positive and three hundred and sixty-five negative *mitzvos* in the Torah. Again, the number six hundred and thirteen represents the combined total of the three hundred and sixty-five days in the year and the two hundred and forty-eight limbs and organs of the human body.

The Rabbis were not just playing a number game like school children. Here they conveyed the whole idea of the Jewish religion.

1. מנחות מ"ג ע"ב.

What they meant was: it is Torah in every day of the week and every day of the year, in every limb of our body, in every element of nature and in every shred of our garment. Judaism means total involvement. The *mitzvos* are a golden chain linking us inseparably to the Master of the Universe, למען תזכרו ועשיתם את כל מצותי והייתם קדשים לאלקיכם, "Remember and do all My commandments and be holy unto your God."

KORACH

קרח

i

Rebellion

No man in history ever put service and community above self as did Moses. Crisis after crisis he weathers in the long and bitter struggle from Egypt to the land of promise, and every time he stands in prayer, pleading the people's cause and seeking to vindicate them. Once, in this week's *Sidrah*, Moses adopts a completely different policy. It has been described as the great mutiny of Korach and his henchmen. Moses' patience reaches exhaustion: ויחר למשה מאד, he burns with anger and denounces their motive. For once he turns to Heaven with the plea אל תפן אל מנחתם, "Do not accept their offering." It is a strange and peculiar kind of prayer, as though God would have been prepared to turn His ear to their claim, and without mercy Moses stands by to see the earth swallow them up. What was it that was so threatening about this mischievous clique? What was it that deadened Moses' sense of רחמנות and silenced his tongue from prayer?

Korach's philosophy was one which to this day has not lost its hold on people. It was a philosophy that led throughout history to ויאבדו מתוך הקהל, "its followers perished from among the community."

It is not death, it is not even punishment; it is a natural consequence. ויאבדו מתוך הקהל is elimination — disappearance from the midst of the people.

Here the crucial problem presents itself: can the Jew survive without מצות מעשיות, without practical religious acts? Will a home survive as a Jewish home without its purity of family life, without its Shabbos table, without its meaningful *mezuzah*? Will a Jew survive as a Jew without *tzitzis* on his garments, *tefillin* on his arm, kosher food in his stomach? Will the Jews survive as one united people if one half of it says, "belief without practice, faith without observance." They talk about God, and they pray to God, and their slogan is כל העדה כלם קדשים, there is good in everybody. They are champions of democracy with a small D, but there is no one law, no one authority to govern Jewish society. Let each one follow his own conscience and the feelings of his own heart, because ובתוכם ה', there is God in the midst of them.

Korach never arose against God; on the contrary, he was ready to make his sacrifice and even spoke about קדושה. That was the difference between Korach and the spies; persons who lose faith in suffering are to be pitied, not condemned, and for them Moses pleads. Korach did not simply arise against the leadership of Moses: that was the rebellion of the עגל הזהב, the Golden-Calf worshippers. The person who looks for outlets of his religious feeling and is unhappy with his guide and teacher is to receive sympathy, not denunciation, and Moses pleads their cause.

No, Korach's was a rebellion against authority as such. That is something different. Who is this man to impose upon us so many מצות מעשיות, practical precepts? He summoned his henchmen and said, "Look at this — here is a widow, she has but one field. She wants to plough the field. Moses says, 'Do not harness the ox and the ass together.' She wants to plant the seed and Moses says, 'Do not sow mixed seed.' She is ready for the harvest and Moses says, 'Leave the corners for the needy, and do not gather in the gleanings, leave them for the poor.' When she is ready to take her meagre produce to the market, Moses says, 'Bring the offerings to the priests and the tithes to the Levites.' So she decides to sell the field and buy a lamb. She is ready to shear its fleece, and Moses says, 'Give the wool to the כהן and bring the firstling to Aaron.' So she decides to dedicate it to the Temple, and Moses demands, 'Give some to the altar, some to Aaron, and only a portion for yourself.'"[1]

Korach, the champion of the masses, denounces religious authority. He asks, בית מלא ספרים, "A house full of sacred books, does it need a *mezuzah*? And טלית שכולה תכלת, a *tallis* all of purple wool, does it need a purple thread in the *tzitzis*?" Any hypocritical pious cry to do away with practical precepts.

Pause for a moment and think, and you will agree that it is not an unfamiliar cry: 'The Orthodox Jew is making too many demands.' These so-called leaders who claim to champion Jewish rights proclaim ובתוכם ה' — so long as you have God in your midst, so long as you have a Jewish heart, you can eat everything and do everything. It may well be that the present generation is not in danger. If you take off the *mezuzah* that you once had, the impression at least is still there. If you cease to eat kosher food that you once ate, the mark is still there. If you cease to attend the traditional synagogue you once knew, the synagogue is still there. But your children will never see בקר וידע ה'; who will survive till the morning?

How long can such a philosophy last? It is a process of elimination; it is a painless extermination. The Torah says of

---

1 ילקוט שמעוני רמז תש״ן ד״ה זהו שאמר הכתוב "אשרי האיש וכו'" מעשה באלמנה ושתי יתומים: בית מלא ספרים וכו' ממדרש תנחומא.

Korach's company, וירדו הם וכל אשר להם חיים שאולה, "they disappeared *alive* into the pit." The Jerusalem Talmud[2] remarks, אף שמותיהם פרחו מתוך טמסותיהם, "even their names that were inscribed on their belongings flew off of them; אפילו מחט שהיתה שאולה ביד ישראל מידם נבלעה עמהם, even their smallest belongings, such as a needle that was loaned to others, was swallowed up with them." ותכס עליהם הארץ, their earthliness covered them completely. Without practical *mitzvos*, life leads only to earthly death in eternity.

That type of rebellion Moses resisted with all his might: אל אלקי הרוחת לכל בשר, he cries out, "God of the spirit of all flesh," reveal Yourself in the flesh of man, not only in the heart of man. Torah is body moulding, Torah is mind shaping, Torah is habit forming. The answer to Korach's question is: you can possess a home full of *sefarim,* but the practical *mezuzah* must still be there.

At the approach of every *Rosh Chodesh* we pray for חיים שיש בהם אהבת תורה; but love of Torah is not enough. There must be אהבת תורה ויראת שמים, love and practice of Torah. Every Jew who is called to the Torah renews the same pledge and offers thanks to the Almighty אשר נתן לנו תורת אמת; but that is not enough — וחיי עולם נטע בתוכנו. There must be Torah and life hand-in-hand. This alone fills a home with joy, gives it a character of eternity, and makes it an example to men everywhere.

ירושלמי סנהדרין פ"י ה"א: טמסותיהם — אוצרות (ראה תורה תמימה). 2.

ii

Demarcation Lines

In Jewish life, הבדלה, distinction, plays an important part, to such an extent that the word להבדיל has become a common Yiddishism. A distinction is drawn between Shabbos and weekday, between *Rosh Chodesh* and other days of the month, between Shabbos and Yom Tov. Prayers are inserted here and there to mark these lines of distinction and demarcation: בין קדש לקדש — אתה הבדלת and אתה חוננתנו and בין קדש לחול. Even our daily prayers mark the הבדלה, the changing of the times at dawn, at sunset, at nightfall — ומבדיל בין יום ובין לילה. The distinction is drawn in food: להבדיל בין הטהור ובין הטמא, between that which is clean and that which is unclean.

The boldest of all distinctions is בין ישראל לעמים, that which separates the Jew from those among whom he lives: כי בנו בחרת ואותנו קדשת מכל העמים, "Thou hast chosen us and sanctified us above all nations." The *Maariv* service is full of it: אהבת עולם בית ישראל, "an everlasting love for the House of Israel"; גאל ישראל, "Who redeems Israel"; שומר עמו ישראל, "Who guards His people Israel." In the עלינו לשבח, the concluding passage of all our prayers, is centred that theme: שלא עשנו כגויי הארצות, "He has not made us like the nations of other lands." So this handful of Jews has from the dawn of its history been drawing the attention of the world to this הבדלה. Jewish distinction, the demarcation line between ourselves and those among whom we live.

Throughout our long and awful history we have never ventured out into fields of missionary activity. The thought of influencing those among whom we have lived to turn to Judaism is foreign to us. Rabbinic law is very clear on the question of admitting proselytes to the fold. Every conceivable obstacle is placed in the way; and whilst the Rabbis are most emphatic in their declaration that the pious gentile has his share in the World to Come, they are even more emphatic on the line of distinction to be drawn between Jew and gentile. Rabbi Akiva used to say, "Beloved is man, for he was created in the image of God, בצלם אלקים." That means every man without distinction. "But Israel is more beloved, for they were called בנים למקום, children of the All-Present."[1] That is a greater distinction, and how jealous we have been of that distinction!

There were times in history when the very clothes we wore were distinguished. Some Rabbis went so far as to argue that the shaving of the beard even by permissible means is חוקת הגוים, a practice of the gentiles, and therefore must be shunned. Assimilation was a terrible fear.

To this day some of the ancient decrees are still obeyed. Touching of the wine in an unsealed bottle or tumbler is a גזרה still honoured by the overwhelming mass of Jews. There are still thousands of Jews who choose black tea rather than make use of the milk which was processed without a משגיח. It was a great Jewish commentator who once said, "When we raise the cup of wine at the Seder table and we proclaim, והיא שעמדה לאבותינו ולנו, we mean 'It was this — this demarcation line, that touching the wine made it a prohibited drink — that stood by our forbears and ourselves and contributed to our survival.'" They were possessed of an immovable faith in God that from persecution He alone could save them, but from assimilation they had to save themselves, and therefore the danger was greater.

If at times they fell a prey to circumstances, and outside the home or outside the synagogue they took wine with the gentiles and ate with them, within the walls of the synagogue they guarded

1. אבות ג', י"ח.

against any tendencies that would affect the demarcation line. Some of our finest synagogue music comes from the Marranos, and some of our grandest prayers were composed in the cellars of Spain, when Christianity had to be practised in the open.

It is a false and misguided view that makes us believe that modernisation of the synagogue service and the imitation of church practices and dress attracts the youth and draws them nearer. Let those who hail from Germany speak up with a fearless voice and tell what one half of Hamburg's Jews looked like, what one half of Berlin Jewry looked like, once these demarcation lines were destroyed and organs and women choirs and Confirmation Services and prayer in the vernacular were introduced. History has not yet repaid in full the honour due to Samson Raphael Hirsch, who with dogged obstinacy and fiery single-mindedness started the fight with a handful of Jews and captured the other half of German Jewry who, without him, would have succumbed to spiritual extinction. American Jewry speaks for itself: the spread of the cancer cannot be controlled.

Various groups and movements have strengthened the demarcation line — they made הבדלה between the Jew and the world. In earlier ages the Jew remained like Abraham, the עברי, of whom the Sages said: כל העולם כולו מעבר אחד והוא מעבר אחר,[2] "Abraham was on one side of the fence and the non-Jews on the other side." They bitterly opposed these shallow compromising attitudes that made the Jew look more and more like his neighbours and the synagogue more and more like the church. The fanatical Rabbi, who was not always right, the fanatical Chassid, they made the הבדלה and drew the demarcation lines that contributed to Jewish survival and guaranteed Israel's future.

2. בראשית רבה מ״ב, י״ג.

Korach's cry was that Moses' laws were hard, impossible to endure: מדוע תתנשאו על קהל ה', "wherefore lift ye yourselves up above the assembly?" It was a modern cry: "Break down demarcation lines; leadership must come from the people; laws must be enacted by the people." What was Moses' remarkable reply? בקר וידע ה' את אשר לו ואת הקדוש והקריב אליו, "Wait until morning, and the Lord will show who belongs to Him and who is holy." Why was it necessary to wait until morning? אמר להם משה גבולות חלק הקב"ה בעולמו, יכולים אתם להפוך בקר לערב? כן תוכלו לבטל את זו,[3] "God has made demarcation lines in His world. There are bounds and there are limits. Can you change the morning into evening?" Just as nature is possessed of its limitations — can an onion grow in a vineyard? can the sun rule by night? — so is humankind possessed of limitations. The Jew makes his contribution and the peoples of the world make theirs; some are born leaders and some have leadership thrust upon them; some are blessed with fortune, some have to toil for fortune. גבולות חלק הקב"ה בעולמו, there are demarcation lines.

The secret of Jewish survival is the strengthening of these lines — to keep on making הבדלה. In the state, in the synagogue, in the home, never to ape and never to mimic, but to retain Jewish distinctiveness, and thus lead the world to righteous thinking. Then בקר וידע ה', with the rising of the sun on a world where each gives of his best, God will be made known and man the world over will live in peace.

רש"י: במדבר רבה י"ח, ר'. 3

iii

A Belated Confession

The Talmud[1] tells of the Sage, Rabbah B. Bar Chana, who was travelling in the desert accompanied by an Arab merchant. The Arab showed him the place where Korach and his companions were swallowed up. There was a crack in the ground, and the Rabbi put his ear to it and heard voices cry, משה ותורתו אמת והן בדאין, "Moses and his Torah are true, and we are liars."

On the ground of Jewish history, across the thousands of miles of desert along which we have travelled through every country of the world, there are so many such cracks into which whole families have been swallowed up; not through persecution but through tendencies of indifference, of apathy and neglect; of following the line of least resistance in the demands that Jewish teaching makes upon us. Rather the Jew who is detached from any synagogue and place of worship; rather the Jew who belongs to nothing — the Jew of the מרגלים type who believes in nothing; for at least there is hope for his children or his children's children. Whereas the Jew who attaches himself to a so-called synagogue or place of worship that permits everything and condones everything turns the Jewish religion into the farce which they have made of it. A generation or two sees the disappearance of all they have lived for and worked for, ויאבדו מתוך הקהל. There is no hope left for children or for children's children.

Let us take the right course: וכל ישראל אשר סביבתיהם נסו לקלם, run away from their attractive voices and disrupting influences. Then will we and our children live to make our mark on the road of history, a mark that will never be erased till the end of all time.

1. בבא בתרא ע׳׳ד ע׳׳א.

iv

The Clever Fool

The Rabbis in their wisdom wonder, קרח שפקח היה מה ראה לשטות זה? Korach, who was a פקח, a prudent person — what made him do such a stupid thing? Did he not know what calamity befell the מרגלים and the מתאוננים, all those who revolted? But his eyes deceived him. He thought he could live in the זכות, the merit, of his children. He saw in his prophetic vision that the prophet Samuel would be his descendant, and a whole generation of pious Levites would spring from him.[1] He made one terrible blunder: children can live by זכות אבות, but it has not yet been seen that parents can live בזכות בנים. Parents can drag children down, but children cannot pull parents up. ויאבדו מתוך הקהל, Korach disappeared from the congregation; but ובני קרח לא מתו,[2] his children held their own.

We are living in an age when בניו עשו תשובה,[3] children are returning to the faith, to the fold, to the glory. Children went out to fight the battle of Israel, children are fighting the battle of religion, children are fighting the battle of ignorance. Parents must try to lend a hand, to encourage, to assist, not to remain indifferent. Let there be no clash between teaching and practice, Korach revolting and the children loyal. Parents should help with good will and co-operation, so that together we may be able to build a better world for ourselves and men all over.[4]

---

1. רש"י; תנחומא ה'.

2. במדבר כ"ו, י"א.

3. רש"י; סנהדרין ק"י ע"א.

4 Given at the Berea Synagogue, S.A., on the completion of the new school.

CHUKKAS

חֻקַּת

i

The Statute of the Torah

Nowadays it is not the thing to accept just because our fathers before us accepted. Implicit obedience to Torah teaching and precepts is old-fashioned. Men and women today want to know *Why?* There is no harm in that, so long as it is prompted by a sincere desire to search for knowledge. Great thinkers and sages have tried to tell us why. But certain fundamentals must first be accepted; otherwise we are never sure of anything. If there is nothing fundamental and everything becomes relative, we will go around and around and come back to where we started. It was once said, "The trouble with our civilisation is that it is all signposts and no destination." We get nowhere if our signposts and destination are invented from our own reasoning. We cannot reason out life: we have to accept or give it up. Faith must come first, that is fundamental. First we must do as we are told, then try and ask why, always bearing in mind that God and His Law are infinite. It borders on insanity to aim to change the law because our feeble minds cannot understand it. We can hardly expect to understand Torah when one hour's study a week is too much; when the synagogue is full for *Kaddish,* but immediately empties out when it is time for an hour's learning. How can we expect to understand Torah when it has become a religion for the dead and not for the living?

This *Sidrah* opens up with one of the most mysterious rites observed in Temple times: the procedure of purification in the event of impurity contracted by coming into contact with the dead. A red heifer had to be ritually slaughtered, its carcass burned to ashes, the ashes mixed with 'living,' i.e., spring water, and the mixture sprinkled upon the unclean person over a period of seven days. The טמא became טהור, the unclean person became purified; but amazingly, the very same priest who performed the purification became himself unclean by touching the very same ashes of purification. Moses was bewildered; Solomon, the wisest of men, cried, אמרתי אחכמה והיא רחוקה ממני, "I searched for an explanation, but it was beyond me."[1] זאת חקת התורה: it is an ordinance of the Torah, beyond the realm of human understanding. A famous commentator once said that the *Sidrah* should have begun with the words זאת חקת הפרה, "This is the statute of the heifer." However, the Sage observed, זאת חקת התורה, "This is the statute of the Torah," implies, This is the statute, not only of the red heifer, but of the whole Torah: אשר צוה ה' לאמר, "to do that which the Lord has commanded." Ours is a do-as-you-are-told, and not an as-you-think, religion.

The secret of Judaism is like the secret of the red heifer. Some it purifies, it brings them nearer. Others it makes impure, it drives them away. If you stand by it with loyalty and obedience, and you have its holiness and its influence sprinkled upon you — not by a mere touch but over a period of days and nights—then you rise from contact with, and concentration on, the deadly things, and you bring yourself into spiritual life. It will purify you and bring you nearer.

1. קהלת ז', כ"ג; במדבר רבה י"ט, ג'.

But if you tamper with it, if you touch and mishandle it, or if it brings fulfilment only in death, but when it comes to living you only want to know why, then the only effect will be to drive you away to be contaminated by the society in which you live.

It would not be impossible for any well-read, scholarly man to get up on the pulpit week by week to try and give reasons for the laws of Shabbos and *kashrus*; marriage and divorce; purity of family life; and a hundred other *mitzvos* which constitute this wonderful Book of ours. But of one thing you can be sure: if one half were to accept the reasoning, the other half would reject it. Independent thinking is every man's prerogative. What an emaciated picture, then, Jewish life and law would present if reasons were put before law and logic before precept. The tragedy of democratic thinking penetrating Divine rulings is plain for all to see. Religion does not mean do as you think; religion means do as you are told.

זאת חקת התורה אשר צוה ה' לאמר, the statute of the Torah is to do that which the Lord has commanded. If you want to understand it, then learn it, study it, toil over it! How long can we expect the Torah to last if all that it is here for is to kiss it, to write about it and to bow down to it? Of course, any show-piece becomes antiquated, and then there is a temptation to change it, to shape it in keeping with the times.

Moses once tried to use his own judgment as against the infinite judgment of God. We find it in this *Sidrah*. There was no water in the wilderness, and the people were crying out for something to drink to quench their thirst. The Divine command came to Moses to take the rod in his hand, but this time he was not told to use it to smite the rock as he had done once before. This time he was to speak to the rock, ודברתם אל הסלע, and the water would flow. The people were impatient and rebellious. In all the confusion, before he had time to calm them down, thinking "Why, then, did God tell him to take the rod?" he repeated his previous action. He smote the rock with the rod and water flowed freely for all the people.

Sometimes it works not to be obedient, but thereby Moses forfeited the greatest prize in his life: his entry into the Promised Land. We may well ask, "Was his crime so great?" After all, he was told to take the rod. No, Moses, you shall not enter the land of your dreams: for one reason only, יען לא האמנתם בי, because you did not demonstrate your belief in Me. You should never have used your own judgment; you should have done as you were told. Here is the challenge of *Sidrah Chukkas:* are we to follow our own reasoning, or have implicit faith? It may well be that now and again our judgment will work. It will quiet the people; they will follow you in making adjustments here or there. It may do no harm for the time being, you will quench their spiritual thirst, you may save them from leaving the fold. But the world must know for all time that יען לא האמנתם בי. . . לא תביאו.[2] In the long run disobedience will mean our downfall.

Possibilities and opportunities are given to man to err. Take the rod, but speak to the rock. Why then take the rod? That belongs to the infinite wisdom of God. First do as you are told, and then ask why. It is by the word of God All-Embracing that we live or die. No *Beis Din*, not even Moses, can change it. By His own Divine Word do we become worthy of His Divine Promise of a Holy Land and a future of purpose and fulfilment.[3]

2, כעין זה נמצא בפירוש "דעת סופרים" מהרב חיים דב רבינוביץ: נאמר כאן לש' יען שפירושו זה המעשה יענה ויעיד שלא האמנתם בי. והוא מציין מקורו מפירוש אבן עזרא על הפסוק "יען אשר עשית. . ." (בר' כ"ב, ט"ז) וז"ל שם, זה המעשה יענה ויעיד.

3 At Edgware Synagogue, 1960.

ii

Aleph-Beis in Reverse

In Rabbinic literature there is an א-ב of which the Rabbis of old occasionally made use for special purposes. They call it the *Aleph-Beis* of א״ת ב״ש. Instead of tabulating the letters in the order that we know them: א ב ג ד ה ו ז ח and so on, the order of the alphabet is completely reversed. They take the first and the last letters, the second and the second to last: א-ת, ב-ש, ג-ר, ד-ק and so on. This reverse *Aleph-Beis* seems especially significant in the light of the experiences and hardships we are presently called upon to endure, especially those in southern England.[1]

We thought we were approaching the end of our troubles, and we were already planning the good times we would have in the good days that soon would be ours. We had gone through the *Aleph-Beis* of war. So characteristic of ordinary people to be lulled into a false sense of security! There are some whose outlook is so narrow and vision so dim, who think the world ends where the sky tilts over the earth. We thought we had endured more than could be expected of us; not, of course, so much as our brethren on the Continent, but it cannot be denied we have had a dose, and we were preparing for the end. Holiday trips as we had never had before, plans for amusements and celebrations. But there is a new kind of *Aleph-Beis*. We begin from א and quickly jump to the ת, thinking it is all over; but soon, very soon, we return to the ב and it is war all over again.

1 A sermon, probably at Brixton Synagogue, after three years of World War II, when hopes were rising for the defeat of Nazi Germany, and in desperation the enemy unleashed an indiscriminate hail of flying bombs on southern England.

Strange though it may seem, only when you tabulate the
Aleph-Beis this way, taking the letters out of their usual order, is יד
the last letter to feature in this process of reversal.[2] Unfortunately,
this seems to be the only way of becoming a יד, a Jew, in the true
sense of the word. The Jew, in the *galus*, begins at the beginning,
going right through all the changes and upheavals, the trials and
tribulations, to reach what seems to be the happy ending — and
then is obliged to begin all over again right from where he began
before. Someone rightly said the other day, "Until recently it was
the aim to have the highest flat in the block, so as to have as much
fresh air as possible; nowadays it is the lowest flat one can get, in
fact the lower the better."

The beginning of the War had a good effect on us: we were
hospitable, we were kind, we shared one another's troubles and
joys. Then a change came over us; with victory in sight, we began
rushing like mad, planning and building and scheming to get the
best out of life. Victory will be ours, there is no doubt about that;
but no one knows what lies ahead, and none can tell what the Jewish
community will yet have to endure. It is a terrible thing when man
fails to submit to a disciplined and righteous order of living in times
of prosperity and honour with the same kindliness that he
demonstrated in times of poverty and indignity. It is a terrible thing
when a man fails to learn the truth from the fullness of life and has
to learn it from the ugliness of death. יען לא האמנתם בי להקדישני לעיני בני
ישראל — man's sole purpose on earth is the fulfilment of God's will:
להקדישני, the recognition of God in all things. If it cannot be achieved
in life, then, sadly, it must be achieved through death. The only
comfort is that such death is never in vain. Moses and Aaron must
go, too, if this purpose of קידוש השם is not fulfilled in their lives. In

2 *Kaf* and *lamed* do not count, as they are normally together.

one word, death must achieve what life fails to accomplish.

Reward and punishment for the things we may do or not do applies primarily to the World to Come. That is a faith in which we are asked to believe, but the Torah is not concerned merely with the world beyond. The Sages, with their profound and Divine insight, do indeed infer from the words of the Torah the existence of עולם הבא, but the Torah as such is a Book of Life. It is a book dealing with practical issues and is concerned with this world and not merely with the next. Reward and punishment in this world are not in the form of a blessing for the good things we do and a curse for the evil. Reward and punishment are the direct consequence of man's own actions. What man fails to do in life must be completed one way or another.

This is the message of the פרה אדומה, the red heifer, in the *Sidrah*. On the one hand it purified and on the other it contaminated. Four conditions, the Rabbis say, were rigidly to be maintained. Firstly, it was to be a פרה; the Rabbis explain, תבא פרה ותכפר על העגל, they sinned with a calf, so let its mother come and atone, making good the mischief of the child. Secondly, it was to be אדומה; it had to be red, שהחטא קרוי אדום, red is synonymous with sin. Thirdly, it was to be תמימה, perfect: שישראל היו תמימים, the Israelites had been perfect, but through the Golden Calf became morally maimed. Fourthly, it was to be לא עלה עליה על, "upon which never came a yoke": שפרקו מעליהם עול מלכות שמים, just as they had cast off the yoke of Heaven from themselves. Thus the red heifer atoned for the sin of the calf.

True, it might be merely symbolic, but it is a sure lesson to mankind: that by the very thing with which he sins, man must atone and make amends. If with the fullness of man's life, in peace and prosperity, there can be no construction and advancement, then by his very destruction will a new world be built. If science failed to bring life to its fulfilment, then by the death which it wrought will science fulfil its purpose. Yes, the red heifer can do both: it contaminates the pure and cleanses the impure — it depends on how you use it. These marvellous things that scale the heights and plumb the depths, which, if not for war, might have taken a thousand years to produce, are not the genius of man but the genius of death, grinding its way bitterly, murderously to its end. It is the fulfilment of a scheme which is unfolding itself and which normal life has been unable to reveal. The oneness of God is being revealed: the complete negation of space and distance, of heights and depths. It proceeds through death because it has not been achieved through life. It is no punishment for sin; that, alas, has yet to come, this we firmly believe. It is the fruits of man's own misdirected labour, nature revolting — total war against total evil.

How many are there, here in this comparative paradise, who are really and deeply concerned about the position of Jewish refugee children, who came over here in 1938, and for whose apostasy we are now paying bitterly? How many practised charity, sharing homes and lives with others as we should have done with refugee strangers in our midst? Today we are glad to make do with any room available in our own meagre homes. What would some of us in southern England pay for a little corner in High Wycombe?[3] How many corners did we offer to the homeless orphans in 1936-1939?

But it is still not too late for a real revival of those Jewish ideals. Like the פרה אדומה, atonement must match the manner in which we erred. Sharing homes and lives, education for ourselves and others, prayer for ourselves and others, Shabbos for all. A revival of Jewish consciousness will alone ensure the survival of our community. Then, with God's good help, war will cease to be and life will fulfil its true purpose.

3 An evacuation area for war-weary Londoners at the height of the Nazi bombing.

iii

Departmentalism in Life

One of the greatest tragedies in human life is what we may call the departmentalisation of God and man. It is the synagogue for Heavenly things and the home for earthly things, Shabbos for God and Monday for man, the *Shechinah* in one compartment and מעשי ידיכם in another. But זאת חקת התורה, "this is the principle of the Torah": to penetrate the טומאה and to bring out the טהרה. Domestic relations with purity, commercial enterprise with honesty, physical satisfactions with sanctity. Open your eyes in the morning, and recognise פוקח עורים, God in your vision. Move your limbs as you rise, and recognise מתיר אסורים, God in your limbs. Dress with מלביש ערומים, eat with הזן את הכל — do all these things, and bring שכינה במעשי ידיכם.

Two deaths are recorded in this *Sidrah*, those of one of Israel's greatest daughters, Miriam, and one of Israel's greatest sons, Aaron. See how vastly different is the description of their passing: ויבאו בני ישראל כל העדה מדבר-צן בחדש הראשון וישב העם בקדש ותמת שם מרים ותקבר שם, "And the Children of Israel came into the wilderness of Zin in the first month, and the people abode in Kadesh; and Miriam died there and was buried there." Five words, that is all, describing the death of this majestic Jewish figure.

Very soon after that, as they continued on their journey, word goes out to Moses that the time has come for Aaron to pass from mortal ken — and in six long verses the Torah gives a full description of his passing in a kind of ceremonial setting: . . . קח את אהרן ואת אלעזר בנו, "Take Aaron and Elazar, his son, and bring them up unto Mount Hor, and strip Aaron of his garments and put them upon Elazar his son; and Aaron shall be gathered unto his people and shall die there." The Torah continues: ויעש משה כאשר צוה ה', "and Moses did as the Lord commanded; and they went up to Mount Hor in the sight of all the congregation, and Moses stripped Aaron of his garments and put them on Elazar, his son; and Aaron died there at the top of the mount." Miriam dies, and there she is buried: ותמת שם ותקבר שם. Aaron dies, and there is no mention of his burial. No parent truly dies whose child takes over.

How beautifully do the Rabbis describe this stripping of the garments, ויפשט, וילבש! Normally Aaron would have to be stripped completely for Elazar to put on the undergarment first. No, the Rabbis say, ויפשט וילבש; as Aaron took off the outer garment it was put onto Elazar. To him it became his undergarment; and as Aaron took off his inner garment, to Elazar it became his outer garment. Happy is the father whose inner life, whose deep sense of Jewish values, whose intimate personal observances are exposed and revealed in the life of his child. Miriam dies with none to take over: ותמת ותקבר. Aaron dies with his son to take over: וימת אהרן . . . וירד משה ואלעזר מן ההר.

Guard and treasure those garments of tradition and observance handed on to us by our fathers. Let the inner sanctity of their lives, the beauty of their Shabbos, the dignity of their worship, the character of their faith, the loyalty of their practice — let them be revealed in all the things we do. Let the inner *Shechinah,* the Divine Presence, rest on the work of your hands, to build congregations and communities and to live a life that will stand out as a living example of true Torah life to Jews the world over.

iii(b)

Internal Conflict: The Greatest Evil

It is strange that after each of the two deaths recorded in the *Sidrah*, different kinds of troubles beset Israel. After Miriam's death the trouble came from within: מי מריבה, the Waters of Strife — trouble among themselves. After Aaron's death trouble came from without: the uprising of enemies, וילחם בישראל . . . וישמע הכנעני. The Canaanites heard that Aaron had died, and they rose up to smite down Israel, to prevent them from occupying the Holy Land.

There is a vast difference between the death of a generation that has no heir, and that of one that leaves its heirs after it. A generation dies and leaves no youth to carry on its glories, no child to take over the priestly garb: ותמת שם מרים ותקבר שם. There where she died she was buried. Hers became a closed book, and the uprising came from within — the cry was "Let us go back to Egypt!" But the generation that dies and leaves a youth to carry forward, children who equip themselves with the garments of their parents — then there is no burial within. There is peace and contentment, and the cry is not "Let us go back to Egypt" but "Let us go forward, and we shall defeat the enemy from without."

We may well wonder which is the worse enemy of the Jewish people, the rot and decay within the camp, or anti-Semitism without. One thing is sure, to cope with both is an insuperable task. There is no object in building fences around the garden to save it from destruction by vagabonds, while allowing it to rot by neglect and carelessness from within. All our defence measures will fail unless we are prepared, by practice and observance, by deeds and by actions, to toil and nurture the vineyard of God: to strengthen the hands of our teachers, to create a link between the home and the Hebrew School. אל תקשו לבבכם כמריבה כיום מסה במדבר: this is the warning that rings out every Friday evening as Shabbos comes. "Harden not your heart as at Meribah, as in the days of Massah in the wilderness, אשר נסוני אבותיכם, when your fathers tried me and proved me, גם ראו פעלי, although they had seen my work."[1] We have seen the work of God in our days, as they saw it in years gone by. The hardening of the arteries of the Jewish heart is as dangerous to the soul of the Jew as it is to his body. "Remember," לכו נרננה calls to us, "the Meribah within: internal conflict is the greatest enemy."

The wells of learning must be re-opened to quench the children's thirst. Then will generations go forward, equipped with all the arms the Jew requires to inherit the Land in a world of peace and calm.

iv

The Three Mountains

(Bar Mitzvah)

The *Sidrah* tells of Israel's march through the wilderness: ויסעו מקדש ויבאו בני ישראל כל העדה הר ההר, "and they journeyed from Kadesh; and the Children of Israel, even the whole congregation, came unto Mount Hor." In a comment which is full of meaning, the Midrash says, הענן הולך לפניהם ומשוה את ההרים, "the pillar of cloud that went before them levelled out the mountains and flattened the hills; but שלשה נשארו בהן, there were three mountains that resisted the shattering clouds: הר סיני לתורה, הר נבו לקבורת משה, והר ההר לקבורת אהרן. One was Mount Sinai, the mountain upon which the Torah was given; the second

---

1 תהלים צ"ה, ח'–ט'.

was Mount Hor, upon which Aaron died; and the third was Nebo, which Moses ascended never to return."[1]

In our long history mountains of all kinds have crumbled to dust. Mountainous fortunes, life and property levelled out, and nothing remained. But there was one mountain that remained: the mountain upon which Aaron stripped himself of his garments and put them on Elazar, his son. The mountain upon which Aaron died and from which Elazar came down to carry on. The mountain of the great take-over from father to son, upon which Moses comforted his brother, saying, אשריך שתראה כתרך נתון לבנך, "Happy are you, Aaron, that you will see your crown placed upon your son's head." Mourning turned into joy. Death, a crowning ceremony: Aaron took off, Elazar put on. That mountain can never be erased.

There was also הר נבו, where Moses went up at the end of his days, placing his spirit in the hand of his God and none knew his burial place. There he is somewhere, the great law-giver, never dead, never buried. It can't be erased. They have tried it a thousand times and more, and he is still holding the hand of God, walking through history. Others have turned the burial places of their masters into shrines. The burial place of our great immortal master is not known. The mountain is there for all to climb, to reach the same heights, to hold the same hand, to walk in eternity.

Yes, everything we built has been erased; but one great mountain remains: הר סיני, that Jewish life that resisted, and still resists, the forces of changing conditions. What a variety of clouds engulfed us, whether they came from without and wanted to deform us, or whether they came from within and wanted to reform us. Not one jot of the Torah, not one pebble of the mountain has been removed. We see it all over: a handful of staunch, loyal Jews bearing

1. רש"י: במדבר רבה י"ט, ט'.

Mount Sinai almost alone on their feeble shoulders, above the dense clouds of ignorance and the still thicker clouds of indifference. Nothing has, nothing will deter that band from holding on, from resisting all pressures.

We are not dealing today with a type of dissident who is intellectually inclined, with the scholarly type for whom one has to have the answers at his fingertips. We can be tolerant of a scholar who reaches out sincerely seeking to understand. Today we are dealing in the main with those who have no knowledge of Rabbinic learning and no scholarship. They break the law to make it easy and make laws to suit themselves. How can one be tolerant of a housebreaker who invades the sacred territory of your home and sanctity, who robs you of your cherished possession handed down by your fathers? Reason alone is very much relative; there is nothing absolute in human reasoning. When there is nothing absolute, everything becomes relative; and when everything becomes relative, nothing is sacred.

Had the Jew made the law, it would have been within his power to change it and to make it anew. But the Jew never made the law — without the law there would have been no Jew. He received it and accepted it, and it made him. A complete law makes for a complete Jew; a broken law breaks the Jew.

As they get older, parents and grandparents tend to think in terms of who is going to follow on, hoping to see that crowning comfort that was given to Aaron when handing on his heritage to his son Elazar. Hoping to see children and grandchildren loyal and devoted to the study of Torah and its observance, bearing Mount Sinai steadfastly and securely. This is what becoming Bar Mitzvah means, as implied in the opening words of the *Sidrah*: זאת חקת התורה אשר צוה ה', "This is the statute of the Torah which the Lord has commanded."

צוה and מצוה are one and the same word, the word featured so prominently in the compound term Bar Mitzvah. It is a call to duty, one's duty as a Jew. Every mitzvah we do begins with a *berachah*: אשר קדשנו במצותיו, "Who sanctified us with His commandments." A mitzvah makes a Jew different. It raises him up; he is not one of the crowd. When you put on your *tefillin* it makes your hands holy, when you wear your *tzitzis* it makes your garments holy, when you eat kosher food it makes your body holy, when you learn Jewish studies it makes your mind holy, when you keep Shabbos it makes your days holy: אשר קדשנו במצותיו.

BALAK

בלק

i

The Future Is in Our Own Hands

(Bar Mitzvah)

It is said of a great general that he never went out to battle without a miniature portrait of his predecessor concealed in his breast pocket. At moments of doubt or perplexity, when victory or defeat hung in the balance, he took the portrait from its treasured hiding place, turned to the character limned therein, and asked, "What would you have done in similar circumstances?"

It is proper that we should turn to the Bible to learn religion. But what is this religion we hear so much about? Is it merely something to do with human emotions, with purity of mind and kindness of heart, but little if anything to do with purity of actions in everyday affairs? In the sphere of so-called religion man turns to Heaven, and in the sphere of daily activity man turns to earth — in a word, God is up above and man is down below. If so, we have every reason, in this world dominated by political influences, to apologise for our attachment to the Bible, to this book of God. But the Bible is more than that. It is a gallery of portraits of individuals and nations, whose lives and activities portray the story of God on earth. It is here to turn to at all times: "What did you do in such a predicament? What would you have done at this turning point in history?" This obstinacy of the Jewish people, our persistence in looking back, has given us hope for the future. Whilst the survival of nations and empires has depended on strength of arms, the survival of the Jew depended on his strength of character.

Historians are mistaken when they say that our will to die for our cause has helped us to survive. No, it is our will to live for our cause. Only on rare occasions have we gone out to fight relying on military weapons alone. Rarely did we succeed when we went out to kill. Balak knew it, as he learnt with horror of the defeat of the mighty Amorites at the hands of this weak, wandering Israel. So what does he do? He employs a master of magic to use his power against this magic people. If gas chambers and concentration camps will not kill him, then we shall kill him with words. Let statesmen make speeches and cast a baleful spell over this mysterious people.

We have seen it in our own day: the men to whom we looked for justice, the prophets of the אומות העולם, turned against us with words. Their sweet tongues have been like a poison; but we must not be dismayed. History will not condone such methods. Our book of records tells us of their failure. וירא בלק בן צפור את כל אשר עשה ישראל לאמרי, "and Balak the son of Zippor saw all that Israel had done to the Amorites." That is all that Balak can see: what Israel did to the Amorites. It pays him to see that side of the picture; but what about all that the Amorites did to Israel? They see the Jew through their own spectacles. To everything else their eyes are closed and their senses numbed. They are ready to condemn, without consideration and without sympathy, any Jewish action committed rightly or wrongly. They are not so ready to condemn the wrongs committed against us. הנה עם יצא ממצרים הנה כסה את עין הארץ, "behold a people has come out of Egypt, it covereth the face of the earth." So narrow was their vision and so selfish their aims that this handful of Jews, these desert-worn bondsmen, covered for them the face of the earth. So much space on this earth, enough for all to live in comfort! Yet to him the Jew covers the face of the earth. Why, even Bilam's ass — this dumb animal, the symbol of man's senselessness and inhumanity — could stand it no longer.

Bilam knows that neither weapons nor magic can destroy this people, whose spiritual strength is indestructible. 'לא אוכל לעבר את פי ה, לעשות טובה או רעה מלבי, he says, "I cannot go beyond the word of God to do either good or evil of mine own mind." Neither good nor bad can come to the Jew from friend or foe. He is neither enriched by the blessings of those who extend to him a hand of welcome, nor is he impoverished by those who aim to destroy him. The future of the Jew is in his own hand. Whatever comes his way he brings upon himself. לכה, "Come," he says to Balak, "I will tell you how to dispose of this people. אלקיהם של אלו שונא זמה הוא, the God of this people hates unchastity. Tempt them with sin."[1] Encourage him, show him friendship, give him freedom, let him mingle with your people and your womenfolk. Make him fall by the sin of unchastity. Aim at his spiritual resources, break up his home life. This is the best strategy. Open your arms to him, let him come within your ranks, let him lose his identity and he will be a prey at your feet.

The Rabbis say that כולם חזרו לקללה, all Bilam's blessings were turned into curses.[2] Throughout our chequered history we were robbed of everything we possessed. Here we are, like beggars knocking at the doors of the world: "Let us in." Deprived of all — מה טבו אהליך יעקב משכנתיך ישראל :but for one exception — כלם חזרו לקללה,

1. רש"י; סנהדרין ק"ז ע"א.

2. סנהדרין ק"ה ע"ב.

"How goodly are thy tents, O Jacob, thy dwelling-places, O Israel."
The beauty of our home-life, the glory of our synagogue life — these
things alone remain with us.

It is noteworthy that the whole of Bilam's rhapsodic praises are
written in the third person. This one verse alone, found on the first
page of our sacred Prayer Book, is written in the second person:
"How goodly are *thy* tents, O Jacob." It is addressed directly to each
individual. This alone belongs to us: our home, our *shul*. The home:
its chastity, its love, its purity, its morality. Take this from us, and
we have nothing left. Break up the home and you break the
backbone of our people. With Jewishness, loyalty, faith, tradition
in the home, we shall survive.

The synagogue: its service, its prayer, its Shabbos, its study
circles, its charitable endeavour; take this from us, and we have
nothing left. Break up the synagogue, its attendances depleted, its
services cut short, its charity cut off, and you break the backbone
of our people. In these two directions this *Sidrah* beckons us to turn
at this turning point in our history. More Jewishness in the home,
more prayer in the synagogue, and we bring blessing upon the
remnant of our people and security to our scattered flock.

כי מראש צרים אראנו ומגבעות אשורנו, Bilam said, "from the top of the
rocks I see him and from the hills I behold him." If one stands on
the top of a mountain and looks down on the valley, everyone looks
so small, none seems to stand out. But looking down upon the world,
Bilam saw the Jewish people distinctly above all others. They did
not mix, they were a people apart, distinguished from all others by
their manner of living, by their laws and conduct. It is a fine thing
to walk among people and to be outstanding by conduct: "Here is
a Jew — someone different." His honesty, his kindliness, his
cleanliness and his respect and his decency. It is a fine thing to rise
in the morning when everyone else rises, but to pause for a while

for *tefillin* and prayer. It is a fine thing to eat with others at the same table, but my food is kosher; and to pause when others rise to say a Grace After Meals. It is a fine thing to be respectful to parents when others show disrespect. You are outstanding. They all look like midgets at your side: כי מראש צורים אראנו, you can be seen prominently, even from the top of the mountains. To such a Jew no harm can come.

This every Bar Mitzvah must try to do. But it can never be done without learning and study. To understand what a Jew really is one must be learned in Torah. Those who follow its path are sure to grow up to be proud Jews, unafraid of hostile tongues, knowing always that none shall curse whom God has not cursed, and all shall bless whom He has blessed.

ii

Think of Others

It is said that some Rabbis are reluctant to preach when this *Sidrah* is read. Conscious of their weakness, they are afraid to express themselves, in case a cynic among the congregation may compare them with Bilam's ass.

The Sages[1] reckon פי האתן, "the mouth of the ass," as one of the ten supernatural phenomena which had their origin in the interval between the close of the work of Creation and the commencement of the Sabbath. Apart from the uniqueness of this miraculous incident, in which a dumb animal expressed itself in language intelligible to a human being, there is indeed something strange

אבות ה', ו. 1

about the speech that the ass made. A renowned Rabbi once pointed this out with a homiletical illustration.[2] He said: the asses once complained bitterly to the Creator, "Why are we regarded as the fool of all the beasts? Are we not the most hardworking? No other beasts are such slaves: some roam freely in the wild, and even those who work have time for rest and are well cared for, but the ass any time of day or night may be called on to be of service, and is frequently whipped. Grant us, at least, a tongue to plead for some consideration from our relentless employers."

"Well," the Creator said, "I will give you the chance of a lifetime, an opportunity that no other animal will ever have. I will give one of you the power of speech, and we will see what will be the result." The opportunity came when Bilam set out to curse Israel. The ass knew how impossible Bilam's mission was, and in spite of its master's anger and rebuke it refused to lead him into disaster.

The Rabbis go so far as to say that the ass had a good speech to make: "Bilam, you intend to kill a whole people by the word of your mouth, but for me, a poor ass, you require a sword!" But an ass is an ass after all. When it opened its mouth to speak for the first time, ותאמר האתון אל בלעם הלוא אנכי אתנך אשר רכבת עלי מעודך עד היום הזה, "am I not the ass upon which thou hast ridden all thy lifetime until this day?" What a fool! As soon as it opened its mouth it started bragging: am I not so and so? Its first thought was of its own importance and its own glory. Whereupon the Almighty said, "If this is what you say when you have such a glorious opportunity, if instead of defending others you defend yourself, if you speak first of your own *yichus* — then you do not deserve to possess the power of speech. Back you

2 The actual source is not indicated in the original notes. One anthology of Rabbinic sayings tells of an incident in which Reb Itzele Ponievezer used this *maaseh* to admonish some fractious individuals who persisted in disturbing an important meeting by arguing about their respective *yichus*.

go to remain for the rest of your days a dumb creature, until you learn to live and speak for others as you speak for yourself."

The power of speech is one of God's greatest blessings. It is intended for the expression of the loftier things of life and thought, not for the creation of a cloak of great praise and vain pride. The test of a person's greatness is how he stands up and speaks for others. Many people, when the faults of others are mentioned, turn round and say, "What's wrong with me? I am so and so." That is not enough. That is the speech of an ass. A sensible human being should find enough words in defence of others, just as many as he can find in defence of himself. The great lesson we have to take from this text is that we don't live and speak for ourselves alone. We represent the other Jew too. And Jews especially must bear this responsibility.

There is another tremendous moral behind this legend. It is a mighty challenge to those among us who rely entirely on the platform to defend the Jew with their power of speech against the calumnies and the libels that are levelled against us. They should speak less of the great things we have done in the past and the contributions we have made to civilisation. Instead they should strive to show the great things we are now doing and the contributions we are now making to civilisation. That we gave the Bible, and we gave the Prophets, and we gave moral standards, is no answer to Bilam, before whose mental vision there looms the present and the future of Israel. We can no longer go on living on the glories of yesteryear; we can no longer endure on the *yichus* of the past. That is the language of the ass: מֵעוֹדְךָ עַד הַיּוֹם הַזֶּה, "from then till now." "What about now?" is the challenge of the moment. It cuts across the minds of those slave-like creatures whose whole being is dependent on the legacy they have inherited from past generations; who possess no independence, no courage to master a situation by their own actions and moral conduct.

iii

From the Top of the Rocks

כי מראש צרים אראנו ומגבעות אשורנו, "from the top of the rocks I see him, and from the hills I behold him."

"I am helpless," Bilam called to Balak; "there is nothing I can do to frustrate this people. אני רואה אותם מיוסדים וחזקים כצורים וגבעות הללו ע״י אבות ואמהות,[1] I see them not only as they are now, I see them from the tops of the rocks, I behold them from the hills — מיוסדים, they are anchored, they are chained, they are pinned down like rocks to their fathers and mothers. They are so entrenched, the foundation is so deep, there is no dynamite in the world that can blow such rocks to pieces. There is one thing I can advise you to do," Bilam tells Balak. "You will never destroy them by physical means. You will do away with them in one country, and they will spring up in another — from the ghettoes of Poland to the highways of Tel Aviv. You will close Mir and Slobodka, and they will open up again in Jerusalem and Bnei Brak. They are unique: הן עם לבדד ישכן, they are unlike any other nation. The only method to attack this people is to come to grips with him from within. Get him to break with his past."

וישב ישראל בשטים. Where there is וישב there is trouble:[2] "and Israel dwelt in Shittim, ויחל העם לזנות אל בנות מואב." Lure them away from their homes, Bilam advises Moab, husbands from wives, children from parents; break the link, snap the chain, detach them from their anchorage, and you will achieve your miserable desires.

Perhaps one of the most profound passages in the Torah is that which tells us that פי האתן, the mouth of the ass, was created ערב שבת

1. רש״י: במדבר רבה כ׳, ט׳ז.

2. כל מקום שנאמר וישב אינו אלא לשון צער (סנהדרין ק׳ו ע״א).

בין השמשות, on the eve of the Sabbath of Creation at twilight. The world was complete; everything was functioning. Friday was drawing to its close. The moon had not yet emerged. It was twilight. The day had gone by and the night had not yet arrived, and the mouth of the ass was then created. Does not this suggest the symbol of the twilight Jew, with his ass-like outlook? He knows neither day nor night. The sun of a devastated Europe has never set on him. His castle of illusions was never shaken by the annihilation of the best we possessed, and the sun of reborn Israel has never dawned on him. The Jew destroyed, and the Jew reborn: neither of them means a thing to him. Yes, that is the בין השמשות Jew, who takes nothing with him from yesterday into today and from today into tomorrow. A twilight Jew, who with his ass-like conceptions wants the best of both worlds: to live like an ass and to speak like a human, תמת נפשי מות ישרים, to live like a heathen and to die like a Jew. We find them all over the Jewish world, those who know not of the task of sanctuary-building on a weekday nor even of the day of rest and the synagogue on the Sabbath.

Build synagogues, establish Yeshivos and colleges, erect day schools; let the spirit of yesterday mingle with the spirit of today, כטל מאת ה' כרביבים עלי עשב,[3] "as dew from the Lord, as showers upon the grass," nurturing, teaching, nourishing a Jewish generation that will bring credit to the glorious past and blessing to its hopeful future.

3. הפטרת בלק, מיכה ה'.

PINCHAS

פינחס

i

The True Man of Peace

In this *Sidrah* we read of the prize awarded to Pinchas, a Divine promise given to no other man: והיתה לו ולזרעו אחריו ברית כהנת עלם, "and it shall be unto him and his seed after him the covenant of an everlasting priesthood." Why was it given to Pinchas? It should have been given to Moses the teacher, or to Aaron the priest, the peacemaker? But this blessing of continuity, this concept of uninterruption does not come from the service in the Temple; neither does it come from the teaching in the synagogue. These certainly help, but they do not forge the links in the chain, they do not make לו ולזרעו אחריו. That comes from the morality, the purity, the integrity of the home.

Pinchas was the one who saw through Bilam's devices. Bilam came to his senses. He realised, after all his futile efforts, that you cannot dispose of the Jew by hate and persecution. On the contrary: gutted synagogues and stolen breastplates have a revitalising effect on the Jew. Everybody gets busy, deputies, ex-servicemen, synagogue vigilantes. The press suddenly turns its attention to the urgency of the problem.

But what of gutted Jewish homes, that are religiously burnt out, where children are completely ignorant of their Jewish heritage? What about the clubs and the synagogue halls; the youth — the friends they bring home! Here is a complete process of disintegration, of ignorance, intermarriage and impurity, against which there is no resistance, no vigilantes and no committees.

Bilam understood it so well so many years ago: הכשילם בזמה,[1] "do not curse them," he said to Balak, "do not fight them; bless them, open your doors to them, give them your sons and daughters." How right he was! וישב ישראל בשטים; that word וישב[2] caused trouble to the Jew so many times. He made himself at home — ויחל העם לזנות, and how long did it take before they began to commit harlotry with the daughters of Moab? And how long did it take after that ויצמד ישראל לבעל פעור, for immorality to lead to idolatry? Had it begun and remained with the masses it might not have been so serious. The masses you can teach, to the masses you can preach. But the leaders were involved. It began at the top, Moses was helpless — who knows, perhaps he was worrying and wondering what had become of his own children.

It is one of the most interesting things in the whole of Jewish law that for this type of harlotry, this form of immorality, court judgment is not prescribed. For something so foreign to Jewish family life it was קנאים פוגעין בו[3]; the pious zealots among the people were to apprehend him and mete out instant punishment. This brazen sin, this outside penetration into our home life is not a sin against man, not a sin against the community, but a sin against God. Joseph said to Potiphar's wife, "how can I do such a thing, וחטאתי

---

1. רש"י; סנהדרין ק"ז ע"א.

2. כל מקום שנאמר וישב אינו אלא לשון צער (סנהדרין ק"ז ע"א).

3. רש"י; סנהדרין פ"ב ע"א.

לאלקים, and I shall sin against God?" Pinchas said to the people, "how can you do such a thing, to commit a crime against God?" The greatness of Pinchas was בקנאו את קנאתי בתוכם, that he was jealous 'for God's sake'; "he took My part." It was not for Shabbos or *kashrus* or *tallis* or *tefillin*; that we would have recognised as fighting for God's sake. Not at all; it was for the purity, the chastity, the integrity, the morality of our human and family relations that Pinchas fought 'for God's sake.'

This it was that made Pinchas great, even greater than Moses. לכן אמר הנני נתן לו את בריתי שלום, "Therefore, say: 'Behold, I give unto him my covenant of peace.'" Not אמר לו, "go and say to him"; this was no private audience; לכן אמר means go and proclaim it to the people. Tell the world who the man of peace is, that the covenant of peace is given not to the ever-ready peacemaker, not to the one whose accessibility makes him beloved by all, not to Moses the teacher or Aaron the priest, but to Pinchas the fighter. Tolerance has its limitations, peace has its price. The greatest peacemaker is the one who fights when it is necessary, the one whose conscience dictates at the point of a spear. No wonder *vav*, in the word שלום, is written in a miniature form, as though the top of it had been chopped off — קטיעא ו', the Rabbis call it. In religious life, peace does not mean surrendering and submitting and giving way for peace's sake, in the name of unity. Real peace, a peace that is handed down from father to son, from generation to generation לו ולזרעו אחריו, is a peace which must sometimes divide the *vav*, the stem of שלום.

ii

A Long-Term Policy

(An Address to Youth)

The story is told of the old man who was planting a seed so that a fruit tree might one day sprout and blossom. When he was called a fool, because he was so old and feeble that he would never benefit from his work, his answer was, "Mine is a long-term policy. The children of the future will benefit from my toil and labours, just as I have benefitted from the toil and labour of my fathers and ancestors."[1]

After the loss of so many of our people in the War there is an especial need today to look to the future with a 'long-term policy.' Our youth must be imbued with the zeal and will to fill the great void in our congregations by re-capturing, with youthful vigour and enthusiasm, the love of Jewish learning and the joy of Jewish living.

That is what happened with Pinchas. He was a young man standing in the midst of the whole congregation of Israel, all the elders and the leaders; none of them moved when they saw a forbidden thing committed in the camp — an immoral deed that caused the profanation of God's name and the blackening of the name of Israel. Everyone stood by, afraid to move, but Pinchas, the grandson of Aaron, could rest no longer. He rose courageously, and in the presence of all Israel took the part of God, of the Jew, of the Torah, and did away with the wicked man and woman who had committed such a crime.

---

1. ראה ויקרא רבה כ"ה, ה': מעשה באדריינוס וכו'.

It was a long-term policy. His reward was not immediate: והיתה
לו ולזרעו אחריו ברית כהנת עולם, "and it shall be unto him and to his children
afterwards a covenant of everlasting priesthood." Out of the
children of Pinchas the world was blessed with great and pious men.
It was courage that did it, and it is this courage that we must train
ourselves to possess. Although some may be against us, we have to
stand firm. Without courage the Jew can achieve very little: courage
to *daven* in Hebrew when others only pray in English; courage to
keep Shabbos when everyone else doesn't care; courage to say, 'I
am not going out playing on Sunday morning because I have got to
attend classes'; courage to do the things that so many neglect, and
not to do the wrong things that so many others do. Courage to be a
true Jew and win the war against wrongdoing. This is our duty; like
Pinchas, we will be playing our part in winning God's covenant of
peace and happiness for our community and for humanity.

iii

Jealous for My Sake

Some find it difficult to understand the opening verses of this
Sidrah, which speak of God's "jealousy" and of Pinchas removing
God's anger. Turning back to the previous *Sidros*, we see in
perspective a sequence of events, spanning virtually the whole
period of the journey in the wilderness, to which the episode of
Pinchas came as a dramatic and vital climax.

In the *Sidrah* of *Shelach Lecha*, the reaction to the report of the
spies reveals a refusal to acknowledge and accept the essential belief
in God's immanence in this world and the guiding hand of Divine
Providence in human affairs. It seems indeed difficult to understand

how men of the calibre of the spies — selected princes of Israel — together with that whole generation, who witnessed the wonders of the Exodus and stood at the foot of Sinai, who daily enjoyed God's bounty, eating the manna from Heaven and drinking the water from the rock, could feel so frightened and abandoned. In spite of all their experiences they seemed to believe that God was remote and indifferent to their fate. As if they were left on their own to fight invincible giants and capture impregnable fortresses! This lack of faith led to the long years of wandering in the wilderness. Those years had fatal consequences for the older generation that came out of Egypt, and they were a constant endurance test of the tenacity and faith of their children.

In the *Sidrah* of *Korach* we find a remarkable contrast. Korach seems to affirm the reverse. He maintains God's immanence: כל העדה כלם קדשים,[1] "all the congregation are holy, every one of them," ובתוכם ה׳, God is in everyone! All are prophets, ומדוע תתנשאו; we have no need for the leader Moses, as the Supreme Authority, and the High Priest Aaron, to exercise exclusive control on the sacred service. There can be a thousand interpretations of the truth; there is nothing absolute.

Against this background the *Sidrah* of *Chukkas* comes as a rejoinder, reminding them of reality. The inexplicable rite of the red heifer is pointedly addressed to Moses and Aaron, reiterating their position as the true vehicle of Divine Revelation. Moreover, the Torah deliberately describes the פרה אדומה as חקת התורה, "the Torah's statute," the prime example of those laws and ordinances whose reason is not disclosed, and which nevertheless demand absolute obedience to the decrees of God. This is a salutary reminder that even in this physical world of ours there are many things that

במדבר ט״ז, ג׳. 1

are unfathomable to the finite mind of man. The *Parah Adumah* comes as the answer to the constant questioning as to the essence of the Divine Being Who is the Creator of the universe, and His relationship with His creatures. It reiterates the great truth that even to Moses it was not given to know that which is unknowable to the human mind. The words זאת חקת התורה אשר צוה ה', "this is the statute of the Torah which the Lord has commanded," affirm that through the Torah, God has, as it were, revealed Himself, and that through Torah He works.

The Rabbis of the Midrash express this in their inimitable manner when they liken the Almighty at the Creation to an architect drawing plans for his constructions: כך היה הקב"ה מביט בתורה ובורא את העולם[2] The Torah is the blueprint upon which the world was built, and faith in its immutability is the Prophets' watchword: צדיק באמונתו יחיה,[3] "the righteous shall live by his faith."

Notwithstanding this great lesson, and the manifestation of God's continuing good will and providential protection by His frustration of Balak and Bilam's endeavours to destroy Israel with curses, Israel persists in its waywardness! At the very end of their long desert journey, at the last stop before the Promised Land they succumbed to the allurement of the daughters of Moab, joining in their worship of Ba'al Peor, a form of licentious idolatry even more objectionable than the worship of the Golden Calf. It was the absolute negation of all they should have learned in their forty years in the wilderness. At this last moment, the glorious prospect that beckoned from across the Jordan, of their becoming settled as a holy people and a kingdom of priests, was in jeopardy.

---

2. בראשית רבה א', ב'.

3. חבקוק ב', ד'.

It was a situation that could only be saved by a mighty act of selfless *Kiddush Hashem*, that would sweep away once and for all the doubts and the disbelief, the weakness and waverings, and imbue the Torah ideal with a true spirit of steadfast loyalty. It was a challenge such as had confronted Moses at the Waters of Meribah; his failure had robbed him of the fulfilment of his cherished hope to enter the land, bringing upon him the Divine reproach, יען לא האמנתם בי להקדישני לעיני בני ישראל לכן לא תביאו את הקהל הזה אל הארץ אשר נתתי להם. In retrospect, we see that if Pinchas had failed to act at this final moment, his failure would have affected the whole course of human history. Israel's abandonment of the Sinai covenant would have led to the aborting of the Torah ideal and its moral values. The very name of God would have been lost to the world, to the eternal detriment of our whole culture and civilisation. Seen in this perspective, it is small wonder that the heroic deed of Pinchas is so boldly described. Small wonder, likewise, that his jealousy for God's sake was rewarded with the Divine promise of a twofold covenant of peace and everlasting priesthood.

We live in times not unlike those of our ancestors in the wilderness. The world is swept with waves of confusion and conflicting ideologies. The advance of modern technology has facilitated an ever-increasing flood of publications. Modern youth is bombarded with so many books about God: 'Where is God?' 'What is God's nature?' 'What is God's name?' It is hardly surprising that some are left wandering in a forest of heresy, and that many of our best have lost themselves in a maze of strange concepts and confused ideas. It only reflects once again those ancient questionings about God's workings and His relationship with men: היש ה' בקרבנו אם אין.[4]

4. שמות י״ז, ז׳.

Amongst those claiming to be proponents of authentic Jewish teaching, there are variations almost as wide as the points of a compass — reminiscent of Korach's cry, "there is more than one Moshe Rabbenu and more than one Aaron *HaKohen*." What one says is acceptable in matters of observance, another condemns, and our sacred tradition is virtually torn limb from limb. Forgotten is the lesson that should be learned from Bilam's perfidy: that God will never allow the Jew to die at the hands of the enemy without. The Jew can only be slain by the enemy within. To tear *Toras Moshe* to pieces, to dismember the Oral Law, is to break with the martyred Rabbi Akiva and all the sacred Sages stretching back to Ezra and beyond. To attempt life without Torah is to break with God and court destruction.

The devout and dedicated Jew must strive to attain the courage and consistency of Pinchas, endeavouring with zeal and selflessness to be jealous for God's name, ensuring that his personal life and his dealings with others, of whatever race or creed, will always be a *Kiddush Hashem*.

iv

A Divine Census

(Bar Mitzvah)

After the plague brought upon Israel by the sin of Ba'al Peor, they were commanded to "take the sum of all the congregation of the Children of Israel." Significantly, in this Divinely ordained census it was the *families* of the Children of Israel that were numbered. How many families were there intact, how many homes were faithful, how many children followed parents? Fathers and sons together, mothers and daughters together were the fighting strength of Israel: משפחת החנכי, משפחת הפלאי — הטיל הקב"ה שמו עליהם,[1] "God set His name upon them," the Rabbis say, not משפחת חנך but משפחת החנכי, a ה on one side of the name and a י on the other side making י—ה, the name of God, attached to each family. Godliness in every home — a Jewish home is a Godly home, a Jewish family is a Godly family. These could go forward into the land of promise. What a wonderful people we would be if our Judaism were something positive, if the name of God encompassed each home, ה"א מצד זה ויו"ד מצד זה.

Of the zeal of Pinchas the Psalmist says, ותחשב לו לצדקה לדר ודר עד עולם,[2] "it was counted righteousness for him unto all generations for evermore." The greatest צדקה that parents can bestow upon children —a צדקה that becomes a legacy לדר ודר, from generation to generation, is zeal, courage, jealousy for God's sake; to attach the name of God to our very own. To this end we must strive together, courageously, fearlessly so that צדקה may be meted out to our children, that they may move forward with honour to their rightful place among men in a world of peace and calm.

The *Sidrah* that tells of Pinchas, the man of courage, is also the *Sidrah* of the sacrifices. It tells first of the two sacrifices that were offered up each day, one lamb בבקר, in the morning, and the second lamb בין הערבים, towards dusk.

A Bar Mitzvah should always remember that the lamb in the morning symbolises the morning of life, when a young person must make some sacrifices to be a good Jew, a lamb without a blemish. It means rising a little earlier in the morning for prayers with *tallis*

1. רש"י; ילקוט שמעוני, פסיקתא.

2. תהלים ק"ו, ל"א.

and *tefillin*, which will help to carry through the day with success. It means a sacrifice to be honest and truthful, never to tell an untruth, to be respectful and kind. It means sacrifices to keep *kashrus* and Shabbos. By learning to make sacrifices in the morning of life, a Bar Mitzvah will grow up without blemish, deserving the unlimited love of parents and family and the genuine respect and admiration of friends and acquaintances at all times. Like Pinchas, have courage to strive always to bring honour upon our people, thus to be worthy of God's blessing of peace and righteousness for evermore.

v

The Possible and the Impossible

(Bar Mitzvah)

A wise man once said that in time to come, when we move on from here and this fight of ours to live and to build and to prosper comes to an end, the question that will be put to every man will not be, "Did you win?" The question asked will be, "Did you fight? Did you try your best?" No one expects the impossible, though there are some people who can achieve the impossible, too. Not every fighting soldier is awarded a V.C.; that is the privilege of a few who dare to risk their lives for a cause, and make what seems to be impossible possible.

There is one dictionary in the world where the term 'impossible' does not exist as a word on its own. It is the dictionary of the Jewish people, the dictionary of Israel. We triumphed over the impossible when we were bleeding profusely after the War. We lost a third of our population, and we went on to achieve the impossible. We established the Jewish State when the entire Arab world was against us. The word 'impossible' just does not exist in the vocabulary of our emotions, and in our religious life it is the same. We honoured the Sabbath and observed it when we could not afford it, for שבת was dearer than anything else in life. We gave of our time for our daily prayers and our *tefillin*; we paid for *kashrus* and for Jewish education though we could ill afford them. It seemed impossible to build synagogues and schools and a state, but the word 'impossible' just did not exist.

The very first verse of the *Haftorah* tells how these impossibles are attained: ויד ה' היתה אל אליהו וישנס מתניו, "and the hand of the Lord was on Elijah, and he girded up his loins." Elijah the Prophet stood alone, ואותר אני לבדי, against a hostile world. False prophets and contemptuous kings — ויבקשו את נפשי לקחתה, he cried, "They seek my life to take it away." It would have been a sad day for the Jewish people, history would have changed its course, had Elijah surrendered and submitted to the crazy fashion of the day; but ויד ה' היתה אל אליהו, "the hand of God was on Elijah, and he girded up his loins." He found strength and courage in the knowledge that God was with him and he could never be defeated. That has been our glory right throughout our history, that the hand of God has been upon us. That hand of God is the Torah, it is the Jewish way of life, our people's sense of purpose and destiny.

We do not expect a Bar Mitzvah boy on joining the ranks of Israel to achieve the impossible; the order of the day as he joins the ranks is not to go and capture hills or wipe out platoons, it is to try his best, do his best, do the possible. In the modern world it is possible to live a complete Jewish life without any hindrance, and to be a fine, loyal citizen at the same time. There is no earthly reason why Jewish study should not continue after Bar Mitzvah; all it means is a little effort. The Hebrew language of the Prayer Book and the Bible is now a recognised subject in public schools and universities. Is it nice to learn the language of other countries and to be ignorant of our own? To know the victories or defeats of William the Conqueror and Napoleon, yet be unaware of Bar Kochva and Rabbi Akiva? To learn of Shakespeare and Dickens, yet be completely ignorant of Isaiah and Amos?

The section of the *Sidrah* dealing with the sacrifices that Israel was duty-bound to bring during the Jewish year concludes, לבד מנדריכם ונדבתיכם, "besides your vows and your free-will offerings." Besides our duties as citizens to be aware of the culture and history of the country in which we reside, we have our duties to our people, our faith, our language and our history. At the end of every day we should ask ourselves the question, "Did I try my best? Did I do that which it was possible for me to do?" Going out of the synagogue, every Bar Mitzvah should feel like Elijah, "with the hand of God upon him," girding himself for the future, resolved to perform his daily duties and his dealings with his fellow men in a manner that will bring credit and honour to his parents and his people at all times.

MATTOS

מטות

i

If We Remember Him. . .

(Bar Mitzvah)

The *Sidrah* tells of Israel's victory over the Midianites and the retribution meted out to them for enticing Israel to sin in the matter of Peor. It tells, too, of the distribution of the captured possessions of livestock and goods, and the thanksgiving offering made by the warriors for their safe return home: ויבאו אתו אל אהל מועד, "they brought it to the Tent of Meeting, זכרון לבני ישראל לפני ה', for a memorial for the Children of Israel before the Lord."

God does not need our gifts; what we give Him is only an expression of our thoughts, it is זכרון לפני ה'. It shows that we have not forgotten Him; על טוב כוונתם is the Rabbinic idiom, 'it is an indication of our good intentions,' it is a way of saying thank-you to God. זכר, remembering, works both ways: if we remember Him, He remembers us. אנשי הצבא בזזו איש לו, "the warriors took the booty each man for himself," but ויבאו אתו אל אהל מועד, they took some of the gold and jewels and brought them to the Sanctuary as a memorial לפני ה'. Judaism does not demand your all for God: enjoy what He provides, but thank Him by making a *berachah* before a meal and *Birkas Ha-mazon* afterwards, instead of getting up from the table like an animal without a word of gratitude. How long does it take to put on *tefillin* in the morning and say a few prayers?

The free-will offering of gold and jewels was not the only thing that the warriors of Israel gave up. There was also the מחצית, the half of the livestock אשר חצה משה, "which Moses divided off" from the warriors for those Israelites who were not sent out to the battle. And then from this half Moses took one out of fifty and gave them to the Levites. חצה means 'to divide'; the Torah teaches the importance of being willing to share: some for God and some for oneself, some for self and some for others. If everyone would realise the significance of the term חצה and the importance of applying it in life, how much better this world would be!

To be a true Jew can be pleasant and honourable, but it means sharing with God. By all means have neat clothes, but have *tzitzis*, too; enjoy nice food, but ensure that it is kosher, too; work and earn, but Shabbos should be God's day of spiritual rest and rejuvenation. Pursue your chosen secular studies, but find a little time for Torah study, too. Keeping pace, hand-in-hand with God, life leads forward from Bar Mitzvah, the threshold of Jewish adolescence, to a fine Jewish manhood, a source of pride and a pillar of strength to our community.

MASSEI

מסעי

i

The March of History

(The Month of Av)

In spite of man's great desire for living, very few people would choose to live their lives over again unless they were given an opportunity of making right the things they have done wrong, of correcting their mistakes and of taking advantage of the countless opportunities they had allowed to pass by on the journey of life. If this is true in the life of the individual, it is much more so in the life of a nation. If the nations of the world could go back only half a century, how much of civilisation could have been saved, how many catastrophes and political mistakes could have been corrected. But history marches relentlessly on, and the world never takes a lesson. No nation has retrieved its losses, no country has made good its defeats. Empires have collapsed and have never risen again. But there is one people, one nation, one country that has risen and fallen, for close on three thousand years. In its ups and downs it has been untouched by its prosperity and unaffected by its ruin.

ויסעו ויחנו, "and they journeyed and they rested"; forty-two times are these words repeated in this *Sidrah*. Not a single letter in this Torah of ours is redundant; why then the use of so much space in this precious book? ויסעו ויחנו — what difference does it make today when they journeyed and where they stationed? משל למלך, the Rabbis say, "This may be likened to a king who had taken his ailing son to a distant place to be cured. On the return journey the king reminded his son, כאן ישננו כאן הוקרנו כאן חששת את ראשך[1] — 'Look, my child; here at this spot we slept, at that place we rested from the heat, at the other place you were overcome with pains.'" It is a profound philosophy: in Jewish life it is not necessary to live all over again to correct mistakes, to make right the wrongs we have done. It can be done on the same journey: כשחזרו התחיל אביו מונה כל המסעות, all you need to do is to look back. Opportunities arise again and again, but keep ever fresh in your mind the places where you slipped. Here we slept: we let an opportunity go by; here we were overcome with pain: we allowed periods of depression to crush us under their weight. Here we rested from the heat and allowed prosperity to spoil us. ויסעו ויחנו is never redundant if every stage in our history serves as a lesson for the future.

Rosh Chodesh Av ushers in the solemn period known as "the Nine Days," during which there is no hair cutting, no amusements, no meat or wine. We remember throughout this period the destruction of the Temple on two occasions in our history, the first time some 2,400 years ago, the second time over 1,900 years ago: days of defeat and despair, so long, long ago, but we keep them fresh as though it had happened today. If we forget one stage in our history we will never make amends. Secular nationalistic movements would never have given birth to a renewed Jewish State were it not for

1. רש״י; במדבר רבה כ״ג, ג׳.

those who prayed and prayed for 1,900 years. No wonder the special *Haftorah* of rebuke for the Nine Days takes precedence over the *Haftorah* of *Rosh Chodesh. Shabbos Rosh Chodesh* will occur again in the cycle of months; but if for one year we shelve this cry of Jeremiah's, שמעו דבר ה' בית יעקב וכל משפחות בית ישראל, if we forget the mistakes of history and silence the voice of the prophet, we will never retrieve the loss or rebuild the ruins.

כל המתאבל על ירושלים זוכה ורואה בשמחתה,[2] "Anyone who mourns for Jerusalem is privileged to behold her joy." It is most interesting that the Rabbis do not say that he who mourns for Jerusalem יזכה ויראה בשמחתה, that he *will be* so privileged. No one can guarantee the future, none can prophesy in whose generation Jerusalem will be built up again; but כל המתאבל זוכה ורואה, he who remembers Jerusalem, he who is ever conscious of Jewish problems, sees in his very thoughts and realises in the midst of his mourning the hope of its joy and the possibility of the redemption.

The month of Av is known as מנחם אב, because its privations and its afflictions, which remind us of history so long ago, are the greatest sign that one day it will be the month of comfort and joy. On Tisha B'Av משיח is born[3] — Tisha B'Av always occurs on the same day of the week as the day upon which Pesach, the festival of freedom, begins. If Tisha B'Av ceases to be, freedom will never come and *Mashiach* will never be born. We need not live over again to make amends, we must look back and ensure that there is no repetition of past mistakes and wrongs. In particular we must be ever mindful of the saying of the Sages: אל תגעו במשיחי — אלו תינוקות של בית רבן,[4] "the Messiahs of our people are the children in the school house." Each

2. בבא בתרא ס' ע״ב.

3. מדרש איכה רבתי נ״ז, פסוק "על אלה אני בכיה".

4. שבת קי״ט ע״ב.

new generation must be taught the Torah and trained in our sacred traditions. They must learn to face the future with loyalty, with pride in our people's history and its Divinely ordained destiny; then Tisha B'Av and the centuries-old period of mourning will be transformed into everlasting joy.

ii

Delivered by Hand

(Bar Mitzvah)

The Torah is not merely a history book; it is a book of wisdom teaching us how to live a life of holiness and righteousness. This is particularly illustrated by the opening passage of this *Sidrah*. At first sight it seems to be nothing more than a list of the resting places and stages of Israel's historic journey from Egypt to the Promised Land. Forty-two times the terms ויסעו ויחנו, "they journeyed and they encamped," are repeated. But on reflection, this repetition, in the Torah in which not a word or even a letter is superfluous, is seen as far more than a mere historic narrative. It emphasises again and again the importance of looking back at the beginning of every new stage in life and learning from experience to avoid previous mistakes. Bar Mitzvah marks a special ויסע, the beginning of an important new stage in the life of every young Jew. It is a time of farewell to childish irresponsibility, and of looking forward to approaching manhood. It is a time to resolve to reach the promised land of good citizenship and worthwhile living, of mature interest in, and pursuit of, Torah guidance to true and abiding happiness.

There is another way in which this *Sidrah* is an important milestone. It is the final portion of the Book of *Bemidbar*. When we conclude the reading we proclaim חזק חזק ונתחזק, encouraging one another to go forward resolutely with our Torah reading and observance. The final verse rings forth with a particularly relevant message for one going forward from childhood to manhood. אלה המצות והמשפטים אשר צוה ה' ביד משה אל בני ישראל בערבת מואב על ירדן ירחו, "These are the commandments and the precepts which the Lord commanded *by the hand* of Moses in the plains of Moab, by the Jordan near Jericho." Should not the Torah have said אשר צוה ה' את משה, "which the Lord commanded Moses"? What is meant by the expression "*by the hand* of Moses"?

People think that to be a good Jew all you have to do is to *think* of God and *pray* to God unceasingly. Not at all; what you *do* about God is of greater importance. Judaism starts with the hands. We put on *tzitzis* with our hands, we put *tefillin* on our hands; before we eat we wash our hands, we take kosher food with our hands. Judaism involves our eyes, our hands, our legs in seeing the right things and going to the right places and doing honest things with our hands. Our religion is a religion of the body; it requires us to do things with our limbs. Limbs need exercising, otherwise they become stiff and atrophied. The מצות and משפטים were ביד משה; if we do not use our limbs for the מצות, constantly without a break, they become spiritually numb, and in later life it is difficult to reinvigorate oneself.

חזק חזק — 'be strong, be strong in body and mind, in heart and soul,' should be the motto of every Bar Mitzvah. Wholehearted and complete involvement in Jewish life ensures a fruitful and successful future.

iii

Kiddush Hashem

The *Sidrah* of *Massei*, with its long list of journeys, bears out its name's implication: it marks the completion of the great saga of Israel's journey to the Promised Land. It must have been a terrific strain, quite unimaginable, for some three to four million souls, among them babes in arms. The sand, the heat, the dryness — the hazards, the food, the water, the sanitation — and it was not for a day or two, or a year or two, but forty years! What an awful prospect; no wonder the prophet Jeremiah sings the praises of the People of Israel: זכרתי לך חסד נעוריך אהבת כלולתיך לכתך אחרי במדבר בארץ לא זרועה,[1] "I remember in thy favour the devotion of thy youth, thy love as a bride, when thou didst go after Me in the wilderness, in a land that was not sown."

Is it surprising that every now and again there were cries and murmurings? To some the idea of returning to slavery in Egypt and dying a natural death of old age appealed more than to live in freedom but to die from thirst and exposure. What a leadership it demanded, not only to imbue faith and instil resistance, but to quell rebellion and to maintain order! In Moses the law-giver and Aaron the peacemaker there was a combination of דין and רחמים, justice and mercy, that is rare to find. In life we usually find either those who deal with דין, administering law, who are usually unpopular, or those who show רחמים, kindliness and mercy, being accessible to all; they are frequently taken advantage of and abused. During Israel's wandering in the wilderness, Moses and Aaron bore the brunt together.

1. ירמיה ב׳, ב׳.

What was the purpose of it all? From the dawn of his history the Jew has been charged with the God-given mission to teach man — כל יושבי תבל, wherever he may be — כי לך תכרע כל ברך תשבע כל לשן,[2] "that all the inhabitants of the world may perceive and know that unto Thee every knee must bow, every tongue must swear allegiance." So Abraham, Isaac and Jacob; Sarah, Rebecca, Leah and Rachel; all were born, and gave birth, out of pain and prayer. There are no shortcuts to God; but if we persevere, He is to be found. In the wilderness a great school of faith was put into operation, to find God and to accept Him. It was the most frightening, yet glorious, epoch in the history of the Jews, that epoch of the wilderness — a 'hide-and-seek game' with God. One day He revealed Himself, another day He concealed Himself. The Jew can get nothing without prayer. The Jew can get nowhere without God.

Three mysterious incidents are portrayed in the *Chumash* of *Bemidbar*. In the *Sidrah* of *Korach* we read of the פי הארץ, the mouth of the earth that swallowed up Korach and his henchmen. In the *Sidrah* of *Chukkas* we read of the פי הבאר, the mouth of the well that opened up in the desert and provided water for three million thirsty marchers. In the *Sidrah* of *Balak* there is another mouth: פי האתן, the mouth of Bilam's ass that spoke to its master. These three mouths, פי הארץ, הבאר, והאתן, were created, the Rabbis say, בערב שבת בין השמשות,[3] at twilight on the eve of the first Sabbath of Creation, when the world had been completed. In a brief interval, a mere second or two, between day and night, the three mouths were produced, amongst other strange things.

Some see God by day. In the words of the Sabbath Psalm, it is להגיד בבקר; for them He appears in victory and in triumph. Some see

2. תפלת עלינו מהפסוק בישעיה מ"ה, כ"ג.

3. אבות ה', ו.

God by night, ואמונתך בלילות, in defeat and in death. The faithful have no difficulty in adapting themselves in accord with God's immutable purpose by day or by night. But in life, and in history, there is a בין השמשות, a twilight: something we just do not understand, a kind of interval that cannot be determined — something incomprehensible. Nothing that one has read or studied or learned can explain it: twilight things. There is no answer to them but faith. They go against all reason, they go against the grain of nature, like פי הארץ, פי הבאר, פי האתן. A mouth in the earth that does what it is told, water that flows freely in the desert, an ass that speaks. There is no explanation to some things. There is never a clash between scholarship and religion; scholarship must admit there are some things beyond it, some things that are בין השמשות, twilight — they are just confusing. Without אמונה, faith, we get nowhere.

Moses — the great Moses — fell into a trap of his own making. Israel had arrived at Kadesh and there was no water to drink, not a drop to moisten the lips of the children and the animals. This time they did more than complain. Miriam, who so to speak mothered them, comforted them, had died. For what they had thought was a trifling offence, her remains were not even taken to the Holy Land. Their faith was shaken, וירב העם: this time they strove with Moses. God called to him to take the מטה, the rod: "Don't use it as you used it before; ודברתם אל הסלע, speak to the rock, and before their eyes water will flow; and you will give them and their cattle to drink."

But Moses, the great lover and defender of Israel, thought it would be a terrible indictment against the people for whom he was ready to lay down his life, if he spoke to the rock and the hard stone obeyed, whereas when he spoke to the quarrelsome Israelites they disobeyed. It was against reason. Had not the rod been used before? Did not history and logic prove that by smiting the rock he would achieve the same purpose? So he smote the rock, and water flowed.

The Jew is not to suffer because of his leader's mistakes, but ויאמר ה׳ אל משה ואל אהרן יען לא האמנתם בי להקדישני לעיני בני ישראל. . . , "and the Lord said unto Moses and unto Aaron, 'Because ye believed not in Me, to sanctify Me in the eyes of the Children of Israel, you have forfeited your right of entry into the Land of Israel.'" יען, the Rabbis say, means more than "because." יענה ויעיד,[4] it will bear testimony to the end of time that you were not מקדש שם שמים ברבים, you did not sanctify the name of God in the eyes of the people.

So many people make the mistake of believing that *Kiddush Hashem* means martyrdom, dying for God's sake, paying the supreme sacrifice. Of course that is the supreme pinnacle of *Kiddush Hashem*; but here is what the Rambam says about it:

כל הפורש מעבירה או עשה מצוה לא מפני דבר בעולם לא פחד ולא יראה ולא לבקש כבוד

אלא מפני הבורא ברוך הוא. . . הרי זה מקדש את השם.[5]

"Whoever turns aside from committing a sin, or whoever fulfills a mitzvah, not for any reason in the world, not for fear nor for gain, only for the sake of the Creator, blessed be He, הרי זה מקדש את השם, he it is who sanctifies the name of God." To obey, to perform a mitzvah, not because you understand, not because history can prove it, though it may go against all your thinking, to do it anyway, only מפני הבורא ברוך הוא — that is *Kiddush Hashem*. Does a house full of books require a *mezuzah*? Korach asked. Does a head full of knowledge require *tefillin*? Can a stone obey a voice? Is it more reasonable to strike the rock? Would it not be more in accord with scientific knowledge? But that is not *Kiddush Hashem*. *Kiddush Hashem* means to do it in spite of everything. *Kiddush Hashem* means faith, just

4 פירוש זה מובא בספר "דעת סופרים" מאת הרב חיים דב רבינוביץ ומציין מקורו באבן עזרא בראשית כ"ב, ט"ז.

5 הלכות יסודי התורה ה׳ י׳.

faith, for no reason, only because God dictates: לא מפני דבר בעולם אלא מפני הבורא ברוך הוא.

יען לא האמנתם בי להקדישני לכן לא תביאו, "Because you did not believe in Me to sanctify Me, that is why you can no longer lead." That *Kiddush Hashem* to which we must strive, which we must teach, and which we must courageously, unashamedly, and boldly preach is the faith that scholarship cannot prove, that science cannot fathom, and that man cannot comprehend. A faith that calls for פרוש מעבירה and עשה מצוה, to turn aside from sin and to observe the commandments. This is true Judaism, the Judaism we must teach our children and practise ourselves. This is the *Kiddush Hashem* that Israel had to learn in that great school of faith in the wilderness, on the way to the Promised Land. This is the *Kiddush Hashem* practised by Jews throughout the centuries of wandering in the wilderness of *galus*. Through this *Kiddush Hashem* we will teach the world to live sanely and righteously, in peace and in harmony.

iv

The Nine Days

(Haftorah)

In spite of our national rebirth, we still conduct a period of mourning from *Rosh Chodesh* until after Tisha B'Av, a long week of *shivah,* as it were. By abstaining from all forms of amusement, and the prohibition of meat except for Shabbos, we express our sorrow for the destruction of the Temple on two occasions and for the final dispersal of our people from their homeland some nineteen hundred years ago.

The Jewish State and Jewish life do not come under any particular political constitution. Vital to our preservation is the ancient charter delivered at Sinai. Our homeland has been gone for nineteen hundred years, our losses through the ages ran into countless millions. Why do the Jews form a solitary exception to the rule which pronounces the end of a nation in such circumstances? The only answer is that our national being is entirely different from that of other peoples. Judea was broken up, but Jews remained; the state was smashed, but Judaism remained intact.

What was essential to their existence and vital to their preservation was the Torah that neither the Roman legions nor the Spanish Inquisition nor the Nazi beasts could destroy. יבנה וחכמיה, the ancient Torah centre of Yavneh and its Sages, left an eternal impression on the course of Jewish history. Why, as far back as the fourth century a non-Jew wrote, "the destruction of the Holy Temple, the ruin of the House of God, the dispersion of the Chosen People into all the kingdoms of the earth, and their continued existence as a nation, notwithstanding every attempt to exterminate them or to compel them to forsake the Torah which distinguishes them from all other nations, is emphatically one of the strongest proofs we have of the truth of the Bible." The new kinds of "temples" in our midst refuse to recognise it, but the Church has, in more ways than one.

The prophet Jeremiah pours out his heart in the *Haftorah*: כי שתים רעות עשה עמי, "for My people have committed two evils, אתי עזבו מקור מים חיים, they have forsaken Me, the fountain of living waters." But that is not all. To turn away from God, to lose hope and faith, is one evil, but there is another: לחצב להם בארות בארת נשברים אשר לא יכלו המים, "they have hewed them out cisterns, broken cisterns that can hold no water." To be unfaithful and disloyal is one half of the tragedy; the other half is to hew out cisterns — broken cisterns that hold no water. To turn from the well of living water and dig wells that are cracked and shallow, a faith that is a sham and make-believe. To build synagogues that are no longer genuine synagogues, to speak Hebrew that is no longer לשון קודש — this is אשר לא יכלו המים: every vestige of Jewish tradition is swallowed up. Mark the prophet's repetition of the word בארות: he cries בארות בארות נשברים. We see such wells — temples built here and there, בארות נשברים, with cracks, in bits and pieces, no uniform service, no particular kind of Jewish practice — a kind of help yourself religion. אשר לא יכלו המים — it holds no water, it leaks, it is unsound; they have no unifying Divine authority.

Right through our history there were elements who lost faith: אתי עזבו. It is to be expected. To suffer heavily as we have suffered, to lose an entire family, to meet death after death and yet to retain faith and say יתגדל ויתקדש, means to be a great Jew; but with all the loss of faith and despair they rarely turned to other faiths. They drank from no other wells. How many משומדים, apostates, do you find in Jewish history? What a glorious record!

השמרו לכם פן יפתה לבבכם וסרתם ועבדתם אלהים אחרים, "take heed to yourselves lest your hearts be deceived, and ye turn aside and serve other gods." This is the great warning of the *Shema*. פן יפתה לבבכם is bad enough, but it is not as terrible as the calamity in וסרתם ועבדתם, "to turn aside" in other directions שכיון שאדם פורש מן התורה הולך ומדבק בעבודה זרה.[1] It was a great Rabbi who once said that there is a great difference between an un-Orthodox Jew and a reform Jew. The un-Orthodox Jew knows at least that he is committing wrong: it is יפתה לבבכם. But the reform Jew thinks he is doing right: it is וסרתם ועבדתם. The one who knows he is doing wrong but cannot resist is much better than the one who believes he is doing no wrong. For one there is some hope; for the other there is none.

---

1. רש"י; ספרי.

There is a constant need to warn the community of the dangers of those elements that try to quench the thirst of the young out of broken cisterns that hold no water. A hungry stomach can be fed; a poisoned stomach is doomed unless it is surgically treated. It needs an operation to cut off completely from those who have turned in other directions. The Nine Days will remain Nine Days and Tisha B'Av will remain Tisha B'Av, with all the sadness that surrounds it, until אם תשוב ישראל נאם ה' אלי תשוב, "if thou wilt return, O Israel, return unto Me" — back into the proper direction; ואם תסיר שקוציך מפני, "put away the detestable things out of My sight" — stop saying, 'this too is Judaism, and this too is the Jewish religion'; ולא תנוד, "and do not waver."

It is to the young that we look during these trying times: the young who have been blessed to be born and to live in this glorious period of Jewish national rebirth. Our youth must be equipped to march in as the older generation are taken out to eternal life. With young people living a Torah-true life באמת במשפט ובצדקה, "in truth, in justice, and in righteousness," ובו יתהללו, in them we shall glory; and the month of Av will become one of joy and thanksgiving.

v

Home Leadership

(The Nine Days)[1]

A learned man, when asked to say something of the wonders of Heaven, replied: "When I get to Heaven I shall see three wonders.

1 An address at the wartime congregation of High Wycombe.

The first wonder will be to see people there whom I never expected to see. The second wonder will be to miss many people whom I did expect to see. The third and greatest wonder of all will be to find myself there."

Many people will readily admit mistakes they have made, for it is only by mistakes that we learn, but how many are there who truthfully and conscientiously believe that whatever they do is correctly done and their every judgment is a just one? Most of us feel without doubt that our conduct of life, at home or in business, is the proper conduct. Nine times out of ten our answer when being taken to task is "Oh, you don't understand." We quickly forget that we are human after all, and our decisions are impelled by our human desires and human inclinations. What a wonder, nay what a shock, it will be to some of us when we reach Heaven, as we hope one day to do, to find that those whom we least expected are there and those whom we surely expected to meet are outside of it.

In כבשת גנב כי ימצא כן הבישו בית ישראל המה מלכיהם שריהם וכהניהם ונביאיהם this *Haftorah,* the second of the Three Weeks, the prophet Jeremiah declares, "As the thief is ashamed when he is found, so is the House of Israel ashamed, they, their kings, their princes, their priests and their prophets." Those whose duty it is to visit places where such people are detained generally find that the גנב, the thief, is not ashamed by the offence he has committed. His victim causes him little concern; the greatest punishment, the greatest shame he suffers is when his deceitful deed is made known to his family, his friends, and acquaintances. The greatest shame is כי ימצא, when he is found out: this man was believed to be honourable, but is discovered to be a thief. What a calamity, the prophet cries out in this pre-Tisha B'Av message, what a calamity, כן הבישו בית ישראל, when the way Israel has fulfilled its Divinely ordained mission will be revealed to the world. They, their kings, their princes, their priests and their prophets; without distinction, rich and poor, wise and ignorant, leader and led, how they will be ashamed when they see who will occupy the "front seats" and who will remain outside. Rabbi and layman, what a wonder it will be if we get there, and what a wonder it will be to see the Heavenly distribution of those allotted positions — כבשת גנב כי ימצא. Yes, like thieves we will be ashamed to face one another.

שמעו דבר ה' בית יעקב וכל משפחות בית ישראל, "Hear ye, the House of Jacob, and all the families of the House of Israel." It applies to individuals, it applies to families and it applies to nations. How we criticise the nation's leaders! Why, every man in the street has something to say about one Cabinet Minister or the other. My way of doing things is, of course, always the right way. Very likely; but what about the leadership of your own home? It is so simple to find fault with others; but you in your home are your own Prime Minister, you are your own master. Who is there to criticise you? The clash of opinions, the meeting of two opposing elements is just as likely in one's own home as it is in one's own country — שמעו דבר ה' בית יעקב וכל משפחות בית ישראל. To the families of Israel and to the nation of Israel the prophet addresses his message. There is the God-fearing child and the Godless child, both under the same roof, so to speak. There must be the God-consciousness of the father to guide and direct those whom he brought into the world. If there is selfishness, there must be self-sacrifice in the parent.

Disruption in the home is disruption in the family, disruption in the family is disruption among nations. Parental leadership no more exists. We have made our growing children into independent units; now when they leave school they are self-supporting. So much a week is given to mother for help, like a lodger, and the remainder — well, one cannot interfere in a child's own earnings. In times gone by to show no respect to parents would have been the end of the world — who would dare to occupy father's seat? What a beautiful link it was between father and son, between mother and daughter. Parental care and guidance was the very foundation of Jewish family life. Today, alas, איש הישר בעיניו יעשה:[2] the young boy and girl control the home, the old man and the old woman take a back seat. The parent is no more a source of inspiration. If they are of the old-fashioned type they are ridiculed, and if Dad can be considered a pal, well, with a pat on the back and "Dad, you don't understand," everything decent is turned aside. When our children are young we idolise and spoil them; when they grow up we despise and ruin them.

If there is no leadership in our own homes, what leadership can there be among nations? Regrettably, כבשת גנב כי ימצא — in later years when it becomes known, when our children have to face the world with its difficulties, we will seem like a גנב, like thieves who have deceived them. They thought it was a right and proper upbringing, but alas, אמרים לעץ אבי אתה ולאבן את ילדתנו, brick and mortar become their idols, these are all they have learned to respect. Where is the father who should guide and lead? Where is the mother who should worry and care? Without the משפחות בית ישראל there can be no בית יעקב. The rush and turmoil of life have swept us off our feet. The very ground we stand on is sinking fast into an abyss from which it is becoming impossible to extricate ourselves. Where is the home-life, that wonderful spirit of a Friday night supper, the *Kiddush*, the *bentshen*? As for the ordinary mid-week supper, it has become, "Quick, Mam, I have got to get out."

Today a new craze has sprung up; people call it psychology. A child is asked, "What would you like to be, a scientist, an engineer, or a lawyer?" To learn to be a Jew — that is purely secondary. If it

---

2. בספר שופטים י"ז, ו', וכ"א, כ"ה.

fits in with the career, well and good. But one's career must fit in with his conditions; what about career fitting in with God and religion? The prophet mourns, פנו אלי ערף ולא פנים, "to Me they have turned their back and not their face." Every nation struggles to maintain its independence, its fatherland and its territory. What are we Jews doing for our spiritual fatherland?

Well may we take this prophetic message to heart during the Nine Days. It is not just for the destruction of two thousand years ago that we mourn; it is for the destruction — the neglect and apathy — of our own times. Our own problems will never be solved if we face others in pride but keep our backs to God in shame. Our cries will go out to the wilderness from which no response will come.

הלוא מעתה קראת לי אבי אלוף נעורי אתה; this is our victory cry, "You are now the Father, the companion of my youth." Conditions will change, nations will rise and fall; but You are now and always the companion of my youth. Let the Nine Days of mourning fulfil their true purpose: to arouse us once and for all from our selfish complacency. Let the משפחות בית ישראל, the families of Israel, once again flourish as they did in days gone by. Then will the world-family see in us the realisation of God's purpose, in happiness and peace.

DEVARIM

דברים

i

A Double Blessing

As Israel's immortal teacher is about to bid farewell to his people, he offers up a two-fold prayer and hope for their future invoking upon them two distinct blessings. Firstly, יֹסֵף עֲלֵיכֶם כָּכֶם אֶלֶף פְּעָמִים, "May God make you a thousand times so many more as you are." Secondly, וִיבָרֵךְ אֶתְכֶם כַּאֲשֶׁר דִּבֶּר לָכֶם, "and may He bless you, as He has promised you." Why the repetition? The first, the Rabbis say, is מִשֶּׁלִי — I give you the blessing that is within my power; but man's blessings are limited. Space is limited and numbers are limited; even אֶלֶף פְּעָמִים, as much as it seems, is limited nevertheless. But if you strive כָּכֶם, to produce generations as you are, with Jewish values undiminished, Jewish living untarnished; if כָּכֶם, if the child of tomorrow is like the father of yesterday, creating an uninterrupted link of Jewish generations, then וִיבָרֵךְ אֶתְכֶם כַּאֲשֶׁר דִּבֶּר לָכֶם, a blessing מִשֶּׁלוֹ.[1] However limited your space or meagre your means, His infinite blessing will be showered upon you.

---

1. דברים רבה א', י"ב.

There is no word in the stupendous volume of Jewish literature so small, yet with so much meaning, as that word ככם. There is no word that has exercised a greater influence on the trend of Jewish history than that word ככם, "as you are." *Nachamu* would never follow *Chazon,* and Israel would never have been reborn, had we not dimmed the lights for nineteen hundred years and mourned for Jerusalem as though it were only yesterday that we were driven out. Every day ובנה ירושלים, and every day תחזנה עינינו, literally ככם, it was as though it happened to us. At every turning in the winding paths of Jewish history, at every crossroad, the question was ככם: will the generations that follow be as we are? Will יסף עליכם be ככם, so that ויברך אתכם כאשר דבר לכם, the blessings of God may follow in the wake of your children's strivings? All over the English-speaking world there are some who are groping to find a middle way, so to speak, between the old bearded grandfather and the young hatless grandchild. All their quack remedies have failed. Why? Because ככם was missing. They were blessed with יסף עליכם, production and prosperity on all sides, but they forgot that Jewish survival is subject to ככם; blessings of today must fit with the pattern of the glories of yesterday.

A famous preacher once cited the opening verses of the Tisha B'Av Torah reading and interpreted them most fittingly for our generation. כי תוליד בנים ובני בנים ונשנתם בארץ — you will be blessed with children and grandchildren, and ונשנתם בארץ, you will become 'old-fashioned' in the land. Your way of life will be a thing of the past, your traditions and customs will become antiquated. העידתי בכם. כי אבד תאבדון . . — the coming generations will never survive the sweeping changes of a society that has lost its way.

This commonplace attitude is anticipated in a remarkable Midrashic exposition of the opening passages of the Book of *Devarim:* אלה הדברים אשר דבר משה אל כל ישראל, "These are the words which

Moses spoke unto all Israel." He is about to bid farewell to the
people whose troubles he had borne for forty years, and calls them
to assemble so that he can repeat to them the entire Torah: his last
will and testament. ?...התחילו מהרהרין לומר תאמר שהוא בדעת שפוי. There
they stood looking into the teacher's face. "Do you think he is in his
full senses?" they whispered to one another. "He is old and senile;
what does he understand of the new country and the new life that
faces us?" היו נוטלין בניהם ובנותיהם קטנים וזורקין לתוך חיקו של משה, "they held
up their children to him and cried, מה הבאה התקנת להן לאלו מה פרנסה התקנת
להן לאלו, these children whom you brought up with these Torah
studies, with these *tallis* and *tefillin*, with this Shabbos — what
pleasures can they enjoy out of life, what careers can they make for
themselves?"[2]

Moses realised that you cannot face such a challenge with a mere
emotional approach. You can appeal to children a thousand times
over to remember the past: "Don't let the old father down!" But ישראל
לא ידע — לא אבו לידע.[3] They do not want to know; he is old-fashioned.
So Moses begins his closing speech, not with an appeal but with an
historical survey. He gives facts and figures, dates and places. Is it
for nothing, he says, that we survived Egypt, Amalek, Moab, Midian
and others? No man is senile who cries, 'Look to history and take
the lesson to heart!'

Sons and daughters of the old traditional fathers and mothers!
Look what we endured, look how we survived, look what we have
saved from the destructions of two thousand years. ככם, build as
they did, live as they lived. יסף עליכם ככם, may your numbers increase
as you are, ויברך אתכם כאשר דבר לכם, and may God bless you that *Chazon*
may turn to *Nachamu*, that mourning may turn to joy, that the

ספרי: ילקוט שמעוני תש"צ ותשצ"ג. 2

הפטרת דברים ישעיה א' ורש"י שם. 3

People of Israel, the Land of Israel and the Torah of Israel may rise to the heights of glory, leading the way to peace and calm among all men.

ii

Order in Jewish Life

(Chazon)

It was during the month of Av that ancient Israel's fate was sealed. The destruction of our homeland and the dispersion into exile began. The collapse of the first and second Jewish Commonwealth on the very same day, though some six hundred years separated them, made it a day of national mourning. With the traditional book of *Kinos* opened before us, the entire picture of Israel's horrifying history stands revealed, and the terrifying story of Jewish suffering and martyrdom, decimated and massacred communities, is portrayed. Even when Israel has blossomed again in all its beauty and grandeur, these days will remain an everlasting reminder of the phenomenon of Jewish history: of a world that lost its balance while the Jew stood undaunted, of the wretched fate of untold numbers, of a people whose hope was never lost. Tisha B'Av is the eternal message to an eternal people that the Jew cannot be measured by the same yardstick as others, that within the framework of society there is a people governed by Divine power.

Hence, even today, in this epoch of reborn glory, these days dare not lose their significance. History has not finished with us yet. The eyes of the world are again turned to the Middle East. To the national Jew as well as to the religious Jew, Tisha B'Av cries out to stop and think. That is the purpose of *shivah*, too: never forget the past. It is the same story but with a different language. The principles of morality and justice have never changed; they are the same today as they were two-and-a-half thousand years ago, because they rest on fixed foundations. Whenever they are tampered with there is danger of collapse. Every nation in the world must know that truth cannot be trimmed to suit the whim or the convenience of an individual or a group.

In the *Haftorah* of *Chazon,* Isaiah speaks out as the implacable enemy of a shallow religion, that relegates God to the place of worship and divorces Him from everyday life and activity: כי תבאו לראות פני מי בקש זאת מידכם רמס חצרי, "when ye come to appear before Me, who has required this at your hand, to trample My courts." It is a strange, but thought-provoking expression: surely one tramples with one's feet, not with one's hands? The prophet should, in that case, have used the expression מי בקש זאת מרגלכם רמס חצרי, "who has required this at your *feet,* to trample My courts." But it was that perverted sense of values that the prophet was attacking: those to whom the Temple was for God and the street for man, those who with their feet walk in silence to God's house but with their hands maul the elementary standards of justice and morality. מי בקש זאת מידכם רמס חצרי, "who has required this at your hand, to trample My courtyards."

If we survey the story of our people today and the story of our people of yesterday; of our rebirth in the sixth century before the Common Era or our rebirth in 1948 C.E.; the destruction of the year 70 C.E. and the destruction of the year 1940; it is the same old story: sects and parties, groups and factions, each claiming the truth, but trampling with their hands on the things sacred to the other. So much pious talk followed by impious action. Everybody, young and old alike, everybody has something to say and holds the key of salvation in his own hand. Isaiah put it so well in three brief words that diagnose the whole disease: ישראל לא ידע, "Israel does not know." Rashi, the immortal commentator, makes but one observation: לא אבו לידע, Israel would know and could know, but לא אבו לידע, Israel does not want to know. Is there anyone today who is not a professor of politics? Everyone has a solution to the Jewish problem and to the world's problems; but the real need is to get to the depth of things, to study history, to practise faith, to honour justice. That is not so easy; ישראל לא אבו לידע — few want to do that.

There is another remarkable comment of Rashi, this time on the *Sidrah*. Moses refers bitterly to the rebelliousness in the wilderness. On two occasions he speaks of the approach made to him by the People of Israel: ותקרבון אלי, "on one occasion you all came to me, כלכם, every one of you, and demanded to send spies to the Holy Land." There he uses the word כלכם, "all of you." On another occasion, at the foot of Sinai, ותקרבון אלי כל ראשי שבטיכם וזקניכם,[1] "you came near to me, not all of you together but ראשי שבטיכם וזקניכם, the heads of your tribes and your elders." There were two kind of approaches to the Jewish problem. One was כלכם בערבוביא: Rashi says, ילדים דוחפין את הזקנים וזקנים דוחפין את הראשים, "the young pushed the old and the old had no regard for the heads." Yes, it was when they stood ready to enter the land of promise, to set up a state, that everyone had something to say. The young pushed the old and the old had no regard for those at the head, כלכם בערבוביא. To what did it lead? They never built the land, they never set foot on it. At Sinai there was a different kind of approach: ראשי שבטיכם וזקניכם, there was respect for authority; the heads had their place and the elders occupied their place. There was study and harmony and there was no ערבוביא. That led to a ממלכת כהנים, a kingdom of priests, a people with a

1. דברים ה', כ'.

visionary character who took their place in the world.

Tisha B'Av calls for a revival of those values, for a return to order in Jewish life. It can never come from trying to capture the political leavings of a decadent society, whether it is the so-called democracy of a Western country or the so-called autocracy of an Eastern society. ואשיבה שפטיך כבראשונה ויעציך כבתחלה, "and I will restore thy judges as at the first and thy councillors as at the beginning"; that should be the order of things. אחרי כן יקרא לך עיר הצדק, "afterwards shalt thou be called the righteous city," bringing peace to yourselves and calm to the rest of the world.

iii

Lost at Sea[1]

(Chazon — Tisha B'Av)

If Yom Kippur is the day of religious communion, then Tisha B'Av is the day of national communion. Whoever refuses to accept it must be considered outside the pale of world Jewry, one whose faith is not pinned to the eventual return of Israel to the Land of Israel, whose mind is not turned from day-to-day affairs to the east, where the heart of the Jewish people will meet again as sure as the sun shines. He is an outcast of our race and must be kept apart. He has relinquished all rights and severed all connections. There is no future for him and his children. If Tisha B'Av achieves nothing more than this feeling of national solidarity it will have been worthwhile.

---

1 A post-war address.

Shall we continue to place our trust in statements replete with political expediency, in the cold logic of international agreements that makes it possible to return by force thousands of people, most of whom are women and children, to shores that are soaked through with the blood of their kith and kin? In the words of the *Haftorah*, אדמתכם לנגדכם זרים אכלים אתה, "your land," the land which is theirs and which they had already reached, לנגדכם, "it is before their very eyes," yet they are sent back to the countries which spat them out, whilst their own country to which their eyes have turned for centuries is being devoured by strangers.

In *Lamentations*, Jeremiah cries out, כי גדול כים שברך מי ירפא לך,[2] "thy breach is as great as the sea; who can heal thee?" A disaster on dry land can be commemorated: the spot is known, a memorial can be set up, a monument erected to remind men of the tragedy that took place on that spot. But if a ship meets disaster on the high seas, the raging waters cover it up. No sign is left, no point can be marked, nothing can be set up to remind men of the tragedy that once took place there. כי גדול כים שברך, "your troubles are great like the sea." One follows the other; each year brings new calamities. Page after page of Jewish history is saturated in blood. In our own lifetime it began with the Kishinev pogroms, then the Russian revolution, the German upheavals, the Polish murders. One tragedy covers the other. The world forgets, we forget. The voice of the Jew must be heard, but it must be one voice, coming from the heart and soul of the Jewish people.

Isaiah urges: רחצו הזכו הסירו רע מעלליכם מנגד עיני, "Wash you, make you clean, put away the evil of your doings from before My eyes." רחצו means washing on the surface, a clean-looking Jew with dignity of race and pride of people. Here walks a Jew, clean, untarnished,

---

איכה ב', י"ג. 2

so that the street-corner scoundrel will never be able to open his mouth against him. הזכו means making clean within one's self — dignity of home and pride of family, so that Jewish home-life should stand out as an example of love and harmony, of decency and respect. הסירו רע מעלליכם מנגד עיני means the things between the Jew and his Maker, in the inner recesses of our lives, where God Himself dwells. A Jew to the outer world, a Jew to our near and dear ones, a Jew to Almighty God. Wash you from without, make you clean from within, put away the evil of your doings from before Mine eyes: a Jew always in every walk of life. Each one in his own way must become an ambassador.

Tisha B'Av, at the height of the summer holiday season, beckons us to stop for a thought on Jewish sorrows, for a curb on the appetite which so often is so un-Jewish. A preacher once said, "The world will ask, 'Did you win?' God will ask, 'Did you try? Did you fight?'" It is unfortunate that the world takes up such an unrealistic stance, but what can we do? We know that our fight is not in vain. Our duty as Jews is to try to do the fighting. Our children after us will not ask, "Did you win?" They will ask, "Did you try, did you fight?"

The fight must begin within ourselves, to keep ourselves clean from within. Nothing in this world can be won without a fight — that is the fight against personal temptation, against greed and lust, it is the fight against the evil-doers, the assimilationists in the camp who stab us in the back. It is a fight against the whole world whose ears are deaf to our cries, whose whole political set-up is centred around their own imperialism and aggrandisement. Alas, the war that has been won was not — as we had hoped — a war that would break down national barriers and racial prejudice. We stand on the brink of another abyss, a mighty melting pot of selfish aims and ideologies. The Jew, scattered as he is over the face of the earth, is a convenient scapegoat for all the world's ills. Whether we shall win through in our time no one knows, no one can predict. But two things are sure: one, that we shall try and we shall fight; two, that we shall eventually win. Ours is and will be a different fight — a fight for moral standards and human values.

With this we shall win through; of that there is no doubt. The question that must be answered by the Jew, each one individually, is "Am I doing my share, am I making sacrifices?" To be ready with the answer is to be moved by the Tisha B'Av message: רחצו הזכו הסירו רע מעלליכם מנגד עיני, "Wash you, make you clean, put away the evil of your doings from before Mine eyes." אחרי כן יקרא לך עיר הצדק קריה נאמנה , "then (and then only), thou shalt be called the city of righteousness, the faithful city." By setting an example of true human values, faith and righteousness, Israel's radiant influence will lead the world back to a sane order, and peace will reign on earth.

iv

The Lesson of Galus[1]

(Tisha B'Av)

In the *Sidrah*, Moses reminds the Israelites of the causes that held them back from entering the Promised Land. The historic survey he makes is not meant merely as an admonition; rather it was intended to lay emphasis on the mistakes they had made and the omissions they had committed, and without which their march

---

1 An extract from a sermon delivered some three years after the War, when a quarter of a million Jews still languished in Displaced Person Camps in Europe.

from Egypt to Canaan would have been a smooth journey from bondage to freedom. Like individuals who forget the rock whence they were hewn; like some great industrialist who forgets the days when he was a small presser or buttonhole maker, or the mansion-dwelling aristocrat who forgets the dilapidated home of his father who struggled for his bread and butter; likewise, nations too forget — very quickly, alas — their climb from small beginnings to the heights of a great power, and all the blood they shed on the road of imperial aggrandisement. But history will not forget, and no human tear is shed in vain. In the long run, evil recoils on the head of its perpetrators.

Remember, Moses called out, to refresh the minds of the people, as they stood at the edge of the Holy Land, remember the murmurings and the rebellions. Remember ויבכו העם בלילה ההוא,[2] that night when the spies returned after exploring the Holy Land, with a report that demoralised the people. Remember how the people shed unnecessary tears. אותו הלילה ליל תשעה באב היה, that night, say the Rabbis, happened to be the ninth of Av — אמר להם הקב"ה אתם בכיתם בכיה של חנם ואני קובע לכם בכיה לדורות.[3] The Holy One Blessed Be He said, "You have wept without cause; the time will come when later generations will weep with good cause." History leaves nothing unaccounted for. No individual, no family, no nation can survive, if on their forward march they have shed innocent blood or unnecessary tears. If you cry for nothing, the time must come when you cry for something.

Despotic nations and wicked men must learn the lesson of history; but we, too, must remember the greatest lesson of our *galus*: that if we cry for nothing, the day must come when we shall cry for

---

2. במדבר י"ד, א'.

3. תענית כ"ט ע"א.

something. So many become low-spirited when confronted with problems. All their senses become occupied by passing clouds, while great Jewish issues are allowed to go by the board. This one cries about business, this one cries about the heavy demands that are made upon his generosity, and this one cries about his heavy workload. Beware that a בכיה של חנם may not become a בכיה לדורות! All tears must be put aside in a great surge forward to ארץ ישראל.

Tisha B'Av must not only renew our hope, but invigorate us with renewed energy to make greater sacrifices for *Eretz Yisrael*, for the rebuilding of the land, for the return of our people to the land of their fathers and for the reconstruction of Torah institutions. Tisha B'Av will then kindle a new light across the horizon of this darkened world, for the redemption of threatened Jewries and the peace of mankind.

VA-ESCHANAN

ואתחנן

i

Man on the Moon[1]

So many things have happened to the Jew and to the world! For us, for Israel, the last few years have been phenomenal, and the enormity of the scientific achievement these last few days is incredible and indescribable.

But did the Six Day War change things for us? Has the moon changed the face of the earth? Is our faith now stronger or weaker? Have these things made any difference to us? Can we still talk from the pulpit about *tallis* and *tefillin*, about Shabbos and *kedushah*, about *kashrus* and *taharah*? Some say our voices are not being heard. There is a strange feeling about, and it seems even to be stimulated by our leadership. It is because we refuse to come to grips with the real problems that beset us. We are preoccupied with remote political and economic issues. We seem to have stepped off our own little world, and we are walking about in space like the men on the moon — no gravity, no anchorage. We ask why, what has gone wrong? We don't know the answers. That is probably why

1 Delivered at the Hendon Synagogue, 1969.

there is a constant careless attitude wherever you turn: a flaunting of authority, a devaluation of cherished values, a rejection of standards. It is because we are directed to look over there, not over here, up there and not down here, for the solution to our problems.

In the *Sidrah* we read of another ascent into the heavens. Thinking men have attempted to explain it: something which was seen by six hundred thousand men over the age of twenty, and has never been denied. אנכי עמד בין ה' וביניכם בעת ההוא, "I stood between the Lord and you at that time." Moses the Law-giver stood between Heaven and earth; his Torah is the living link between them. There is no conflict between science and religion. On the contrary, they are supplementary. Read the *Haftorah* of *Nachamu* and see what the prophet Isaiah said about the heavenly constellations as he stood on earth and looked up above. The fundamental principle of the Unity of God, שמע ישראל ה' אלקינו ה' אחד, "Hear O Israel, the Lord our God, the Lord is One," proclaimed by Moses when he came down from Sinai, is Israel's first and greatest contribution to civilisation. Unity of space, of time, of man and of God: the heavens are within reach of the earth, the earth is within reach of heaven: ואתם הדבקים בה' אלקיכם חיים כלכם היום. The greatest unity of all, the greatest harmony, the greatest oneness, is Heaven and earth combined in one, man and God together. When we cleave to Him we are linked with eternity; we never die. This was the great discovery made on that first ascent Heavenwards.

Like the astronauts, Moses too brought down stones: ויכתבם על שני לוחות אבנים, the two tablets upon which the Ten Commandments were written. Would it not have been more impressive to bring down samples of stone from above? Torah written on chunks of sky, pieces of moon-rock, of angels' wings? What an impression that would have made on the Jew and the world! But God wrote the Torah on earthly stones. The Jewish ideal is to bring earth up to Heaven, not to bring Heaven down to earth. We want to turn men into angels, not angels into men. ‏וראו כל בשר יחדו כי פי ה' דבר‎, "so that all flesh will see together that the mouth of the Lord has spoken" — in these words of the *Haftorah*, Isaiah reiterates the message of Moses, the father of the prophets, in our *Sidrah*: God in the life of men, and God on earth.

There is a beautiful Midrash regarding the origins of the two tablets of the Ten Commandments. One tablet, it is said, was the stone upon which Jacob rested his head when he fled from his brother Esau. He gathered stones round about him, and when they vied with one another for the honour of being Jacob's pillow they were miraculously welded into one. That unified stone was one of the two upon which the Torah was written. The other stone was the one upon which Moses sat with hands held high as Amalek waged war against Israel. These two tablets of stone Moses took up with him to be engraved with the Ten Commandments.

One represented the conflict from within: ‏עלי יניח צדיק את ראשו‎,[2] each one wanted Jacob's head; all kinds of Judaism, left, right and centre; all kinds of education, Sephardi and Ashkenazi, modern and ancient. All kinds of marriage, all kinds of *kashrus*; conflicts and splinter groups. Upon the stone that was turned into one, Moses wrote the Torah. With more Torah, more Shabbos, more *kashrus*, more learning, more *kedushah*, the stone becomes Heaven, the home becomes a paradise, and children become angels.

The other tablet of stone represented the fight with Amalek. Judaism does not mean that Israel is to close itself up in an ivory tower with no technological development or scientific advance. Israel must go forward, fighting its battles; but on the stone must be written the Torah. Here lies the greatness of Torah: ‏כי הוא חכמתכם‎

2. ‏חולק צ"א ע"ב‎.

ובינתכם לעיני העמים, "it is your wisdom and your understanding in the sight of the nations, who, when they shall hear all these statutes, shall say, 'Surely this great nation is a wise and understanding people.'"

In the technological age in which we live, when men scale the heights and plumb the depths, exercising an influence on our children, the *Sidrah* calls out, פן תשכח את הדברים אשר ראו עיניך . . . והודעתם לבניך ולבני בניך, "lest you forget the things which *your eyes* saw . . . make them known to your children and your children's children." Make known to them that *your* greatness supersedes all man's might on earth. Then וכל בני בשר יקראו בשמך להפנות אליך כל רשעי ארץ, all abomination will be removed from the earth, לתקן עולם במלכות שדי, and the world will be perfected under the Kingdom of the Almighty to the end of time.

ii

Born Civilised

A well-known Rabbi once wrote to the famous author, George Bernard Shaw, that he believed that in one of his plays Mr. Shaw had said, "the Jew is born civilised." Could he please tell the Rabbi in which play this passage was to be found? Shaw replied that he could not lay his finger on the passage, and in fact he could not remember the occasion on which he gave utterance to that notable saying. But, Shaw continued, "Let me assure you, dear Rabbi, that if I did not say it, I ought to have said it."

It is undeniably true: the Jew is born civilised. I wonder what it is. The Jew also seems to be possessed of a sense of destiny which he has passed on to successive generations. I wonder what it is and where he got it from, buffeted as he has been between the heavy seas, suffering reverses and misfortunes. Yet his sense of destiny has never waned. He seems to be in possession of a tremendous reserve that can never be exhausted. The very destruction of the Temple that we commemorate on Tisha B'Av immediately gave birth to *Shabbos Nachamu*. Sorrow and perils stimulated a new and vivid consciousness of Jewish solidarity. That *Mashiach* is born on Tisha B'Av is perhaps the most striking Rabbinic comment about these days. It sustained and it nourished, it inspired and it encouraged that sense of Jewish destiny. It was the greatest factor in our survival, proclaiming, and thereby ensuring, that salvation would spring from sorrow and reconstruction out of destruction. We have seen it in our own day. The rivers of blood in Auschwitz have been transformed to streams of living water in Haifa and Tel Aviv. Is not that a kind of *Mashiach* born out of Tisha B'Av?

When a mourner is ushered into the synagogue on Friday evening, we greet him with the traditional formula associated with those who mourn for Zion and Jerusalem. We express the hope that as *Nachamu* follows *Chazon* in our national life, so will comfort follow sorrow in our individual life. It is a profound testimony that in Judaism, joy and grief, Zion destroyed and Zion rebuilt, is our common destiny. That is why we use the expression המקום ינחם, which literally does not mean Almighty but Omnipresent: He Who is everywhere, wherever a Jewish heart beats and wherever it has ceased to beat. In this infinite unity of God, space, time and numbers have no meaning. It can be sorrow yesterday and joy today; each has its purpose. More than anything in life, it is our common attitude towards things and our common consciousness that shape the common destiny.

In Jewish life, strange though it may seem, it has not always been the observant Jew whose future generations have been retained to the faith or to their people. One wonders sometimes, 'Where are the children and grandchildren of those pious and saintly men we possessed?' To take religion for granted is a dangerous thing. It can become a kind of outward garb that can be discarded to suit the fashion of the hour unless it is a life-pulsating force. When our ancient teachers asked, Why are not the children of the scholars always learned in the law, their answer was שלא ברכו בתורה תחלה,[1] "Because these scholars rose in the morning to learn without making the *berachah* on the Torah."

There is more here than what the simple translation implies. A *berachah*, too, can become a mechanical, meaningless act. Even an observant Jew must have an attitude, for once religion becomes mechanical it becomes dangerous. What we require more than anything else is an attitude, a Jewish attitude. That was the approach of the prophet in the *Haftorah* of Tisha B'Av. Religion in his day was relegated to the Temple — empty formalism — whilst day-to-day things went on their own way. Wealth without an attitude, misspent — give where you should not give, do not give where you should give. Wisdom misguided — lecture where you should not lecture, and imbibe knowledge from those to whom you should refuse to listen. Strength misused — you fight with those with whom you should have no quarrel, and refuse to raise a voice against those with whom you should quarrel. אל יתהלל חכם בחכמתו ואל יתהלל הגבור בגבורתו אל יתהלל עשיר בעשרו,[2] "Let not the wise man glory in his wisdom, neither let the mighty man glory in his might, nor the rich man glory in his riches." We cannot believe that Jeremiah belittles these blessings; life would become extinct without these gifts; but he continues, כי אם בזאת יתהלל המתהלל השכל וידע אותי, with these blessings there must be

---

1. נדה פ"א ע"א.

2. ירמיה ט', כ"ב.

שכל and awareness of God. Given Divine intent and Divine content, everything in Jewish life becomes an act of worship.

The thing that made the Jew born civilised was his attitude to life. God was in his wisdom, and God was in his strength, and God was in his riches. The judge on his bench and the carpenter at his bench: neither was superior. The Rabbi who speaks the truth, the judge who acts impartially, the tailor who does not deceive, the shopkeeper possessed of integrity — בזאת, in whatever you occupy yourself, השכל וידע אותי, have שכל and know Me. It was not always the leaders of the community that gave birth to leaders; it was often the rank and file, who shared this common Jewish destiny. The mother over her kitchen table and the father over his counter, the simple folk whose attitude towards life was to create a God-consciousness. לא מרבכם מכל העמים — You were chosen as God's people, Moses proclaims in this *Sidrah*, "not because you were greater in numbers"; on the contrary, כי אתם המעט מכל העמים, "ye are the fewest, the smallest in numbers." The Rabbis in a beautiful comment say: — כי אתם המעט המממעטין עצמכם,[3] "You are the ones who hold yourselves small." Abraham said אנכי עפר ואפר, "I am dust and ashes"; Moses and Aaron said ונחנו מה, "What are we?" All the riches and wisdom and strength in the world are but transitory things, passing fancies. Without an attitude they mean nothing, and we leave nothing.

The greatness of the Jew is not in what he possesses, but in what he is: כי מאהבת ה' אתכם. It is that partnership with God that makes the Jew born civilised. Great men rise from obscurity, just as gold is extracted from the earth and not from the skies, and just as trees grow from the soil, not from the heavens. It is the humble, everyday life in which God finds a place that shapes Jewish destiny. From the murky soil of *Chazon* will spring forth *Nachamu*, and that tiny

3. רש"י; חולין פ"ט ע"א.

struggling state will become a glory to mankind. This tiny little
nation will rise high, if we remain civilised and share the destiny of
one God, one faith, one people and one land.

iii

Do What You Can

The *Sidrah* begins with a prayer that Moses offers up to God
when the time comes for Israel to take possession of the Holy Land.
The burden of leadership has now fallen to Joshua, and Moses
realises that it will not be his good fortune to lead the people to
whom he had been so faithful into the land of promise. He pleads
to be allowed to cross the Jordan only to see the land, its mountains,
its scenery, its landscape and its beauty. But his prayer is rejected,
and here he now stands on the east side of the Jordan, making his
farewell broadcast before his departure. He recapitulates all the
happenings in the wilderness and exhorts the people to be mindful
of their duties to God and to man.

It would seem that his task had now come to an end, but he
suddenly interrupts his farewell speech by fulfilling one more duty
which seemed to have no connection with his preceding or
subsequent remarks. אז יבדיל משה שלש ערים בעבר הירדן, "Then Moses
separated three cities beyond the Jordan, towards the rising of the
sun." Altogether six cities were set aside as ערי מקלט, cities of refuge:
three west of the Jordan, in Palestine proper, and three east of the
Jordan. These were to serve as a refuge to a murderer whose deed
was not premeditated. It was to these cities that the manslayer was
entitled to escape, there to find a sanctuary from the vengeance of
the victim's relatives, who naturally would pursue him to the ends

of the earth. Why did Moses do this before he died? אַף עַל פִּי שֶׁאֵינָן קוֹלְטוֹת עַד שֶׁיִבְדְלוּ אוֹתָן שֶׁבָּאָרֶץ כְּנַעַן אָמַר מֹשֶׁה מִצְוָה שֶׁאֶפְשָׁר לְקַיְּימָה אֲקַיְּימֶנָה,[1] "although they did not become effective until those in Canaan had been designated, Moses said, 'Any mitzvah that it is possible for me to perform, I must perform.'"

There is a vital and profound lesson in this, Moses' last assignment. It is true that for the time being this mitzvah — the selection of cities as places of refuge — had no significance. He knew they could not yet be used. But his duty was to do what he could, and leave the rest to history: לֹא עָלֶיךָ הַמְּלָאכָה לִגְמוֹר וְלֹא אַתָּה בֶן חוֹרִין לִיבָטֵל מִמֶּנָה,[2] "It is not thy duty to complete the work, neither art thou free to desist from it."

To refrain from doing a mitzvah because we cannot complete it is not a Jewish way of thinking. We do what we can, and leave the rest to God. Those of our friends with commercial enterprises will, I am sure, go in search of smaller dividends if larger dividends are unobtainable. To say 'either all or nothing' is a fallacy that gets us nowhere. הִשָּׁמֶר לְךָ וּשְׁמֹר נַפְשְׁךָ מְאֹד, "take heed of yourself and take heed of your soul," is man's twofold responsibility. That amount of service and that amount of care that one spends on oneself, on לְךָ, must equally be spent on נַפְשְׁךָ, on one's soul. The same attitude we adopt in our business undertakings must be adopted in our spiritual undertakings. No one would be stupid enough to refuse to take one hour's business in the morning and enjoy the little profit he can make; and no one can afford, in religious life, to refuse to do the little he can because he cannot do the whole. Such a state of affairs would lead to spiritual bankruptcy and losses that would never be retrieved.

1. רַשִׁ"י; מַכּוֹת י' ע"א.

2. אָבוֹת ב', מ"ז.

A saintly Rabbi was once asked by a religiously inclined traveller to advise him what to do because there were some days in the week when his travels made it impossible for him to carry out all his religious functions. הִשָּׁמֶר לְךָ וּשְׁמֹר נַפְשֶׁךָ, the Rabbi said; "do as much for your soul as you would do for your body." Make it a fifty-fifty arrangement: your busy time for yourself and your free time for God, and you will have done your duty. אל תרחק עצמך ממדה שאין לה קצבה וממלאכה שאין לה גמירה,[3] "Do not depart from something which has no limit and from work which has no end." Our duty is to try and to leave it to God to judge the sincerity of our actions. One should always say מצוה שאפשר לקיימה אקיימנה. To give nothing to charity because one cannot give much, never to *daven* because one cannot *daven* always, to spend no time in *shul* because we cannot attend always, for a כהן to refuse to דוכן because the rest of the year he does things he should not do, to serve on no committee because one cannot give up all his time — this attitude to religious duties and communal functions would bring about a complete disintegration of traditional Judaism. The other elements who say "do what you like" would thrive, indeed as they do on the negation of Jewish values in our life and in our homes.

The faith of our fathers demands that we honour and respect our religious duties, and if for some reason or other we fail in some respect, in other respects our loyalty should not be questioned. To do otherwise would be to expose ourselves to a grave danger. For we live our Jewish life on our parents' capital. We remember the customs and the traditions we saw practised and observed in the rich spiritual life of the homes in which we were reared. So far as we are concerned, the failure to observe this mitzvah or that is not so serious. At least we know they exist. But our children face life

3. אבות דר' נתן כ"ז, ג'.

with no equipment or experience. If our own stock is low, if we fail to give them the little we can show in practical life, the whole religious structure will collapse in the next generation. What a profound effect it has on our children when they see Daddy doing the things he can do! But give them nothing and they will know nothing. It is their knowledge that these things exist that gives us hope that one day in the future they may return to our original glory.

We won back our national heritage, and we celebrate *Shabbos Nachamu* because for two thousand years we commemorated it with *Shabbos Chazon.* It is חזון that gave birth to נחמו. That Palestine existed and we mourned its loss brought us to this period of hope and comfort. Remember, its light was never extinguished from Jewish prayer and Jewish yearning. If the light of Jewish practice and Jewish observance, if only a spark of it is kept alight, there will be hope for the children. But do away with them because you cannot observe them all, discard the lot because you cannot observe a little, then the glory of Jewish tradition and the beauty of Jewish faith will come to an end. Keep the light aglow! Let us do what we can when we can, and then, we hope, there will one day be a return to Jewish values and a complete resuscitation of Jewish ideals.

iv

The Shema

The *Shema* is the first prayer of the innocent child and the last utterance of the dying Jew; its hold on the Jewish people is beyond any verbal description. On one occasion, as chaplain to a number of prisons, it was my unpleasant duty to attend the execution of a Jew on the gallows. Difficult as I found it to get him, practically the whole night before his doom, to utter a single Hebrew word, yet seconds before the final drop he shouted out שְׁמַע יִשְׂרָאֵל. A great preacher once said, "It is strange how those few words have clothed the Jew with invincible, lion's strength. We stood up to the most terrible tortures."

We hear lectures and we read papers on the hackneyed subject, 'the Jewish contribution to civilisation.' So much energy, money and paper have been devoted, in recent years particularly, to showing the world the extent of our contribution to every human effort. We tell of our great war heroes, our great scientists and our great communal men; but there is never a distinction drawn between the Jewish contribution and the contribution by Jews.

It is difficult to understand what the word Jewish means when put in front of a word. We speak of Jewish art, Jewish music or Jewish culture — for that matter, we might as well talk of Jewish science, Jewish medicine or Jewish psychology, since famous Jews have influenced the whole course of human thought in those spheres. We have been guilty, right through our history, of diverting the attention of the world, and of our own people particularly, from our specifically Jewish contributions. No one would dare belittle the great part our people have played in all branches of progress, and there is every reason to be proud of belonging to such a people, whose genius has left such an impress on the progress of life. But we have not done it as Jews, and as Jews we had nothing out of it; we left it all behind.

We have no right to sap from the minds of our children the pride they must feel in the contributions Jews made as Jews — the Jewish contribution to civilisation that has laid the foundation of the world. What would the world have looked like, with all its scientific genius, had paganism, polytheism, pantheism, and dualism not been challenged by the Jewish people, with its proclamation of שְׁמַע יִשְׂרָאֵל

ה׳ אלקינו ה׳ אחד? The barbarisms of our own age would have been child's play had not the prophet's words struck deep into the hearts of men: הלוא אב אחד לכלנו,[1] "have we not all one Father?"

The only fight we ever took up was against those evil powers that preached and practised idol-worship of one kind or another. For ה׳ אחד we gave up all. It was practised by Abraham, it was brought to a glorious climax at the *Akeidah* by Isaac and it was uttered for the first time by Jacob. For countless generations it was the watchword for the myriads of martyrs who agonised and died for the unity of God. אשר בחר בנו מכל העמים— that we are the Chosen People is a fact that we shall never surrender, because whatever the world possesses in the field of religion, which is the only restraining influence on man's bestiality, it all comes from us. The nations talk of one who died for the salvation of the world; we have got millions who died for that cause, because not one man but every one of us is part of that great unity.

The *Kaddish* stresses the unity of the dead with the living, the oneness of the human spirit in life and in death. שמע ישראל stresses the unity of that spirit with God, which means that there is no beginning and there is no end. As a great scientist said: "Every fresh discovery confirms the fact that in all nature's infinite variety there is one single principal at work, one controlling power." It is astonishing, but the Patriarch knew it before the splitting of the atom was even dreamed of. He knew it when he took his axe to break down his father's idols, and when he took his knife to surrender his only son to the will of that great Unity. He realised that the fulfilment of the Divine Will in death is of as much value as life itself; we know so little about both. Would brother ever compete with brother, and would man ever raise a sword against

מלאכי ב׳, י׳. 1

fellow man, if that unity were felt and the love of God came before the love of self?

A well-known *Maggid* said that he once wanted to define the word love, the meaning of ואהבת את ה' אלקיך, "and thou shalt love the Lord thy God." So he went to the market-place, and there he heard someone say, "I love fish." The *Maggid* followed him. Here, he thought, I will find out what love means. He saw the person select a choice fish; he took it home, cut its head off, scraped off its scales, tore out its bowels, and cooked it and ate it. "Did you say you loved fish?" he asked the man. "You love yourself." Love means something that transcends nature. בכל לבבך, "with all thine heart," means בשני יצריך,[2] to subject earthly passions and personal ambitions to God's will and thus make them instruments of his Divine service.

The first paragraph of the *Shema* is known as the keynote of Judaism: קבלת עול מלכות שמים, bending our neck, as it were, to the yoke of the Kingdom of Heaven. It includes the *mezuzah* which implies the house, it includes the *tefillin* which imply the limbs of man, it includes transmission of the Torah to children, which implies the surrender of the child to the will of God. ובלכתך בדרך ובשכבך ובקומך — it includes the whole of life: when you walk, when you lie down and when you rise up. In short, a human being who is one with his Maker and one with his fellow men.

Can you imagine what a wonderful place this world would be to live in, if that first paragraph of the *Shema* became the keynote not only of Judaism but of human life? That is the Jewish contribution to civilisation; that is why so many die with those words on their lips — because without them living is not worthwhile. What does it mean, another slice of bread with a slab of butter, for what purpose? To leave nothing behind but squabbles and conflict over

2. ברכות נ"ד ע"א.

who will take what? To die out of unity with God is to be cut off in death as one was cut off in life. There is nothing in it unless we believe in that unity in our lives, unless we believe that we go back to that unity when it is all over. That is why the *Shema* became the last solemn utterance of the dying Jew. That is why Rabbi Akiva prayed that he might be granted the opportunity of dying a martyr's death for God's sake. It is not philosophy and it is not religion; it is logic.

How proud the Jew should feel, and how much of this pride should be instilled in his children, that it was the Jew who brought meaning to life and glory to death! It needs courage for a small group of people — this handful of Jews in a world of mighty nations — to defy the belief of countless millions and to proclaim אחד when the others say there are more, gaining nothing from our belief but martyrdom and suffering. With nothing in our place of worship but scrolls of Law in the Ark, we throw out an open challenge that each and every one has access to God — more even than that, that everyone is actually united with Him. This is our contribution, this is our glory, and in this we must take pride.

The great disaster of the Golden Calf that overwhelmed our people was due to one thing, that they assumed a superhuman belief in Moses and imagined him to be a kind of God incarnate. The moment he turned his back they lost faith and ran amok. Hence the message of שמע ישראל ה' אלקינו ה' אחד is, it is not only Moses, but you and you, each and every one can reach the peak of Sinai. God's back is never turned. There is a unity between Him and mankind, but practise that unity also between yourselves. Let that unity bring about a ואהבת, an unselfish love, a bending of passion and nature to His Divine Will. Then, and then only, will His love towards mankind manifest itself in a world of true peace.

v

Today

(Bar Mitzvah)

Everyone knows that a boy of thirteen is only a boy, after all, and he cannot assume all the responsibilities of a man. But we are told to start our Jewish adulthood at Bar Mitzvah age, so that when we grow up we may reap the benefits of our early years. This message is reflected in the last verse of the *Maftir* portion of this *Sidrah*: ושמרת את המצוה ואת החקים ואת המשפטים אשר אנכי מצוך היום לעשותם. "You shall keep *the mitzvah*" — that means, of course, the בר מצוה; otherwise the Torah would say מצות, commandments, in the plural. *The mitzvah*, in the singular, refers to the duties and the observances that become incumbent on one particular day — היום, this day, the day when you start doing them. היום לעשותם ולמחר לקבל שכרם,[1] do them today so that when tomorrow comes you will receive the reward. If you do not start a thing today, the morrow never comes; but if you start it today, tomorrow you enjoy the benefit. When we look around and see young men who take an interest in their studies, in the synagogue, in the life of Israel, they are those who started with היום. But those who have grown up and forgotten even how to make a *berachah* over the Torah, who come into synagogue like strangers — they are those who never started. There was no היום, so there can be no מחר.

There is a story told of a soldier who during the War was given the task of crossing over into the enemy lines. He was warned by his commanding officer to kill every bloodhound he came across on

1. עירובין כ״ב ע״א.

his way. He saw a little dog, he picked it up, and was going to get rid of it when he heard a voice shouting, "That is not a bloodhound!"

"Ah," he said, "but I must remove it anyway, because who knows what it will turn out to be if I leave it behind?" No one in the world knows what a בר מצוה will turn out to be, but of one thing we can be sure: if he starts well, if he starts his post-Bar Mitzvah Hebrew studies, if he starts the day with *tallis* and *tefillin*, if he starts the week with Shabbos, if he starts showing respect for his parents and teachers, then there is every hope that he will grow up to be a good man and a good Jew. היום לעשותם, to do them today, means למחר לקבל שכרם, to take the reward tomorrow. It is the start that counts — היום, this day.

In Hebrew literature and in Rabbinic writing we usually find the words לקבל שכר used, not ליטול שכר. לקבל means to receive reward, whilst ליטול means to take reward. You only receive what others give, but to take means that it is always there to take. A good boy never waits לקבל שכר, to receive reward. He never waits for people to give him honour, he just takes. Wherever he goes there is distinction waiting for him; with whomsoever he mixes he stands out as above the ordinary. To be a real and true Bar Mitzvah it must be היום, today. Then when the morrow comes the Bar Mitzvah of today will be a man, worthy ליטול שכר, and a credit to the whole of our people.

vi

A Highway to God

(Bar Mitzvah)

Isaiah, in the *Haftorah* of *Nachamu*, gives a Divine message of comfort and a promise of restoration to Israel in exile. He calls for it to be more than a physical return: קול קורא במדבר פנו דרך ה' ישרו בערבה מסלה לאלקינו, in the great wilderness of your lives clear a way for God to come down. Where there is no learning — learn; where there is no practice — practise; where there is no faith — have faith. ישרו בערבה, make a straight, honest, upright life that alone will create מסלה לאלקינו, a highway to God.

If we wanted to say in three words what Bar Mitzvah means we could not do better than quote those three wonderful words of the *Haftorah*: פנו דרך ה'. It means, "Clear the way for God." There is a way, a path in every man's life. It can be full of rubble and dirt, with no room on it for God. Getting up in the morning without a prayer on one's lips — from bed to breakfast; off to school and lunch, no word of God on one's lips; from lunch to the sports-ground, no word of Hebrew study. Home for dinner and homework and then games or television; day after day, night after night. At home and in the street, all over, wherever he goes, nothing Jewish, no Shabbos, no Yom Tov, no Hebrew book — a way of life that is full of triviality and nonsense. That is turning Bar Mitzvah into a big joke.

פנו דרך ה'; make room for God! the prophet cries. ישרו בערבה, straighten things out. Take your pleasure and fun by all means, but make time for God, too. *Tefillin* in the morning; a few words of Grace when you eat; prayer before going to bed. A little study in the afternoon; respect for your parents; Shabbos once a week — מסלה

לאלקינו, we create a highway to God, ונגלה כבוד ה', the glory of God is revealed, וראו כל בשר כי פי ה' דבר, and everybody can see there is something different about this boy.

There is a very interesting expression in the *Maftir* of this *Sidrah*. Twice the words אל פניו are repeated: ומשלם לשנאיו אל פניו, God pays him who dislikes Him to his face, לא יאחר לשנאו אל פניו ישלם לו. The Torah seems to imply that you can recognise a good, loyal, faithful Jew by his face. The student, the *talmid chacham*, the type who keeps the *mitzvos* — of them people say, "See, the *Shechinah* is on his face." The one who knows no synagogue, no prayers, no charity, and no study loses his Jewish characteristics. He loses his Jewish face and appearance: ומשלם לשנאיו אל פניו להאבידו. That is what the prophet means in the *Haftorah*: ונגלה כבוד ה', God will reveal Himself. God's glory will be revealed in us if we are honest, faithful and loyal Jews.

vii

Lift up Your Eyes

(Bar Mitzvah)

Bar Mitzvah does not mean that parents no longer bear a responsibility to their child. Their responsibility remains, but it means that a boy's own responsibility has begun too. Every child is born of three partners: his father, his mother, and God. God gives, and they provide, and becoming Bar Mitzvah demands nothing else of a boy but to remember that partnership. If all Jewish boys went through life with that partnership in mind we would have a perfect community; neither God nor parents would have any cause for complaints. But, as in so many partnerships that do not last long, one buys out the other: the Bar Mitzvah boy sells out the Almighty. His Hebrew books, his *tefillin*, his synagogue attendances, sometimes even his respect for his parents — all go by the board. Then what happens — he grows up, and Hebrew, the language of Israel, of our prayers, of our Bible and great literature, is strange to him. Amongst his own people he is like a stranger.

The way to avoid this tragic betrayal is to think of the last verse of the *Haftorah* of *Nachamu*. The prophet bids his people שאו מרום עיניכם וראו מי ברא אלה, "Lift up your eyes on high and see who hath created these." Isaiah could find only one hope for the Jewish people, who even when in their own land were surrounded by enemies. They lost faith and thought the world was coming to an end for them. God calls to Isaiah נחמו, "Comfort them." With what words does he comfort them? He says, "lift up your eyes," look up to the skies; you will see the sun, the moon and the stars. Everything is working according to a plan. לכלם בשם יקרא, everything in Creation has a name and a purpose. Who did it all? God! Who else could have made this wonderful world? If God has given all these creations a purpose, surely He gave a purpose to man and to the Jew.

The human being is the only creature who walks about with his head turned upwards. All other creatures turn their eyes downwards, their face to the ground. If they want to look up to the skies they have to turn their head upside down. The prophet says, 'All you have to do is שאו מרום עיניכם — lift your eyes up, and you will acknowledge God.' The man who never lifts up his eyes to Heaven, who always keeps them down, is like an animal. When we open our eyes in the morning, just lift them up and think of God with a prayer. That will help us to think of our parents and our people, our duties and our loyalties. To go through life selfishly, without learning something about our past, the struggles and the victories of our people, is an awful thought.

Keep your head high and be proud that you are a Jew. Never forget your God and your people. איש לא נעדר — every Bar Mitzvah who does that will never fail.

viii

The Fifteenth of Av

נחמו נחמו עמי, "Comfort ye, comfort ye my people." The prophetic message of Isaiah beginning with these momentous words has sustained and fortified the Jew during centuries of ordeal and persecution. We felt assured that no death will have been in vain and no tear will have been shed for nothing. הנה שכרו אתו, "behold, his reward is with him"; it will come. ופעלתו לפניו, "and his recompense before him"; that will come, too.

Shabbos Nachamu comes always in close proximity to another significant day in the Jewish calendar, the Fifteenth of Av. They have something in common: they both stand in marked contrast to the mood of the earlier days of the month of Av. The Mishnah[1] tells us, לא היו ימים טובים לישראל כחמשה עשר באב וכיום הכפורים, "There were never happier days than the Fifteenth of Av and Yom Kippur." On the Fifteenth of Av the *bnos Yisrael*, dressed in white, would go out among the vineyards and dance. Those blessed with beauty would say, "Young men, turn your eyes to beauty." The מיוחסות, those blessed with יחוס, family pride, would say, "Turn your eyes למשפחה, to noble family." Those blessed with neither יופי nor משפחה would say, שקר החן והבל היופי אשה יראת ה' היא תתהלל, "Neither beauty nor family be your choice, but let the God-fearing

we lead. If millions died for this, it is surely because life is not worthwhile without it. An American psychologist once said: "There is mighty little difference between one man and another, but what little difference there is, is mighty important." There is that little difference that makes all the difference in civilisation.

It has been said again and again, and we must never tire of repeating it, that Judaism is a religious civilisation with its own language, its own literature, its own history, its own customs and its own institutions. It has resisted all forms of suppression and changed the course of history, and no one can change a course and make others follow unless he is in the fore. The time has come when we must realise that education and culture, seminars and colleges, Zion and faith, have no place in this procession of civilisation unless they are deeply-rooted in the concepts and precepts, in the tenets and observances of historic Judaism; in the ideals and proclamations of the seers and the Prophets, the teachers and the Rabbis, the students and the scholars, from whom this civilisation emerged.

This religious civilisation of ours is not the concern of Rabbis and teachers alone; it is the concern of each and every individual and group. The *Sidrah* of *Ekev* concludes with a mighty promise for Israel's success as it is about to enter the Promised Land, but it begins with the premise כי אם שמר תשמרון את כל המצוה הזאת, "for if you shall diligently keep all this commandment. . . ." This prompted the Rabbinic comment: הרבה שמורים כתיב כאן, "the word שמר, 'keep,' is repeated many times in this *Sidrah*." Why? שמא תאמר יש בנו זקנים יש בנו גדולים יש בנו נביאים תלמוד לומר כי אם שמר תשמרון שהכל שוין בתורה,[1] "Lest you should say, 'There are elders among us, there are great men among us, there are prophets among us; so what need is there for us to keep?' שמר תשמרון, says the Torah; no! You must keep it, too, שהכל שוין

1. ילקוט שמעוני עקב סימן תתע״ג.

בתורה, because in this Torah of ours, in this civilisation of ours, everyone is equal."

It is a tragic fallacy in Jewish life to departmentalise our Jewish duties, as if they were like a big store where there is a department for garments, a department for provisions, one for men's wear and another for ladies' wear. יש בנו זקנים, we have got old people — let them *daven* and keep Shabbos. יש בנו גדולים, we have great scholars — let them learn. יש בנו נביאים, we have prophets — let them reproach. A new expression was coined during the last War, "combined operations": the Navy, the Army, the Air Force hitting at one target, unification of effort. It was the secret of success. The secret of Jewish success is combined operations: laymen and Rabbis, teachers and parents — הכל שוין בתורה. It will be a sad day in the life of our community when one body deals with prayer and another with culture, one with Zion and another with education — divided operations that separate the sacred from the secular. We are not dealing with cashbooks in which figures are divided into various columns. We are dealing with religious civilisation, and everything is part of that civilisation. It is a combined operation.

The *Sidrah* begins with a seeming grammatical inconsistency. First it is phrased in the plural, addressing the congregation as a whole; but the same verse concludes in the singular. והיה עקב תשמעון את המשפטים האלה ושמרתם ועשיתם אתם, "And it shall come to pass because you hearken to these ordinances, and keep and do them" — that is in the plural. ושמר ה' אלקיך לך את הברית ואת החסד, "and the Lord thy God shall keep with thee the covenant and the mercy which he swore unto thy fathers" — that is in the singular. The safeguarding of those values, the observance of those duties, are communal matters: mass responsibilities. No one individual, group or body has a greater claim than any other. They cannot be dissected like figures in a ledger; it is a combined operation. But as a result of that united effort, by marching as a people in the procession of civilisation — when the larger look after the small, the rich after the poor, the wise after the ignorant, when הכל שוין בתורה, everyone plays his part — then ושמר ה' אלקיך לך, the fruits of that service, the benefits of that universal application, are enjoyed by each individual. Life becomes worthwhile.

There is a profound truth in that seemingly confused Biblical verse. It is the community that influences the individual, and not the individual who influences the community. For countless centuries the synagogue, the בית הכנסת, and the בית המדרש, have been the home and the cohesive force of the masses of our people. Here religion must vibrate and from here it must spread. The synagogue and its associate bodies must be the centre of all Jewish activities. The synagogue is the only security for our religious survival, and it must be given all our devotion and support.

Years ago Gladstone wrote: "The great triumph of our day, a triumph in a region loftier than that of electricity or steam, will be the enthronement of the idea of public right as the governing ideal of the European policy." For that ideal millions imperilled their lives.

The great triumph of our time will be in a region loftier than that of the comet and the atom. It will be the spread of a mass Jewish civilisation, with Jews preaching, learning and practising the glories of a wonderful faith that has outlived every other ideology and given birth to the finest ideals of mankind. Thus we will lead the whole world in a glorious procession to a sane order and righteous thinking.

iv

The Message of Religion

During the last War a great statesman once said, "There are three sorts of people: there are those who will, those who won't, and those who can't. The first effect everything, the second oppose everything, and the last fail in everything." In every field of human activity, it is the go-to-it man who invariably achieves success in whatever he undertakes. You will find that the man who is prepared to take a chance is usually the most successful, but the man who stops to ask why and wherefore misses opportunities.

What would the world look like today if we had not been blessed with such men, who had foresight, who had faith in themselves and faith in their cause. The submarine that plumbs the depths and the airplane that scales the heights would never have been brought into being. They might still be blueprints in the hands of those who fashioned them. Mind you, one cannot tell; the world would perhaps have been better off that way. But who is to blame if these things have been misused? What a wonderful place the world would be to live in if all this human genius had been used for construction instead of destruction! But be that as it may, the daring men with a pulsating sense of their own capacity to achieve have set the world in motion. The driving force in life, in all spheres of human endeavour, is heroism: trying to overcome the impossible. Because there is no such thing as impossible if man can see in it something he can reach and grasp with his hands. Wherever there is a will, the word "impossible" disappears.

Much has been written of the men who, in civil and national life, grasped what seemed to be the impossible and succeeded. You will find monuments dedicated to their undying names in every city in the world. Yet very little has been written or erected to commemorate those great and saintly men who, in the religious life of our people, paved the way, with sacrifice and with blood, to bring to mankind the knowledge of God and respect for His teaching. Our history teems with the names of such men, without whom the Torah, the Bible and the Prophets would have remained but a blueprint with no bearing on practical life. Oh, what a poorer place the world would have been to live in! And what would the Jew have looked like today?

Just pause for a moment and think what a spectacle the scattered Jewish communities would present today, if throughout all these years of our wanderings we had been captured by the glamour of the changing conditions under which we lived. The death warrant of Jewry would long ago have been signed and sealed. The trouble is that whenever any change is commended to us, we do not stop to think. It is attractive, and we are captured by it. No wonder קידוש השם became the watchword of Israel down the ages. Those whose lives embodied it are the silent heroes of mankind, for whom monuments of brick and mortar, that the winds of time demolish, are no fitting tribute.

The Jewish people themselves are the living monuments to these immortal men. How many were burned on the stake rather than allow one letter of the *Sefer Torah* to be erased? For centuries the Jew has striven to resist a Torah-less society and a faithless nationalism. כי תאמר בלבבך רבים הגוים האלה ממני איכה אוכל להורישם, "If you should say in your heart, 'These nations are more than I, how can I dispossess them?' לא תירא מהם, do not be afraid of them." Fear is the greatest danger, for it breaks down all resistance. כי תאמר בלבבך, "If you should say in your heart," means to be guided by the heart, by sentiment and emotions and not by conscience and history. Fear means to belong to the third category, the cannots, who fail in everything. Without courage to overcome difficulties and battle opponents, life would become monotonous: everything would seem impossible. The very birth of a child against natural walls of resistance, as it breaks through into the open, is the greatest proof that life cannot be faced with a take-what-comes attitude. It is a struggle to be born, it is a struggle to live; yes, and it is a struggle to die.

The Talmud[1] relates that the Sages once seized the יצר הרע and imprisoned him, hoping thereby to better the world. The Rabbis soon found that all was not well with the world. Ambition was dead. Right only exists where there is wrong, and good can only be where there is bad. When there is no evil and no temptation, good ceases to be an achievement. Take away the יצר הרע and ambition is dead, passions and interests come to a standstill. Man's greatest glory is freedom and will; the capacity to fight and to struggle against all odds to achieve what seems to be the impossible. That distinguishes man from the beast. It is the obstinacy of evil and suffering that produces in man the driving force for good. What satisfaction, what interest would there be in life if we met no resistance wherever we turned? What pleasure would there be in the rays of the sun if darkness never set in? When the Almighty created the light of the sun, He also created the shadow. The warmth of the sun is so pleasant and beneficial that we may be forgiven for thinking that it would be better to have uninterrupted, constant sunlight. But on reflection, with the sun must go the shadow, and with good must go evil; the great thing in life, that is man's glory, is to penetrate the shadow and get to the light! מי יתן טהור מטמא,[2] to bring out cleanliness from uncleanliness, to extract the good from the bad, to make that

1. סוטה ס״ט ע״ב.

2. איוב י״ד, ד׳.

which is impure, to say 'I will' and to make the impossible possible — that is the great message of religion.

We frequently speak about things we can do and should do, but there are times when we must be mindful of the things we think we cannot do but must try to do. In this *Sidrah* we read how Moses gives an historical survey of Israel's march through the wilderness, the great event that brought them to the land of promise. Here they were, virtually in Paradise all over again: water from stones, food from Heaven, even שמלתך לא בלתה מעליך, garments were provided for them. ורגלך לא בצקה, their feet never swelled during forty years' wandering; whatever they were short of was provided without any effort. All they had to do was to go and take it, a take-what-comes attitude. ושני לוחת הברית על שתי ידי, Moses said: even the tablets of the Covenant were not בשתי ידי, "in my hands," but על שתי ידי, "on my hands." Everything so easy; even religion, education and Divine worship, laid out on top of his hands. They just had to take it without any resistance.

But it did not last. סרתם מהר מן הדרך, "You turned aside quickly from the way which God had commanded, ואשליכם מעל שתי ידי ואשברם לעיניכם, and I cast them off from my two hands and broke them before your eyes." What a deep and profound lesson is here, particularly for us in the times in which we live. People say, "Money quickly made is quickly spent." There is little value in its achievement. But hard-earned money is hardly spent. Ambition breaks down resistance; "I will" makes the impossible possible. A religion that seems to be hard and difficult is a religion that can stand the test of time; a religion that comes the easy way holds no water.

בעת ההוא אמר ה' אלי פסל לך שני לוחת אבנים... ועשית לך ארון עץ, "At that time the Lord said to me...." בעת ההוא, "At that time," whenever it happens that men preach an easy religion, where no sacrifice and no demands are made for the observance of faith and tradition — then

פסל לך, you must take the hard way: "hew out for yourself two tablets of stone." פסל לך: "out of your own means," say the Rabbis;[3] and ועשית לך, "make for yourself an Ark" — your own effort and your own labour. Work for religion, spend on religion, guard your religion. There will be no value in its achievement unless you work for it, sacrifice for it, and spend on it. The stronger the resistance, the greater your effort, the more lasting its influence.

Moses abides by God's wish: with his own hands he hews out the stone. This time when he comes down the mountain it is no longer על שתי ידי, "on his hands"; this time it is ושני הלחת בידי: the tablets are "in his hands." Whoever wants them must break down resistance and grasp them. With will-power and determination they will be handed down from generation to generation to the end of all time.

v

The Yoke of Mitzvos

(Bar Mitzvah)

This *Sidrah* contains one of the most important portions in the entire Torah. It embodies everything in Jewish life that a Jew must know. That is why it was chosen to be read every morning and repeated every evening. It is the second paragraph of the *Shema*.

The first paragraph of the *Shema* is contained in the previous *Sidrah*. These passages are part of the last message by Moses to the People of Israel before he parts from them. A teacher cannot accompany his pupil throughout life, just as a parent cannot

ראה דברים רבה ג', י"ד: אתה שברת ואתה מחליף אותן; וברש"י שמות ל"ד, א'. 3

accompany a child through life, but there are things they say and do which we should never forget. That is why these two portions of the *Shema* bear a special name. The first paragraph is known as קבלת עול מלכות שמים, "the acceptance of the yoke of the Kingdom of Heaven." The second paragraph is known as קבלת עול מצוות, "the acceptance of the yoke of the *mitzvos*."

The Hebrew word עול, translated as "yoke," usually means something tangible and physical. It can be vegetable or mineral, or have animal connections; but it can also be abstract. A yoke is a burden on a man's neck, a yoke restricts movement. It makes one keep one's head to the front and one's eyes in the right direction. With a yoke on one's neck, one cannot easily turn where one would like to turn or do what one would like to do.

The first portion of the *Shema* is described as the yoke of God's sovereignty; it is always around the Jew. It is to make him always conscious that he is never alone, in life or in death, in joy or in sorrow. It gives hope and faith. We are reminded of this by the wonderful Jewish tradition of keeping one's head always covered. A *cappel* or a *kipah* is not a burden, but it is like a yoke over us, helping us always to realise that God is with us all the time, that we are in His care. He is always watching. If we feel that way, then we can hardly do wrong, because He is listening and watching.

It is a good thing never to do wrong; it is much better to do no wrong and to do good. So from עול מלכות שמים we come to מצוה, the yoke of the *mitzvos*.

When a boy becomes Bar Mitzvah it means one thing: that the yoke is placed on him, and from that moment he just cannot do what he likes. He is in harness, so to speak; he is surrounded on the left hand by his *tefillin*, on the right hand of the door the *mezuzah*, on his garments his *tzitzis*. In his food, *kashrus*; in his speech there must be honesty. In his daily occupation, his study or his work,

Shabbos observance. A Bar Mitzvah has the yoke of *mitzvos* on his neck; to throw off the yoke is abandoning responsibility. It removes the signs of direction, it detaches him from the People of Israel.

A Bar Mitzvah does not become a man overnight; he is still a boy. He will become a man gradually, stage by stage and year by year. It is a process of development in body and in mind. Bar Mitzvah means you have begun to become a man.

והיה אם שמע תשמעו אל מצותי; remember those immortal words. The usual English translation is, "And it shall come to pass if you shall hearken diligently unto My commandments." But that is not the literal translation; the literal translation is והיה אם שמע, "And it shall come to pass if you hearken, then תשמעו, you shall hearken." You have to begin listening. If you hear once then you must hear twice; you begin and you continue. If you don't begin, you will never continue. It is continuity that makes a man. You will begin today with Shabbos, and next week you keep Shabbos again. You begin tomorrow with your *tefillin,* and you follow on the next day with your *tefillin,* and so with everything you do as a Jew. The *mitzvos* never take a holiday. It is an עול, a yoke you have got on you all the time. That is why Bar Mitzvah can never become a dream. It is a reality, and you cannot get out of it unless you abdicate and abandon the Jewish community.

If only we will listen, God promises in the *Shema* to reward us with all the good things in life: עשיתם מה שעליכם אף אני אעשה מה שעלי,[1] "if you will do your duty I will do Mine." This is the message of the *Shema* to the Jew every day, morning and night. A Bar Mitzvah must live up to it. He must hold on to it and never abandon it; and in so doing he will become a man, a real man, bringing pleasure to parents and credit to the community.

1. רש"י מספרי דברים י"א, י"ד.

vi

Parents and Friends

(Bar Mitzvah)

והיה עקב תשמעון את המשפטים האלה. The word עקב can be translated in different ways. The English Bible version puts it very well: "And the consequence will be, if you will hearken to the laws of God, that ואהבך וברכך והרבך וברך פרי בטנך, He will love thee and bless thee and multiply thee, and He will also bless your issue, your children." Blessed children, good sons and daughters, are not a gift or a reward. In a sense they are not a blessing; it is עקב, the consequence of parents' deeds. If parents listen, children listen, and if parents practise, children practise. Of course there are mishaps sometimes, but generally speaking, והיה עקב תשמעון . . . וברך פרי בטנך. Rashi says that עקב means "a heel," a footstep, and the verse could well mean that children follow on the heel, or in the footsteps, of their parents. On many a Bar Mitzvah occasion the hope is expressed that the son should follow in the footsteps of the father; but it is not always appropriate. Sometimes, however, it is all that needs to be said: "Walk in the footpaths that have already been paved by your parents."

In this world of strife, competition and envy, with so many attractions that sometimes lure away a child from the finest home, something even more than good parents and a good home is needed to mould character and strengthen determination. It is essential, therefore, not only to remember this opening passage of the *Sidrah* but also never to forget the closing passage: כי אם שמר תשמרון את כל המצוה הזאת אשר אנכי מצוה אתכם לעשתה לאהבה את ה' אלקיכם ללכת בכל דרכיו ולדבקה בו, "for if ye shall diligently keep My commandments which I command you to do them, to love the Lord your God, to go in all His ways and to cleave to Him. . . ." The Rabbis asked אפשר לומר כן, "Is it possible to say that a man should cleave to God? He is not physical or material and fleshly; how, then, can a man cleave to Him? אלא הדבק בתלמידים ובחכמים ומעלה אני עליך כאלו נדבקת בי, it means to cleave to students, to scholars, to teachers and to wise men, and it will be as though you cleave to God."[1] A good home is a great blessing, a wonderful gift, but good friends are an even greater blessing. If you cleave to the Torah and those who teach you the Torah, if you associate with a *talmid chacham*, a pious and learned man, it is as if you would associate with God Himself.

We see boys from the finest homes who have been a bitter disappointment, children of the most wonderful parents who have broken their parents' hearts. The people with whom you associate sometimes at school or college or university, or in business or at play, have a greater influence over you than anything else in life. They can talk you into anything, to go anywhere, to eat anything, to do anything. It is like cleaving to the devil: you cannot get out of their clutches. If there are good boys whose homes are not so good, it is because their friends have been good; and if there are boys who are not so good, though they come from good homes, it is because their friends are not good.

Remember, ללכת בכל דרכיו ולדבקה בו, "to walk in the ways of God and to cleave to Him," means להדבק בתלמידים ובחכמים. If a man works in a tannery all day, he smells of leather when he comes out; if a man works in a perfume store, he smells of scent when he comes out. If you are friends with your Hebrew teacher, your Rabbi, your synagogue associates, if your spare time is spent in study and learning, you come out a *talmid chacham* and a Jew to whom

רש״י; ספרי; כתובות קי״א ע״ב. 1

everyone looks up, a pride and blessing to all.

vii

The Highway to Heaven

The *Sidrah* and *Haftorah* of *Ekev* are read as the year is drawing to a close. The month of Elul approaches, and it will not be long before the shofar and the *kittel* will remind us of the time when all holidays come to an end. A famous *Maggid* once made a telling comment on a passage in the *Rosh Chodesh bentshen*. We pray to the Giver of all things for חיים של ברכה חיים של פרנסה . . . חיים של שלום., "a life of peace, of blessing, of sustenance." When it comes to the prayer for יראת שמים ויראת חטא, "the fear of Heaven and the fear of sin," the preacher continued, we add two little words: שיש בהם, "that there may be in *them*" — as if we were saying, "Let us go on our own sweet way, and let others be blessed with יראת שמים ויראת חטא." But just in case it might be thought that this is indeed our intention, we conclude חיים שתהי בנו אהבת תורה ויראת שמים, "a life in which *we* may be blessed with the love of Torah and the fear of Heaven." It is a different kind of יראת שמים, the fear of Heaven has a different meaning, when it springs from אהבת תורה, love and admiration. A child who loves his father has a different kind of respect for him than the child who dreads his father. If there is no שמים in life, how can there be יראת שמים?

The Rabbis say that the word Elul is an acrostic. Each letter signifies a word: אני לדודי ודודי לי, "I am for my Beloved and my Beloved is for me." The approach to God, the highway to Heaven, is not aloofness, keeping one's self away from Him, it is by getting near: קרוב מצדיקי, "he that is near justifieth Me," is Isaiah's prophetic call in the *Haftorah*. Can you debate the validity of science by discarding its study? Those who have rejected faith cannot argue about faith. מִי יָרִיב אִתִּי נַעֲמְדָה יָחַד, "who will contend with Me, let us stand up together." Can you question the influence of *tefillin* if you have never worn them? Can you doubt the beauty of family purity in life if you have never tried it? Can you pass an opinion about Shabbos if you have never tasted it? מִי בַעַל מִשְׁפָּטִי יִגַּשׁ אֵלָי, "who is Mine adversary, let him come near to Me." To break marriage laws and then plead for tolerance from those who uphold them is a stupid argument. It is being intolerant. To abrogate the law that makes a man a Jew, and then seek new definitions of 'what is a Jew,' is not sane thinking. מִי יָרִיב אִתִּי נַעֲמְדָה יָחַד; a challenge has to be faced, not bypassed.

In the *Sidrah*, Moses relates how he returned from Sinai with the new tablets of the Ten Commandments: וּשְׁנֵי הַלֻּחֹת בְּיָדִי, "and the two tablets were in my hand." בְּיָדִי — one hand was free to fight off the lawbreakers, and the other safely grasped the tablets of the Torah. What a wonderful message that is! From that day down to this it has been a constant struggle, one hand helping to maintain the other, to fortify its resistance, to build up its strength.

A new expression is coined in this *Sidrah*: וּשְׁמַרְתֶּם וַעֲשִׂיתֶם, "and you shall guard and you shall observe." וּשְׁמַרְתֶּם means to study it, to learn it, and to support it. Faithful guardians are never on holiday. Those who patrol the borders of Israel and guard its soil against invaders, for them there is no rest. For those who build and maintain the institutions of learning there is no relaxation, there is a constant daily struggle. Ignorance, עַם אֲרָצוֹת, is the greatest problem that confronts our community. Where there is ignorance there is no will-power and no resistance. It is a disease that brings every calamity upon us.

The greatest fear of Jewish parents used to be the thought that the child will grow up an *am ha'aretz*. A home without a *Shas,* without *Mishnayos* was a rarity. Today there are thousands of children to whom the words *Tanach*, *Mishnah* and *Gemara* sound like foreign terms. Without ושמרתם, how long can עשיתם last? No less important than the guardians of the borders of Israel are those guardians of the Torah of Israel. Every effort must be made to support the Yeshivos, the guardians of Torah learning, וישם מדברה כעדן, "so that the barren, Torah-less wilderness shall become like Eden, וערבתה כגן ה', and her desert like the garden of the Lord." ששן ושמחה ימצא בה תודה וקול זמרה, "then shall joy and gladness be found therein, thanksgiving and the voice of song."

viii

A New Link

(Bar Mitzvah)

Continuity is all-important in Jewish life. It is like a chain linking generations to one another by faith, practice and tradition; fathers and sons, mothers and daughters, right down the ages. If we can look back and see the straight line unbroken, there is every hope that we can look forward to its continuation. That is probably what the prophet meant in the *Haftorah*, when he tried to find words to comfort the people after their terrible ordeals: הביטו אל צור חצבתם, "look unto the rock whence you were hewn, ואל מקבת בור נקרתם, and the hewn pit whence you were dug out, הביטו אל אברהם אביכם ואל שרה תחוללכם, look unto Abraham your father, and unto Sarah who bore you." The word הביטו in Hebrew generally means to look from afar. No people in the world can trace their origin so clearly, right back for thousands of years without a break. If you can see right down the line, every link in the chain, then the prophet expressed the hope that the future will be bright and secure, come what may. But there is no guarantee; it is not something that comes naturally. In the links of a chain there is usually a very narrow gap. Sometimes the watchmaker has to put on a special magnifying glass to find it, then he widens it and fits in a new link and tightens it again so that it should not fall off.

When speaking of this ancestral chain, Isaiah begins with an introductory summons: שמעו אלי, "listen to me, stop to hear." There is so much noise about! Science is shouting, politicians are shouting. There is the radio, television, the press, and there is noise at home and at work, records and music; we can hardly hear each other's voices. Who stops to listen? It is true that science has made tremendous progress and has every reason to shout and be proud of its achievements. But do you know why that is? It is because the best brains in the world are concentrated on it.

Men are trained for years to endure all conditions, air pressure, spacelessness, no gravity; they are prepared physically and mentally to face it. They must know every bolt and screw in that colossal machine that takes them up. The slightest diversion or error would mean the end. Everybody is captured by it. There is no time for goodness, righteousness, God, faith and religion — they could not care less. Men who preach about God are deported, and men who teach about God are hounded.[1] The prophet does not denounce the arts and the sciences, but שמעו לי, he pleads, "stop for a moment to listen to me, you רדפי צדק." רדפי צדק does not mean "followers of righteousness," as the English version puts it; רדפי means "pursuers," those who run after it. Try and catch righteousness, מבקשי ה׳, "seek after God," try and find Him. Give a little of your mind to it. Give of

1 This address was delivered in 1962, when space exploration began with the first Russian Sputnik.

your time to it. Just as you must learn to endure all pressures, just as you must keep yourself fit to live under all kinds of conditions, make an effort, too, to pursue religion that way. Men train themselves to go around the world above it: train yourself to walk round the world in it, to be a pious man, a good man, loyal, faithful and disciplined. Condition yourself; שמעו, you have to listen. Shut out the noise for some moment of the day. ורדפי, you have to pursue it. Do not spend all day in running after everything else, spend a little of the day in pursuing your faith and your religion. Be מבקשים: look for it, study it, find it.

Bar Mitzvah means condition yourself physically, mentally, and morally. On your head your *tefillin*, on your garments your *tzitzis*, inside of you your kosher food. In your conduct, respect; in your dealings, honesty; in your work, Shabbos. Yes, you have to train yourself to endure trouble sometimes for Shabbos. A good scientist learns to endure, a good Jew must learn to endure. That has been the greatness of the Jew right down the years. We have been around the world, and we have endured all kinds of pressures, and we are still here; and we can look right back אל אברהם אביכם, to Abraham our father. כי אחד קראתיו, he was one man against the whole of society, but ואברכהו וארבהו, "I blessed him and multiplied him." So it has been handed down right to our fathers' day and to our own day. The same Torah, the same Bar Mitzvah, has added links to the chain that could not be broken.

As we welcome each new Bar Mitzvah and fit in a new link in the chain, he must tighten and strengthen it, and not let it get loose or snap. Thus we may hope that he will grow up a healthy, staunch and observant Jew, bringing credit and joy to all.

RE'EH

ראה

i

A Crucial Choice[1]

In a recent historic scientific manifesto, scientists gave a warning to the world of the dangers involved in nuclear warfare. Shall we put an end to the human race, or shall mankind renounce war? There lies before us, if we choose, continual progress in happiness, knowledge and wisdom. Shall we instead choose death, because we cannot forget our quarrels? The world lies before a new paradise; but if you cannot forget, there lies before you the risk of universal death.

The world must choose one of two alternatives: life or death. In the opening verse of this *Sidrah* we have the words of Moses addressing mankind in those far-off days: ראה אנכי נתן לפניכם היום ברכה וקללה, "Behold, I set before you this day a blessing and a curse."

היום means this day, every day. If you believe that this is wishful thinking — an old man speaking to his children, giving them good advice before his death — look a little further in the Torah,[2] where

1 Delivered at Young Israel of Los Angeles in 1956.

2 נצבים ל', ט'ו.

he repeats the same warning. This time he seems like a scientist who understands the laws of nature, whose mind has penetrated the physical pattern of the universe. ראה נתתי לפניך היום את החיים ואת הטוב ואת המות ואת הרע, "behold, I set before you this day life and good, death and evil." This time the great Jewish mind does not stop there: העדתי בכם היום את השמים ואת הארץ החיים והמות נתתי לפניך הברכה והקללה ובחרת בחיים למען תחיה אתה וזרעך,[3] "I call heaven and earth to witness against you this day, that I have set before thee life and death, the blessing and the curse. Therefore choose life, that thou mayest live, thou and thy seed."

How do you think the silent heavens and the speechless earth can testify against man? Theirs is the ancient voice of brimstone and fire, of Sodom and Amorah. Theirs is the modern voice of radioactive dust, of the atom. At last man is beginning to realise that we cannot separate the conduct of the physical from the conduct of spiritual nature. The progress of atomic science cannot be considered in isolation: העדתי בכם היום את השמים ואת הארץ החיים והמות נתתי לפניך, "I call heaven and earth to witness against you this day that I have set before thee life and death." There is a close relationship between atomic science and man's ethical and spiritual standards. It depends on you, how you harness the forces of nature — ובחרת בחיים למען תחיה. "Choose life that you may live"; but, like the scientist, Moses does not stop there: למען תחיה אתה וזרעך, "that you may live and your seed" — universal life or universal death. Never before has religion come so near to science. There is hardly a bridge to be crossed; we are nearly there — at the time when heaven and earth stand poised for life or for death.

If Rosh Hashanah means anything, it means the acknowledgment, on the birthday of the world's Creation, of the sovereignty of God. It means that God is the King, and all human beings His subjects, heaven and earth His messengers. But where there is majestic kingship there must go with it the majesty of law. There is a system of living whereby God and man and nature can live in harmony and bring about the fulfilment of the Creation. את הברכה אשר תשמעו, the blessing is the very fact of abiding by these laws; והקללה אם לא תשמעו, the curse is itself the rejection of these laws.

In a remarkable interpretation of the opening verse of the *Sidrah*, the Sages say that the blessings for obedience and the curses for disobedience were not given all at one time. את הברכה is written in the singular: ונתת את הברכה להקדים ברכה לקללה... ברכה אחת קדמת ברכה לקללה ואין כל הברכות קדמות לקללות.[4] They were given individually: for the acceptance of each מצוה, one ברכה, to which the people answered אמן; for the rejection of one מצוה, one קללה, and the people answered אמן.

One blessing, one curse; one blessing, one curse. There is a profound thought in that Rabbinic interpretation. You cannot reach perfection in one single effort. One Rosh Hashanah will not do it and one Yom Kippur will not achieve it; there must be a gradual process of operation, striving to fulfil each mitzvah as it comes your way.

In an international sense, President Eisenhower was right. You cannot turn suspicion into trust at one conference alone. The converse is true, likewise: the קללה, the curse of society has not been the result of one conflict alone. Evil is like a cancer: it begins with the maltreatment of one little people, somewhere on the map, to which the nations of the world only once answered אמן, and it resulted in a world conflagration that may well bring the whole of human society to universal disaster.

4. דברים י"א, כ"ט; סוטה ל"ז ע"ב; וראה תורה תמימה שם.

How true this is in our own religious life! We stood by and we saw the weakening of the Shabbos, and we said אמן; then again, for the deterioration of *kashrus* and the disappearance of Jewish family purity; and this gradual process of elimination has changed the whole appearance of Jewish life. We must get back, little by little, to Jewish values. We are no mere onlookers upon the world's arena. As the prophet proclaims in the *Haftorah*, הן עד לאומים נתתיו, we are witnesses of the eternal truths which alone will bring back the nations of the world to sanity and order, that man may live in peace and tranquillity.

ii

A Challenge to the Individual

The Vilna Gaon gives a thought-provoking interpretation of the opening verse of this *Sidrah*, in which Moses makes an impassioned appeal to the Children of Israel before his departure: ראה אנכי נתן לפניכם היום ברכה וקללה, "Behold, I set before you this day a blessing and a curse." Here it is: ברכה וקללה. There is no in-between for the Jewish people: you are either the dust of the earth, for everyone to trample upon, or the stars of the heaven, for everyone to look up to.

ראה is written in the singular: the Torah addresses itself to each and every individual. In the final analysis, man is not judged by the actions of society; ועל המדינות בו יאמר,[1] for society there will be a different judgment. אל תשגיח על העולם, the Gaon says, "do not be concerned with the world." Abraham was one man alone; he is called the עברי because כל העולם מעבר אחד, "the whole world was on

---

1. בתפלת מוסף דר"ה ממה דתניא בתקיעתא דרב; ראה סידור "עבודת ישראל" בבאור שם.

one side of the fence and he alone on the other." But because אנכי, I am with you, ראה, with vision you will never be alone. נותן, I give you, in the present; let no man think that it is ever too late. It is never too late to choose between right and wrong. Freedom of choice is man's greatest blessing; it distinguishes him from the animal. היום, I give you today — Elul comes every year to remind man, as the year comes to a close, that if his year was filled with sin and corruption, with apathy and indifference, ראה אנכי נותן היום, "Look, I give you an opportunity today." Every day you are free to choose; and remember, אנכי נותן לפניכם — not לכם but לפניכם: you can reject it if you wish, that is your privilege. בחירה, the choice is לפניכם, it is set before mankind: you can turn the world into a גיהנום, a jungle, or you can turn it into a paradise.

The *Sidrah* warns of the temptations and allurements that will put you to the test. הישכם אהבים את ה' אלקיכם בכל לבבכם ובכל נפשכם — how much heart, how much soul, how much sacrifice are you prepared to make, so as to hold on at all cost to those principles of faith and practice that no power in the world can change? Think of all the things that surround us: the temptations to break the Shabbos, the attractions to turn away from a service that follows the Shulchan Aruch, the modern shower that makes the *mikveh* seem unattractive. כי מנסה ה' אלקיכם אתכם — every day new things arrive to test our spirit of resistance. This is the message of the *Sidrah* of *Re'eh*: it calls to the individual, Do not be swamped by mass opinion, for Elul is coming with its plea, אני לדודי ודודי לי, reminding us to consider our personal relationship with God.

iii

Ani Le-dodi

The month of Elul has been singled out for one purpose and one purpose only: to pave the way for the arrival of Rosh Hashanah. Rosh Hashanah, too, has but one purpose: the recognition by humankind, on the birthday of the world's Creation, that God created the world. But that does not mean a matter of mere belief and speculative opinion about some supernatural force that made itself felt at the beginning of all things. It means that א-ל is מלך, that God is King and humankind His subjects. This conviction dominates the entire New Year Prayer Book. It must enter into daily life, regulate our mode of living, determine our ideals, inspire and control our actions.

Elul is not concerned with national issues and international problems, though it would solve those problems, too. Elul is not concerned with moral values and ethical principles; it is concerned with the dependence of moral values and ethical principles on God the King. אני לדודי ודודי לי — it is concerned with the link, with the proximity, with the nearness between man and his Maker. דביה סליק משה לטורא למבעי רחמין, "in this month Moses ascended the mountain to plead for mercy," as though he could not beseech the throne of God with his feet on the ground; but Elul is a process of spiritual climbing for each and every one of us. אני לדודי ודודי לי, "I am for my Beloved and my Beloved is for me," implies the spiritual climb of the individual, who alone can create his own salvation and assist in the salvation of humankind.

כי יקום בקרבך נביא או חלם חלום ונתן אליך אות או מופת, "If there arise in the midst of thee a prophet or a dreamer of dreams, and he give thee a sign or a wonder." The *Sidrah* deals with what is known as the

religious seducer: a false prophet or a dreamer of dreams who will
entice the people away from the path of God and Torah living. He
will show signs and work miracles that will come to pass.

We do not deny anyone the right to pose as a prophet or a
dreamer of dreams. On the contrary, the Torah recognises a dream
as a medium through which God sometimes communicates with
those who are near to Him: בחלום אדבר בו,[1] a dream is a vehicle of a
Divine message. But there is a vast difference between a dreamer
who dreams of reality and applies the dream and its message to
himself, inspiring others to follow, and the dreamer who applies the
dream to others — ונתן אליך אות או מופת, he applies it to you, not by
inspiration nor by example nor by personal conduct. This dreamer
must be removed from the camp. אות בשמים או מופת בארץ,[2] he makes
signs in the heavens and miracles on earth, but אפילו מעמיד חמה באמצע
הרקיע,[3] "even if he can make the sun stand still in the middle of the
sky," you have to remove him from the camp.

We may well wonder why phenomenal power should be granted
him; the Torah answers, כי מנסה ה׳ אלקיכם אתכם, it is God putting you
to test. Can you withstand the most insidious seduction from the
revealed will of God?

False prophets who entice you away from the paths on which
your father before you walked — מעמיד חמה באמצע הרקיע, such prophets
can make the sun stand still constantly to shine above your head.
Jewish life sometimes presents difficulties; sometimes a cloud is
spread over the home. A disciplined life means to be able to say "no"
when the need be, and to say "no" means sometimes to make a
sacrifice. When a sacrifice has to be made, the sun might have to

1. במדבר י״ב, ו׳.

2. רש״י; ספרי.

3. סנהדרין צ׳ ע״א.

set for a short period. No dreamer can come along to make the sun stand for you, and abrogate Biblical precepts, and accommodate Judaism to all conditions. These are the men to whom religion remains a חלום, a dream, never brought into reality, a religion that makes no demands. כי מנסה ה' אלקיכם אתכם, these things come to prove you, הישכם אהבים את ה' אלקיכם בכל לבבכם ובכל נפשכם, "whether you love God with all your heart and all your soul."

The test of moral strength and religious vitality is to what extent you can be influenced by the religious seducer, to what extent you are prepared to follow the man to whom God has become a חלום and is no longer reality. Blood and sweat and tears, the statesman said, were required to fight the common enemy when he was standing with his wings spread over the English Channel — miracles will not do it. The Rabbis say, בנביא אתה מבקש אות, "if a prophet arises make him give you a sign, ואי אתה מבקש אות בתורה דכתיב בה על פי התורה אשר יורוך,[4] the Torah of God can give you no signs." The Torah is not a miracle-performing book; it cannot make the sun stand still always to spread its rays. ככל אשר יורוך is a hard way, but it is the way to glory.

Nations have collapsed and empires have crumbled that turned their leaders into demigods, dreamers who ונתן אליך אות או מופת, who wanted to turn the country into a paradise the easy way. All you had to do was to follow, and your Messiah had been born. Oh! and how much carnage had been let loose. Homes have gone to rack and ruin, children have turned their backs on their parents, and brother has set face against brother, because they have dreamt of the day when מעמיד חמה באמצע הרקיע. Their false prophecies dethroned God and put personal whims in his place.

There are all kinds of religious seducers. They dream of unity and ask for the sacrifice of conviction; they dream of tolerance and

4. ירושלמי ברכות פ"א ה"ד על הפסוק בפ' שופטים י"ז, י"א.

ask for the sacrifice of conscience; השמר לך פן תנקש אחריהם, "take heed of them that thou be not ensnared to follow them." This is the stream of events that in our days allows the suppression of conscience in the interests of the state. Give up your language and give up your political ideologies in the interests of the Party, and now give up your individualism in the interests of communal cohesion. In other words, take off the crown of God's kingdom from your own head so that the Kingdom of God may reign on earth.

Never before in the history of world Jewry has the message of Elul been so vital to our survival as today. The Jewish state, on the one hand, is buffeted between political parties and economic systems, while the Jewish communities in the Diaspora are buffeted between religious and cultural differences. They are led by prophets who dream dreams of God and of unity, but forget that unity lies in God and that God must become a reality. Elul calls out אני לדודי ודודי לי. Attune your thoughts, get yourselves into step, find your own personality, and let no one influence you to deviate from it. Then, when the new year comes, the crown of God will rest upon your head, your own salvation will be assured, and with that the salvation of mankind.

iv

Stop and Look Back

(Shabbos Rosh Chodesh)

Nothing in the world can stop the march of time. Neither the *koved*-hunter nor the pleasure seeker: no one can stop it. A politician, a scientist, the Kremlin or the White House — no one, no one can stop it.

אתה יצרת עולמך מקדם כלית מלאכתך ביום השביעי, "Thou didst form Thy world of old, Thou finished Thy work on the seventh day." What is the meaning of this *Rosh Chodesh* prayer? Are we not taught that God created the world in six days and on the seventh day He rested? What, then, is meant by the words כלית מלאכתך ביום השביעי?

No task is complete whilst the machine is still in motion, and no job is finished whilst the labourer still stands over his bench. The emergence of light, strength and beauty as the Creation appeared on the scene would have been but a gigantic piece of lifeless mechanism spreading senselessly into unknown space, had there not been one final act of Creation: the power to say, Stop! it is enough! The greatest moment in the story of Creation was that moment of כלית, of saying "Stop" to the universe. Then could the Divine architect look back to see if it was good.

Ask the dress designer, and he will tell you that the greatest thrill of his new design is when he stops and reflects on the work of his hands. Ask the author, and he will tell you that his most moving moment is when he has written the last word and turns back to reflect on the expression of his thoughts. Ask the preacher, and he will tell you, too, that when his peroration comes to an end and he glances at the faces of his listeners, that is his greatest moment. Every month, as the moon disappears behind the clouds and the new moon is about to set his face on the world, the Jew is reminded כלית מלאכתך ביום השביעי — "Stop, look back." This will be your greatest creation; you will then adjust the wrongs, fill in the omissions, and repair the mistakes.

With the commencement of Elul the year nears its end, and, if God wills it, a new year will take its place. Has my work this year been complete? Can I say that it was good, as God said at the beginning of all things and at the end of His Creation? Twenty-nine more days to repair the work. Have I given offence? Yes; I must make it right! Have I been dishonest? Yes; I must make amends. Have I *davened*? No; I must now begin. Have I given what I should and can give? No; then I must give now. This is all that Elul stands for, this and naught else. It is a man-and-God affair, this last month of the year, a truly personal matter between man and his Maker. Here is a month; take Me into your confidence. Save yourself from the grasp of sin and despair. As Rosh Hashanah comes, and we pray for the restoration of Zion and for the recognition of the Kingdom of God, each one becomes part of that restoration. The world is made up of individuals, and unless the individual puts his house in order the world's house becomes a restless place to live in.

ראה אנכי נתן לפניכם היום ברכה וקללה, "Behold, I set before you this day a blessing and a curse." The opening word of the *Sidrah* is written in the singular: ראה, "see"; and, strange though it may seem, the Divine Author switches over immediately to the plural: not לפניך but לפניכם. The lesson is clear: 'Let each one see for himself.' The life and death of Israel as a community depends on the individual. No home can be happy unless every child in it makes for its happiness. No business can be successful unless every employee helps in its progress. No synagogue can bear fruit unless every member gives of his best, and no Israel will be restored unless every Israelite adds his quota to its restoration: ראה אנכי נתן לפניכם היום. It all depends on each single individual's vision; so much and no more will the community benefit. This is Elul's purpose. Make ready for Rosh Hashanah to bring down the Kingdom of God on earth, but bring Him down first into your own life — אני לדודי ודודי לי. Then will this last month bring an end to Israel's sorrow, and the first month of the new year be the beginning of Israel's joys.

v

Science and the Soul

Prayer in Jewish life is associated with fixed times and fixed seasons, because in the first instance prayer is not pleading for things but establishing things. First, it is to affirm that God is the Creator; it is to recognise God the Owner. He Who made it can give it, He Who owns it can grant it. So שחרית and מנחה and מעריב, at sunrise, sundown and sunset. Shabbos, marking the end of the work of Creation and the beginning of the physical universe. *Rosh Chodesh*, the renewal of the elements; the festivals, the seasons; Rosh Hashanah, His sovereignty; Yom Kippur, man's submission. So, at these times and these seasons, acknowledge and pray. Man is the agent, not the owner; man is the instrument, not the maker; man is the crown, not the king. He has access to all the secrets, he can scale the heights and plumb the depths, so long as he makes no claim of ownership, so long as the throne remains uncoveted.

In the *Sidrah* we read the warning that the day may come when כי יקום בקרבך נביא או חלם חלום ונתן אליך אות או מופת, "there will arise amongst you a prophet or a dreamer of dreams, and he will give you a sign or a wonder" — אות בשמים ומופת בארץ,[1] either a sign in the heavens or a wonder on earth. Through the genius of his technology and through the power of his material might, as our Sages expressed it many many centuries ago, אפילו מעמיד חמה באמצע הרקיע,[2] he may reach out even beyond the moon, and make the sun stand still in the middle of the sky. If such things happen, some are bound to say נלכה, "let us go after this new revelation." If you listen to them you will be

1. רש"י; ספרי

2. סנהדרין צ' ע"א.

captured by the wave of enthusiasm, and you will be persuaded to turn away from the truth — לא תשמע אל דברי הנביא ההוא, "take heed, do not be influenced by that man, כי מנסה ה' אלקיכם אתכם לדעת הישכם אהבים את ה' אלקיכם, for the Lord your God putteth you to proof, to know whether you do love the Lord your God with all your heart and with all your soul."

No man and no nation can impose their will on history. They are, as someone once said, only the material of history; whether their aspirations are realised or rejected by history depends entirely on whether or not they are in harmony with its inherent direction. In the Divine scheme of things it is not man that makes history, but history that makes man. We don't own the world, the world owns us. There is a combined operation between God, man and nature. There is another science into which man must probe, and other forces into which man must delve: the science of the soul, the forces of the heart — the science of self, לדעת הישכם אהבים. This is rather an unusual Biblical expression, this הישכם; it speaks of a knowledge that lies deeper down than the knowledge of technology. הישכם — it is something that man possesses within himself, an atom that cannot and will not be split. God and man operate in it; it is a Divine-human capsule — הישכם, it is there in the personality of man.

The intrinsic tragedy of society is that man has gone beyond himself before finding himself. Everybody is on the run: נלכה אחרי אלהים אחרים, "let us go after other gods." Standards are swept away and traditions uprooted. The serenity of living, just living, is fast disappearing. Homes are shattered because foolish men try to find happiness outside, though they can well find it inside. They run away from themselves. Communities disintegrate, states collapse, the world is on the brink of disaster; because men set themselves up as idols who will show signs and wonders. They crush individuality, they turn men into things and human life into a commodity. So it is with the vain politician, so it is with the conquering industrialist, so it is with the powerful statesman; and everyone is on the run at home, in the community, and in the state. Each is trying to find the biggest idol, the wonder-maker in whom he can place his loyalty, confide his faith, and invest his means, to earn for him what he believes to be the security and the happiness he seeks.

If Elul means anything, it means first אני לדודי ודודי לי, "If I am for my Beloved, then my Beloved is for me." Every human being possesses that Divine personality. It has got to be found before Rosh Hashanah comes, so that every man can adorn himself with the crown of God's kingdom. We are not commodities, we are human beings.

There is a remarkable Rabbinic passage concerning the Torah portion read from the second scroll on *Shabbos Rosh Chodesh*. That portion details the sacrifices brought to the Temple on the New Moon, amongst them a sin offering: ושעיר עזים אחד לחטאת לה', "one he-goat as a sin offering to the Lord." The Rabbis say that this could be understood as "a sin-offering *for* the Lord," and explain: הביאו כפרה עלי על שמיעטתי את הירח,[3] "God calls to Israel, saying, 'Bring an atonement offering for Me, for My having diminished the moon.'"

At the beginning of Creation, the two luminaries, the sun and the moon, were of equal size, and subsequently the moon was reduced to a size suitable to its task, to rule by night, while the sun retained its original size and strength, so as to rule by day. But men were misled: because the sun was the more powerful, greater in size, it became a god of light, a symbol of idol-worship to those who search for God. With the imaginative study of human guilt and Divine judgment, the Sages strike a note that echoes through

3. חולין ס' ע"ב.

history: "I am guilty," says God, "for man having turned away from Me. I gave him the means — I diminished the moon in size; I gave more to one than to the other. I made room for human error. Therefore, every *Rosh Chodesh* הביאו כפרה עלי על שמיעטתי את הירח, bring an atonement for Me for this sin" — שעיר עזים אחד לחטאת לה', "one he-goat as a sin offering to the Lord."[4]

What profound thinking lies in that amazing Rabbinic passage! The blessings given to us were never intended to be used for self-aggrandisement, for idol-worship. Every element must play its part, every man must find his place.

ראה אנכי נותן לפניכם היום ברכה וקללה; here is the significance of the *Sidrah*'s opening up in the singular and continuing in the plural. ראה, "behold, let each man find salvation in himself; let each one contribute to the fortunes of mankind. If you have wisdom, share it; if you have means, distribute them; if you have time, give it. The world depends on me, and I depend on God." Thus will His luminaries bring in their rays the light and hope of tranquillity and peace for men the world over.

v(b)

Your Soul's Desire

(Bar Mitzvah)

The blessings of God are given us for a purpose; they are not to be wasted. Enjoy life to the full, בכל אשר תאוה נפשך, "in anything you may desire," but never forget that the purpose of these blessings is

4. כעין זה ברבנו בחיי פ' פנחס.

למען תלמד ליראה את ה' אלקיך כל הימים, "in order that you may learn to revere God, to acknowledge Him, to recognise Him all the days of your life." No one knows what the future holds for any of us, and especially for the new and growing generation, but למען תלמד: if you learn now, when the opportunity presents itself, you will realise כל הימים, throughout your life, that all the time we are dependent on God. So now is the time to learn every day, to thank God for every kindness, to look in the proper direction, which *tefillin* every day help to do. To put aside one day a week for Shabbos, for thought, for prayer, for contemplation. To share your blessings with those less fortunate, הגר היתום והאלמנה, the stranger, the orphan, and the widow.

There is nothing finer in life than the great industrialist, or the great businessman, or the great scientist, who is a great Jew. למען יברכך ה' אלקיך בכל מעשה ידך אשר תעשה, "in order that God may bless you in all the work of your hands that you do." It is not what a man does with his hands that matters, but how he does it. It is what prompts him to do it; it is the thought behind it. If God is to bless the work of your hands, then He must be with you all the time, in your thoughts and in your prayers.

vi

Beware of a Mixed Blessing

The most precious thing in human life is the ability to reason and to exercise freedom of the will. It is that something in us that comes from God Himself. It is even more than that: it is part of Him. The most sacred privilege is to be free to obey or to disobey, to do or not to do, to kill or to let live. There are so many things in which there is little to distinguish between man and animal — we say it every morning in our *Shacharis* prayer: ‎ומותר האדם מן הבהמה אין כי הכל הבל‎,[1] "and the pre-eminence of man over beast is naught, for all is vanity." But a great sage once said that this ‎אין‎, this seeming nothing, is an acrostic: the "‎א‎" stands for ‎אדם‎, the "‎י‎" stands for ‎יש‎, and "‎נ‎" stands for ‎נשמה‎, making the three words ‎אדם יש נשמה‎. The pre-eminence of man over beast is that ‎אדם יש נשמה‎, that man has a soul. That is the most precious of all gifts.

The Torah tells us that at the Creation man was made in God's image and in His likeness. We often hear people say of a child, "He is just like his father"; sometimes people say, "He is the image of his father." There is a vast difference between these two. Being his father's image means that to look at him you would think it was his father. To be 'like him,' however, can mean in character or in nature. You can sometimes see a saintly person, a ‎צדיק‎, of whom you would say that he has the *Shechinah* on his face. To be like Him means to choose between right and wrong.

‎ראה אנכי נתן לפניכם היום‎, "Behold, see, that 'I' am put into each of you; it is ‎לפניכם‎, before you: everyone has the same choice, ‎ברכה וקללה‎, blessing and curse." This last phrase is usually taken to mean, "I put before you two things, a blessing and a curse, between which you have to choose." It should, however, be translated in another way, because if you translate it this way, that there are two separate and distinct things, ‎ברכה‎ or ‎קללה‎, then only a fool would choose the ‎קללה‎. But ‎ברכה וקללה‎ can be rendered literally, "a blessing *and* a curse"; it is all one thing, for in every ‎ברכה‎ there is always the possibility of misuse turning it into a ‎קללה‎, a curse. We all hear of people endowed with wealth and fortune, who shower all this upon their children, only to find that it has been their ruination. Their very good fortune

<hr/>

1. ‎קהלת ג׳, י״ט‎.

leads them astray. A choice must always be made in one's career, but what career did fortune drive their children to follow? How many fortunes have driven husbands from wives, fathers from children? A ברכה misused has within it the making of a קללה. The reverse can also be true: sometimes, even often, a קללה can turn into a mighty ברכה.

Is not this what is meant in our *Rosh Chodesh bentshen* prayer? We ask for חיים שימלאו משאלות לבנו לטובה, "a life in which the wishes of our hearts will be fulfilled for good." Is the extra expression, "for good," necessary? Does anyone wish for something that is not "for good"? But sometimes what is good in our eyes is not good in God's eyes. He knows better, so we plead of Him, "may the good wishes of our heart be good for You too." Then the month will indeed be a happy one. May all our hearts be turned towards Him, that we may be worthy of true blessing and good for Israel and all mankind.

vii

The Soul's Holiday

A holiday is a good thing, not only for the physical faculties of man, but equally for his mental faculties. It helps to balance one's mind. The constant and uninterrupted grind of our daily preoccupations makes it impossible to sit back as one would wish and just think for himself. There is nothing better, nothing healthier, than to stop this headlong rush of ours and to take account of our own affairs.

It is the same for each one of us in his own intimate sphere. Each of us is a slave to something or other. There is no denying that we are held in bondage by certain habits; we are enslaved to our

businesses or homes or amusements. What we need, and need not
too infrequently, is a so-called break: a taste of something different,
something we are not accustomed to do or to see or to have. Even
governments recognise the need for holidays to ensure better and
increased production. Our habits need a change, our pursuits need
a vacation, our surroundings need a break. We go on day in and day
out, week in and week out, with the same monotonous routine.
Why, just pause for a moment and think: we are no longer masters
of ourselves.

What shall I do? Shall I do that to which I am accustomed, or try
a change? Ask it of yourselves and of the man in the street. You will
find that in most instances you cannot act differently. It has all
become second nature. The thing we are most afraid of in life is the
change of routine, a change of surroundings and a change of habits.
A real holiday means to become fearless of these things: to make
our common and everyday affairs secondary, incidental to the
uncommon and unusual. Our limbs and our senses need a rest from
the drab routine which has become second nature.

Man is the most precious element in the great universal make-up.
The world belongs to him, every part of it and everything in it. He
is to make the best of himself and the best of all that he can enjoy.
"A man will be held accountable," the Rabbis say,[1] "for refusing to
enjoy the things that he is permitted to enjoy." Self-neglect is one
of the greatest dangers to which man can expose himself. Who
knows what opportunities he loses by being afraid to change his
way of life, by enjoying one thing at the expense of another, by
satisfying one of his senses and neglecting the others?

---

1 ירושלמי סוף קידושין: וראה גם בבלי נדרים י׳ ע״א ובתורה תמימה על הפ׳ במדבר ו׳, י״א
מה שמביא מהרמב״ם ועוד.

There is another side to the picture. If we dare to say that man's physical being needs a change of surroundings, and no part of it is to be neglected, is it too daring to assert that man's spiritual being needs a holiday, a change from the usual? Dare we penetrate so far into the designs of God as to say that He too — His part in us, the soul — requires an airing? For days, for weeks and for months it is enslaved in this fleshly frame of ours, following blindly the selfish whims and desires of man, until it breaks through and can stand it no longer. Is it fair, in the partnership of spirit and flesh, of God and man, to neglect that part in us that cries out, too, for a change of surroundings? צמאה לך נפשי,[2] "my soul thirsts for Thee," is the Psalmist's innermost yearning. Why not take it in its literal sense? The Divine in man wants a holiday. הטו אזנכם ולכו אלי שמעו ותחי נפשכם, "Incline your ear and come unto me, hear and your soul shall live," the prophet pleads in the *Haftorah*. The soul is dying of thirst; only hear, and it shall live again. It is perhaps significant that the month of Elul, the last month of the year, with its shofar reminding us of the coming days of awe and judgment, follows on the heels of the summer months. Tammuz and Av, the holiday season for the flesh; Elul and Tishrei, the holiday season for the soul.

In the midst of life, this dark and miserable wilderness of ours, there stand two mountains. One belongs to God, the other to man; one is life, the other is death; one is Heaven, the other is Hell. ראה אנכי נתן לפניכם היום ברכה וקללה, "Behold, I set before you this day a blessing and a curse." One need not be a philosopher, a scientist or even a Rabbi to make the choice. ראה, see! You cannot reason, you cannot argue with a phenomenon that your own eyes can behold. Which other people has seen it as we have seen it? For us there has been no in-between; it has been either ברכה or קללה, life or death. We are

_____
2. תהלים ס"ג, ב'.

different: to us it is one or the other. There is no standing at the crossroads; we reach the heights or we are dragged down into the mire.

If you hearken you shall live, if you refuse to hearken you shall die. I cannot explain it, but ראה, I can see it. If God becomes an equal partner in life, then blessing must be; if we take all for ourselves and refuse to share with Him, then we must suffer the inevitable consequences. Those about to build a new home, those who will soon bring Jewish lives into the world, take this message with you: ראה אנכי, "see Me," God pleads; then ברכה, you shall be blessed. With the arrival of Elul let us determine to make it a month for God. Let us give Him a change from the usual surroundings: more prayer, more devotion, more charity, more purity. Then will the new year bring with it the dawn of a new era of peace and happiness for all men.

SHOFTIM

שפטים

i

Be a Judge in Your Gates

(Bar Mitzvah)

שפטים ושטרים תתן לך בכל שעריך, "Judges and officers shalt thou make thee in all thy gates which the Lord thy God giveth thee." This opening verse of the *Sidrah* means, of course, that when Israel entered the Promised Land, they were to appoint judges to ensure the keeping of law and order. שפטים are דיינים who rule and give instructions in accordance with the teachings of the Torah; שטרים are the police, the officers to administer the law and see that it is carried out in Israel.

How seemingly strange are these opening words! Surely the Torah should just have said שפטים ושטרים תתן; why לך, addressing the individuals? And surely the right word would be not תתן but תשים, you shall set or appoint judges? You don't give judges, you appoint them. This seems to suggest that before there can be law and order in the country, שפטים ושטרים תתן לך, you must give unto yourself judges and officers. Control your actions, give justice to yourself; appoint yourself an officer in your gates.

We are full of gates. The mouth is a gate, it opens and closes; the eyes open and close. Not everything our eyes see can our mouths enjoy. Close your mouth and do not let it in. Close your eyes and do not let them see. Become a judge and officer over yourself. Your ears have gates; the Rabbis say[1] that the lobes hanging down from the ears are not really for piercing for earrings, but to close like gates over the opening in the ear so as not to hear things we should not listen to. We are full of שערים, gates, that open and close. The hands — close them before we think of taking something that does not belong to us. What a fine set of Jews we would be if we appointed ourself as policemen over our gates!

A strong man is not a heavyweight boxer or weight lifter; a strong man, our Sages say, is הכובש את יצרו,[2] one who can control himself. He is strong in character; he polices himself. A Bar Mitzvah boy should train to be a spiritual heavyweight: to be strong not only in bodily health but in character, in determination, in will-power, and in Jewish loyalty and observance.

The *Haftorah* is the fourth of the seven prophetic messages of comfort that follow Tisha B'Av. It begins with the words אנכי אנכי הוא מנחמכם, "I, even I, am your comforter." What is the significance of this repetition? It implies אנכי לא נשתניתי, אנכי כמקודם, "I have not changed, I am the same now as before." I saw you before the Destruction and I see you after the Destruction. I never change, says God, but I look at you, and מי את, "Who are you? I can recognise you no longer." The prophet even uses the feminine gender, not מי אתה but מי את — you have changed completely, you are not the same person I knew. מי את, "what has become of you, ותשכח ה' עשך, you have forgotten the God Who created you." Sometimes we see former Bar

1. כתובות ה' ע"ב.

2. אבות ד', א'.

Mitzvah boys, and we feel like crying out like the prophet, מי את,
"who are you, you have changed." Of course, we wish we could say
"you have changed for the better." Some do change and improve
year by year for the better. The way to do it is by applying the lesson
of the *Sidrah*, by imposing self-judgment, by guarding the gates and
exercising will-power and growing strong in a truly Jewish way.

ii

Worldly Judaism

There has been a lot of talk in recent years about the place of
religion in life. Books and articles have been published asking
whether or not the religious sentiments in which we have been
nurtured still have a meaning in the world in which we live. Can
the spirit of the twentieth century fit in with the opinions that were
entertained by our fathers? The question is even asked, "Can
Judaism help the perplexed Jew?" Some say that the Psalms, the
Jewish Book, the Talmud, have had their day, their place and their
admirers, and today they are an episode of a past that has gone. The
function of Jewish education, these people say, is to bring it about
that the Jew in his personal life shall delve to the depths of
Jewishness and elevate it to a major factor of his life. How this can
be done, how a Jew can be made to feel what he misses and how
the depths of Jewishness can be reached without the Book, if the
Psalms and the Talmud are an episode of the past, is beyond my
comprehension.

These views reveal the restlessness of those who are concerned
about questions of Jewish preservation. So frightening is their
outlook that they advocate the retention of Jewish values and ideas

in which they do not really believe, because it is only in the books that we find them. Some talk of a meaningless װעלטליכע אידישקייט, worldly Judaism, but there is no such thing as Jewishness without the Book. To the books we must turn in order to check the oncoming wave of materialism that otherwise will surely crush the body and soul of human society.

The most essential factor of Rosh Hashanah is מלכות, the enthronement of God the King. What are we going to do about it? Should we apologise to those who want to push us into the background, and throw out the Psalms and the Talmud into the limbo of bygone days? Can anyone affirm that Karl Marx has made the world a happier place to live in than that which Moses tried to make? Have Freud or Einstein made our lives more comfortable than Saadiah Gaon or Maimonides? The Karaites of the eighth century, or the reformers of the nineteenth century — have they been able to fill the spiritual void or assist in Jewish preservation?

There are a thousand quack remedies to the world's ills; and the more remedies we find, the more widespread is dishonesty, the greater is the decline in respect for age and authority, the more black is the licence that besmirches civilisation. קסם קסמים, מעונן ומנחש ומכשף וחבר חבר ושאל אוב וידעני ודרש אל המתים, here is a list of some of them: spiritualists, sorcerers, enchanters, magicians, wizards, and necromancers. We have been inflicted with them right through our long history: some who attempt to investigate the future, others who speak with the dead, false messiahs and lying prophets; but none of them has ever calmed the restless soul of man.

There is nothing in the realms of Heaven that can be proved or disproved. If the wicked have prospered and the righteous have suffered, how many times in history have the tables been turned? There is only one way out of all this perplexity: faith, simple faith. That was the greatest message ever to the Jew, proclaimed by

Israel's ancient teacher whose Divine Book so many wish to throw aside today: תמים תהיה עם ה' אלקיך, "you shall be perfect with the Lord your God." תמים תהיה—if you want perfection, peace of mind, serenity of thought, calm in your soul, they can only be achieved when עם ה' אלקיך, when there is simple faith in God. התהלך עמו בתמימות ותצפה לו ולא תחקור אחר העתידות אלא כל מה שיבוא עליך קבל בתמימות ואז תהיה עמו ולחלקו.[1] "Do not attempt to investigate the future, because it will get you nowhere. Whatever it may be that comes upon you, accept it wholeheartedly; then will you be with Him and become His portion." Without faith, there is a colossal vacuum that nothing can fill. There is a hunger that nothing can satisfy, unless we are prepared to make dust our destiny and the entail of four planks (i.e. the coffin) our ultimate goal.

What is the use of this ridiculous talk of Jewish self-preservation if we are not prepared to believe in the first instance that preservation is for a purpose? What difference will our survival as Jews make if we have no contribution to make to civilisation? We commit a crime against children that we bring into the world if we do not give them some indication of what their life means and what it stands for. If the first thing in the morning is מודה אני, faith; if the last thing at night is שמע ישראל, faith; then whatever onslaughts may be sandwiched in between, we will withstand them. If the day has not been too good, then 'Thank God — it could have been worse'; if the day has been successful, then 'Thank God — it is due to Him.' If life is empty, if there is a void somewhere, the first thing put in must be faith.

No wonder we pray with the Psalmist during these Elul days ה' אורי וישעי ממי אירא,[2] "The Lord is my light and my salvation; whom shall

1 . רש"י; ספרי

2 . תהלים כ"ז

I fear?" Take God out, and what perturbation we get in all this darkness that surrounds us! There is no light that can direct us to our salvation. Science cannot kindle it. It could, if it were devoted entirely to construction instead of destruction. Atomic energy is the greatest proof, so far, of the Power behind nature. But if it is not used for establishing the things in which to believe, then it is like tampering with a machine of which you know next to nothing — generally the end is that we wreck it. Humanity will learn to its bitter cost that if you detach science from God, if you conceive life without faith, if you dream of Jewishness without the Book, you will live selfishly and brutally, and a darkness of a kind we have never yet seen will engulf the world.

The Psalmist knew it; after the battles he had fought, after the defeats he had suffered and the victories he had won, there was one flicker of light that could illumine the darkness, one ray of hope: ה' אורי וישעי, "The Lord is my light and my salvation." Moses knew it as he bade farewell to a people who were to take their place in the comity of nations. You will come across all sorts of sorcerers and magicians, he told them, who will offer you new lights and new ideas, who will say that the Book is antiquated, that it has no future. But none of them will fill the vacuum. תמים תהיה; if you want tranquillity, then it must be עם ה' אלקיך, it can only come with God — עמו ולחלקו. With Him there is no perplexity. It is a grave mistake to ask, "Can Judaism help the perplexed Jew?" The real question is, "Would the Jew be perplexed if he were living with Judaism?"

This is the demand of the hour: faith, simple faith in God the King. That is the first gem you must pick out of the depth of Judaism. Elevate that to a factor of your life, and Jewish preservation will no longer be a problem. The Jew will become a living force in human society and a light unto the nations of the world.

iii

When Waging War

The Torah is an all-embracing civilisation, and as such it envisages the possibility of a מלחמת מצוה, an obligatory war, when sacrifice for the cause is a mitzvah. The *Sidrah* implies that there are two ways of going into battle. First the Torah speaks in the singular: כי תצא למלחמה על איבך, "When thou goest forth into battle against thine enemies." Then the Torah speaks in the plural: והיה כקרבכם אל המלחמה, "and it shall be when you draw near unto battle." In the first instance it delivers the exhortation, When you go forth into battle you must go as one man; united, strengthening each other's hearts, supporting each other's hands, governed by one purpose, directed towards one goal. וראית סוס ורכב, "and you will see a horse and a chariot" — have you ever heard of an army that goes out to fight with one horse and one chariot? Ah! But if you go as one, then all their horses and all their guns will appear to you as if just one.

When there was unity among the people, the army commander needed to make no appeal to them. He simply made a statement — an order of the day — לא תירא מהם כי ה' אלקיך עמך, "you shall not be afraid of them, because the Lord your God is with you." But כקרבכם אל המלחמה, if you, in the plural, go out to war, if your forces are split, if your strength is divided — then ונגש הכהן ודבר אל העם, "the priest shall approach and speak to the people, ואמר אלהם שמע ישראל, and he shall say unto them, 'Hear O Israel.'" At least let שמע ישראל hold you together. Remember the cry of the martyrs who died for our cause; remember the myriads whose only purpose in life was שמע ישראל, unity with God in life and in death. If you are animated by selfish desires; if you have built a new home and your own whims come first; then you will lose — don't fight. If you have prospered in business and your heart will not be in the fight — don't go, you will lose. If you have recently married and your emotions are not set on battle — stay at home.

Last, but by no means least, מי האיש הירא ורך הלבב, if you are afraid and faint-hearted, go home. Here the Rabbis add that this means more than being afraid of war and the naked sword of battle; also הירא מעבירות שבידו,[1] he who is afraid that the sins he committed will bar the way to victory must leave the field of battle. These are not ordinary sins, for after all there is no perfect man, and no one would be left to fight; but הירא מעבירות שבידו, he who is afraid of sins committed by his own hands. Sometimes circumstances drive man to sin, sometimes social conditions and environment are the instruments of shaping character and moulding conduct. That type of sinner is not to be condemned: teach him, encourage him, sympathise with him. The unforgivable sin that is contagious and can influence the whole battle of life is עבירות שבידו: the one who has the power in his hands to help, but refuses to help; the one who has the means בידו, and holds back.

What a sad situation faces us when בקרבכם, we fight the battle of Torah life in factions, torn to pieces. עבירות שבידו — we know better, and have it in our power to do better, and we sit back complacently as though nothing concerns us. ילך וישב לביתו, we are complacently concerned only with our own home life. As Elul moves forward, let us be united in purpose, determined to join the battle, with a clear consciousness that we have done our duty. Then God will grant us all a new year of joy and fulfilment.

1. סוטה מ׳ד ע׳א.

iv

The Power of Prayer[1]

והיה כקרבכם אל המלחמה . . ., "and it shall be, when ye draw nigh unto battle, that the priest shall come nigh and speak unto the people, and shall say unto them, 'Hear O Israel! you approach this day into war against your enemies: let not your hearts faint, fear not, and do not tremble nor be terrified because of them; for the Lord your God is He that goes with you, to fight for you against your enemies, to save you.'" These are four admonitions, the Rabbis explain: אל ירך לבבכם, let not your heart faint; אל תיראו, fear not; אל תחפזו, do not tremble; and אל תערצו, be not terrified because of them. These four behests correspond to four things with which the warriors of other nations fight their battles. They clash their shields and thereby make a loud noise; they trample the ground heavily with the beating of their horses' hooves, again in order to make a noise; they shout aloud; and they blow trumpets and other noisy instruments. Against these four methods of waging a frightening war, the priest was to enjoin the people: let not your hearts faint, fear not, do not tremble, nor be terrified, for the Lord your God is He that goes with you. They come to war relying on the conquering strength of man, but you come relying on the unconquerable strength of Almighty God.[2]

What a fitting thought this is on the *Yahrtzeit* of this terrible war! True, the methods of war have changed, but the Biblical behests remain unchangeable through the ages. There is no concealing the fact that many speak lightly, perhaps too lightly, of a national day

1 Delivered at Brixton Synagogue on the 4th anniversary of the outbreak of World War II.

2. רש"י; סוטה מ"ב ע"ב

of prayer. I have heard it from Jew and non-Jew alike; "It is
somewhat overdone," they say. "Too many of these, and they lose
their novel value." There are many religiously inclined people who
feel that this repetition of days of national prayer is dangerous. We
remember the packed places of worship during the early months of
the War, when prayer days were instituted. When the French army
collapsed and the sun set over Dunkirk; when Jews were being
massacred on a scale unprecedented in human history and darkness
fell on every Jewish home. Yet with the dawn of victory in sight and
light breaking through the clouds, there is so much to thank Heaven
for and so much to pray for.

If science has found new methods for fighting battles and waging
war — if the clashing of shields has been replaced by guns and the
beating of hooves by tanks, if bombs have taken the place of noisy
instruments and bayonets the shouting of the warrior — the power
of the spirit remains unchangeable. It is the same spiritual force that
spoke to the Jews in their fight for justice thousands of years ago.
It is that same recognition of the triumphant power of the spirit that
gives strength to the faint-hearted: "let not your heart faint." It is
the conviction of the unconquerable spirit of truth and justice that
gives courage to the weak: "fear not." It is the calm and determined
sense of duty in the cause of righteousness and faith that gives the
capacity and energy to transcend all feelings of fear and pain: "do
not tremble nor be terrified because of them."

Who can deny that this has been the secret of our
indestructibility? שמע ישראל, "Hear O Israel," has been our war cry;
שמע ישראל has given us the strength to withstand and overcome all
onslaughts. What then is it, if not the power of the spirit, that has
infused in the people of this island a calm, determined sense of duty
and an unshakable belief in the value of the things for which they
are fighting? God was not on the side of the big battalions and tiger

tanks, but on the side of those who by their unselfish living and honest endeavour have brought His spirit into everyday thinking and His force into everyday undertaking. Music while you work? Yes, but prayer while you work, too.

We thank God for the mercies of the past and we beseech Him for the mercies He must yet shower upon us. Life expended in such a way is not in vain. Life is measured in spirit as well as in years. To this end let us continue the struggle — in this end there is no death. Let our prayers be real and sincere, so that the day may come, and come soon, when the better world for which we are fighting will be established, to the happiness of men and to the glory of God.

v

The Inner Battle

Our ancient teachers liked to compare the battle referred to in the *Sidrah* to the battle we wage within ourselves:[1] the battle for religion and battle against social conditions, the battle for knowledge and the battle against ignorance, the battle for religious practice and observance in spite of difficult economic circumstances. Likewise, we can perhaps think of the four classes of exemption mentioned here in terms of our own experiences. מי האיש אשר בנה בית, a house built somewhere where it cannot be dedicated, so far is it removed from Jewish life. ומי האיש אשר נטע כרם, one whose choice of livelihood is such that it makes observance

---

1 ראה אור החיים כאן: אולי שרמז הכתוב מלחמת האדם עם יצרו ובא להסיר מלבבו מורך ואמר כי תצא למלחמה הידועה שאין גדולה ממנה וכו׳ וכעין זה בגמ׳ ברכות ה׳ ע״א: לעולם ירגיז אדם יצר טוב על יצר הרע וכו׳.

well-nigh impossible. ומי האיש אשר ארש אשה, one whose wife, whose home-life, does not fit in with the requirements of faith and practice. Finally, מי האיש הירא ורך הלבב, one who is not strong enough to resist temptation — a faint-hearted Jew whose spine has snapped. Those are the types who cannot put up a fight against heavy odds, and who succumb to the enemy. To the stalwarts, to the Jew who is staunch and fearless, the Torah calls out אל תיראו: however few in number you remain, do not fear. Numbers and circumstances mean nothing, כי ה' אלקיכם ההלך עמכם: so long as you go with God in your heart, the battle will be won.

We live not for ourselves but for the Divine purpose for which we have been placed on earth. והיה ככלת השטרים לדבר אל העם, "and it shall come to pass, when the officers have made an end of speaking to the people, ופקדו שרי צבאות בראש העם, they shall appoint captains of the armies to lead the people." Let the 'captains' take their place at the head of the people, to guide and direct, to teach and to guard the glories of faith and culture, of language and of observance; and let them lead the people to the goal of God's glory, speedily and in our days.

vi

A Kind Cover-Up

The *Sidrah* lists four types of exemptions from military service in the event of war in the Jewish homeland. This, too, is encompassed in the all-embracing civilisation of the Torah; ואם לא תשלים עמך, if all efforts for peace fail, וצרת עליה, there must be mobilisation. War has a code, legitimate bloodshed is to be governed by law and order. Even on the battlefield human kindness is to be displayed. Beastly savagery, wanton destruction, are a crime. Even when you go out to kill, therefore, selected elements of the community are to be exempt from military service. One who has recently set up a home, one who is betrothed, one who is faint-hearted, one who has just entered into a commercial transaction, who has bought himself farms and they would remain uncultivated. How many fighting troops would remain after these exemptions matters not. If the cause is a righteous one, if you fight בנצחונו של מקום,[1] for God's sake, then numbers do not count. The spirit wins in the face of the heaviest odds.

There is another interpretation on the last of those exemptions, מי האיש הירא ורך הלבב ילך וישב לביתו, "What man is there that is fearful and faint-hearted, let him go and return unto his home." רבי יוסי הגלילי אומר. זהו המתיירא מן העבירות שבידו ... Rabbi Yosi says that the Torah's words are not to be taken literally: הירא ורך הלבב means one who is afraid of the sins he has committed. He is fearful of the retribution that might be meted out to him in war, so he too is to return home, he is to be demobilised. Kindness is shown to the sinner. That is not all; the Rabbis do not stop there. לכך תלתה לו תורה לחזור על ביתו וכרמו ואשה לכסות על החוזרים בשביל עבירות שבידם;[2] surely, Rabbi Yosi wonders, if exemption is given the sinner, is it necessary for the Torah to enumerate the other three causes, the one who has built a home, who is betrothed, or planted a vineyard? But the other causes are there only to provide a cover-up for the sinner: שלא יבינו שהם בעלי עבירה והרואהו חוזר אומר שמא בנה בית או נטע כרם או ארס אשה,[3] those three veil the motive of the sinner's return home. People who see him returning home from battle will say, "Perhaps he has built a house, or planted a vineyard, or betrothed a wife." What magnanimity is shown

1. רש״י; סוטה מ״ב ע״א.

2. רש״י מהמשנה סוטה מ״ד ע״א.

3. רש״י שם.

the man who returns from the battlefield because of his misconduct! Let others go back who should not go back, so as not to expose the sinner to society. Let people think he is one of the others. What a cover-up to make the בעל עבירה look like a *mentsch*!

On Yom Kippur pious and sinful alike will beat their breasts על חטא שחטאנו לפניך, as though the righteous and the wicked are tarred with the same brush and the sins committed by one were equally committed by the other. But the sinner cannot be exposed; so we stand together in bowed humility, not knowing who is who, but leaving it to God, Who knows the hearts of all men, to judge. The danger is when we cover up our own sins, and excuses are found for every wrong we commit.

עבירות שבידו is a very striking expression: the sins which are in one's own hand, to avoid or to commit. The Rabbis say[4] that the angel who supervises the birth of man takes the seed which is to become a human and brings it before the Creator and asks, "What shall become of this in life? Will it be strong or weak, wise or simple, rich or poor?" He does not ask whether he will be pious or sinful, good or bad; these things are left to the free will of man. Man is judged not according to that which is hardly in his own hands but rather according to that which God put entirely in his own control. שפטים ושטרים תתן לך — judge yourself: are you honest about the things you can do and cannot do, or are you covering up?

Elul is the month of searching of the heart, tapping of the conscience. אני לדודי ודודי לי, it is communion with God; cover-up and excuses are His affair, otherwise we should all be put to shame. עבירות שבידו can be avoided and must be avoided, so that when the day arrives the Divine call will come, סלחתי כדבריך, and the year will be one of joy and happiness.

4. נדה ט'ז ע"ב.

KI TETZE

כי תצא

i

Temptation

This *Sidrah* is the most remarkable of the whole cycle of the *Sidros* in the year. The Torah contains 613 *mitzvos*, comprising 248 מצות עשה, positive precepts, and 365 negative precepts, מצות לא תעשה. This *Sidrah* contains a higher number of *mitzvos* than any other single *Sidrah*: a total of 74 *mitzvos*, made up of 27 positive and 47 negative precepts. (Next is the *Sidrah* of *Emor*, containing 63.) The 74 *mitzvos* of this *Sidrah* cover practically every aspect of daily life, save for those practised in Temple times and the *mitzvos* between man and God, like *tefillin*, Yom Tov and Shabbos. Here we have laws concerning children, marriage and divorce, family, commerce, employer and employee.

One of the greatest tragedies in Jewish life is that religion has come to be something to do solely with emotions; it has lost its halachic dimension. All kinds of remedies are used today as a means of trying to cure our spiritual ills. There is everywhere a tendency to break away from the ancient Jewish landmarks. Believing in God has come to mean talking about Him, as if faith were some kind of intellectual persuasion, like music, that appeals to the intellect and moves the emotions. One can go these days to places of so-called Jewish worship to hear עבודת הקדש, where the very words have no meaning, where Jewish עבודה is torn to pieces, where fundamentals of faith and practice have been uprooted, where sanctities for which our forbears gave up all, which define the very purpose for which we live, are trampled upon.

Yes, intellectually it is a good way of escape. Emotions can be satisfied; but for how long? There are a thousand ways of satisfying one man's emotions. Can we accept the individualistic standpoint which measures every aspect and detail of Jewish life by a person's own whims and caprices?

A great preacher spoke wisely when he once said, "They condemn tradition when they ought rather to condemn themselves." This must be made clear from every Jewish pulpit and platform. In Judaism, faith in God is bound up indissolubly with our ethical teachings and religious practices. God is not a formula; you cannot separate Him from the movement of the limbs and from the day-to-day affairs of society. Religion involves all the faculties of human life. If religion were to become something more than seat booking and preaching, if religion operated in every sphere of human life, in state, in home and in communal relations, there is no telling how many of the great problems of mankind would be solved. The great message of this *Sidrah* is, God in life: dispense with the attractions, put off the thrills, set aside the emotions. Get down to the root of things in the depths of your own personality, find God deep down and lift Him up to the surface.

כי תצא למלחמה על איביך . . . וראית בשביה אשת יפת תאר, "When thou goest out to battle against thine enemies and seest amongst the captives a woman of goodly form." You will be captivated by her outward beauty. You will find among the captives something that your heart desires. The Torah recognises the overpowering influence of man's surroundings: לא דברה תורה אלא כנגד יצר הרע,[1] the Torah speaks of contingencies that arise from time to time in the life of man. There is sometimes a clash between conscience and heart; should one give way to the יצר הרע, to passing fancies, and abandon his conscience, or should he hold back, so that time will tell and conscience will prevail? Napoleon once said, "The only victories which leave no regrets are those which are gained over oneself." When values are made cheap and morals are brought low, the יצר הרע takes control.

One of the greatest proofs of the truth of the Torah is that it never conceals human weakness. The Patriarchs were no angels, and Moses was no demigod, and David's sin is frankly exposed. The Torah does not condemn; it sympathises. If you see something that tempts you, because war demoralises even the elated victor, if you are moved by emotions and swept off your feet by temptation — wait! Do not rush headlong into the mire: והבאתה אל תוך ביתך. Here will be the test. Bring the woman of goodly form into your house; what will she look like when the colour is removed and the glamour dies down? וגלחה את ראשה ועשתה את צפרניה, "and she shall shave her head and pare her nails."

Not all that glitters is gold — a luxurious house does not mean a happy home, a beautiful temple does not mean sanctity. Neither do prayers in English and the one-day Yom Tov, the violation of marriage laws, the policy of eat what you like and do what you like when you like. Bring this יפת תאר, these attractions, into your home, and see how long that home will last, how stable that home will be, what generations will issue from the loins of such relationship. וישבה בביתך; how long can vain attraction endure? Cut off the frills and let emotions die down; רואה בבכייתה רואה בנוולה,[2] see that kind of beauty

1. רש"י; קידושין כ"א ע"ב.

2. רש"י; ספרי.

in all its facets and you will realise one day סופו להוליד ממנה בן סורר ומורה,[3] the home built on it will be a home torn to pieces, father talking in one voice and mother talking in another. But on one thing they will agree: בננו זה סורר ומורה. From such an emotional setting there arises a stubborn and rebellious generation that will throw off the authority of parents and the authority of God.

What a dismal picture is painted by the Torah's Divine Author of the home in which conscience gives way to heart, religion to convenience, and discipline to passion. Children are reared who halt between two opinions: neither church nor synagogue, neither Jew nor gentile. Children who want the best of both worlds, but who in the long run have access to neither. The secret of Jewish survival is the ability to stand the test of endurance. Israel's homeland has withstood the test of time; our eyes were constantly focused on it; we never lost hope and we never lost faith. We never willingly surrendered a single *dunam*. We prayed day and night and we struggled to the last. Now we must beware lest we fall into the trap of a glamorous setting: a state that has grown out of the debris of a confused society. While others are still destroying, we are building. It is the only thing we have captured from the spoils of a war-ridden world. וישבה בביתך, we must take it into our life and into our homes. We must cut out the glamour of political ambition, never relaxing until our land has risen so high as to be beyond the reach of political strife and international squabble.

This Torah of ours has withstood the test of time. There is nothing in the world to compare with it. In all these years and through so many oceans of blood, not one letter has been erased, not one fundamental practice has been reformed. Shabbos and Yom Tov, *tallis* and *tefillin*, *kashrus* and dignity; we never lost hope and

3. רש"י.

we never lost faith. Today let us beware, lest we fall into the trap of an attractive setting painted by men who openly defy Jewish conscience and desecrate Jewish values. Bring it home, and see if it will withstand the test of time! Cut off the frills, set aside emotions, go to the depths and see it in its true colours; and you will drive it out, lest it poison the spiritual nerve centres of our very existence.

The enemy from without cannot be minimised: כי תצא למלחמה על איביך, "when you go *out* to war against your enemies," is as true today as it was when the great teacher bequeathed it to Israel, when they were about to take possession of their land of promise. But if the fight is to be כי תצא, a fight from without, then be confident that ונתנו ה' אלקיך בידך, "God will deliver the enemy into your hands." No one but the Jew has ever won the last battle. But the basic tragedy is not כי תצא; the basic tragedy is ושבית שביו, the penetration of the evil influence into our home and life. The glamour and the attraction that capture our imagination, Christianising Judaism, churchifying the synagogue. Sunday School making the classes *treifah*, the home becoming a shallow sham; a make-believe kind of religion that penetrates no depths and strikes no roots; a religion of outward beauty and inner decay. Israel's teacher warns, והבאתה אל תוך ביתך, before you surrender to it, bring it אל תוך ביתך, right into the home. What is its effect on the inner sanctum of your life, what kind of children will emerge, what generation will grow out of it? Religion and faith, practice and observance, are no fleeting fancies that can be cut to shape and made to fashion. Unaffected by climatic conditions, unchanged by outer influences, the Jew transmits from generation to generation his glories and his high ideals, until that great day when mankind will learn from him the true way of life, and thus bring about a sane order to this troubled world, peace and tranquillity to all men.

ii

The Triple "Yoke"

The Rabbis speak of three "yokes": firstly, the all-important עול מלכות שמים, the yoke of the Kingdom of Heaven, the acknowledgment and acceptance of the sovereignty of God; and flowing from this, the עול תורה ועול מצות, the yoke of Torah and that of *mitzvos*, the devotion to the study of God's teachings and obedience to His commandments.

A yoke is not an implement imposed upon animals to torture them. On the contrary, to harness animals without a yoke would mean greater pain. A yoke helps them to share the weight, to spread the load and pull together. It is in this favourable sense that we say each day in our *Shacharis* prayers וכלם מקבלים עליהם עול מלכות שמים זה מזה, "and they all accept the yoke of the Kingdom of Heaven one from the other." Why do we make reference in our daily prayers to the prophet Isaiah's vision of what goes on in Heaven? It is to teach us that קבלת עול מלכות שמים is measured by זה מזה, how much reciprocation there is, how much partnership in pulling together. The greater the number attending a daily *minyan*, the greater the power of the *Shechinah*, because the עול, the yoke becomes that much bigger. The more that listen attentively to the קריאת התורה, the reading of the Law, and attend *shiurim*, the greater is the עול תורה, the yoke of the Torah.

There is no religion in the world that bears so much sympathy and gives so many concessions to human weakness. The first paragraph of this *Sidrah* is the most outstanding manifestation of sympathy ever heard for the one who in wartime turns his back on his own people to satisfy his passion with a woman of foreign birth. But even in sin you must have some kind of עול, you must bear some responsibility to your God, your people and your family.

After a long procedure that might help passions to cool, only then does the Torah concede. If one has to sin, let him at least sin like a Jew and be conscious of his duty to carry the triple yoke of Judaism. All that is expected of the Jew is to pull his weight in every facet of Jewish life.

The Talmud[1] cites the words of Isaiah, ועזבי ה׳ יכלו,[2] "they that forsake the Lord shall be consumed," and applies them to המניח ספר תורה ויוצא, those who go out of the synagogue when the Torah is being read. Rabbi Abahu, we are told, נפיק בין גברא לגברא: he went out only between the *aliyos*. Later halachic commentators[3] quote the ruling of a renowned authority that this is only permitted באקראי, only as a rare occurrence in compelling circumstances; אבל כשעושין זה תדיר נראה פירוק עול תורה, "but if it becomes a regular practice, it is as though he throws off the yoke of the Torah," and to him may be applied the prophet's denunciation: ועזבי ה׳ יכלו, "they that forsake the Lord shall be consumed." In a wider sense this awesome reproach applies to המניח ספר תורה ויוצא, those that throw off the yoke of Torah, who leave it to others to uphold its study, who do not pull their weight and leave it to the faithful few.

Of the overburdened beast of burden that has collapsed beneath his load the *Sidrah* says, לא תראה את חמור אחיך או שורו נפלים בדרך והתעלמת מהם, "Thou shalt not see thy brother's ass or his ox falling down by the way, and hide thyself from them; הקם תקים עמו, thou shalt surely help him to lift them up again." עמו, says the Torah, "you shall help him" — say the Rabbis, . . .הלך הבעלים וישב לו,[4] if the owner leaves it entirely to you, you are not obliged to do it yourself. This insistence on working together applies equally to the bearing of the burden of

1. ברכות ח׳ ע״א.

2. ישעיה א׳, כ״ח.

3. ראה משנה ברורה או״ח סי׳ קמ״ז סעיף א׳ בביאור הלכה בשם תשב״ץ.

4. רש״י; ספרי.

Torah itself: הקם תקים עמו. We must not shirk our responsibility to ensure that Torah and mitzvah institutions are firmly established and exalted. We must bear the yoke and pull our weight; then God will add His הקם תקים עמו, so that our age-old hope may be fulfilled: לתקן עולם במלכות שדי, "when the world will be perfected under the Kingdom of the Almighty, ויקבלו כלם את עול מלכותך, and all will accept the yoke of Thy Kingdom."

iii

Learn and Reap Reward

The Sages who handed down the traditions and teachings of the Oral Law made an astonishing statement regarding the passage of the *Sidrah* dealing with the stubborn and rebellious son. It occupies four complete verses in the *Sidrah*, and a full chapter of the Talmud, Tractate *Sanhedrin*, is devoted to it. This is the case of a boy who has just reached the age of maturity, who, although so young in years, throws off all authority, of God, parents, and elders. He is full of vice and insubordination, a glutton and a drunkard, and is beyond parental control. If he were allowed to reach full growth, he would be the greatest danger to society. The Torah says, Better to let him die sinless, and have an opportunity of living in the Hereafter, than to let him become so sinful that there would be no hope for him. His parents bring him to the *Beis Din*; they must be the prosecutors and they must say בננו זה, this is our son. איננו שמע בקול אביו ובקול אמו, "he does not listen to the voice of his father nor to the voice of his mother" — here lies the fault, this is the cause of the tragedy. If only there had been one voice! If there had been קלנו, one voice, instead of קול אביו וקול אמו — if there had been one ideal, one background — a different child would have grown up.

The Sages see this passage as related to the previous two passages of the *Sidrah*, the laws of the victorious warrior who takes an alien captive as a wife and the law of the hated wife and the rights of her first-born son. The Torah tries to be sympathetic; in wartime life is cheap, values are low. The elated war heroes take their captives. They are lonely; they are only human, and the Torah consents under certain conditions. There is heart-break for both of them before their objective is reached. Even after all that, there is the danger of two backgrounds, two grandparents' voices; sooner or later it results in mixed-up children, neither here nor there. Nevertheless, so exacting are the conditions that the Oral Law lays down before this penalty can be imposed that it is virtually inapplicable: בן סורר ומורה לא היה ולא עתיד להיות[1] "Why, then," the Rabbis ask, "was the law written? דרוש וקבל שכר, study it and receive reward." There are some things in life that we must learn and learn and never get tired of learning, because life depends upon them. דרוש וקבל שכר, learn as much as you can, try and reach down to the depths, וקבל שכר, and you will find it most rewarding! It will be so rewarding; you will realise that there is so much in life we cannot understand.

Each morning as we approach the climax of our *Shacharis* prayers — just before we proclaim the *Shema*, the unity of God's Name — we call out אבינו מלכנו בעבור אבותינו שבטחו בך ותלמדם חקי חיים, "Our Father, our King, for the sake of our forefathers who trusted in Thee, and whom Thou didst teach the laws of life, כן תחננו ותלמדנו, we beg Thee, be gracious to us and teach us, too, those חקי חיים, those statutes of life." The חקי חיים are the statutes in this Torah of ours, which is the blueprint — the plan — upon which the world was established.

1. סנהדרין ע״א ע״א

These "statutes of life" comprise unfathomable decrees such as לא תזרע כרמך כלאים, "Thou shalt not sow thy vineyard with mixed seeds." The resultant crop has to be destroyed. לא תחרש בשור ובחמר יחדו, "Thou shalt not plough with an ox and an ass together." לא תלבש שעטנז, "Thou shalt not wear a garment made of mixed stuff, wool and linen together." You must not even use it as a blanket. It is said that the saintly Chofetz Chaim would not sit on the seats in a train because it consisted of mingled materials! There is also the prohibition of בשר בחלב, boiling milk and meat together. Also that a child born out of a forbidden, adulterous relationship is illegitimate and bears an impediment through his life and for all future generations. These are the חקי חיים, the statutes of life that prompt us to say with the Psalmist לתבונתו אין מספר,[2] "His wisdom is infinite."

This is what we say and accept every day of the week. We follow it with the psalm which says חק נתן ולא יעבור,[3] "He gave a law to Creation and it cannot be transgressed." These words of the Psalmist are uttered as the climax to his poetic portrayal of the praises for God's wonders evident in the immutable workings of the heavenly hosts. הללוהו שמי השמים והמים אשר מעל השמים, "Praise Him, heavens of heavens, and you waters that are above the heavens." The Hebrew term for heaven, the Sages say, is in the dual form שמים, implying that it is a composition of two elements: אש ומים,[4] fire and water. The two conflicting elements combine harmoniously in obedience to His will: חק נתן ולא יעבור. By the Divinely ordained 'laws of nature,' עושה שלום במרומיו,[5] "He makes peace in His high places." By these same 'laws of nature' we see on earth the mixing of fire and water, resulting in volcanic eruptions and such atmospheric disturbances

2. תהלים קמ״ז, ה׳.

3. תהלים קמ״ח, ו׳.

4. חגיגה י״ב ע״א; רש״י בראשית א׳, ח׳.

5. איוב כ״ה, ב׳.

as hurricanes and tornadoes. These physical manifestations of a Divinely ordained order — חק נתן ולא יעבור — of statutes that shall not be transgressed, are a sure indication that in human life too there are mixtures that make eruptions in family life, disturbances in human nature resulting in violence, murder and robbery. In our own day we hear constantly of stubborn and rebellious youngsters who are the product of disturbed lives and broken homes.

From the beginning of Elul till the end of the Holy Days we recite psalm 27 morning and evening. In it we pray הורני ה' דרכך ונחני באורח מישור למען שררי, "Teach me Your way, O Lord, guide me in a right path." Why the repetition? If we pray that He may teach us His way, why do we go further and pray for guidance "in the right path?" The Psalmist may well have been mindful how many interpretations there are of God's teachings. This is the same Psalmist who cries חק נתן ולא יעבור, "He has set the world on חק, on law and order, ולא יעבור, they cannot be transgressed." With all the sympathy in the world it cannot be done; the mixture will not hold; but some so-called interpreters want tolerance above all else! They think they are the only ones who understand tolerance; not Hillel, not Shammai, not Rabbi Akiva and not Rabbi Yochanan ben Zakkai! Hence, when we ask Him הורני ה' דרכך, "Teach me Thy way, O Lord," we further implore Him ונחני באורח מישור, "guide me in the right path."

The Torah law of the stubborn and rebellious son is written to urge us דרוש וקבל שכר, learn those laws that are beyond your reasoning וקבל שכר. Build your life on the חקי חיים, those statutes which alone make for a wholesome society, at home, in the family, in the community, and in the state. Thus you will show the world the only way to peace and tranquillity.

iv

A Holy Camp

כי תצא מחנה על איביך ונשמרת מכל דבר רע, "When you go forth in camp against your enemies, then keep yourself from every evil." Besides the previous passages dealing with the laws of warfare, the Torah here has a further passage with a significant variation of expression. It does not seem to be speaking of physical war: the term used is not מלחמה, it is מחנה. The Camp of Israel is in danger, our unity, our peace of mind, our spiritual loyalties — our מחנה, not the enemy's — so "keep thee from every evil."

The Rabbis ask a pertinent question: וכי אם אינו יוצא אינו צריך לו שמירה? "Is it not a duty at all times to keep away from every evil? אלא מכאן שאין השטן מקטרג אלא בשעת הסכנה,[1] this teaches us that the Satan is active in times of danger, and therefore beware." The word שטן is never referred to when speaking of the belligerent forces who from time to time come up against us, aiming at our physical destruction. The Satan works more subtly; he is the one who aims at the camp from within, when values are at stake, when the מחנה, the way of life, is being threatened. Be careful כי תצא, when you are outside the camp, not to do anything that could besmirch the good name of traditional Judaism.

If adverse and cynical elements in social, vocational and communal life can be avoided, אם אינו יוצא אינו צריך שמירה, if you do not stir out of your circle, your 'camp,' the need to be careful is not so great. But כי תצא מחנה, if you do have to go out as a camp to strive for the preservation of cherished ideals — which is sometimes inevitable, living as we do in a modern society where communal

1. ירושלמי שבת פ״ב ה״ו.

and social conditions make it necessary — then be careful ונשמרת מכל דבר רע אפילו מדבור רע,[2] watch your step, guard your mouth even more than at home. Anything you might say or do might besmirch the good name of the Orthodox Jew. Any flaw in the precious jewel of traditional Judaism may make a blot on the pure faith of our fathers.

ויד תהיה לך מחוץ למחנה; the Targum interprets יד as אתר, "you shall have a *place* outside the camp." When you are חוץ למחנה, outside the camp in their company, let them look up to you with respect and admiration for the place and position you hold amongst them with dignity. It is a sad reflection, sometimes bordering on the grave sin of *chillul Hashem,* when one who is reputed to be an Orthodox Jew, who never neglects his synagogue and pays due regard to the things which stand בין אדם למקום, between himself and his Maker, seems at times to by-pass (perhaps unwittingly) the things בין אדם לחבירו, between man and his fellow man. It may be small and insignificant, a careless word or a thoughtless deed which none of us can avoid; but what do they say, these cynics who stand around the camp and want to push us out? They will not speak of us as individuals, they will speak of the "*frumer* fanatics." They think that only those who have discarded *tallis* and *tefillin* and have closed the *Gemara* for all time are entitled to tell an untruth or make a rash statement. But the God-fearing man is to be blameless!

Do we not hear it in many circles? Others can do what they like, but at any misdemeanour by a religious Jew they whisper, "look at them, the *frumer Yidden.*" How right the Rabbis were, how well they understood human nature when they suggested an alternative reading to the verse כי תצא מחנה . . . ונשמרת מכל דבר רע: "if you go out among them, be careful of the least thing you say," lest it shed darkness on the ideals you are supposed to represent.

כתובות מ׳ו ע׳א; ספרי. 2

This is the message for anyone who finds himself assaulted: at home do your best and let God be the judge, for He knows your heart; but outside remember, man is the judge. If you carry your faith with dignity and respect, ויד תהיה לך מחוץ למחנה, then you will create a place for yourself outside. If the faith you bear is revealed in your personality, if they see no hypocrisy in you, ויצאת שמה חוץ, then you may take that place consistently. If you expect others to give, give yourself; you will show by deeds the courage of your convictions. Then והיה מחניך קדוש, your 'camp' will remain holy and intact; no assault from outside will penetrate it. Your faith will never wane and you will stand out as an example to friend and foe, leading men back to the faithful path of Judaism that will become a light to the whole world.

v

Enlarging the Tent

(Bar Mitzvah)

In this *Haftorah*, the seven weeks' dialogue[1] of consolation with which the year ends reaches a significant stage: the prophet Isaiah looks forward to the time when Zion's suffering and humiliation will be forgotten in her glorious future. The exiles returning to repopulate and rebuild Jerusalem and the devastated homeland will be more numerous than the inhabitants of old. הרחיבי מקום אהלך, "enlarge the place of thy tent, האריכי מיתריך, lengthen thy cords." Make them expandable to make room for the increased population, but

1. ראה אבודרהם בסדר הפרשיות וההפטרות (דפוס ירוש', דף ש"ג).

ויתדתיך חזקי, "strengthen thy tent-pegs." See that the foundations remain immovable. When there is expansion and progress, alien influences and foreign tendencies might weaken the foundation. ויתדתיך חזקי, strengthen the stakes to weather the winds of changing conditions.

The joyful prospect of expansion envisaged by Isaiah is in stark contrast to another kind of expansion referred to in the opening passage of the *Sidrah*. The victorious warrior's espousal of an alien captive conjures up the prospect of an expansion that is menacing to Jewish survival and calls even more urgently for a "strengthening of the tent-pegs." Alas, it is a form of expansion that is contemporary, too. It threatens the boundaries of the Jewish home: the law and the tradition that shape and mould Jewish living; the boundaries of the *mitzvos* that encircle the Bar Mitzvah; the קדושין that cements the marriage; the טהרה that pervades the home and produces the child. Of these boundaries the Psalmist's words must be said no less than of natural boundaries: גבול שמת בל יעברון,[2] "thou hast set a bound that they may not pass over."

It is a shocking mistake that people make who think they can live a Jekyll-and-Hyde existence, a Jew at home and a heathen in the street. In the long run we will never change the street; we will never shape the street to the pattern of our home. We will only find that we begin shaping our homes to the pattern of the street. The whole philosophy of the Torah is to "strengthen the tent-pegs," to set bulwarks against such invasions. That is why we have *tefillin* on our arms and *tzitzis* on our garments, *kashrus* in the food and Shabbos in work and laws of purity in family life. That is living Judaism: following the Shulchan Aruch every day and ensuring that every action fulfills our duties and devotions. Once the boundaries

2. תהלים ק״ד, ט׳

of *halachah* are broken, one may think that he can remain a Jew with a good heart and good intentions — a Jew in heart and a heathen in action, a kosher kitchen but a *treifah* stomach. Yes, he will satisfy his appetite: ושבית שביו, he will expand the territory, he will become contemporary, but at the expense of a clash of loyalties — a clash between his wants and his loyalty to the community. Religious faith and practice are not fleeting fancies, nor are they like cloth that can be cut to measure. ויתדתיך חזק, strengthen the tent-pegs; only then וזרעך גוים יירש, will your children dispossess the alien influences and grow up to be loyal sons of Israel.

This prophetic message has a particular relevance to those on the threshold of adult life. Concerning them the prophet's exhortation has a special significance: אל תיראי כי לא תבושי, "do not be afraid, for you will not be ashamed." Every new Bar Mitzvah boy is a new branch on the family tree of the House of Israel, which we hope will grow and spread in beauty and in splendour, so that parents and earlier generations will not need to be afraid or ashamed. Manhood brings with it many challenges, alluring attractions and tempting associations that wean away even some of our best and brightest. However steadfast the upbringing, we can never be sure.

It is so easy to be drawn away, and it is so hard to get back. In the words of the *Haftorah,* ברגע קטן עזבתיך וברחמים גדולים אקבצך, "For a small moment have I forsaken thee, but with great compassion will I gather thee in." One turn off the well-worn track of our sacred traditions needs רחמים גדולים, "great mercy," to get back. Only by strengthening the pegs, ensuring that each new generation is firmly fixed, with a solid grounding in Jewish education and an ongoing attachment to the tent of Torah learning and Torah living, can we hope to see the fulfilment of Isaiah's joyful vision, Israel's expansion and God's promise: כי ההרים ימושו והגבעות תמוטינה וחסדי מאתך לא ימוש וברית

שלומי לא תמוט אמר מרחמך ה', "for the mountains may depart and the hills be removed; but My kindness shall not depart from thee, nor shall My covenant of peace be removed, saith the Lord that hath compassion on thee."

KI TAVO

כי תבא

i

Measure for Measure

The *Sidrah* begins with a graphic description of the first-fruit offerings which the Israelites brought to the Temple in thanksgiving for God's beneficence. העשירים מביאים בקלתות של כסף ושל זהב, the Rabbis say, "The rich brought their fruits in baskets made of gold; the poor in baskets made of cane." ולקח הכהן הטנא — the Rabbis explain[1] that the priest was to take not only the contents, fruits of the vine or barley or figs, but the container, the basket, too. Why? That was not the purpose of the בכורים; why the basket?

נטמאו הבכורים הסלים נתנים לכהן,[2] "In the event of the fruits becoming unclean for one reason or another, and so uneatable, the basket at least remained the possession of the priest."[3] If there were no fruits, then at least the טנא, the container, was a satisfactory contribution. It is a wonderful lesson for us all. Some come to God's house with fruits; some offer their labour, some their time, some their energy;

1. משנה בכורים ג׳, ח׳.

2. ירושלמי בכורים פ״א ה״ז.

3. ראה תורה תמימה בענין זה.

some learn, some give services, others give gifts; but whatever you do, do not come empty-handed. אם נטמאו הבכורים הסלים נתנים לכהן, if the fruits are unobtainable, then give something else, give of yourself. When all the various gifts and tithes had been given, this prayer was offered up: השקיפה ממעון קדשך מן השמים, "look down from Thy holy habitation, from heaven, and bless Thy people Israel." The Rabbis make bold to supply the intent lying behind that prayer: עשינו מה שגזרת עלינו עשה אתה מה שעליך לעשות,[4] "We have done our share; now You, Almighty God, do Yours." We who have been able to give have given, we who have been able to serve have served; we have done that which is within our power — now You do that which is within Yours.

Religion is no magic lamp that lights up when you press the button. It is measure for measure: give and you will be given in return, deal justly and justice will be meted out to you. The nations of the world, who never raised a finger to stop gangsterism when it affected the struggling State of Israel, are learning that bitter lesson![5] It is a kind of justice that will never work. The ways of God are by means of reciprocation: you take out as much as you put in. Occasionally He gives something for nothing; now and again there is a dividend. But it is one of life's cardinal principles: עשינו מה שגזרת עלינו עשה אתה מה שעליך לעשות, "We have given, now it is Your turn; we have acted justly, now others will act justly with us." Let none who is guilty point a finger of guilt at others; let none who comes empty-handed expect to receive a gift in return.

What a challenge this is as we prepare for the Holy Days! We shall stand with bent back and open hands, pleading "Give, give פרנסה, give us our needs, give health, give Israel strength and peace." Make lighter and easier the burden of those who have consecrated

4. רש"י; משנה מעשר שני ה', י"ג.

5 This sermon was delivered at the time of the Suez Crisis.

their means to the religious education of their children, to the needs of the poor, to the observance of *mitzvos*, to the building and strengthening of Israel, and to the maintenance of our religious and communal life.

Throughout the whole of this *Sidrah*, which is known as the *Sidrah* of תוכחה, there are long lists of blessings and curses: blessings for obedience and curses for disobedience. Nowhere do we find in the *Sidrah* that God Himself blesses the obedient and punishes the disobedient. The blessings and curses came not from the lips of the Divine — no voice was heard from Heaven — they came from the lips of men. אלה יעמדו לברך, one half of the people shall stand on Mount Gerizim, ואלה יעמדו על הקללה, and the other half shall stand on Mount Ebal. One half for the blessings, and all responded אמן; the other half for the curses, and again all answered אמן. All confirmed the declarations. Joy and sorrow, war and peace, cannot be bought or avoided at a price. You cannot buy happiness, you cannot run away from suffering; והשיגוך, it catches us, it pursues. There are obligations and responsibilities that we owe each to the other, that we shoulder each for the other. ברוך אתה means man himself must become a blessing and spread that blessedness upon others; ארור אתה, man himself becomes a curse and spreads his miserable influence upon others. We say אמן to one another's actions.

No nation in the world can live on its own; no individual can build a castle for himself. Blessing and curse come from within. Those who give that others may enjoy, those who build schools and synagogues, state and community, for one and for all — these are a blessing to human society.

May those who give inspire others to do likewise, so that darkness and hardship may be ended. ועליך יזרח ה' וכבודו עליך יראה, "Upon thee — Israel — the Lord shall shine, and His glory shall be seen upon thee, והלכו גוים לאורך, as a light unto the world."

ii

Thanksgiving and Confession

There are two interesting *mitzvos* referred to in this *Sidrah*, the mitzvah of בכורים and the mitzvah of מעשר. Both applied only when Israel entered and occupied the Holy Land. First is the bringing of the first fruits, those for which Israel was acclaimed: wheat, barley, grapes, figs, pomegranates, olives and date honey. The first fruits were brought to the Temple in joyful procession, and the Rabbis spare no effort in describing at length the beauty of the ceremony of הבאת בכורים, the bringing of the first fruits. The second mitzvah is the giving of מעשר, the tithes to the Levite, the widow and the orphan. Another tithe was to be brought to Jerusalem and eaten with family and friends in joyful celebration, this time without pomp and without ceremony.

The fulfilment of each of these *mitzvos* was to be accompanied by a prayer. One prayer was known as מקרא בכורים, the reading of the verses of thanksgiving for the first fruits, and the other was known as וידוי מעשר, the confession and declaration concerning the giving of the tithes. The מקרא בכורים was to be read only in לשון הקדש, in Hebrew; וענית ואמרת בקול רם, it was to be read in a loud voice; but וידוי מעשר was to be recited in a קול נמוך, a quiet and humble manner, and בכל לשן,[1] in any language. What is the difference? Both were an expression of thanksgiving for God's beneficence; why was one a וידוי and the other a מקרא? One בקול רם and the other בקול נמוך, one בלשן קדש and the other בכל לשן?

There are two kinds of blessings. One is the blessing that comes from God Himself — the blessings of the land, of the soil and nature:

ויבאנו אל המקום הזה ויתן לנו את הארץ הזאת, "He brought us to this place and He gave us this land, so now ועתה הנה הבאתי את ראשית פרי האדמה, now I bring You the first fruits of the earth אשר נתתה לי, which You, O Lord, have given me." That is מקרא בכורים: acknowledging what God does, proclaiming to the world His goodness. It calls for the loudest acclaim. His wondrous deeds in the workings of nature are testimony to His celestial and Divine Being. They bespeak the prophetic truth מלא כל הארץ כבדו,[2] which is one of the three aspects of God's Holiness: קדיש על ארעא עובד גבורתה, "holy upon earth, the work of His might," to which we give expression in our daily prayers.[3] Hence it requires not merely the loudest acclaim, it must also be in the Holy Tongue as befits its holy message.

In contrast to this, in the declaration concerning the giving of tithes man speaks of his own deeds. One should never brag and boast out loud about his virtuous doings; it must always be בקול נמוך, in a low voice: יהללך זר ולא פיך,[4] "let another man praise thee and not thine own mouth." Furthermore, man is sometimes motivated by promptings of self-interest: כי אדם אין צדיק בארץ אשר יעשה טוב ולא יחטא,[5] "there is no righteous man upon earth that doeth good and sinneth not." Even the noblest of human acts are not always all-holy; not all man's avowals of his good deeds are fit to be expressed in לשן הקדש!

In the וידוי מעשר there are expressions that have an eternal relevance, and they are never more topical than in the days before the season of Divine judgment. There is the bold declaration, בערתי הקדש מן הבית, I am keeping nothing for myself which I should give to Jerusalem. לא נתתי ממנו למת, I leave nothing after me which I should

2. ישעיה ו', ג'.

3. בקדושה דסידרא בתפלת ובא לציון.

4. משלי כ"ז, ב'.

5. קהלת ז', כ'.

give to the needy. While I live, my hands are clean, my conscience is clear. Can we say this to God before Rosh Hashanah in our own language, and with our personal confession be sure we tell Him the truth?

Equally relevant today is the difference between the things to be said out loud and those to be said in a hushed voice. As in the מקרא בכורים, we must proclaim בקול רם, in a loud voice, our attachment and our giving to our God-given Land of Israel. We must let the world know that it is הארץ אשר נשבע ה' לאבתינו לתת לנו, "the country which the Lord swore to our fathers to give us." On the other hand, we must suppress any temptation to boast out loud, and we must only speak בקול נמוך, in a quiet voice, if speak we must, of our own giving to our community. Actions speak louder than words in sharing with others the blessings that a benevolent God has bestowed upon us.

Only thus can we approach the Heavenly Throne of Judgment, confident that we may merit a favourable response to that ancient prayer: השקיפה ממעון קדשך מן השמים וברך את עמך את ישראל ואת האדמה אשר נתתה לנו, "look down from Thy holy habitation, from heaven, and bless Thy people Israel and the land which Thou hast given unto us."

iii

Preaching to the Converted

(Selichos)

The confession of tithes contained in the *Sidrah* was to be made by the Israelite at the end of a three-year cycle. There were three tithes to be set aside: one tenth of one's produce was to be given to the Levite, a second tithe was to be given to the needy, and a third tenth was to be taken to Jerusalem. At the end of the third year, when these offerings had been discharged, it was the duty of the Jew to make a solemn declaration: בערתי הקדש מן הבית וגם נתתיו ללוי ולגר ליתום ולאלמנה ככל מצותך אשר צויתני לא עברתי ממצותיך ולא שכחתי, "then thou shalt say before the Lord thy God, 'I have put away the hallowed things out of my house, and also have given them to the Levite and unto the stranger, to the fatherless and unto the widow, according to all Thy commandments which Thou has commanded me. I have not transgressed any of the commandments, neither have I forgotten.'" Forgotten what? the Rabbis wonder: לא שכחתי מלברכך ומלהזכיר שמך עליו,[1] "I have not forgotten to offer thanksgiving to You and to be conscious of my gratitude to You."

It seems strange that this kind-hearted and faithful Jew, who is ready to give up three tenths of his produce to Israel's needy, and to travel from one end of the land to the other as a manifestation of his gratitude to God, is asked in his declaration to say, I have not forgotten מלברכך, to bless You at all times. We are always criticised that we preach to the converted, and that our message would serve a more useful purpose if it were given to those who make no appearance in God's house. But here it is right in the *Sidrah*: it is of those who are alive to Israel's needs and are conscious of Jewish values that the Torah demands the confession.

It is to the committed stalwart that the summons to *Selichos* goes out, a summons that attunes our thoughts to the solemnity of the Holy Days. Now is a season of preparation for the great day of forgiveness and atonement, which can have a tremendous influence on our lives in the confines of our own homes. Because of the *Selichos*, Yom Kippur comes as the culmination of a constant day-to-day confession, and the על חטא of *Kol Nidrei* night makes a deeper impression.

1. מעשר שני ה', י"א.

Whilst the nations of the world plod restlessly on, endeavouring to find healing for a world that is sick unto death, let us find a healing in our lives and homes, with a return to *Selichos,* expressing in them a real sense of confession for wrongs committed. Two things the *Sidrah*'s confession demands of us: 'I have given to the stranger, the fatherless, and the widow,' and 'I have not forgotten the Torah's precepts in my own life.' Then must the answer come from the Giver of all things: "You have done yours, I will now do Mine." May He bring succour and comfort to a stricken world[2] and peace to all men.

iv

Spiritual Discernment

There is a profound thought in the declaration and prayer that was offered up by the ancient Israelite after giving his tithes. Amongst the things to be said was: לא אכלתי באני ממנו ולא בערתי ממנו בטמא ולא נתתי ממנו למת, "I have not eaten thereof in my mourning, neither have I put away thereof being unclean, nor have I given thereof for the dead." There is a type of Jew whose religious life is centred around his period of mourning, and even that much is becoming a burden and is cut down by some to the minimum of one night. There is also the type of Jew with a mixed sense of values: he is as good as gold and can refuse none, but he cannot discern between קדש and טמא, between holy and unclean. He allows his generous enthusiasm to get the better of him, and gives indiscriminately to all and sundry. Then there is the third type of Jew, whose whole *Yiddishkeit* is centred around the dead: the funeral, the tombstone, and the

2 This sermon was given in 5708 (1948).

employment of a *Kaddish*-sayer. That is his whole religion. We speak sometimes of the man who sins without שכל. He is religious, but does not know when to be religious; he gives, and does not know to whom to give.

Against these three peculiar weaknesses the Torah guarded the Jew who made his periodical pilgrimage to the Temple. לא אכלתי באני ממנו, 'I never made the period of mourning my main religious practice.' ולא בערתי ממנו בטמא, 'I never gave to all causes alike.' ולא נתתי ממנו למת, 'and I never allowed my religious sentiments to be centred around death; I exercised a sense of spiritual discrimination.' The finest thing in Jewish life, a blessing which is within reach of each of us, is the mental capacity of spiritual discrimination. Not everything that appears good is good, and not everything that appears bad is bad. There would be no romance in life and no greatness if that sense of discrimination were taken from us. If evil, for instance, were banished, then the struggle of achievement would be abolished with it.

If Rosh Hashanah means anything, it means to stop the cycle of the year for a brief moment, to take ahold of oneself, to show greatness; not to abolish evil — that you will never do — but to take hold of it, break through it, and allow the crown of God to rise upon your head. What did the pilgrim say when he came to God's Temple? בערתי הקדש מן הבית, I have made a clearance in my own home and life. I have drawn a line between clean and unclean, between holy and unholy; I have distinguished between right and wrong. We prepare at this time of the year for our pilgrimage. An extra little prayer each day; an extra little study; a little more charity, and clean thoughts in keeping with the solemnity and spirit of the occasion. Then when the sun of the new year rises, we shall be ready to be blessed by its radiant light, to go forward resplendent, adorned by the crown of Divine Kingship, revealing a brightness that will illumine the way to all men.

v

Sin and Punishment

(Shabbos Before Selichos)

With the commencement of *Selichos* we begin familiarising ourselves with some of those old-fashioned words: סלח לנו, חטאנו, אשמנו. These terms of liturgical confession seem quite out of date in this age of ours. It does not seem right, in these days of rebellion, to search one's conscience, to beat one's breast and pray for repentance. Only an old-fashioned Rabbi dares to stand up and talk of these things. Only he is unashamed and not the least embarrassed, ready to talk about sin and punishment in an age when sinners have become martyrs, murderers have become politicians, immoral people teachers, and social misfits publishers. There is a song that is sometimes sung on *Simchas Torah*: מדוע העולם הפוך וכו', "Why is the world upside down? What should be high is low, what should be low is high, what should be black is white and what should be white is black."

But when I pause for a moment to think, I feel so proud and so good because we have this *Selichos* period of preparation, a week or ten days before the new year. Other people, everywhere else in the world, have their bars filled with drink and their ceilings with bunting. They run out of beer and paper hangings; we run out of seats in the synagogue and *machzorim* in the bookshops. There will be hundreds of thousands of Jews all over the world beating their breasts with the first call of אשמנו before the Days of Awe and Repentance. Pious Jews, thousands of them, in the early hours of the morning as dawn breaks, queuing up for the *mikveh* to purify themselves for the first call to Heaven. . . שמע קולנו חוס ורחם עלינו, "hear us, have pity on us."

It is precisely this conscience-pricking idea, this soul-vexing conception, this sense of guilt now and again, this feeling of humility, that fills me with a sense of pride and nobility. Thank God I was born into this people! It is because I am something that my life means something. It is because I am what I am that I feel so badly about the wrongs I have committed: the things I do but should not do, the things I do not do and should do. If I were a nobody, I would not care a penny; but I have such connections, such associations, such relationships!

We have only to glance at a few lines in this *Sidrah*: ה׳ האמירך היום להיות לו לעם סגלה, "the Lord has exalted you this day to become His own treasure, ולתתך עליון על כל הגוים, and to make you high above all nations, לתהלה ולשם ולתפארת, in praise and in fame and in glory, והלכת בדרכיו, and you will walk in His ways: וראו כל עמי הארץ כי שם ה׳ נקרא עליך, and all the peoples of the earth shall see that the name of the Lord is called upon you." Then there are these remarkable words of the *Haftorah*: וכבוד ה׳ עליך זרח, "and the glory of the Lord is risen upon thee"; ועליך יזרח ה׳ וכבודו עליך יראה, "upon thee the Lord will arise, and His glory shall be seen upon thee"; נצר מטעי מעשה ידי להתפאר, "you are the branch of My planting, the work of My hands wherein I glory." When I read these verses, do you wonder that I feel so humble and yet so great? I want to weep and to rejoice. See who I am, and yet so unworthy!

Selichos are not merely prayers for forgiveness, pleading for pardon; of course, they are that too, but they are essentially expressions of failures. See the heights we could have attained, and how low we remained. Rosh Hashanah is approaching, the coronation day when we crown God the King; then Yom Kippur, when we swear allegiance to Him and become His loyal subjects; Sukkos, the culmination, when we take Him by the hand — out into the open, His crown on our head — hand in hand, ישראל אשר בך אתפאר,

to show Him off to the world. *Selichos* are cleaning-up exercises, getting fit for the occasion. Ours are not services of confession; in Jewish life there is only one service of confession: וידוי, before the end. When it is finished, there is no time to clean up then, when it is late; just before the heart stops beating, that is called וידוי. These other services are סליחות. We ask Him to look to the good and not to the bad, we pray to Him not to break off relations with us, never to turn aside.

It is one of the most interesting features in Jewish religious thought that although we find this *Sidrah* full of the promise of reward for good behaviour and punishment for bad, curses, ארור, for disobedience, and ברוך for obedience; yet we hardly find anywhere in our liturgy, "please, God, do not punish us for the wrong we have committed, let us not suffer for the sins we have wrought." It must be made clear that reward and punishment is a fundamental doctrine in Judaism. There is no doubt about that: אפילו שיחה יתירה שבין איש לאשתו,[1] there is a Heavenly record of everything, and it will be taken into account, "even small talk between husband and wife." But that has to do with the Hereafter, יענער וועלט. It is part of the Divine pattern which will unfold itself there one day. Reward and punishment is not for the here and now.

One may well ask: "Well, what about all those verses in this *Sidrah*?" Look again at the *Sidrah*: ארור and ברוך, blessings and curses, never come from Heaven. אלה יעמדו לברך את העם על הר גרזים, ואלה יעמדו על. הקללה בהר עיבל . . . "These tribes shall stand upon Mount Gerizim to bless the people. . . and these shall stand upon Mount Ebal for the curse." The proclamations came not from the lips of God, not from Heaven, but from the lips of men here on earth. If you run across the road without looking and get run over, it is not punishment. It

1. חגיגה ה' ע"ב; ויקרא רבה כ"ז, ז.

is your own fault and the consequence of your own action. If you plant a seed and it flourishes, it is not reward: it is a natural consequence of your action. ברוך does not mean 'may you be blessed,' or even 'be blessed': ברוך means 'blessed *is*.' ארור does not mean 'be cursed': it means 'cursed *is*.' ברוך means, 'He becomes a blessing who is obedient and disciplined; he becomes a curse who is disobedient, a rebel.'

Religion says, 'You are what you are, you produce what you are, you take out what you put in.' You cannot expect from a child more than you put into him. You cannot expect from God more than you put into God. If there is nothing in the home, there will be nothing in the child, and that is not punishment, it is only natural. If there is something in the home, there will be something in the child; it is not reward, it is natural. Very few sons go wrong where there has been *tallis* and *tefillin*, Shabbos and *kashrus*, Yom Tov and charity. Very few daughters go astray when there has been a home-loving mother with Shabbos and with purity. You take out what you put in; that is religion, do not blame God.

There is a lovely comment on this *Sidrah*. Each Israelite was to bring the first fruits to the Temple in thanksgiving for Heaven's favours of produce. He was to put the fruit in the basket, ולקח הכהן הטנא מידך, and the priest was to take the basket with the fruit. What material was the basket made of? העשירים... של כסף ושל זהב עניים בסלי נצרים,[2] the rich brought baskets made of gold and those of the poor were made of cane; but נטמאו הבכורים הסלים נתנים לכהנים,[3] say the Rabbis, if the first fruits were not fit, having been rendered impure, then the basket at least will belong to the priest. You cannot come empty-handed and expect Him to give; religion is no jackpot. He

2. משנה בכורים ג', ח'.

3. ירושלמי בכורים פ'א ה'ז.

does not give without the asking. Sarah gave birth to Isaac, Rachel gave birth to Joseph, Chanah gave birth to Samuel — on Rosh Hashanah.[4] Not one of them had it easy. Prayer, pain and suffering — He wants us to pray, to plead, to ask for what we want.

Selichos stress the unique relationship between God and man and the need for each other, the dependence of each upon the other. Homes are broken up when husband and wife no longer feel a need for each other. Children leave home and break parents' hearts when there is no longer a need and a feeling for each other. Brotherhood and friendships are shattered when we want to do without each other. It is the same when there is no feeling for God, no need for God, no prayer, no giving, no paying, no feelings of regret, no חטאתי. *Selichos* are a way of showing the need for getting attuned and showing regret. It is an opportunity for re-opening relations with God, bringing Him into heart and home, life and living. Then, as happened to Sarah, to Rachel, to Chanah, He will respond to prayer by giving all we need and deserve in a year of peace and blessing.

vi

Upholding Torah

The *Sidrah* portion of the blessings and curses concludes with an implied blessing on anyone who upholds the Torah and a similarly comprehensive denunciation: ארור אשר לא יקים את דברי התורה הזאת, "Woe to the one who will not uphold the words of this Torah." The Talmud Yerushalmi[1] asks, וכי יש תורה נופלת, "what does the Torah

4. ראש השנה י׳ ע״ב.

1. ירושלמי סוטה פ״ז ה״ד.

mean by יקים, hold up? Is there such a thing as a Torah that falls?"
The Ramban (Nachmanides) refers to this question posed by the
Yerushalmi with a significant rephrasing of one of the answers given
there. He says: אפילו היה צדיק גמור במעשיו והיה יכול להחזיק התורה ביד הרשעים
ולא החזיק המבטלים אותה הרי זה ארור. One can be the perfect צדיק גמור — he can sit in
his home praying and studying, practising and observing — a צדיק
גמור! Imagine what that means in the estimation of the Ramban. But
if he does not go out of his way to lift up the Torah, to do everything
in his power to make it live in the hands of men who have been
breaking every law in it, he is included among the cursed. If a
Yeshivah has no place to learn and doors are not open to it, if children
roam the streets without *Aleph-Beis* and a *Talmud Torah* is not
established, if boys and girls want to learn and we do not provide
the means, we can be real צדיקים, we can be pious in our own
surroundings; nevertheless, הרי זה ארור, we are included among those
who are doomed. It is an awful prospect.

Conversely, those who support Torah and its institutions with
whatever means are within their power, are worthy of the blessing
that preceded the curse. The opportunities that exist today in Israel
and throughout the Diaspora are many and varied, and those that
support and uphold Torah are legion. By the merit of all those who
work למען תינוקות של בית רבן, may the whole House of Israel be worthy
of blessing and prosperity, joy and happiness.

vi(b)

Each According to His Ability

The concluding pronouncement of the blessings and the curses,
which is so significantly paraphrased by the Talmud Yerushalmi and

incisively crystallised by the Ramban,[1] is more than a comprehensive summary of the duties of the Jew. It is a warning on its own, independent of all others. Whatever the secrets of our hearts may be, however pious our actions, a special duty is imposed upon us: להקים את דברי התורה, to uphold Torah in the hands of others from whom it has fallen. כבד את ה' מהונך,[2] "Honour the Lord with thy substance," says King Solomon; אל תקרי מהונך אלא מגרונך,[3] expound the Sages, "Read not מהונך, with your substance, but מגרונך, with your voice." אל תקרי מהונך אלא מחונך,[4] "Read not מהונך, with your substance, but מחונך, with whatever God has blessed you" — this is another Rabbinic interpretation. Some have been blessed with means; then hold the Torah up with your means. To judge one's contribution by the standards of others' contributions is not honouring God from that with which He has blessed us. Some have been blessed with speaking ability, and to remain silent because others are silent is not מגרונך, using the voice with which God has blessed you.

This is the great message of the Shabbos before *Selichos*: ארור אשר לא יקים את דברי התורה הזאת לעשות אותם. No blessing is confirmed upon the man who is not prepared to hold up the Torah, לעשות אותם, to do those things which are in his power to do. וכי יש תורה נופלת, asks the Talmud; if, God forbid, a *Sefer Torah* were seen falling from the hands of one who is holding on to it, would we wait and see what the next man would do? Or would we rush forward to save it from his weakening grip? לעשות אותם, each one must use the ability with which God has blessed him. The preacher in the pulpit, the reader at the reading desk, the industrialist in his office, the communal worker in his sphere of activity: irrespective of his private and personal conduct,

1 See the previous section.

2 משלי ג', ט'.

3 פסיקתא רבתי עשר תעשר ב'.

4 פס"ר כ"ה ב'.

אם יכול להחזיק ואינו מחזיק הרי זה בכלל ארור, if he can help to hold it up and refuses to do so, he is precluded from the blessing.

There are two problems that are of constant concern to the Jewish community. One is the state of the Jewish faith; the other is the spiritual well-being of the Jewish State. All other problems pale before the magnitude of these two eternal issues. If we are to be counted among those who are to be blessed, then let each one of us, with whatever God has blessed him, hold up the weakening hands of those who are struggling hard to maintain them. If we openly display the courage of our convictions, with voice and with means, then כל מי שיכול להחזיק ומחזיק הרי זה בכלל ברוך, we shall be included among those who merit the Torah's blessings of peace and prosperity.

vii

The Fountain of Life

The world cannot reconcile pain and suffering with an omnipotent God. Agnostics grope in darkness with this question, and what an abyss faces them! World wars, with the blood that pours like torrents, have shaken their assumed stability of mind, and they too are beginning to wonder whether or not there is not something deeper in it all. The Jew has no such religious perplexities. He never asks why there is suffering, for such a question arises only when salvation is sought through a force outside of one's own being.

ברוך אתה בבאך, "Blessed shalt thou be when thou comest in," is the Torah's promise; בביאתך לעולם, "when you come into the world," the

Rabbis remark.[1] From within our own being blessing emerges. ברוך is derived from the word בריכה, a well. Man is linked with the Divine Source of life: he draws from the fountain of life, and if the water is untainted, if his life is pure and clean, then the water flows endlessly; there is a living companionship that goes on and on. ברוך אתה בצאתך, ביציאתך מן העולם [2] — even when you go out, out of the world, life continues undiminished, without end.

This is the philosophy of the Jew: it all comes from within, from us alone can salvation spring. If the link in the companionship snaps; when we cease to be בריכה, a well of life; if the water becomes contaminated and impure; then ארור אשר לא יקים את דברי התורה הזאת, "Cursed be he that confirms not the words of this Torah." He himself becomes a curse to mankind. There is no in-between for the Jew; he can be either ברוך or ארור, a blessing or a curse. Reward and punishment are no mere gains or losses for obedience or disobedience: מפי עליון לא תצא הרעות והטוב.[3] It is as if they have no connection with God. There is no such thing as reconciling God with pain and suffering; הרעה באה מאליה, suffering comes from itself, of its own accord. והטוב לעושה טוב,[4] happiness too is no reward from Heaven; both are the inevitable consequences of man's own actions: we reap as we sow. This is the mighty power of God in us. This is man's purpose as ordained by God.

The Jewish conception is that you cannot go out to find happiness, that there is no seeking after it. Nor can you evade unhappiness; there is no running away from it. There are two paths of action. One is אם שמע תשמע...ובאו עליך כל הברכות האלה והשיגך, "If you will hearken diligently unto the Lord... all these blessings shall come

1. בבא מציעא ק"ז ע"א.

2. שם; רש"י.

3. איכה ג', ל"ח.

4. רש"י, איכה שם.

upon thee and overtake thee." What a strange utterance! והשיגך, blessings will overtake you, happiness will pursue you and overtake you! אם לא תשמע, "If you will not hearken unto the Lord, ובאו עליך כל הקללות האלה והשיגך, then these curses shall come upon thee and overtake thee." Yes, precisely the same expression: unhappiness will pursue you and overtake you. ודבק ה׳ בך את הדבר, "pestilence will cleave unto thee"; there will be no running away from it.

This is the plan of life. The choice can be glorious or terrible, and there can be no questioning 'why?' because ואמר כל העם אמן: the people ratified it. We accepted it as our mission; this is the Jewish purpose. The sufferings of our people are the most remarkable proof of the truth of this portion of the Torah. Who has ever denied the Divine interposition in our history?

Shall we not, then, turn first to ourselves, wherein the course of our destiny lies, to stem the drifting further and further away from the truths of the Torah, which alone can bring us blessing? Elul is the time to revitalise ourselves from the fountain of life, with more prayer, more devotion, more honesty and more decency, more God in our everyday lives, so that our children may see and learn. Then, when כי שם ה׳ נקרא עליך, "the name of God is called upon you," when the word Jew has become synonymous with everything that is Godly, then will Divine blessing rest upon our lives.

viii

The Divine Alternative

יצו ה׳ אתך את הברכה באסמיך ובכל משלח ידך, "the Lord will command His blessing *with thee* in thy barns and in all thou puttest thy hand unto." Here is a beautiful verse, but a very strange one. We always read of

God "giving," "granting," or "conferring" a blessing; but what is this about "commanding" a blessing? At least if the Torah would say יצו ה׳ לך את הברכה, "God will command the blessing *unto you*," we would not be so surprised; but יצו ה׳ אתך את הברכה, that God will "command the blessing אתך, *with you*," is a rare expression indeed.

All the good things in life are really blessings from God. Good sons and daughters, good health, a good year, good fortune: these are all blessings that God gives by His Divine Grace. These are gifts that come to us from outside. If these good things are taken away from us, who are we, what have we?

A person with riches enjoys a blessing, but he himself is not always a blessing. יצו ה׳ אתך את הברכה, "the Lord will command the blessing *with you*," means that you yourself will become a blessing to society. People will look upon you, be inspired by you: the way you live, the way you conduct yourself, the way you hold yourself as a Jew. יצו ה׳ אתך, with you God will command respect.

About the word באסמיך the Talmud says, בדבר הסמוי מן העין,[1] "you will be blessed in those things in your life which no one can see," things that are inside you, a clean mind, clean thoughts. Going out into the world in places of secular studies and work, there are those whose minds are full of rubbish, whose thoughts are poisoned by the media. יצו ה׳ אתך את הברכה, God's blessing should be באסמיך, in your innermost parts and your innermost being. The verse continues ובכל משלח ידך, "and in everything to which you put your hand." His blessing will be made manifest by your honesty, your integrity in the work of your hands. כי תשמר את מצות ה׳ אלקיך והלכת בדרכיו, "if you will keep the commandments of the Lord thy God and walk in His ways" — that is what the Torah means by אתך: your every limb will be blessed. וראו כל עמי הארץ כי שם ה׳ נקרא עליך, "and all the peoples of the earth shall see that the name of the Lord is called upon you."

The Rabbis say that two things came down together from heaven: ספר וסייף ירדו כרוכים מן השמים אמר להם אם עשיתם את התורה הכתובה בזה אתם נצולים מזה ואם לאו הרי אתם לוקים בו,[2] "The book and the sword came down together from heaven." The People of Israel, the Land of Israel and the Torah will live and never die. Alas, there have been times in our history when we have been obliged to defend ourselves with the sword. The עמי הארץ, the peoples of the world, have seen Israel's military prowess; but we must never forget that the סייף, the sword, is also מן השמים. However great our relief at the salvation by the sword, we must realise that there is a Divinely ordained alternative. Our great mission is the ספר, this Torah that was given us to live by. וראו כל עמי הארץ כי שם ה' נקרא עליך ויראו ממך: the verse can mean, as the English version has it, that all the peoples of the earth shall see ויראו, "and they shall be afraid of thee." A preferable translation would be ויראו ממך, "they shall revere you," respect you and learn to be God-fearing from your example.

The *Sidrah* concludes: ושמרתם את דברי הברית הזאת ועשיתם אתם, "Observe, therefore, the words of this covenant, and do them, למען תשכילו את כל אשר תעשון, so that you may prosper in all that you do." תשכילו means in order that whatever you do, you will do with שכל, with wisdom and understanding. The Torah gives wisdom, understanding, שכל, to choose between right and wrong. This true שכל is also באסמיך, a rich inner storehouse and a true source of good fortune and blessing for a happy and prosperous future.

ספרי עקב י"א, י"ב. 2.

NITZAVIM

נצבים

i

Living Monuments

אתם נצבים היום כלכם לפני ה' אלקיכם ראשיכם שבטיכם זקניכם ושטריכם כל איש ישראל, "You stand this day, all of you, before the Lord your God; your captains of your tribes, your elders, and your officers, with all the men of Israel."

היום, "this day," it is said, recurs each year on Rosh Hashanah[1] and Yom Kippur. Yes, Rabbis and laymen, rich and poor, wise and ignorant: all are equal at the bar of judgment.[2] אתם נצבים, the Torah says; not אתם עומדים, the usual Hebrew word for standing, but נצבים, which means firm, unbending. You are the מצבות, as one commentator puts it, you are the living monuments of an unchangeable Torah. You who recognise the frailty of man and the sovereignty of God, who go out to welcome the new year with new determination to rally around the Torah, to rally around those who learn the Torah, to rally around those who uphold the Torah.

---

1. זהר; והשוה איוב א', ו' ברש"י, ושם ב', א' שעליו נאמר שהוא י"ב.

2. מדרש תנחומא

The prophet Isaiah, in the *Haftorah*, proclaims על חומתיך ירושלים הפקדתי שמרים, "upon thy walls, O Jerusalem, I have set watchmen, כל היום וכל הלילה תמיד לא יחשו, day and night they shall never hold their peace."[3] What are the defensive walls of ירושלים when the city is besieged by a sworn enemy? What are חומתיך ירושלים to those in the countries of the Diaspora? חומתיך ירושלים הן תורה שבכתב ותורה שבעל פה,[4] the walls of Jerusalem are the impenetrable walls that guard the sanctities of Jewish life, the Written and Oral Law, the faith and tradition, the customs and the observances. On those walls of Jerusalem God has set watchmen to guard and to defend, to honour and to observe. כל היום וכל הלילה לא יחשו, by day or by night there is no rest. There can be no relaxation in sunshine or in storm, in war or in peace. המזכירים את ה' אל דמי לכם, "You that remember God, take no rest," Isaiah calls across the ages to a world that has lost its sense of values. You who remember God even in the darkest darkness of the night, be the watchmen over Jewish defences. Guard the sanctities, observe the laws, take no rest until Jerusalem is rebuilt, the Torah restored, and God recrowned.

ii

Divine Justice and Mercy

The Tetragrammaton, the ineffable name of God, ה', denotes the Divine attribute of mercy; אלקים is the name representing the Divine attribute of justice. The human kind would never stand up to the

3. ישעיה ס"ב, ו'.

4. ראה פסחים פ"ז ע"א.

test of דין in its strictest form: אם עונות תשמר י-ה א-דני מי יעמד,[1] "if Thou shouldst mark iniquities, O Lord, who could stand?" How we should cover our faces in shame if a record of our activities of the year that has passed was replayed; nay, we could never stand it. The secret of human survival has been this: אתם נצבים, "you stand," and face life with all its difficulties, only because לפני ה' אלקיכם, there is a combination of Divine justice and mercy.

If the Rosh Hashanah days of judgment go well, if the days of *teshuvah* are well spent, if Yom Kippur day is one of devotion, then we can be confident in the mercy of God's judgment כי הוא אלקינו ואנחנו עם מרעיתו וצאן ידו,[2] "He is our God and we are the people of His pasture and the sheep of His hand." He will surely help; He will lead us in mercy to the goal of our desires. היום אם בקלו תשמעו,[3] if we will only take Rosh Hashanah seriously and with devotion, feeling that אתם נצבים היום לפני ה' אלקיכם, then we will be granted, for ourselves, for our children, and for men all over, a year of peace and prosperity.

iii

The Order of Rank[1]

The Shabbos before *Selichos* has been from time immemorial an awe-inspiring day to the Jew. From the early hours of the morrow, in every Jewish place of worship, wherever freedom of worship exists, Jews and Jewesses gather together in solemn prayer, and with the High Holy melody intone the *Selichos* Service. No matter

1 .תהלים ק"ל, ג'
2 .תהלים צ"ה, ז'
3 .שם

1 From a wartime sermon at Brixton Synagogue.

how well the Jew lives, he sees gaps, omissions and sins. Deep down
in the Jewish heart there is a desire to fill in the gaps, to rectify the
omissions, and to repent for the sins. I remember the *Selichos* days
abroad, when the *shammash*, the town's beadle, went at dawn from
door to door beating his stick against the walls, rousing the Jew
from his slumber, calling him to rise לעבודת הבורא, to the service of
God. Those were wonderful days. Nothing else mattered but to make
peace with God, Who alone was to witness and judge the earth. He
alone was to distribute to each one his share and allot to each one
his portion. Each *Selichos* Service was a committal service, a
wholehearted confession for the past and an unyielding
determination for the future.

I could never understand, in those youthful days, the agonising
cry that came from the lips of those saintly Rabbis: אשמנו מכל עם בשנו
מכל דור,[2] "We are more guilty than any other people, more ashamed
than any other generation." Surely their sins were lighter, and their
shame in God's eyes not so blatant! But they knew well that in the
presence of Almighty God there is an order of rank. אתם נצבים היום כלכם
לפני ה' אלקיכם ראשיכם שבטיכם זקניכם ושטריכם כל איש ישראל, "You stand all of
you this day before the Lord your God, the heads of your tribes, your
elders, your judges, all the men of Israel." החשוב חשוב קודם,[3] our Sages
remark: they stood before the Lord in order of their rank, the heads,
the elders, the judges, then the people of Israel.

When wrong is committed at home, you take the eldest son to
task first. The generals are blamed for misfortunes in the war. In
the misfortunes of mankind, it is the Jew who is first in the order of
rank. The Jew should know better; the Jew must know better. For
four thousand years the words of Moses in this *Sidrah* have been

2. חדי מסדור רב עמרם גאון.

3. רש"י.

echoing through the world: העדתי בכם היום את השמים ואת הארץ החיים והמות
נתתי לפניך הברכה והקללה, "I call heaven and earth to witness this day
against you, that I have set before you life and death, blessing and
curse." As man cannot scale the heavens above or fathom that which
is below — as heaven and earth abide forever — so do these sublime
principles of life and death outlast all changes of human life and
outlive every system which man may choose to build: לאהבה את ה'
אלקיך לשמע בקלו ולדבקה בו, "to love the Lord thy God, to hearken to His
voice, and to cleave unto Him, כי הוא חייך וארך ימיך, for that alone is thy
life and the length of thy days."

Life must be dominated by a ceaseless striving to cleave to the
Divine force. Life divorced from God, civilisation detached from its
spiritual foundations, becomes rotten and decadent. This is the
eternal message of Rosh Hashanah, the anniversary of the world's
Creation. God is the beginning and the end. Rosh Hashanah calls
for the rededication of human life to Him Who willed the beginning
of all things. It calls for the return of man to the Divine order which
alone can bring happiness and length of days.

iv

Leadership Priorities

The Rabbis notice that when Moses assembled the People of
Israel to deliver his farewell message, first came the heads of the
tribes, the princes and lay officers, then came the זקנים, the elders
who had acquired much Torah knowledge. But when Joshua, his
successor, summoned the people to his side, he put the זקנים in the
fore, and the ראשים followed — משה הקדים ראשים לזקנים וביהושע כתיב ויקרא

לזקני ישראל ולראשיו.[1] Moses addresses the people before they enter the Promised Land to conquer it, to overcome the enemy, to build the land, organise it, set it up, fight for it, and pay for it. The זקנים take second place when there is need to give, to sacrifice, to create, to build. הקדים ראשים לזקנים, young leadership takes precedence over aged counsel. Joshua addresses the people when the land has been established. When all was conquered and the tribes had been settled, the preservation of ideas, the maintenance of values — the elders — took precedence over young leadership: הקדים זקנים לראשים.

It may well be that these two contrasting policies in establishing seniority in the Jewish community are two schools of thought with which we are not unfamiliar throughout Jewish history — the old sage versus the young fighter. Happy is the generation that can send forth its young to re-establish the ideals of the old. Happy is the father who throughout his long life set standards and honoured them, who can hand over the care of them in his lifetime to his son and to the generations that follow him: his *Shacharis* and his *Musaf*, his shofar, his Shabbos, his Jewish living. It was a sad day in Joshua's life to see, as his own life was drawing to an end, that he could not hand over to the ראשים, but the זקנים had to take priority. They had to ensure that the land he had conquered and established should not be torn to pieces by irresponsible judges and leaders.

מה היום פעמים כלכם, "ye stand all of you this day" — אתם נצבים היום מאיר ופעמים מאפיל אף אתם, "just like the day: sometimes bright, sometimes dim; so is your history, sometimes light and sometimes dark." But עתיד להאיר לכם אור עולם, the time will come when light will never darken, בזמן שתהיו כלכם אגדה אחת,[2] when you are נצבים כלכם, when you hold yourselves together, ראשיכם זקניכם, young and old, father and children

---

1. יהושע כ"ד, א'; ירושלמי הוריות פ"ג ה"ה; וראה תורה תמימה על פס' אתם נצבים.

2. תנחומא.

maintaining the same synagogues, living the same faith, holding each other's hands like a chain, generation to generation. Then the old live on and never die, as son follows father and generation follows generation, as year follows year, in happiness and joy to the end of all time.

v

The High Festival Timetable

A famous journalist, presumably recalling a wartime experience, once wrote: "I lay on the ground while death held me in its clutches. I was twenty-three years of age. Did my past life appear to me? Yes, it did; and I regretted that I had not squeezed more out of my time. Then a great feeling of curiosity filled me. Fear of death I did not feel; yet I am not a brave man. There is only one thing worth repenting, and that is the harm you may have done to others." It is a wonderful thought for the last Shabbos of the year and the approach of our annual season of repentance: "There is only one thing worth repenting, and that is the harm you may have done to others."

It is a grave mistake to think that Rosh Hashanah, Yom Kippur, and the *Selichos* days that precede them are concerned only with the violation of religious precepts — only with *kashrus*, Shabbos and the like. Far be it from us to belittle these Divine injunctions; but let it be said, for the benefit of those who criticise Rabbinic Judaism, that in the order of Jewish life these religious precepts come second on the list. The harm we may have done to others comes first: עבירות שבין אדם לחבירו אין יום הכפורים מכפר עד שירצה את חבירו.[1] The relationship between man and fellow man is of the utmost concern to our Sages in the timetable of the Holy Days. They condemn in no uncertain language those who fail to make it up, so to speak, with a fellow man, before the approach of Yom Kippur. That glorious day has no effect, it passes by as though it had never been, unless our fellow man has been conciliated for the sin committed against him.

קשה גזל הדיוט מגזל גבוה,[2] "to defraud a human being is a graver sin than to defraud the Almighty." This is something we must still learn, and learn to our bitter shame, if we are to bring to bear the gracious influence of these Holy Days. Ignorant people who have never taken the trouble to study accuse Rabbinic Judaism of being concerned with religious practices alone, and by this accusation are responsible for a perverted conception of Judaism in the minds of the younger and more ignorant members of our generation.

We cannot answer for the so-called Orthodox Jew who wraps himself in his *tallis* every morning and considers himself at peace with his Maker, and then for the rest of the day and the week is engaged in evil practices of lying and deceiving and harming others. It is sometimes argued in his defence that perhaps two thousand years of homelessness has made him lose his faith in man, whereas God has never failed him, so that his sense of duty to his Maker has remained unshaken. To man, however, he has no sense of duty, and treats him as he himself has been treated for so many centuries. Of course, this is no excuse, but it is understandable nonetheless. History is to blame for this man's inverted sense of values; the struggle for bread and butter in the ghettoes of a selfish and cruel world have upset his mental balance.

1. משנה סוף יומא

2. בבא בתרא פ"ח ע"ב

But this is not Torah Judaism; neither is it Rabbinic Judaism. There can be no relationship with God without the relationship with fellow man. The practical ceremonial that we cherish, the *mitzvos*, whether religious, ethical or ceremonial, are the means to bring life to a state of perfection. Practical Judaism is to permeate life with a purpose that can only be achieved by a live, virile sense of duty to man. To pronounce a benediction over a stolen *lulav*, to hear the sound of a stolen shofar, is as treacherous as it is hypocritical. Not by artificial devices that cover religion in a veil of hypocrisy do we do our duty as Jews. The first duty of a Jew is to do no harm to others. To harm an orphan, to abuse a widow, to offend a stranger, to dishonour an obligation, to break a word of honour: these are criminal offences in Jewish law, and take precedence in the order of repentance. To this end we must direct our thoughts during the days of *Selichos*.

The tasks confronting the Jewish people are so enormous that we would despair utterly of their accomplishment without unity amongst ourselves and a measure of good will from others. Only in this spirit can we go forward to welcome the new year. אתם נצבים היום כלכם לפני ה׳ אלקיכם, "You stand all of you this day before the Lord your God." Rich and poor, ignorant and wise, leader and led, all stand stripped of such vain, annoying qualities as eagerness for financial gain and prominent position. What do these mean to the Divine Judge, Who penetrates the heart and reads the mind? It is the spirit that counts: character, conduct, decency, honesty and humility. Before coming to God on Rosh Hashanah we must answer the question: "Have I committed any wrong against my fellow man, have I harmed a widow, have I offended a stranger?" We can still make it up. In this spirit let us go forward to the High Festivals and welcome a new year. Then will it bring us joy in place of sorrow, peace in place of war, and happiness to men the world over.

vi

Who Can Judge?

אתם נצבים היום כלכם, "You stand all of you this day לפני ה׳, before God Himself." Outward things do not count; to Him to Whom the *neshamah* belongs, כל איש ישראל, every man is a Jew. It is not our affair to judge men, it is not our concern to condemn. What do we know of men's thoughts? What right have we to pass judgment? How do we judge? By actions, by garments, by outward influences. Who can read the tale, perhaps a bitter tale of woe, graven on another man's heart? לפני ה׳ אלקיכם כל איש ישראל, before God, Who knows man's thoughts, all are alike; כל איש, every man, is a ישראל. If you are arrogant, forget your arrogance; if you are wise, forget your wisdom; if you are wealthy, forget your riches. Turn to one another before the day comes, forget the petty things that divide us, and think better of the greater things that unite us. Our first duty before coming to God is to come to fellow men. Do not be ashamed; say to one another, "Forgive me if I have wronged you." Before we can claim to stand with God we must first stand with each other; it must be כלכם, "all of you"; then have we the right to come לפני ה׳.

What a wonderful sight Jewry would present if each of us turned to his neighbour in modesty and sincerity, and instead of finding fault found cause for praise! There is some good in every human being; that good we must seek out, instead of seeking evil; for is it not this that we ask God to find in us? Let us be determined, not merely by lip-service but by deed and thought, to create a solemn bond of friendship between Jew and Jew, between man and man. The women in their sphere of influence, the men in their sphere, let them go about sowing seeds of fellowship and friendship. Tell whoever speaks evil of another to try and find the good in him.

Then, and then only, will God find the good in us.

There are so many ways in which we can each help the other. There are so many places where so many meet, so much talk about so many people; let us be determined never to talk evil of another, for who knows what others say about us? Let us create a real fellowship of men, a real bond of friendship. Let us feel that we are all alike, children of one father with one common heritage, forgiving one another, loving each other. Then will God our Father take us under his Divine wings, to shield us from sorrow and grief, that all men may look upon our people as the harbinger of brotherhood in the world, and peace and tranquillity may be the destiny of the new world to be born in the new year.[1]

vii

On the Highway of Life

There are some words, or their connotations, that have disappeared from the vocabulary of human emotions nowadays: חטא, "sin," פשע, "transgression," and עָן, "iniquity." Now people do not sin anymore, they are merely frustrated; it is not their fault, it is the failure of human society, it is broken homes, it is diminished responsibility. People turn increasingly to psychiatrists, and meantime sins are accumulating and frustrations are beyond repair. Mind you, our Sages, too, say of a sinner that "no man would do wrong unless נכנס בו רוח שטות.[1] But רוח שטות does not mean frustrated or unbalanced; that is a שוטה. רוח שטות is stupid, misguided thoughts.

1 From a wartime sermon at High Wycombe.

סוטה ג' ע"א. 1

We are still old-fashioned enough, millions of us all over the world, from the temples of New York to those little, narrow streets in the Meah Shearim area of Jerusalem, in all kinds of places of worship — we are old-fashioned enough to chant together על חטאים ועל עונות ועל פשעים, "for sins and iniquities and transgressions, סלח לנו מחל לנו כפר לנו, forgive us, pardon us, grant us remission." For weeks before Rosh Hashanah we plead every morning at *Selichos* for forgiveness for the sins we have committed, beginning with each letter of the *Aleph-Beis*: אשמנו, בגדנו, גזלנו. When we reach the *tav*, the last of the twenty-two letters, we say three times *tav*: תעבנו תעינו תעתענו. Maybe we missed some out in between the letters of the alphabet.

On Yom Kippur, beginning with *Minchah* on *erev* Yom Kippur until after *ne'ilah,* it works out to some 255 confessions. Are we all unbalanced, are we all frustrated? Why do we not stop to think what it is all about? Do we improve, do we get any better when it is all over, or is this too just a habit, like sin itself? We just cannot or will not stop to think. We are like motorists on a highway or free-way: we are geared up and cannot slow down. We cannot make a U-turn because there is so much traffic at the back, and there are no side turnings, not to the left nor to the right. We go on and on until there is no petrol left, no כח in the engine; and then what?

Oh, and that is not everything; we *shlep* others with us, the passengers in the car: the family, the children. Where we go they go, what we do they do, how we live they live. As the old Yiddish saying puts it, "The apple does not fall far from the tree."

In the *Sidrah*, Moses looks forward to the future with a warning: פן יש בכם איש או אשה או משפחה או שבט אשר לבבו פנה היום, "lest there be among you a man or woman, or family or tribe, whose heart turneth away from the Lord your God, שרש פרה ראש ולענה, a root that beareth gall or wormwood." The Ramban (Nachmanides) explains these figurative expressions in a most meaningful way: שרש רע שיפרה... ובימים הבאים יוציא

פרחים רעים, "bad roots producing bad growths, ויצמיח מרורות, and bitter things result." Nachmanides continues, האב שרש והבן נצר משרשיו יפרח, "the father is the roots, the son is the produce of the spreading roots." Habits are formed at home, character is shaped at home: what the child sees, what he hears, where he goes, who are the guests at home, who are his friends, what does he eat. פן יש בכם איש או אשה, משפחה או שבט — man and woman, family and tribe; they are the roots. What Dad and Mam do becomes the nature of the child. הבן נצר משרשיו; it is a wonderful expression. The son is formed, נצר, in the very roots, he cannot be expected to change!

What an awful indictment Moses makes against the people in his address! He continues, כי ידעתי אחרי מותי כי השחת תשחתון.[2] He does not say "I think," or "I prophesy." He says ידעתי, "I *know* that after my death you will become corrupt, and will turn aside from the way which I command you, and evil will befall you in the end of days." He looked at that generation and he knew what the next generation would look like; he saw the roots and he was able to behold the branches. But one thing a Jew must never forget, the greatest thing God ever conceived for human society; if it is forgotten, there is no hope for this so-called religion in the world. That thing is that in Judaism there is no such thing as "paradise lost." There is no room in our thinking for a 'hopeless situation.' We cannot accept the philosophy of no return: it is false, it is not true, it is a lie. Moses never concluded his farewell message with the words that evil will befall you in the end of days. Heaven forbid, וזאת הברכה אשר ברך משה לפני מותו, he gave utterance to his greatest blessing before he died.

This sentiment is echoed by the prophet Joel in the final words of the *Haftorah* for the Sabbath of Repentance: וידעתם כי בקרב ישראל אני, "you shall know that I am in the midst of Israel." When He is

2. וילך ל״א, כ״ט.

there, there is continuity, there is perpetuity, there is eternity.

In an amazing passage in the Talmud Yerushalmi[3] it is said:

אמר רבי יודה בן פזי מלא תרווד אחד נטל הקב"ה ממקום המזבח וברא בו אדם הראשון אמר
הלואי יברא ממקום המזבח ותהא לו עמידה הדא הוא דכתיב וייצר ה' אלקים את האדם עפר מן
האדמה. Whence was the dust for man's creation taken? "From the
place where the altar would someday be built," say the Sages.
Maimonides adduces it, significantly, not in his philosophical
writings but in his practical Code of Jewish Law, the *Yad
Hachazakah*:[4] אדם ממקום כפרתו נברא, "Man was created from the place
where his כפרה, his atonement, will be granted." This is the most
powerful declaration in Rabbinic literature, indeed in the entire
orbit of theological and philosophical thought, of man's innate
power of rehabilitation. Man has it in himself, within his own being;
it is part of his original make-up to return and make atonement.
Animals too are born out of dust, but from any part of the earth:
וישרצו בארץ, "let them swarm upon the earth." There are all kinds of
animals, in their hundreds, but the unique being, man, came from
a selected part of the earth: ממקום המזבח, ממקום כפרתו נברא.

Men may have different features, different characters; but they
are the same humans, hewn from the same rock, taken from the
same soil. Take hold of this flesh that sins, that wants, that will not
relent; control the hands, control the eyes, control the tongues. No
wonder the prophet calls out during these *teshuvah* days, קחו עמכם
דברים — it is עמכם, it is within you. There is nothing you need bring
except what you have within yourself to do — determination: make
up your mind to put the brakes on. It is עמכם: your hands for *tefillin*,

---

3. ירושלמי נזיר פ"ז ה"ב.

4. הלכות בית הבחירה ב', ב'.

your palms for honesty, your work for Shabbos, your lips for peace. Take your limbs and ושובו, return to God. You will take your children with you, others will follow you. As the Almighty says: וידעתם כי בקרב ישראל אני, "you will know that I am in your midst," and you and yours will go on and on to the end of all time.

viii

Thought and Action

(Selichos)

In this practical world of ours it is our practice, not theory, that counts. It is not what we believe, but what we do; it is not how we think, it is how we act. This, according to the commentators, is the meaning of the familiar verse in this *Sidrah*: הנסתרות לה' אלקינו והנגלות לנו ולבנינו עד עולם. Those things that are concealed within us, thoughts not expressed — לה' אלקינו, they belong to God; He knows the thoughts of men. They exercise no influence on the course of life. But הנגלות, things that are exposed, thoughts put into practice, the conduct that men and women see — לנו ולבנינו עד עולם, they are handed on from generation to generation, they go on to the end of time. A good Jew's head is God's business; a good Jew is man's business.

A famous Rabbi was asked why it is that the Shulchan Aruch, the code of Jewish life, omits הלכות תשובה, Laws of Repentance, whilst the Rambam, in his code, the *Yad Hachazakah*, finds a prominent place for הלכות תשובה. "The Rambam," the sage replied, "includes in his code all the laws that govern Jewish life, past, present, and future, אפילו אינם נוהגים, even those that are not practised in present times; whereas the Shulchan Aruch contains only the laws which

are practised בזמן הזה, today. *Teshuvah* is not in fashion today," the
Rabbi said, "so the *Shulchan Aruch* omits it!" That is a scathing,
sarcastic remark from the lips of a saintly man, but it is far from
being untrue. How many approach the *Yamim Noraim*, the Days of
Penitence, Rosh Hashanah and Yom Kippur, with a serious
endeavour to make right their wrongs and not to commit them
again? People do not realise that from the "slot-machine" of religion,
the Giver of all things only gives out an amount of return
corresponding to what we put in: שובו אלי ואשובה אליכם,[1] "Return to Me
and I will return to you," is the philosophy of Jewish life, measure
for measure. Do not expect more than what you put in, any more
than you would from an automated machine.

   Teshuvah does not mean to repent; *teshuvah* means to return. It
is automatic: if we turn away He turns away, הסתר אסתיר פני; if we turn
back, He turns back. There is a connection between Heaven and
earth. There is a link, and so long as it has not snapped there is hope.
אדם שיש בידו עבירה ומתודה ואינו חוזר בה למה הוא דומה לאדם שתופס שרץ בידו שאפילו
טובל בכל מימת שבעולם לא עלתה לו טבילה.[2] One can confess his sins a
thousand times, but if his hands are still unclean his slate is not
cleaned either; if he does not come back, he is still miles away.

   No one has ever realised more than the Rabbis, the authors of
the great *Selichos* book, what are the frailties and weaknesses of the
human kind. It is hardly possible for a man to come straight into
Rosh Hashanah and stage a come-back of any lasting character, so
they instituted *Selichos* for a minimum period of four days before
the new year. Why four days? שכן מצינו בקרבנות שטעונים ביקור ממם ד' ימים
קדם הקרבה,[3] "This we find was the case with the animal sacrifices on

---

1. מלאכי ג', ו'.

2. תענית ט"ז ע"א.

3. משנה ברורה סי' תקפ"א ס"ק ו' בשם אליהו רבה.

Israel's ancient altar: the animal was set aside and kept under observation for four days before the appointed day of the קרבן, to be sure it was free of any blemish." So the Jew, like the קרבן, is to set aside four days for introspection, for a searching of the heart, a ביקור ממום, to cleanse himself of his blemishes before God comes down on Rosh Hashanah to proclaim Himself King. That is why, if Rosh Hashanah occurs during the first half of the week, *Selichos* commence on the second Saturday night before the new year, but if it occurs in the latter part of the week, the first *Selichos* night is after the Shabbos immediately before Rosh Hashanah, for then follow four days, Sunday, Monday, Tuesday and Wednesday. *Selichos* is intended for ביקור ממום, to "operate" on the blemishes, to clean the sins and to prepare for God the King.

The greatest menace to the human kind, threatening the world with destruction, is the shamelessness of sins. Today there is no shame in telling a lie. Leaders and statesmen today have no בושה; yet בושה is one of the greatest characteristics with which men are blessed. It seems to have disappeared. No people in the world have the guts to get together as we do and cry from our hearts לך ה' הצדקה ולנו בשת הפנים,[4] "You are right, and we should be ashamed of ourselves." כל העושה דבר עבירה ומתבייש בו מוחלין לו על כל עונותיו,[5] "If someone commits a sin and is ashamed of it, all his sins are forgiven." The first prerequisite to *Selichos* is shame for the wrongs we have done. At least to be ashamed of חלול שבת; at least to be ashamed of not paying dues to the local synagogue; to be ashamed that we could help Israel and we do not. ביקור ממום is the purpose of *Selichos,* to find our blemishes, to recognise our mistakes and then to try and make amends. Determined so to do, we shall approach Rosh Hashanah

דניאל ט', ז. 4

ברכות י"ב ע"ב. 5

with clean hands and pure hearts, confident in a generous response from Heaven.

Concluding the year in this frame of mind, we can look forward to the coming year with hope: may we be worthy to see the fulfilment of the final message of the season of consolation, with which the *Haftorah* concludes: בכל צרתם לו צר ומלאך פניו הושיעם באהבתו ובחמלתו הוא גאלם וינטלם וינשאם כל ימי עולם, "In all their affliction He is afflicted, and the angel of His presence saved them; in His love and in His pity He redeemed them and He bore them, and carried them all the days of old." May His pity and His love be with us, to bring an end to the affliction of Israel and of the world, that the dawn of a new year may bring with it rays of salvation and peace to men the world over.

VAYELECH

וילך

i

A New Leader

ויקרא משה ליהושע ויאמר אליו לעיני כל ישראל חזק ואמץ, "And Moses summoned Joshua and said to him in the presence of all Israel, 'Be strong and of good courage.'" Moses is about to depart and take leave of his people and of his successor Joshua; but was it necessary for Moses to say good-bye to Joshua in public? Did he have to say, Be strong and of good courage, in the presence of the whole community? Did he have to embarrass Joshua לעיני כל ישראל?

Moses wanted them to know of the courage required and the strong will needed to resist the fads and whims of כל ישראל — the crazes of the masses. Any young man who is not strongly set can fall prey to these temptations, and embark on ambitious ventures that sweep away every traditional landmark. Why, even trained spiritual leaders sometimes bend over backwards and break their resistance against the demands of a livelihood, and so have turned synagogues into theatres and Holy Day worship into showpieces. What, then, can one expect of a young student, physicist or scientist, doctor or lawyer? Can we expect him to sacrifice a career that dangles its anticipated fortunes in front of his eyes? ויאמר משה ליהושע

לעיני כל ישראל, so Moses tells Joshua in the presence of all Israel: "Irrespective of what they may say, regardless of your environment, notwithstanding all moral pressures, חזק ואמץ, be strong and of good courage; וה' הוא ההלך לפניך, God will be with you, לא ירפך ולא יעזבך, He will not fail you, neither will He forsake you." You are never alone. Great ideals are not preserved by the masses; לא תירא ולא תחת, do not fear the weight of mass opinion and do not be dismayed by the pressures of the environment.

ii

Rehabilitating the Soul

(Shabbos Shuvah)

A saintly Jew once said, at the commencement of the Ten Days of Penitence, that the whole year round a Jew's mind is engaged with the enemy from without, but during these days of *teshuvah* his mind needs to be engaged with the enemy from within. One form of enemy or another has exercised the attention of the Jew in every generation, and in every country wherever the Jew has set foot throughout his long and unhappy exile — the Russian, the German, the Pole, the Arab. During these days of *teshuvah* we are asked to divert our attention from these enemies that surround us, and to concentrate on the enemy within ourselves, the *yetzer hara*: the sinful tendencies in man called the evil inclination.

אלקי נשמה שנתת בי טהורה היא,[1] "My God, the soul which Thou hast given me is pure." The impurity of sin stains the soul of man. It is

---

1. תפלת שחרית.

with the annihilation of this enemy within that the *teshuvah* days are concerned. It requires the mobilisation of all the moral forces at our command to wash away the stains and to rehabilitate the soul in the body of man. Just as in every physical battle victory must be planned with strategy for attack and defence, so in this battle, too, there must be confession, repentance and return. A soul that has become defiled by the recurring, accumulating acts of sinful wrongdoing must first be purified by an admission that one's actions have been the cause of shame. This must be followed by repentance, addressed by one's awakened conscience to his Maker, and by a definite change of conduct away from unrighteousness, made manifest by action and deeds of a reverse nature. A complete transformation of mind and character purifies the soul from all the dross of past offences against man and God. This is *teshuvah*.

In the words of the prophetic portion for *Shabbos Shuvah:* שובה ישראל עד ה' אלקיך כי כשלת בעונך, "Return, O Israel, unto the Lord your God, for thou hast stumbled in thine iniquity." How can the return be effected? The prophet continues: קחו עמכם דברים, "take with you words," implying confession — I am sorry for what I have done. אמרו אליו כל תשא עון, "say unto Him, Forgive all iniquity," implying repentance; וקח טוב, "accept that which is good" — this is complete return: the resolve to act differently, determined to do good.

The doctrine of *teshuvah* is one of the greatest and finest of Jewish conceptions. We reject outright the theory of the "fall of man," as interpreted by theologians of other faiths: that man is unable, by reason of his original sin, to return to God by his own natural strength. It is their confusion over this dilemma that led them to accept a false doctrine of the suffering of one for the sins of all. We believe (as a great thinker once put it) in the rise of man and not in the fall of man. The door is always open, and every single member of the human family can enter. Every man is capable of realising the highest potentialities of the moral and spiritual life.

It is a great pity that preachers today, in their desire for popularity, to reach down to the level of the masses, have eliminated discussions of sin and repentance from their pulpit vocabulary. Why, it is an embarrassment even to refer to them in this so-called modern age. A candidate for a ministerial office these days would never succeed in obtaining the popular vote if he were to preach about sin and repentance. Rather should he preach about common themes of anti-Semitism, the national home, or the virtues of the United Nations; or he should express the everyday platitudes of moral standards and ethical values, that do not mean a thing in these immoral and unethical times in which we live.

These days people pin their faith on political or social theories to influence the course of human society; but where is that God in Whom they believe? רם על כל גוים ה',[2] somewhere high up — beyond the reach of man; no direct contact with the human kind, no link between Heaven and earth. What have they created to satisfy that natural human religious urge born in every child? They have an organisation, a church-oriented religion, with vested interests, with little or no influence on the life of the individual. They have severed the link that binds man to God, that brings Heaven down to earth. What has been achieved in the nineteen hundred years since the establishment of this pseudo-religion? Read the reports of their conventions and convocations, and see how gravely they review the future. Today a spiritual bankruptcy lurks before them. The way to *teshuvah* has been blocked, and the storms that ravage the world are bringing about the dismemberment of human society. This is the result of organised religion which can claim no truth and is void of foundation.

תהלים קי"ג, ד'. 2

שובה ישראל עד ה' אלקיך, "Return, O Israel, to the Lord your God." This verse is written, mark you, in the singular, because it is the potential of each single unit of the family of man. Return to the path that leads right unto Him! No impediment, no obstacle lies in the way.

הקהל את העם האנשים והנשים והטף וגרך אשר בשעריך למען ישמעו ולמען ילמדו ויראו את ה' אלקיכם ושמרו לעשות את כל דברי התורה הזאת. Here is the great Jewish heritage, the legacy of Moses: "Assemble the people." The word of God concerns the entire people. Who are these people? Not the clerics alone, but אנשים ונשים וטף וגרך אשר בשעריך, whoever comes within the gates to embrace this way of life, whoever stands in line with these conceptions. Our Sages say,[3] אנשים באים ללמד, the men come to learn; הנשים לשמוע, the women to hear; והטף לתת שכר למביאיהם, and the infants to provide reward for those who bring them. To hear means to submit to the word of God; to learn means to understand the word of God. To do the word of God means not merely to honour moral and ethical principles, but to apply them to everyday life — to create the link between man and his Maker by incorporating these principles into a binding, active code. These Heavenly qualities are to be given an earthly application.

There is no word in the Hebrew vocabulary equivalent to the word "religion." That is a foreign word to the Jew, because there is no such thing as religion in our set-up. I make bold to say that this concept of "religion" has been the curse of humanity. What crimes have been committed in its name; what suffering has been caused to millions through what they ignorantly call religious experience! הלואי אותי עזבו ותורתי שמרו [4] is an old Jewish cry: "Would that they left

רש"י; חגיגה ג' ע"א. 3

ירושלמי חגיגה פ"א ה"ז; וכזה גם בפתיחתא דאיכה פסוק "מי האיש החכם"; וראה בקרבן 4 העדה וציון ירושלים על הירושלמי הנ"ל.

Me alone, would that they forsook Me" is the Divine message;
"better that they just keep my Torah and my commandments."
'Believe in me and you will be saved' is nonsensical. 'Live with me
and you will be saved' must be the slogan.

The *Sidrah* tells us ומצאהו רעות רבות וצרות, a time will come when
many evils will come upon Israel. ואמר ביום ההוא הלא על כי אין אלקי בקרבי
מצאוני הרעות האלה, "In that day they will say: are not all these evils come
upon us because our God is not among us?" This is the test: an
acknowledgment of guilt, not for having failed to believe in Him
but for having failed to bring God among them. בקרבי means right
in their middle: in my very self, in my everyday actions. This is
teshuvah. God is here; all we need is to turn. You can leave religion
out of the picture — it does not mean a thing. וצדיק באמונתו יחיה,[5] "a
righteous man *lives* by his faith." Faith without living is absurd, it
has no meaning.

The prophet, in the *Haftorah*, concludes with the message וידעתם
כי בקרב ישראל אני,[6] "you shall know that I am in the midst of Israel."
God is down here, among the people, not just up above among the
angels. Turn to Him with this threefold plan: confession, repentance
and return in all our actions. Then ולא יבשו עמי לעולם,[7] "My people shall
never be ashamed." We shall stand out as an example among the
nations of the world, showing the true way, radiating the true light
that will, with God's help, lead to the salvation of mankind.

5. חבקוק ב', ד'.

6. יואל ב', כ"ז.

7. שם.

iii

Within Reach of Heaven

It is sometimes said that a Jew never gives a direct reply to a question put to him. He usually gives another question as the answer. A Rabbi, for example, once questioned his pupil about the existence of God. "Tell me," he said, "where is God?" "Tell me," the pupil replied, "where is God *not*?"

This, in fact, is not merely a question to avoid a reply: it is the only reply to the question. Where is God? — Where is God not? Here is expressed one of the major features of these *teshuvah* days worthy of comment: the view expressed by our ancient teachers that the spirit of God hovers over Israel's camps during the Ten Days of Penitence. He draws closer and nearer; and if for twelve months he has been merely God the Father, now he becomes God the King, and reigns in the very hearts of His mortal subjects. דרשו ה' בהמצאו קראהו בהיותו קרוב,[1] "Seek ye the Lord while He may be found, call ye upon Him while He is near." These are the days when Heaven comes within the earth's reach, when the voice of man pierces the Divine ear.

If ever there has been a Jewish contribution to civilisation — which as Jews we can rightfully claim — it is in the realm of religious thought and knowledge. Other contributions have come from Jews as individuals, but coming from the Jewish people as a whole it is this profound principle of the nearness of God to man. With this mission we Jews have been charged: to teach man with the Bible; to show man by example; to manifest to man in our history that God is not merely a force in life, a power, as it were, behind the scenes

---

1. ישעיה נ"ה, ו'.

or even in front of the scenes, but that God is part and parcel of man's make-up. Whilst others believe that על השמים כבדו,[2] His glory is in Heaven, we conceive Him בשמים ובארץ, in heaven and on earth.

How wonderful is the Rabbinic comment, ישראל בגלות שכינה בגלות,[3] "When Israel are in exile, the glory of God goes with them." Put plainly, though rather sweepingly, on this earth there is no *Shechinah* without man, nor is there man without *Shechinah*. This is Israel's contribution to the world of religious thought. There is no intermediary between man and his Maker; here is God and here is man. When Moses, the greatest seeker after truth, asked for the revelation of God, הראני נא את כבדך,[4] "Show me Your glory," the Divine finger pointed to man. Here he is and here we are.

In the *Sidrah* we find the Divine premonition: ואמר ביום ההוא הלא על כי אין אלקי בקרבי מצאוני הרעות האלה, "On that day they will say, 'Are not these evils come upon us because our God is not among us?'" בקרבי means not merely hovering over the camp but right down here among us. We may put it this way: men are accustomed to saying, "God will help, God will save, God will spare." It is a common expression of men. It is not entirely true; more than that, in fact, is the case. When He is בקרבי, in our very being, help is not required, for evil does not exist. Only when והסתרתי פני מהם והיה לאכל, "I will hide My face from them and they shall be devoured," only then is His help and mercy invoked; only when His presence is turned away.

The greatest curse of this generation has been — even with the religious class of men, even those who still believe in the Divine Spirit as a dominant force and a guide in the affairs of men — that religion as such, God as such, has become something outside of

2. תהלים קי״ג, ד׳.

3. מגילה כ״ט ע״א.

4. שמות ל״ג, י״ח.

man's make-up. Ask any God-fearing man: "Do you believe in God?" He will be astonished at your question: "Of course I believe in God." Ask the same man, "Do you feel God in your senses and in your limbs?" Very few will be able to answer. It is as true of the Jew as it is of others. Religion gives a sense of comfort and satisfaction, but rarely does it give a real sense of joy and elevation. This — shall we call it — insensible faith has been the cause of the sad neglect of religious practice. Why, to most people religious practice is a burden, a need perhaps because of its traditional value, but so unnecessary to true religion. Yes, even to the pious practising Jew, his ten or fifteen minutes' prayer in the morning, his washing, his *bentshen*, are simply matters of course, because it would seem strange to do away with them.

But there are people, and these, alas, constitute the majority, who have been brave enough to be original and revolutionary. "Why do it because I have been used to it, or because my father did it? Religion is a thing of the conscience; I am a good Jew at heart." This conception of religion cannot be explained nor understood. It is a belief in a Supreme Being Who is far away from man, yet a Being in Whom men believe. But it is only half of the real need. With this conception, however noble it seems to be, we get the conflict of two diametrically opposed forces. One is the conscience, which they call God, or the spirit, that desires one thing; and the other is the body, that yearns for other things. The only way in which the modern believer can conceive unity between these two forces is by training the body to live with the conscience by being honest and decent, clean and moral. How different is the true Jewish conception! To us God is part of our very make-up: He is in the movement of the hands, in the movement of the legs, in the seeing of the eyes and the hearing of the ears. He is in the stomach of man and in all his limbs. Oh, what a glorious creature man would be, what an angel on earth, what a God-like being in the flesh, if he knew, nay if he felt, that he walked with God and slept with God, talked with God and ate with God.

Our Sages would have us talk always in the plural, and never in the singular first person. The well-known Kelmer *Maggid* once said, "To say, 'I will do so and so,' even with 'P.G.,' is a degree of אפיקורסות." There is no "I" in the vocabulary of the Holy Tongue; it is "we," God and I. שובה calls for a return to God; not with the conscience, that is inadequate, but שובה ישראל עד ה' אלקיך, return unto Him, right unto Him. With your mind or with your conscience you can of course return — you can be a good Jew at heart — but you can only go to a certain limit: עד ה', until God. You can, as it were, reach the door, but it is not enough. קחו עמכם דברים, take with you your whole beings — your senses, your limbs, everything you have; then ושובו אל ה', you can go a step further. There is a difference between עד and אל; עד is limited, and אל is unlimited. If you have alienated the love of your child, and for months he has refused to return, how great is the joy when he comes back to your home. How incomplete is that joy when he comes עד, as far as the front gate, and still refuses to enter the house. With his conscience he has returned, but he still remains on the outside. How complete is the happiness when אל, he walks right in and returns to you in person.

It will be of little avail if we decide to make a religious come-back, but in conscience alone. We hear so much from press, from pulpit, and from platform, of the need for Jews to be honest, decent and truthful. These things we have to do as men and women of reason and understanding. That is merely a return in mind and conscience. *Shuvah* calls for still more.

קחו עמכם דברים ושובו אל ה'; we must stage a full religious come-back. Let us be old-fashioned — and let people laugh — the truth will prevail as it has done in the past. We need more religious practice, *tallis, tefillin,* and *tzitzis, kashrus* and Shabbos, washing and *bentshen,* prayer and synagogue. Enough of serving God with our mind! We must serve Him with our limbs, with our hands, our lips, our ears and eyes: קחו עמכם דברים. Let us try these things — מי חכם ויבן אלה, "Who is wise and understands these things? For the ways of the Lord are right and the just shall walk in them." Only as wise and just men shall we walk God's world; only with God reigning in our hearts will His kingdom be established.

iv

Mitzvah Power

A young student once said, "What if I return home and make it up with my parents? What if I repent and am no longer the sinner you judge me to be? Will the world change? If I mend my ways, will the world's statesmen mend their ways?" There is a deadly moral danger in thinking that way. We must agree that it is difficult to understand how the world would become a better place to live in if an individual changed his ways. After all is said and done, the hope of society today rests with the leaders of the world and the force of collective action. What is the answer? How can my little חטאתי, עויתי, פשעתי achieve anything in a world where the epicurean has come to life? "Snatch what you can, because you will never have it so good." Moral values are so, so low that there is hardly anything left to hold on to, not on the international scene, not on the national scene, and not on the domestic scene.

On the international scene, agreements are frequently not worth the paper they are written on. Political parties and national organisations break their solemn pledges. On the home scene the marriage undertakings — "I faithfully promise I will be a true husband unto thee" and "the bride pledges her troth unto him in sincerity"—are often untrue. The Bar Mitzvah boy's implicit pledge, in his blessing on the Torah, has become meaningless. This might well be the meaning of the prophetic call to *teshuvah*: קחו עמכם דברים, "Take with you in your repentance, in your return to God, the things you said; look back and reflect upon them: did I honour them? Was it worthwhile? Can I retract? ושובו אל ה', and return unto God!"

What then does it all mean, this אשמנו, בגדנו, in a world that has gone off the tracks? We have no power to hold it back. In fact, some of our best homes and many of our young people are shaken to the very foundations. There is a remarkable Rabbinic comment on a verse of the fifteenth psalm, which describes the Jewish ideal of human character. "Who shall sojourn in Thy tent, who shall dwell upon Thy holy mountain?" asks the Psalmist, and goes on to detail the qualities required of this ideal character: 'walking uprightly and working righteousness, speaking truth in his heart and having no slander on his tongue, nor doing evil to his fellow.' He concludes, עשה אלה לא ימוט לעולם, "He that doeth these things shall never be moved." The Talmud[1] relates, כשהיה רבן גמליאל מגיע למקרא הזה היה בוכה, when Rabban Gamliel came to this verse of the Psalms, he used to cry and say, מאן דעביד להו לכולהו הוא דלא ימוט, "Is it only he that does *all* these things who shall never be moved? הא חדא מינייהו ימוט, does it mean that he who does only one of these things shall be moved?"

"No, no," came the reply; "the Psalmist does not say עושה כל אלה, he who does *all* these things; עושה אלה כתיב, even if a man observes one thing; if he stands by one thing only, אפילו בחדא מינייהו, but he does it because God tells him to do it, then he shall never be moved for all eternity!" The Rambam makes this clear: כשיקיים אדם מצוה מתרי"ג מצות

1. סנהדרין פ"א ע"א; מכות כ"ד ע"א.

כראוי וכהוגן ולא ישתף עמה כוונה מכוונות העולם בשום פנים אלא שיעשה אותה לשמה מאהבה...זכה בה לחיי העולם הבא,[2] "If a person fulfils any one of the 613 Torah precepts as it should be fulfilled, without any ulterior motive or improper intention בשום פנים, of any possible kind, but purely for the sake of the mitzvah and for the love of God's commands, he thereby becomes worthy of life eternal."

Maimonides continues that Rabbi Chanania ben Tradyon, one of the Ten Martyrs of whom we read in our prayers on Yom Kippur, gained his share in the great beyond not by his martyrdom, but because of one mitzvah he performed completely לשמה, without any thought in his mind except the love of God and the fulfilment of His command.

This is one of the most profound thoughts in authentic Jewish religious teaching. A mitzvah done for no other reason but for God's sake brings God into play in daily life. It touches our home- life, making it אהלך, a tent of God. The *Shechinah* at that moment pervades and permeates life; it keeps the wheels of the world in motion. This is precisely what the Rabbis mean: it is within the power of any single Jew, with one good deed, one mitzvah, to bring the *Shechinah* to abide within us, to sway the balance in favour of good instead of evil. This is how Maimonides considers a Jew to be a צדיק, cleaving, as it were, to the *Shechinah*, the Divine Presence. He forges a link between Heaven and earth.

This Rabbinic teaching presents a great challenge to each individual, especially in the light of the Almighty's warning in this *Sidrah*: ואנכי הסתר אסתיר פני ביום ההוא, "I will indeed remove My *Shechinah* from them on that day." With the proper performance of one simple mitzvah, every Jew has a wonderful opportunity to bring the *Shechinah* into his life, to see God face to face. Could not this be

2. פירוש המשניות לרמב״ם, סוף מכות.

another interpretation of the *Haftorah*'s call, קחו עמכם דברים, "Take with you things"? You cannot do the whole at once. God does not do package deals; if you promise the lot you will do little. Let each one of us do one mitzvah; but it must be done thoroughly and correctly, with no other thought in mind but that God requires it. You will see what influence that will have on your home and life, and on the world at large.

v

Turning Away

We frequently find in the Torah expressions of Divine favour figuratively phrased as, "God turning His face towards us," or "lifting up His face to us": ישא ה' פניו אליך or ופניתי אליכם. In this *Sidrah* we find the reverse, too: אסתיר פני, והסתרתי פני, "I will hide My face" or "I will turn away My face." The significance of this expression can best be understood with a simple illustration. If two people are standing face to face in the street and one turns away from the other, leaving him standing, and walks a foot away, there is now a gap between them. Then if he decides to return, he has to go back one foot. But if the second person also turns away and both walk a foot away from one another, then a double journey has to be made to return and catch up. If we left God, so to speak, when He was near, and we turned our back on Him, that would not be so bad, it is half the battle to return. But if, when we turn our backs on Him, He also turns His back on us, then the task of return is ever so difficult. It is a double journey unless He also comes back to meet us.

This is probably what Malachi meant when he closed the prophetic era with the Divine call, שובו אלי ואשובה אליכם,[1] "Return to Me and I will return to you." It is a Heaven-sent gesture of conciliation: the Almighty offers to meet us halfway if we make the effort to return, repentant! The conciliatory tone of the last of Israel's Prophets seems to be in sharp contrast to the doom-laden vision of the future revealed to Moses, the father of the Prophets, when he is told of the impending end of his leadership of Israel. In the *Sidrah*, Moses is told הנך שכב עם אבתיך, "Behold, thou art about to sleep with thy fathers." (Incidentally, we notice here the implication that good Jews do not die, they sleep.) Moses was about to move on, וקם העם הזה וזנה אחרי אלהי נכר הארץ, "And this people will rise up and go astray after the foreign gods of the land." והסתרתי פני מהם, "and I will hide My face from them." Many evils and troubles shall come upon them, and they will say the reason is because אין אלקי בקרבי, "our God is not among us." They drove God out, they drove the *Shechinah* away, they turned their backs on Me. ואנכי הסתר אסתיר פני ביום ההוא, "And I will surely hide My face on that day, for all the evil which they shall have wrought."

We may well ask, Why this sharply contrasting harshness to Malachi's message? Would it be the first time they had sinned? If they turned away, should God turn away too? Is there such a thing in Judaism as man's fall never to rise again?

The answer to these challenging questions seems to lie in the opening verse of the *Haftorah* for *Shabbos Shuvah*. The prophet Hosea calls out, שובה ישראל עד ה' אלקיך כי כשלת בעונך, "Return, O Israel, unto the Lord thy God, for thou hast stumbled in thine iniquity." When one falls it is difficult to get up without help, but כי כשלת, when one stumbles he just picks himself up and walks on. The future sins of Israel revealed to Moses were different. The Torah describes them in a far more forceful and meaningful way: וקם העם הזה וזנה, "this people will *rise up* and go astray after the foreign gods of the land." The Torah does not say the people will stumble, unwittingly losing their self-control, but וקם, they will rise, they will stand, they will do it brazenly and with *chutzpah*. When people are ashamed and embarrassed by their wrongdoing, there is hope of reconciliation; they can be met halfway. But brazen defiance and deliberate turning away evokes similar Heavenly response.

It was this defiant posture that prompted the *Ha'azinu* Farewell Song of warning and the repeated threat of God's turning away: ויאמר אסתירה פני מהם אראה מה אחריתם. It is comforting to know that in spite of everything foretold, we are assured that Divine mercy will prevail, and His reconciliation with Israel will be made manifest to all the nations: הרנינו גוים עמו כי דם עבדיו יקום ונקם ישיב לצריו וכפר אדמתו עמו, "Sing aloud, O ye nations of His people; for He does avenge the blood of His servants and doth render vengeance to his adversaries, and doth make expiation for the land of His people."

vi

Get Talking!

(Shabbos Shuvah)

שובה ישראל עד ה' אלקיך כי כשלת בעונך, "Return, O Israel, unto the Lord thy God; for thou hast stumbled in thine iniquity." To stumble means to slip, to miss a step, to fall by accident from not looking, perhaps. God is so understanding of the stumbling! You cannot always get up and walk, it takes time for adjustment. He does not expect people to become pious overnight. קחו עמכם דברים, that is all He asks, "take with you words." Get talking about it, אמרו אליו, "say to Him." Do not be shy, turn round, look where you are going. The worst thing in life is to get into a rut, to stumble; not to say a word and to keep on crawling. In the end you forget what it means to walk straight. It becomes your natural way of doing things.

There is an interesting comment on a word in the early chapters of the Torah that deals with the first sins of man. Of course, Adam could not say "If it was good enough for my father it is good enough for me." He slipped for the first time, and I do not suppose he knew how to get up. וישמעו את קול ה' אלקים מתהלך,[1] "and they heard the voice of the Lord God walking"; it was a new experience, God on the move. They became frightened like children in the dark, ויתחבא, so they hid themselves; in a moment of fear all senses are numbed. Foolish man! He thought he could hide himself from God.

ויקרא ה' אלקים אל האדם ויאמר לו איכה, "And the Lord God called to the man, and said unto him, איכה, 'Where art thou?'" What a strange question from the Knower of all things; as though He did not know where Adam was! Of course He knew; ידע היה היכן הוא, you cannot play hide and seek with God. אלא ליכנס עמו בדברים,[2] God wanted to have a talk with him — just to get him talking, even if it was only to say, "Hello, here I am"; just a word of contact. The tragedy is when there is no contact with a child who has moved away, no telephone call, no "hello," nothing at all: the relationship broken.

ליכנס עמו בדברים; God wanted just to have contact. It is not the sin that man commits, it is not the wrong — we are not angels. It is losing the relationship. It is forgetting who you are, where you are,

---

1. בראשית ג', ח'.

2. רש"י; בראשית רבה.

איכה. The Rabbis[3] suggest a play on the word איכה, "how," of the Book of Lamentations. The same letters, but different vowels; איכה, if you only know where you are, then איכה, how can you do it? Cain was not punished for murdering his brother; he was punished because he had the temerity to say השמר אחי אנכי, "Am I my brother's keeper?" Ezra the Scribe, the founder of the אנשי כנסת הגדולה, cries out with us in our *Selichos* בשתי ונכלמתי להרים פני אליך,[4] "I am ashamed to lift up my face unto Thee." The real sin is to forget where you are and who you are, and to stop feeling ashamed.

Once upon a time people were at least ashamed of their sins. Like Adam they hid their faces: they put the shopping bag behind their back, they hid the cigarette, they stopped the car in a side-street. For such people there is hope, as the prophet says in the *Haftorah*: ארפא משובתם אהבם נדבה, "I will heal their backsliding, I will love them freely." We can talk to them, we can reason with them. From such people God does not turn away; it is man who turns away, and all that is expected is שובה.

But there is the other type of sinner: the sinner with *chutzpah*, the one who has no shame. In the *Sidrah* we read, ויאמר ה' אל משה, "And God said to Moses, הנך שכב עם אבתיך, you are about to sleep with your fathers, וקם העם הזה וזנה אחרי אלהי נכר הארץ, and this people will rise up and go astray after the foreign gods of the land." To go astray is not so terrible; it is a natural weakness, and God is compassionate and forgives; but וקם העם וזנה, this people will rise up with arrogance, he will sin shamelessly, barefacedly. He will put a *Magen David* on the shop window and say that the *treifah* meat is kosher. He will sell goods as kosher-for-Passover when they are known to be *chametz*. He will claim that his *Kiddushin* are valid when in fact they

3. פתיחתא למדרש איכה רבה.

4. עזרא ט', ו.

conflict with the laws of marriage. He openly declares himself opposed to תורה מן השמים, yet he calls himself Orthodox. He openly reforms and deforms the whole structure of Judaism, yet demands to be recognised as a religious Jew.

This is not a sinner who stumbles, who has slipped up. He is not the sinner for whose return God waits: ועזבתים והסתרתי פני מהם, "and I will forsake them and turn My face from them." There is a vast difference between man breaking off relations with God, and God breaking off relations with man. When man breaks off relations, God waits for man to return: שובה ישראל, "Come back — don't be shy." But if God breaks off relations, ועזבתים, if He turns His face, והסתרתי פני מהם, the process of *teshuvah* is long and agonising. There is a difference between a crack and a break: a crack can be repaired, but a break can necessitate a new wall.

The Sages say that the word וקם, in the phrase וקם העם הזה, "and the people will rise," can be read in two different ways: אין לו הכרע.[5] It can be attached to the preceding words, הנך שכב עם אבתיך, thus yielding "you will sleep with your fathers and will rise up"; or it can be read as normal: וקם העם הזה חנה. These alternative readings seem to suggest the key to Jewish eternity. It depends on what we leave behind when we move on to the Hereafter. If וקם is not attached to חנה, to wilful going astray; if there is no brazen turning away with *chutzpah*, with arrogant demands and the making of self-righteous conditions, but instead there is a genuine effort to return with shame and embarrassment for any wrongdoing, and a genuine resolve to make good; then הנך שכב עם אבתיך וקם, "Behold, you will sleep with your fathers and rise to תחיית המתים." Your relationship with God, your link with eternity, is not severed. Despite their lapses, children will carry on; generation will follow generation.

5. יומא נ"ב ע"ב.

But if וקם is not attached to שכב and there is no filial loyalty; if וקם is attached to חנה and those who are left behind have lost all vestiges of *derech eretz*; if they sin with arrogance, seeking only to satisfy their unbridled desires, and brazenly turn away from parents' traditions; then הנך שכב עם אבתיך, "Behold, you will sleep with your fathers," and that will spell the end of the line: there will be no וקם, the link with eternity will be severed.

The prophet pleads in the *Haftorah* וידעתם כי בקרב ישראל אני, "and know that I am in the midst of Israel." I have not turned away My face — you have turned yours away, but I am still here, ואני ה' אלקיכם ואין עוד, there is no other way: "I am the Lord your God." Come back, ולא יבשו עמי, "do not be ashamed, come back to tradition." Come back to *tallis* and *tefillin,* come back to Jewish learning, come back to Shabbos. Do not be ashamed; walk hand in hand with God through all time.

vii

About Turn!

(Shabbos Shuvah)

The Ten Days of Repentance, the first ten days of the year, are intended to be the foundation upon which our conduct in the new year is to be built. Their purpose is the creation of a personal relationship between man and God. Here is a sweeping philosophy that leaves no room for any intermediaries, that refuses to raise one and lower others. It is a tremendously uplifting outlook on life, one that eases so much sorrow and calms so much grief. It gives one a sense of nearness and lifts up the most humble to feel himself with

God, to feel that no man is ever alone. The importance of this confidence and conviction is implied in the Divine warning conveyed to Moses before he bade farewell to His people, who were about to set up an independent state. The time would come when they would say כי אין אלקי בקרבי; when God would no longer be felt among them.

Israel's ancient teachers emphasised the significance of the terms הארת פנים or, God forbid, הסתר פנים, the presence of God or His absence. As a famous Chassid once put it, שובה simply means to return. If you have turned your back on someone, you only have to turn and you look him in the face. *Shabbos Shuvah* calls to us, "turn round and face Me!" But it must be made clear that the repentance to which we repeatedly refer during the Ten Days does not refer to the sins committed against our fellow man. For such sins there is only one way out: find your victim and crave his forgiveness. If he is no longer in the land of the living, then gather a *minyan* and go to his grave and there make a public confession. It is not a pleasant thing to do. But it is a serious mistake that some of us make who believe that "from nine to five" during the day we can conduct ourselves as our interests dictate, then come to *shul* to *daven Minchah* and do as God dictates.

That, unfortunately, has been the canker eating away at religious life: we have separated the sacred from the secular. We will have much to answer for, on our day of judgment, that we never stressed sufficiently the בין אדם לחבירו, the sins we commit against one another.

In the business world so many things are taken for granted; and our people are not worse in that respect. In the wilderness of old, there was very little cause for sin against fellow man. There were no shops and no communal enterprises. Yet the cry went up from Moses' dying lips, כי תעשו את הרע בעיני ה' להכעיסו במעשה ידיכם, "You will do

evil in God's eyes and provoke Him through the work of your hands"
— Divine feelings of provocation arising not merely from the
disregard of religious duty, but from the disregard of human duty.
Once upon a time one had the impression that the approach to God
was through man: through having a good heart, a generous hand
and an honest word. Religion as such was taken for granted. The
home had God in it, the synagogue was full of Him. There was no
determined, organised opposition: some observed more, some less.
Consequently, if someone claimed to be a good Jew at heart, it was
an acceptable point of view. But the impact of society is far too great
today. Nowadays it is a question of God or no God.

Economically, the conflict between exploitation and honesty can
also be summarised as God or no God. Domestically, the conflict
between home and street influences and attractions; shattered hope
and broken loves; that, too, is a question of God or no God. It is
nonsensical to believe in God on the one hand, and yet refuse to
bring Him into the sanctum of life on the other. Religiously, it is
absurd to suggest that one can believe in God, portray the shofar in
the press, exhibit a *Sefer Torah* in the Ark, and yet abrogate the
Torah's laws and pervert the message of the shofar. It is a public
deception of the first order. Make no mistake about it: that is not
an ideology, it is the same question, God or no God.

We have got to get back to the beginning again: שובה ישראל, about
turn. Religion, religious acts and religious observance must come
back into their own again. It must become a living force. Without
the acceptance of God, moral life has no future. It may continue to
exist for some time, but without the continuous power of religion
it must deteriorate and after a time perish altogether.

The Ten Commandments were so divided as to provide the first
five for בין אדם למקום and the second five for בין אדם לחבירו. Those who
think that from "Thou shalt not steal" they can reach all the way to

אנכי ה' אלקיך, "I am the Lord your God," are making a grave mistake. It is a fallacy; "I am the Lord your God" must come first. שובה ישראל עד ה' אלקיך כי כשלת בעונך, "Return, O Israel, to the Lord your God, for thou hast stumbled in thine iniquity." First turn to Him, then קחו עמכם דברים. From the confines of His house, from the sanctum of your lives, you can take with you into the open the power that will help you resist temptation and overcome passion. "About turn!" is the message of *Shabbos Shuvah*, face to face with God, religion all over again. Then we will set a foundation upon which the year ahead will be built, and which will bring credit to each and every one and glory to the community.

viii

An Annual Bar Mitzvah Address

תשובה means to go back, to return to where we started, to become Bar Mitzvah again. Start again today keeping Shabbos, start again tomorrow morning putting on the *tefillin*. There is one difference between a thirteen-year-old's Bar Mitzvah day and ours: we are receiving no Bar Mitzvah presents, no pens, no vouchers, and no cheques. But there is one thing we want to receive, something that nothing in the world can buy: a year of life and of happiness, of peace and of blessing.

The prophet Hosea, in the *Shabbos Shuvah Haftorah*, gives a Bar Mitzvah address to Jews all over the world. He tells them two things. First of all, שובה ישראל עד ה' אלקיך, "Return, O Israel, unto the Lord thy God." The precise meaning of עד is 'towards, in the direction of.' First you have to set a goal, a target, and you aim your sights and your actions in the direction of that goal. But that is not good enough; resolutions without deeds do not mean a thing. So the prophet continues, קחו עמכם דברים ושובו אל ה', bring your resolutions into operation, translate them into practice. Take 'things' with you and return אל ה', right unto God. Hold Him by the hand as the year begins, with *tefillin*, with honesty. Live with Him as the year begins, with Shabbos and with *kashrus*. Honour Him as the year begins with Jewish decency, respect, discipline and dignity. Thus, as the year begins we flock to our synagogues to become Bar Mitzvah again, and we ask Him to give us our great gift that only He can give: to inscribe us in the Book of Life.

There are all kinds of books. Some are full of rubbish, not worth the paper they are written on. Some are worth their weight in gold, for their every word has meaning and every page is a volume. There are books that leave no impress, and there are books that go down to posterity. All of us are pages in the book of life that our parents wrote. How long these books last depends on how we live and how much we hand on to those who follow us. The parents are the covers and the binding of the book; children are the pages. זה ספר תולדת אדם[1] may be rendered as "The book of life is the generations of man." Most parents offer up a very special, silent prayer; they hope that each of their children will write a fine page in their book of life. Sometimes parents fail to produce a creditable book of life, not because of the children but because of the parents; the covers of the book are no good, the binding is weak, and before the boys and girls grow up, the book falls to pieces and the pages scatter!

Moses, in his last and final message to the people, before he bids them farewell, conveys to them one final mitzvah: ועתה כתבו לכם את השירה הזאת ולמדה את בני ישראל שימה בפיהם, "Now write this song for you and teach it to the Children of Israel — put it into their mouths."

---

1. בראשית ה', א'.

Write this song, Moses begs them; what a strange word with which to describe this Torah of ours! (There is quite a discussion in the Biblical commentaries regarding which song Moses was referring to; but he was referring to the whole Torah and he called it a song.)

Ask any composer what happens to a musical composition if one note is changed, if one variation is made in the notes or the rhythm. The whole thing loses its taste. The whole orchestra collapses. The Torah is called a song not only because it brings music into life, it gives meaning to life, it makes the most sorrowful event a joyous event, because it brings God into life. Even more than that, it is called a song because if one mitzvah is taken out, if one letter is dented, if you reform it or liberalise it, changing it to suit your whims, then the whole Divine Composition loses its taste. It is no longer Torah.

Moses calls the people and instructs them to write this song, to teach it to the children and שימה בפיהם, put it into their mouths. Let them sing it and live by it. Bring the music of Torah into the soul; live by it, practise it, and study it. Let the pages children write in their parents' book of life be this שירה, and so bring eternal joy to them, credit to the community, and glory to God.

HA'AZINU

האזינו

i

Our Father, Our King!

(Shabbos Shuvah)

Shabbos Shuvah is the link between Rosh Hashanah and Yom Kippur. Rosh Hashanah is Coronation Day, when we proclaim God the King, when הא-ל becomes המלך; we acknowledge His majestic sovereignty. That is Rosh Hashanah: מלכות, the Kingdom of God. But what good is a king without subjects? Yom Kippur is Submission Day, when we pay homage and prostrate ourselves before Him, when we submit to His will. That is Yom Kippur: אנו עמך ואתה מלכנו, "We are Your subjects and You are our King." This is the simple philosophy of Rosh Hashanah. There is nothing mysterious about it. On the birthday of the Creation, man must learn that the world belongs to Him and this is His creation. God the Creator, man the creature; God the King, man the subject. Year by year, at this time, we reaffirm our faith and we proclaim it to the world.

But that is not enough. Heaven above and the earth below as separate entities are not good enough. We can stand all day in salutation and worship, we can read about Him and study Him, we can even believe in Him; that is still not enough. The trouble is that in what we call religion there is so much that has no meaning. They have become colloquial figures of speech, 'heaven and earth,' a kind of up and down, representing that which is far removed and that which is near at hand. But if we look into the source when heaven and earth are first mentioned, they are spoken of as being created in one act: בראשית ברא אלקים את השמים ואת הארץ, in one מאמר, one Divine utterance, in one day. When man came on the scene this oneness was consummated. He was formed out of dust, put into shape, and something from Heaven breathed into him.

When Israel stood at Sinai we read again of this fusion, of the heavens opening up and the word of God coming down. Do you think that the Ten Commandments were written on chunks of sky, on pieces of heaven inscribed with 'thou shalt' and 'thou shalt not'? Not at all; there was an even more remarkable fusion of Heaven and earth, Heavenly words written on tablets of stone. Even more expressive of this fusion is the description of earthly human beings standing at Sinai, men and women like you and me witnessing the Heavenly revelation. They neither submitted nor surrendered: it was ואתם הדבקים בה' אלקיכם.[1] They were at one with God; Heaven and earth combined.

The word *mitzvah* means more than commandment; it means attachment. The hand became the instrument of God with *tefillin*; the body with *kashrus*, the limbs with purity, and the senses with morality; work with Shabbos; seasons with the festivals; earnings with charity; times with prayer; garments with *tzitzis*. Around-the-clock with God, King and subject, Creator and creation, a unique at-oneness involving the whole of life. Not a mere intellectual persuasion, an attitude or a conception or a theory, but

דברים ד', ד'. 1

Heaven and earth brought together in man. Time and eternity, finite
and infinite, body and soul, in a living communion: King and subject,
God and man.

This *Sidrah* of *Ha'azinu* is not just a song — lovely words that
are sometimes orchestrated and put into music. האזינו השמים ואדברה
ותשמע הארץ אמרי פי, "Give ear, ye heavens, and I will speak, and let the
earth hear the words of my mouth." Strange words, are they not?
"Let the earth hear the words of God." What do you think this is? A
kind of poetic licence in the Bible, to make it rhyme and make it
look nice on parchment? Heaven forfend, not at all. True, this *Sidrah*
is called a song: כתבו לכם את השירה הזאת.[2] For in a song, if a curve is
missing, one note out of place, the whole composition collapses.
This Torah is a song: one jot changed, one letter removed, and it is
no longer Torah. It is to penetrate the whole of life's activities; not
a single facet is left out of this all-embracing Judaism which we call
Torah. The earth responds to the voice of God, and this dust-clinging
man with all his frailties and weaknesses can reach out to eternity.
In such oneness with God, death becomes a mere passing phase. In
such oneness the bitter cup, if it comes from Him, is sweet.

No man paid a more costly and painful price for one sin than did
Moses. What anguish must have been his as he was to close his eyes
for the last time! Yet no man sang with such fervour as he did, as
he wrote the *Ha'azinu*-song with utter devotion in those last
agonising moments. This is the religion of the Jew: the mitzvah that
penetrates everyday living forges a link and creates a communion
that knows no end.

שובה ישראל, the prophet calls out in the *Haftorah*, "Return, O Israel,
עד ה' אלקיך, unto the Lord your God, כי כשלת בעונך, for you have stumbled
in your iniquity." To return to God still does not mean to reach Him.

2. דברים ל"א, י"ט.

עד means towards Him, in His direction. You can be walking towards Him, and if you are not looking where you should look you can stumble and fall. There are some who go about preaching and teaching and philosophising about God and religion, telling you why you should believe and how you should believe, saying "Turn your eyes towards Heaven." They take your eyes off the road, and you can stumble and fall. They suggest changing everything: the Prayer Book, the Shabbos, the references to animal sacrifice in the Temple service. They want to change everything except their own lives. They are worried about animal sacrifice when the Temple will be restored, as though they had already solved the tragic problem of human sacrifice.

By all means, the prophet pleads, "return unto God," in His direction. But remember that it is not good enough, כי כשלת בעונך; with your eyes off the ground you will stumble in your iniquity. קחו עמכם דברים ושובו אל ה', "take with you words," put your beliefs into action. Take your practical *mitzvos* — your *tallis* and *tefillin*, your Shabbos and your Yom Tov and your family; and you will return not just עד but אל, right up to Him. You will become one with Him. אמרו אליו, "Say unto Him, כל תשא עון, forgive all iniquity, וקח טוב, and accept that which is good." Not a good Jew only in heart, but וקח טוב, good in the hands, in action and in deeds. God in action through man makes Heaven visible on earth. The King Whom we crowned on Rosh Hashanah, to Whom we paid allegiance on Yom Kippur, becomes one with us through our desire to fulfil His *mitzvos* and to become attached to Him. Thus we can face the future, fortified by the faith that in this we will find true joy and happiness.

ii

This Is Your Life

(Bar Mitzvah)

Moses, the great leader and teacher, concludes his Farewell Song with a final plea to Israel to 'charge' their children "to observe to do all the words of this Law, כי לא דבר רק הוא מכם, for it is no vain thing for you; because it is your life." The Hebrew word רק, usually translated as 'vain,' literally means 'empty'; and in this sense the phrase לא דבר רק הוא lends itself to a significant alternative meaning. If you take a container and fill it, it is full; then when you empty it, it is referred to as an "empty container," but it is still a container, retaining its potential use for a similar purpose. לא דבר רק הוא implies that if a Jew is empty of his Torah, he is *not* like a thing that is empty. A gentile without Torah is a gentile — he can be somebody; a Jew without Torah is nothing at all — he has no meaning, no value. כי הוא חייכם, the Torah is our very life. Empty the Jew of his Torah, take his *mitzvos* away from him, his *tallis* and his *tefillin*, his Shabbos and his festivals, and there is nothing at all Jewish about him. He loses his real significance. To be a true Jew, life must be filled with something. He cannot be a דבר רק, an empty vessel.

The שירת משה, the Farewell Song of Moses, with its plea for spiritual loyalty and Torah observance, is sometimes followed with the *Haftorah* of שירת דוד, the magnificent Song of Thanksgiving of King David which he sang on the day the Lord delivered him from all his enemies. After all his battles and struggles he declared, ה' סלעי ומצדתי, "the Lord is my rock and my fortress."

A Bar Mitzvah, on the threshold of Jewish manhood, can hardly fail to feel inspired by these historic songs, to endeavour to be strong and steadfast like a rock, defending like a fortress the great ideals and way of life of our holy people.

iii

Give and Take

During the Days of Penitence we repeatedly refer to God in many of our prayers as אבינו מלכנו, "our Father, our King." A father has children, a king has subjects. The relationship between a father and a child is love and compassion. The relationship between a king and his subjects is loyalty and allegiance. אבינו and מלכנו go hand in hand. In Judaism that is basic. אבינו, Father, we ask for compassion; מלכנו, our King, we offer You our allegiance.

When a child leaves home and there is never a card or a phone call, the love between parents and the child frequently becomes very cold, and the will to give and to help is slender and shaken. But how warm is the love and how keen is the desire to help when the child is in touch, when the link is never broken. Happy is the home where love is combined with respect, loyalty and obedience. The world was created in pairs — the Hebrew terms for the basic elements of the universe are all in the dual form: חיים, מים, שמים — and similarly we have heaven and earth, man and woman, in twos. Life is give and take; life is forgive and give. It is not give alone; it is not all heaven. He does not want angels on earth, He wants men and women; but it is not you alone, it is not all earth; He does not want animals, He wants human beings. If heaven gives to earth, earth must give something in return to heaven; that is the simple ABC of religion. אבינו, God the Father — He loves and He gives; מלכנו, God the King — He demands loyalty and obedience. You cannot have one without the other.

Our trouble is that we have turned religion into a theology, into a philosophy, into a theory. We want Rabbis to be scholars and laymen to be intellectuals. The truth is, we need Rabbis to teach us and to show us how to practise, and we want laymen to practise and to learn how to do it. We want our womenfolk to see to it that it is done. Religion to the Jew is one thing and one thing only: it is a form of living that makes us God-conscious all the time. We cannot just think of Him and read about Him; we must be in touch with Him every day like a father. You *daven,* you make a ברכה, you say ברכת המזון, you keep Shabbos — that is keeping in touch. To forget God is bad enough, but there are those who even hope to dislodge Him and to replace Him. That is an awful thing. The prophet in the *Haftorah* for *Shabbos Shuvah* yearns for the time when לא נאמר עוד אלהינו למעשה ידינו, "Never again will we call the work of our hands our gods, אשר בך ירחם יתום, for in Thee the fatherless will find mercy."

The Rabbis say, משה היה קרוב לשמים,[1] "Moses was near to Heaven," a man who was out of reach of the מלאך המות. Because of this, when his time came to leave this earth he had to be ordered to ascend Mt. Nebo, ומת בהר אשר אתה עלה שמה, "and die on the Mount on which thou goest up." מת is a rare grammatical form of the word in Biblical literature; it means "die of your own accord." Take off your garments, stretch out your hands, straighten your limbs; you must do it yourself, על אשר מעלתם בי בתוך בני ישראל במי מריבת קדש, "because you trespassed against Me in the midst of the Children of Israel at the Waters of Meribah."

Can you imagine Moses, this man of God who was akin to the angels, *trespassing* against God in the midst of the Children of Israel? He was told to take the מטה, the rod: קח את המטה...ודברתם אל הסלע,[2] and

1. ספרי האזינו.

2. במדבר כ', ח'.

speak to the rock, and water would flow. In his modesty, Moses never believed for a moment that he could bring God down, right down בתוך בני ישראל, just by calling with his own voice to the rock for water. So he found himself unable to speak, in which case he should have kept quiet. To keep God out is bad enough; at least leave room for Him to return. מעלתם, 'trespass,' conveys the idea 'to dislodge' — he never spoke to the rock, he smote the rock, and in so doing he replaced God. על אשר לא קדשתם אותי בתוך בני ישראל, "you never sanctified Me in the midst of the Children of Israel," you took Me out and put a stick in My place — a religion of gimmicks. You turned me into a culture, a science — if you cannot do the *mitzvos* say so, but do not put something there in their place!

These Judgment Days in the Jewish calendar call to the nations of the world as well as to ourselves: ועל המדינות בו יאמר.[3] We have seen in history how nations have reached their peak, then suddenly they come tumbling down. They say they believe in Him, but they have put Him away on high and they have replaced Him with their false 'isms' and cultures.

To us the prophet pleads שובה ישראל: "If you have forgotten, come back." No home can be without Me. A world without God is a jungle, a home without God is a stable. וידעתם כי בקרב ישראל אני, "You shall know that I am in the midst of Israel"; bring Me into your home and lives. I will help you with your needs. First things first: spend on God and God will spend on you. Some things are not easy: Shabbos and *kashrus*, synagogue affiliation and the children's Jewish education; it is giving to Heaven. Be assured that in return God will give peace and contentment, salvation and tranquillity.

---

3. תפלת מוסף לראש השנה.

V'ZOS HA-BERACHAH

וזאת הברכה

i

The Strong Hand

ולכל היד החזקה ולכל המורא הגדול אשר עשה משה לעיני כל ישראל, "And in all the mighty hand and in all the great terror which Moses wrought in the sight of all Israel." These words conclude the greatest of all books. What was the might revealed in the hands of Moses? שקבל את התורה בלוחות בידיו,[1] "that he received the Torah in his hands." Education and knowledge are absorbed in the brain and transmitted by teaching. Not so the Torah; it was received by hand and handed down by hand; ולכל היד החזקה, Moses' hands bore the weight of showing God in the flesh, God in society, God in civilisation. In Jewish life you cannot separate the mind from the body. This alone brings about the realisation of בראשית ברא אלקים את השמים ואת הארץ, that the earth is as much to do with God as the heavens.

We are not a people who worship the dead; we only respect them. We pay our respect to the departed with *Yizkor* on Shemini Atzeres, and then we go on to celebrate the completion of the annual Reading of the Torah, taking out the scrolls from the Ark, bearing

1. רש"י; וראה תורה תמימה מהירוש' תענית פ'ד ה'ה.

the weight of them on our shoulders, combining the souls of the dead with the flesh of the living. It is perhaps significant that the last few lines of the Torah relate the death of Moses. An account of his burial is not even recorded. No one knows how and where his burial took place; ולכל היד החזקה is not the hand that carried the coffin, but the hand שקבל תורה, the hand that bore the Torah in the sight of all Israel. We are concerned with hands that bear the living: those hands reveal God on earth. We too could have gone out into the world, when we took our place among the nations, crossing the Jordan into the Holy Land, with that remarkable story of Moses' death. A man who had God in him and who disappeared without trace of his burial place! But the Divine Author of the last eight verses of the Torah knew well what kind of faith a world could build up and what kind of a religion it would be if its foundation were a dead Jew. See what a mess the world is in; do you call that religion?

Moses died, of his grave nothing is revealed; but what remains for all time are his achievements אשר עשה משה: the things he did, the glory he left behind. The living Jews took the Torah from him and bore it in their hands and transmitted it from generation to generation. The wisest of men said: ושבח אני את המתים שכבר מתו מן החיים אשר המה חיים עדנה,[2] "I praised the dead that are already dead מן החיים, from the living אשר המה חיים עדנה, who are still alive." The only praise one can give the dead is מן החיים, to see what kind of living men they left behind them; חיים עדנה are their generations still alive. The *Yizkor* on Shemini Atzeres is not a mournful ritual but a joyful remembrance, because אשר המה חיים עדנה, the glories they left are still alive.

The phenomenon of Jewish history has not been our survival; we survived because never at any time has the Jew been

קהלת ד', ב'. 2

concentrated in one place. When we were threatened in one country, we survived in another. The miracle of our history has been our independent character. Wherever we lived we remained a self-contained unit. We were the reservoir from which the nations of the world drew their life-blood and possessions; we drew nothing from them, we took nothing in return. Is there a people like ours, blessed with such a superiority complex, unbendingly independent and self-supporting? With all the troubles in our Jewish communities of intermarriages and conversions, there is hardly a single case of any Jewish young man who surrendered his faith to the one to whom he surrendered his affections. How many genuine apostates will you find right through our history? Yes, there have been assimilationist tendencies from time to time, movements to change the law, to give dispensations, to bind the heavens to us rather than bind ourselves to Heaven. But שמד, apostasy — never. Social climbers and hypocrites occasionally, but genuine, convinced apostates — perhaps a dozen since the beginning of our history. No Jew has stooped so low. What prospect have they to offer? נישט די וועלט, נישט יענע וועלט.

הוא עשך אומה,[3] הוא עשך ויכננך "He made thee and established thee"; באומות,[4] "He made you a nation among nations." You lived among them and you retained your independence. That has been the marvel of the world: ויכננך — בכל מיני בסיס... מכם כהנים מכם נביאים מכם מלכים כרך שהכל תלוי בו,[5] "He made you self-contained — all human resources come from you: priests from you, prophets and kings from you, כרך שהכל בו, like a city which contains everything that man requires." The annals of our history tell no story of imperial pomp and military

3. דברים ל"ב, ו'.

4. רש"י.

5. רש"י; חולין נ"ז ע"ב.

conquest: ours is a story of intellectual pomp and spiritual conquest. Prophecy is ours, democracy is ours, religion is ours, the Bible is ours. Take away their dollars and their oil, their tanks and their bombs; what will you have left? But מי כמוך, "who is like unto you, Israel, אשר חרב, whose sword is not the sword of the nations of the world, but גאותך, thine excellency."[6] Our whole history, our whole life has been a glorious combination of שמים וארץ, Heaven and earth. In their לכם, their self-seeking, there is no עצי: nothing holds them back from their evil-doing. In our לכם there is an עצרת, in our very flesh, in the food we eat and in the wine we drink, in the pleasures we enjoy — in the earth there is Heaven.

This is the great message of the *Sidrah* which tradition has associated with Shemini Atzeres and Simchas Torah. It is a message of Jewish pride and Jewish glory, not in what we possess, but in what we are: a light unto the nations of the world. With the *Sefer Torah* in one hand and with our children in the other, we rejoice on these two days as on no other occasion in the year. The deeper the mire in which the world is plodding, the greater becomes the message of the Jew. Materialism without God can never succeed, earth without Heaven can never survive. God in our Hebrew language; God in our school, through Jewish knowledge and Jewish culture; God in our home discipline; God in life — Torah leading the world back to a sane order and righteous thinking.

דברים ל"ג, כ"ט. 6

ii

In the Sight of All Israel

לעיני כל ישראל; the marvels of Jewish history have been manifest not only to the Israel of Moses' day, but לעיני כל ישראל, to the Israel of all generations. The Egypt that rose and fell has been followed by Babylon, Persia, Greece, Rome and Spain. Yes, Nazi Germany too, that rose and fell, and all the others who will follow, whose torches will burn out. לעיני כל ישראל — we have seen them, and our children will continue to see them soar high but crumble to pieces.

No sooner does the *Chasan Bereishis* conclude לעיני כל ישראל than we turn to בראשית ברא אלקים, proclaiming "In the beginning God created." What God hath made, none can destroy, notwithstanding every attempt to exterminate us. To use the words of a fourth-century churchman: "Exiled and dispersed, reviled and persecuted, often denied the commonest right of humanity and still more often made the victim of ruthless fanaticism and bigoted prejudice, the Jews are Divinely preserved for a purpose worthy of God." Sixteen hundred years ago these words were uttered, and how true they are today. But centuries before him, the Rabbis disclosed it! בראשית — בזכות ישראל שנקראו ראשית שנא' קדש ישראל לה' ראשית תבואתה,[1] Israel and Israel's message were the Divine purpose of God's creation. This Israel, like the first fruits, waved hither and thither on the altar of every human endeavour, has preferred the Torah to the thousand freedoms the world could offer it. This Israel, the children of the Patriarchs and the descendants of the Prophets, has been the greatest benefactor to the world's cultural thought and ethical standards. Without the genius of the Jew, without the

---

1. ילקוט שמעוני בראשית רמז ב' על הפסוק בירמיה ב', ג'.

teachings of the Jew, without the blood of the Jew, no light would ever have penetrated the thick darkness of this jungle world. We brought the light into the world; no one can deny that we are the chosen of all peoples.

On Shemini Atzeres and Simchas Torah, holding the Scroll of the Law, whose precepts and duties we shall never abrogate, we rejoice in our lot, singing אשריכם ישראל אשר בחר בכם א-ל. Do as they will, these nations of the world, none will destroy what God hath made. Seen in this perspective a new light is cast on the Rabbinic question, best expressed in the words of *Koheles*: ולשמחה מה זה עשה,[2] what occasions this eighth Day of Rejoicing, as Israel leaves the *sukkah* again to wander the face of the earth? This question is answered with a parable. After the offering of seventy sacrifices, during the days of Sukkos, for the well-being of the peoples of the world, the Almighty says to Israel on this final festival day, "Make one sacrifice for yourselves." Like a king who calls to his closest and most intimate friend, after the conclusion of a public banquet for all his courtiers, saying עשה לי סעודה קטנה — קשה עלי פרידתכם,[3] "Make a small repast just for you and for me, your parting is difficult for me to bear." Let the world see that the Jew is inseparable from God, that the Jew is wedded to one conception. We are still Thine, though our limbs are torn.

קשה עלי פרידתכם, "your parting is difficult for Me," is the Simchas Torah call: "Hold fast to Me, let nothing crush your נשמה, your spiritual strength and your inner values." Live for My sake. Let the weekly toil and labour not squeeze out the Shabbos spirit. Let not the daily grind and routine squeeze out your שמע ישראל. Let home comforts not squeeze out your moral values and pure living. Let not

2. קהלת ב', ב'.

3. סוכה נ"ה ע"ב ורש"י ויקרא כ"ג, ל"ו.

gentile hatred squeeze out your Jewish courage. Living for My sake, קשה עלי פרידתכם — there will be no place in the world for God without you and there will be no place for you without God. Make your life a *Kiddush Hashem*. And if death there must be — then let it be על קדוש השם, for the sanctification of God's name.

ואהבת את ה' אלקיך בכל לבבך, "Love the Lord your God with all your heart," does not mean merely to be a good Jew at heart — it means with life itself. ובכל נפשך does not mean by selling your soul for the gifts that the nations of the world can bestow, it means giving up everything for your soul's sake, because only then is life eternal. ובכל מאדך does not mean sacrificing your soul in pursuit of fortune and the false security that money can buy. That is not the way of Jewish life; קשה עלי פרידתכם, "do not part from Me." בכל לבבך, with all your heart to God. ובכל נפשך, with all your soul to God. ובכל מאדך, with all your might and main to God. Take Me into life, practise Me, live by Me. Make Me the source of your joy and spiritual strength. Only then will the world's conscience be stirred by a Jew who not only dies but lives for God's sake. כתבו לכם את השירה הזאת,[4] make this Torah the song of your life — this was Moses' message at the end of his days. Make Jewish life a song: Shabbos and Yom Tov, charity and learning. Then will God grant that we see an end to Jewish sorrow. ויהי ערב, the evening of sorrow in our lives will disappear; ויהי בקר, the dawn will rise, bringing light and salvation to our people the world over.

iii

To the End of Time

It is customary to conclude the Reading of the Torah with song and dancing. With joy and gratitude we proclaim our pride that we

---

4. דברים ל״א, י״ט

have been blessed with the unique distinction of being chosen to be the People of the Book. Our feelings are expressed in words such as those from the daily morning prayers: אשרינו מה טוב חלקנו, "Happy are we! How good is our portion!"

The Torah testifies: כי אתם המעט מכל העמים,[1] "You are the fewest of all peoples." Yet, thanks to the Torah's inspired wisdom and understanding, ours has been the greatest contribution of all to the world's thinking, cultural, ethical and moral. As has been said, "Israel is a small nation, but it has been chosen to accomplish world-embracing and eternal things." In the scientific world, too, we have never fallen short of a much higher proportional percentage of achievement than any other people. Verily we can say מה טוב חלקנו, how goodly is our share of those things that are of eternal value in human life. But for too long we have taught the world how to die for a cause; we must yet show them how to live for a cause. Ours is a religion of life — כי הם חיינו[2] — not of death; it is a Law to live by, not to die by.

The Jew in every age must be vigilant to uphold the Torah, like Moses, ביד חזקה, with all our strength, with will-power and determination to do it even against the heaviest odds. Then, like the Torah itself, we will never end. When we finish our life-span here we will go on to בראשית in eternity. So Jews and Jewesses, lift up your hearts; honeymoon with God, you, your children and grandchildren. With the Torah we will go on to the end of time.

1. דברים ז', ז'.

2. תפלת ערבית.